中国传统文化

中英双语

Understanding Traditional Chinese Culture

欧阳美和◎译著

中国政法大学出版社

2025·北京

声　　明　1. 版权所有，侵权必究。

2. 如有缺页、倒装问题，由出版社负责退换。

图书在版编目（ＣＩＰ）数据

中国传统文化：汉文、英文 / 欧阳美和译著. -- 北京 ： 中国政法大学出版社，
2025.4

ISBN 978-7-5764-0857-7

Ⅰ. ①中… Ⅱ. ①欧… Ⅲ. ①中华文化－汉、英 Ⅳ. ①K203

中国国家版本馆 CIP 数据核字 (2023) 第 107824 号

出 版 者	中国政法大学出版社
地　　址	北京市海淀区西土城路 25 号
邮寄地址	北京 100088 信箱 8034 分箱　邮编 100088
网　　址	http://www.cuplpress.com（网络实名：中国政法大学出版社）
电　　话	010-58908285(总编室) 58908433（编辑部）58908334(邮购部)
承　　印	北京旺都印务有限公司
开　　本	720mm×960mm　1/16
印　　张	23
字　　数	370 千字
版　　次	2025 年 4 月第 1 版
印　　次	2025 年 4 月第 1 次印刷
定　　价	99.00 元

序 言 / PREFACE

　　文化的概念多种多样，一般认为有广义与狭义之分。广义的文化范围非常广泛，包括政治、经济、社会、制度、法律、科技、文学艺术等，可以说，我们日常生活的方方面面都是文化的映射，如饮食文化、服饰文化、茶文化、养生文化、交通文化等，实际上是指物质财富和精神财富的总和；狭义的文化主要是指文学艺术、法律制度、集体无意识等意识形态诸现象。一个时期的文化反映了一个时期的社会发展和经济状况。不同的民族有不同的文化，不同的时期有不同的文化，并且以不同的文化形式呈现。文化发展的历史延续性使不同时期、不同民族和国家的文化具有自己的时代特色和语义特征。文化是一个国家或民族区别于其他国家或民族的特色符号，具有历史性和时代性。"文化是一个国家、一个民族的灵魂"，要了解一个国家或者是一个民族，就要了解其文化。在国际交往中，对他国文化的了解，是文明互鉴的基础，也是民心相通的前提。习近平指出，"中国传统文化博大精深，学习和掌握其中的各种思想精华，对树立正确的世界观、人生观、价值观很有益处。""学史可以看成败、鉴得失、知兴替；学诗可以情飞扬、志高昂、人灵秀；学伦理可以知廉耻、懂荣辱、辨是非。"对中国文化的了解，有助于国际人士更好地了解今日中国的方针政策、国家治理和发展成就。我们相信："他山之石，可以攻玉"。

　　中国历史悠久，中国文化源远流长。习近平指出，"中华文明绵延数千年，有其独特的价值体系。中华优秀传统文化已经成为中华民族的基因，植根在中国人内心，潜移默化影响着中国人的思想方式和行为方式"[1]。沿着

---

〔1〕 习近平在北京大学师生座谈会上的讲话。

历史的发展脉络，从历史深处走向当代中国，就会对中国文化、中华民族、中国人民有比较全面、客观的了解。中国文化的根基来源于农耕文明，与游牧文化和海洋文化不同，是中华民族在独特的地理环境下生产生活的实践总结，并且以不同的形式延续下来的精华浓缩并传承至今的一种文化形态，具体表现为中华民族崇尚的传统美德，如爱国主义、自力更生、爱好和平、集体至上、尊老爱幼、吃苦耐劳、艰苦奋斗、勤俭节约、邻里相帮等中国文化传统和核心价值理念，这些即使在物质文明高度发达的今天，也值得充分肯定和借鉴。中国文化兼容并包，经过了多次的不同区域或民族文化的交汇与融合。早在秦统一中国前，不同区域的文化之间就有着密切交流。《尚书·尧典》中就提出"协和万邦"的理念，主张不同国家和睦共处，彼此包容。

中国文化的核心理念之一是"天人合一"，指的是人与自然要和谐相处，物质环境和精神环境要相融相合；中国文化非常重视内外平衡、阴阳协调，"天人合一""知行合一""情景合一"表现的就是这种理念。中国传统文化中理想的家庭模式是"耕读传家"，这种家庭模式推崇自然和谐、乐天知命和合作包容，与今天的和谐发展理念也甚为契合。中国古代的启蒙读物《三字经》中就有"三才者，天、地、人"，这表明中国文化强调人本位，将天、地、人三者并列，以人为宇宙的中心，认为人是"万物之本""最为天下贵"。中国文化更多的关注今世、此岸，而不是来世、彼岸，人们尽可能地在现实生活中实现人生的自我价值。伦理道德修养在中国传统的文化人中处于核心地位，视"修身"为立命之根本。"德高望重"就是对一个人的高度评价。中国历来在国家治理中视道德感化为政治统治的重要手段，用道德去教化民众，以规范社会成员的思想与行为，即"以德治国"；强调个人的伦理义务，要求个人服从整体；个体只是整体的一个有机组成部分，个体利益必须服从家庭、社会以及国家的利益。

中国传统文化对教育理念和方法具有深远影响。"师者，所以传道、授业、解惑也"，这是中国人耳熟能详的关于老师的解释，实际上反映了中国传统教育文化的理念，即"政治—伦理—教育"三位一体，学校教育与现实社会应该融为一体，"学以致用"；注重历史与现实紧密结合，"以史为鉴"；注重个人道德修养，"以德为先"。中国传统教育思想和方法，如因材施教、启发诱导、学思结合、教学相长和有教无类等依然贯穿在当代中国教育中。因材施教就是根据不同教育对象，选择符合实际的教育内容和教育方法，使学习者能各尽其才。因材施教最早的实践者是孔子，因材施教的方法被中国历史上许多教育家所采用。启发诱导就是教师要充分调动学生的学习积极性，当学生碰到棘手的问题时，教师要启发引导学生，做到"循循善诱"；学生则要能举一反三、互帮互学，做到"触类旁通"。学思结合就是在学习的过程中既要重视学习，又要重视思考，"学而不思则罔，思而不学则殆"，学思并重、相互促进，以提高自己的认识、思考和辨析问题的能力。教学相长，教师在教授学生的过程中，自己也能从学生身上学到东西，教学活动不是单向的知识传授，而是师生都能受益的互动过程，在这一过程中师生双方都能得到提高，正所谓"三人行，必有我师焉"。有教无类就是不管是什么人都应该受到教育，不能因为某些人贫穷、出身低下、不聪明或者是性情顽劣等原因而把他们排除在教育对象之外，而且在教学的过程中要做到"诲人不倦"。

习近平曾说："讲故事，是国际传播的最佳方式。""讲故事就是讲事实、讲形象、讲情感、讲道理，讲事实才能说服人，讲形象才能打动人，讲情感才能感染人，讲道理才能影响人。"[1]《中国文化传播系列丛书》坚持历史维度、国际视野、他者视角。既"以史为系"，系统梳理了中国风土人情、人文地理、文化典籍和社会变迁；又"以史为证"，从历史的角度佐证了当代中国文化发展的内在逻辑，延伸了文化的内涵；同时还"以史为镜"，立足于中国和世界文化发展史，选取最具有典型性的民族文化元素和世界文化交流案例，通过历时性分析概括出超越时空的经验和方法，为世界文化多维度交流互鉴提供了详实资料和理论分析。本丛书系列的译著者具有针对国际学生的中华文化教学的实际经验和思考，能基于读者对象对中华文化的客观诉求、阅读习惯和审美习惯，尤其是国际人士了解历史中国与当代中国的需要，充分发掘和利用中国的地域、经济和文化优势，吸收已有的中华文化研究成果，以民族性和世界性为准则，通过精心科学的内容安排，更适应国际人士了解和认识中国的实际需要，使国际人士更好地了解和理解中国文化，从而在情感上和认知上拉近与中国文化的距离，消除对中国文化的陌生感。

本丛书各部分相互衔接，构成了颇为完整的中华文化丛书系列，其知识

---

〔1〕 习近平：讲好中国故事，传播好中国声音，www.9stheory.cn/zhuanqu/2021-06/02/c_11275 22386.htm，最后访问日期：2022年9月22日。

点对焦国际人士对中华文化了解的需求，能够满足国际人士对历史中国与当代中国了解的需要。本丛书充分考虑到读者对象的中文能力和对中华文化的理解程度，采用中英双语形式呈现，语言通俗易懂，更便于国际人士对中国文化的理解，不失为中国文化国际交流的一种有益探索。

2024 年 9 月 26 日

前　言 / PREFACE

　　谈到中国，人们常说的是历史悠久，地大物博。的确，中国是世界上四大文明古国之一，中华文明是世界上四大文明之一，历时五千余年且绵延不断，在四大文明中绝无仅有。文化是一个国家一个民族的灵魂，也是一个国家一个民族的生命。在 5000 多年文明发展中孕育的中华优秀传统文化，积淀着中华民族最深层的精神追求，代表着中华民族独特的精神标识，是中华民族的集体无意识。中华文化在其发展过程中，兼收并蓄，体现了极大的包容性：从赵武灵王胡服骑射，到北魏孝文帝汉化改革；从"洛阳家家学胡乐"到"万里羌人尽汉歌"；从边疆少数民族习用"上衣下裳""雅歌儒服"，到中原盛行"上衣下裤""胡衣胡帽"等，无不展现了中华文化的互鉴融通。

　　文化的定义甚多，文化包含的范围甚广，很难有一个准确的定义和界定。费孝通认为中华民族是一个自在的民族实体，呈现的是"多元一体的格局"；中华民族经过漫长历史过程形成的文化就是中华文化或中国文化。中华文化大概包含哪些内容？中国文化史的开山之作、柳诒徵先生创稿于二十世纪二十年代的《中国文化史》，可以让我们一窥端倪，该书内容丰富，从中国的典章政治、教育文艺、社会风俗，到经济生活、物产建筑、图画雕刻之类，均有详述。在该书的近代文化史部分，作者以史学家的严谨谈到了西方学术之输入、法制和经济之变迁以及近代之学校教育，进一步体现了中华文化的包容性和发展性，这是中华文化既历史悠久又生机勃发的生命源泉和根本动力。

　　对中国文化的传承与传播方面影响甚大的一本书是中国国学大师钱穆先生所著的《中国文化史导论》。该书从中国文化之地理背景谈到中国国家的形成、民族融合、宗教发展、中华民族的精神特质和性格特征，对中国人和西方人面对外部环境的反应从本质上进行了分析，对中国传统文化之演进从中国文化与欧洲文化的区别入手进行了简明扼要的归纳总结，具有很强的说服力：中国文化是"人类主义"的即"人文主义"的，既不只想求一国的发展，也不想一步步向外扩张其势力，而是具有"世界大同、天下一家"的大观念。热衷向西方人宣传东方的文化和精神并产生了重大影响的辜鸿铭先生在他所著的《春秋大义》一书中指出了中国人的性格和中国文明的特点是"深沉、博大、淳朴、灵敏"。林语堂认为中国文化的精神就是人文主义的精神。中国的人文主义者相信人生的意义，不在于死后来世，而在于享受淳朴生活，尤其是家庭生活的快乐和睦；这样淡朴的快乐，实为人生追求幸福之目标。这是林语堂尽心翻译《浮生六记》的最好注脚，也是普通中国人的普通追求。

"讲好中国故事，传播好中国声音，展示真实、立体、全面的中国"，让国际人士了解中国传统文化是一条有效的路径，这样不仅能增加中华文化的感召力，也能让世界更加了解今日之中国。中文是世界上使用人口最多的语言，英语是世界上使用范围最广的语言，用中英双语介绍中国文化，不仅会降低国际人士通过语言理解中国文化的难度，而且对国际人士通过英语理解中文本身也有裨益，在语言上达到互学互鉴之效。林语堂用英语创作的作品曾经轰动欧美文坛，在用英语向西方介绍中国文化方面取得了杰出的成绩，所著的《生活的艺术》影响深远。精通西学的辜鸿铭，认为中国传统的儒家学说乃仁义之道，可以拯救丛林世界竞争中出现的冷酷与毁灭，他不遗余力地向世界推广中国传统文化，翻译了"四书"中的《大学》《中庸》《论语》等中国传统典籍，在西方引起极大反响。如果辜鸿铭和林语堂两位大师的英语大作是中英对照的，可能对中文国际教育也有意料之外的臂助效果。罗常培先生在其所著的《语言与文化》一书中就说过"语言所反映出来的文化因素显然对于文化本身的透视有很大帮助"。

用英语来讲述中国的文化，就不可避免地涉及文化翻译问题。文化翻译殊非易事，因为仅就文化和翻译之一而言，就不是简单的事。然而也不能因此就裹足不前，因为翻译是一种凭借语言转换的文化传播手段，文化翻译是翻译内在的任务和功能。刘宓庆在他所著的《文化翻译论纲》里就指出"文化翻译的任务不是翻译文化，而是翻译容载或含蕴着文化信息的意义"，文化理解的最大障碍是文化视差，因而翻译文化理解就要注意其整体性和多维性。

为了达到比较好的文化传播效果，不同的译者在翻译中国文化典籍时都会采取种种他们认为有效的翻译策略，今人对利玛窦、理雅各、霍克士、辜鸿铭、林语堂、杨宪益等的翻译策略已有诸多研究。2019 年上海外语教育出版社出版了史志康教授的《〈论语〉翻译与阐释》，杨仁敬先生认为该书有三大特色：其一，面向海外读者，方便欧美读者；其二，采用学术型和通俗型相结合的方法，使译文语言简洁、平易和流畅；其三，在"欣赏与评说"中将《论语》的思想观点与欧美思想家、哲学家、文学家和批评家的重要看法进行比对和参照，"借帆出海"，让中西文化磨合，增进英语读者对《论语》的理解和接受。这种做法拉近了英语读者的文化心理距离，部分地消除了理解中国文化的文化视差，从而较好地达到民心相通的效果。中国文化内容丰富。本丛书分为《中国传统文化》（Understanding Traditional Chinese Culture）、《中国现代文化》（Understanding Modern Chinese Culture）、《中国当代文化》（Understanding Contemporary Chinese Culture），从不同方面用中英双语介绍中国文化，"展现可信、可爱、可敬的中国形象"，以便国际人士更好地理解中国、了解中国，从而更好地知华、友华。感谢中国政法大学出版社的编辑魏星老师对本书的出版付出的智慧和辛劳，感谢史志康教授、胡开宝教授、孙宜学教授等提出的宝贵专业建议。文明互鉴，文化交流，需要更多有志之士的共同努力。

欧阳美和

2024 年 10 月 29 日

目　录　/CONTENTS

第一章　文化与中国文化 ·· 001

Chapter 1　Culture and Chinese Culture

第二章　中国的传统地理文化 ·· 018

Chapter 2　Traditional Chinese Geographical Culture

第三章　中国文化的历史源头 ·· 028

Chapter 3　The Birthplace of Chinese Civilization

第四章　中国的传统政治制度文化 ·· 043

Chapter 4　Traditional Chinese Political System Culture

第五章　中国的传统经济制度文化 ·· 064

Chapter 5　Traditional Chinese Economic System Culture

第六章　中国的传统教育文化 ·· 080

Chapter 6　Traditional Chinese Education Culture

第七章　中国的传统饮食文化 ·· 096

Chapter 7　Traditional Chinese Food Culture

第八章　中国的传统酒文化 ·· 106

Chapter 8　Traditional Chinese Drinking Culture

第九章　中国的传统茶文化 ·· 122

Chapter 9　Traditional Chinese Tea Culture

第十章　中国的传统建筑文化 ……………………………………… 132

Chapter 10　Traditional Chinese Architectural Culture

第十一章　中国的传统绘画文化 …………………………………… 146

Chapter 11　Traditional Chinese Painting Culture

第十二章　中国的传统书法文化 …………………………………… 167

Chapter 12　Traditional Chinese Calligraphy Culture

第十三章　中国的传统舞蹈文化 …………………………………… 181

Chapter 13　Traditional Chinese Dancing Culture

第十四章　中国的传统戏曲文化 …………………………………… 199

Chapter 14　Traditional Chinese Opera Culture

第十五章　中国的传统音乐文化 …………………………………… 209

Chapter 15　Traditional Chinese Music Culture

第十六章　中国传统文学的文化精神 ……………………………… 225

Chapter 16　The Cultural Spirit of Traditional Chinese Literature

第十七章　中国的传统武术文化 …………………………………… 255

Chapter 17　Traditional Chinese Martial Arts Culture

第十八章　中国的传统姓名文化 …………………………………… 273

Chapter 18　Traditional Chinese Name Culture

第十九章　中国的传统节日文化 …………………………………… 282

Chapter 19　Traditional Chinese Festival Culture

第二十章　中国的传统中医文化 …………………………………… 299

Chapter 20　Traditional Chinese Medicine（TCM）Culture

中国文化类词汇中英对照表 ………………………………………… 323

参考文献 ……………………………………………………………… 352

文化与中国文化

一、文化的概念 The Concept of Culture

文化（拼音 wénhuà，英文 culture），是中国语言系统中古已有之的词语。"文"的本义，指各色交错的纹理。"化"，本义为改易、生成、造化，指事物形态或性质的改变，同时"化"又引申为教行迁善之义。

Culture（wén huà in Pinyin, culture in English）is an existing word in the Chinese language system in ancient times. The original meaning of "Wen" refers to the interlaced texture of various colors. "Hua", whose original meaning is change, generation, and creation, refers to the change of the form or nature of things. At the same time, "Hua" is also extended to the meaning of teaching people to behave well.

"文"与"化"联用，较早见之于战国末年儒生编辑的《周易》："观乎天文，以察时变；观乎人文，以化成天下。"意思是：通过观察天象，来了解时序的变化；通过观察人类社会的各种现象，用教育感化的手段来治理天下。"天文"，即天道自然规律。同样，"人文"，指人伦社会规律，即社会生活中人与人之间纵横交织的关系，如君臣、父子、夫妇、兄弟、朋友等。这段话说，治国者须观察天文，以明了时序之变化，又须观察人文，使天下之人均能遵从文明礼仪，行为止其所当止。在这里，"人文"与"化成天下"紧密联系，"以文教化"的思想已十分明确。

The combination of "Wen" and "Hua" was seen earlier in the *Zhouyi* (*The Book of Changes*) edited by Confucian scholars at the end of the Warring States period: "To observe natural phenomena, to observe time changes; to observe humanities, to civilize the people around the world. " It means: by observing astronomical phenomena, we can understand the changes in time sequence; we govern the world by observing various phenomena in human society and using educational methods. "Natural phenomena" refer to the laws of nature. Similarly, "humanity" refers to the social laws of human relations, that is, the intertwined relationships between people in social life, such as the relationship between kings and officials, fathers and sons, husbands and wives, brothers, friends, etc. This passage says that the ruler of the country must observe celestial phenomena to understand the changes in time sequence, and also observe the humanities, so that everyone in the world can obey the civilized etiquette and act as they should. Here, "humanity" is closely related to "civilize the people around the world", and the idea of "educating people with culture" is very clear.

传统的观念认为：文化是人类在社会历史发展过程中所创造的物质财富和精神财富的总和，包括物质文化、制度文化和心理文化三个方面。物质文化是指人类创造的物质文明，包括交通工具、服饰、日常用品等，它是一种可见的显性文化；制度文化和心理文化分别指生活制度、家庭制度、社会制度以及思维方式、宗教信仰、审美情趣，它们属于不可见的隐性文化，包括文学、哲学、政治等方面的内容。人类所创造的精神财富，包括宗教、信仰、风俗习惯、道德情操、学术思想、文学艺术、科学技术、各种制度等。

The traditional view is that culture is the sum of material wealth and spiritual wealth created by mankind in the process of social and historical development, including three aspects which are material culture, institutional culture and psychological culture. Material culture refers to the material civilization created by mankind, including transportation, clothing, daily necessities, etc. It is a visible and explicit culture; institutional culture and psychological culture refer to life system, family system, social system, and way of thinking, religious belief, and aesthetic taste. They belong to the underlying invisible culture, including literature, philosophy, politics and other aspects. The spiritual wealth created by mankind includes religion, belief, customs, moral sentiment, academic thought, literature and art, science and technology, various systems, etc.

人类文化内容具体指族群的历史、风土人情、传统习俗、生活方式、宗教信仰、艺术、伦理道德、法律制度、价值观念、审美情趣、精神图腾等。

文化可分为三个层次：高级文化，包括哲学、文学、艺术、宗教等；大众文化，指习俗、仪式以及包括衣食住行、人际关系各方面的生活方式；深层文化，主要指价值观的美丑定义，时间取向、生活节奏、解决问题的方式以及与性别、阶层、职业、亲属关系相关的个人角色。高级文化和大众文化均植根于深层文化，而深层文化的某一概念又以一种习俗或生活方式反映在大众文化中，以一种艺术形式或文学主题反映在高级文化中。

The content of human culture specifically refers to the history, local customs and practices, traditional customs, lifestyles, religious beliefs, art, ethics, legal systems, values, aesthetic tastes, spiritual totems, etc. of an ethnic group. Culture can be divided into three levels: high culture, including philosophy, literature, art, religion, etc.; popular culture, which refers to customs, rituals, and lifestyles including clothing, food, housing, transportation, and interpersonal relationships; deep culture, mainly referring to the definition of beauty and ugliness, time orientation, pace of life, way of solving problems, and personal roles related to gender, class, occupation, and kinship. Both high culture and popular culture are rooted in deep culture, and a certain concept of deep culture is reflected in popular culture as a custom or lifestyle, and reflected in high culture as an art form or literary theme.

二、中国文化的生成背景 The Background of Chinese Culture

（一）地理环境特征 Geographical environment characteristics

中国地势西高东低，呈阶梯状下降，山地、高原和丘陵约占陆地面积的69%，盆地和平原约占陆地面积的31%。山脉多呈东西和东北——西南走向。地形多种多样，山区面积广大，地势西高东低，向海洋倾斜，一方面有利于海洋上湿润气流深入内地，形成降水；另一方面使许多大河滚滚东流，沟通了东西交通，方便了沿海和内地的经济联系。河流自西向东，逐级下降，河流落差大，水能蕴藏丰富。多种多样的地形为因地制宜发展农、林、牧、副多种经营提供了有利条件。山区在发展林业、牧业、旅游业、采矿业等方面具有优势；但山区地面崎岖，交通不便，不利于农业生产发展。

The terrain of China is higher in the west and lower in the east, descending in a step-like manner. Mountains, plateaus and hills account for about 69% of the land area, and basins and plains account for about 31% of the land area. The mountains are mostly east-west and northeast-southwest. The terrain is diverse, the mountain area is large, the terrain is high in the west and low in the east, and it is inclined to the ocean. On the one hand, it is conducive for the moist air to flow from the ocean to penetrate the inland to form precipitation; on the other hand, many big rivers flow eastward, so it is convenient for east-west transportation and to establish economic ties between the coast and inland. The rivers descend step by step from west to east. Many rivers have a large drop and are rich in water energy. The diverse topography provides favorable conditions for the development of diversified operations in agriculture, forestry, animal husbandry, and sideline according to local conditions. Mountain areas have advantages in the development of forestry, husbandry, tourism, and mining. However, the rugged terrain and inconvenient transportation are not conducive to the development of agricultural production.

中国东濒大海，背靠高山大漠。从帕米尔高原的东南，由北支喀喇昆仑山——阿尔金山——祁连山和南支喜马拉雅山——横断山包围形成了世界上最高、最大的青藏高原，其平均海拔在 4000 米以上，冰山雪峰，直插云汉，成为中西陆上交通的巨大屏障。从帕米尔高原向东北，天山——阿尔泰山——萨彦岭——外兴安岭横亘在蒙古高原外围，成为中国西北和北方的一道天然长城。这两条由帕米尔高原分别向东南和东北向延伸的巨大山系，对于地处亚欧大陆东端的中国来说，恰恰形成了"人"字形的包围之势，它们构成了封闭中国的骨架。而在中国的西南，中缅、中越边境同样山峦连绵，澜沧江、金沙江、乌江等大江大河从峻岭峡谷中奔腾而下，构成山高水险之势。加之热带丛林瘴疬盛行，风雨水泛，地广人稀，在古代与中原交往极为困难。

China faces the sea to the east, backed by mountains and deserts. From the southeast of the Pamirs, the northern branch of Karakoram-Altun-Qilian Mountains and the southern branch of Himalayas-Hengduan Mountains form the world's highest and largest Qinghai-Tibet Plateau, with an average elevation of more than 4000 meters. Icebergs and snow peaks, high into the sky, have become a huge barrier for land traffic between China and the West. From the Pamirs to the northeast, Tianshan Mountain-Altai Mountain-Sayan Mountain-Outer Hinggan Range stretches across the Mongolian Plateau, becoming a natural Great Wall in northwest and north China. These two huge mountain series extending from the Pamirs to the southeast and northeast respectively, for China, which is located at the eastern end of the Eurasian continent, have formed the encircling trend of the "人" (meaning man) shape, and they constitute the framework of the closed China. In southwest China, the China-Myanmar and Sino-Vietnamese borders are similarly mountainous. Large rivers such as Lancang River, Jinsha River, and Wujiang River rush down the steep gorges, forming a potential of high mountains and dangerous water. Coupled with the prevalence of tropical miasmic jungle, wind and rain, and sparsely populated land, it was extremely difficult for these countries to communicate with the Central Plains in ancient times.

这种一面临海，其他三面与域外陆路交通极不便利的地理环境，造成了中国与外部世界相对隔绝的状态，一方面妨碍了中国与外部世界的文化交流，另一方面也有助于中国文化按其自身规律而自我发展。首先，相对封闭的地理环境，造就了华夏中心主义的心理定式，以华夏为天下的中心，四周的则是蛮夷之邦。这种视栖身之地为天下中央的观念，主要缘于古代中国人与外部世界缺少交流，疏于了解。历史上，古希腊、两河文明通过地中海有着频繁的交流，而在中国早期的古籍中，很难找到有关其他文明的记载。其次，偏居一方的地理位置，形成了中国文化的"保护反应机制"，使中国文化具有超常的连续性和稳定性。与中国同处近似纬度地带的古老的尼罗河流域文明、两河流域文明和印度河流域文明，在其发展过程中相继中断，唯有中国文化在与外来文化的碰撞中，虽数度受到异质文化的冲击，却表现出对异质文化的巨大涵摄能力，最终将其融入本土文化中，其重要原因之一，在于中国与外部世界虽相对隔绝，但疆土广袤，腹地纵深，有着极为宽绰的回旋余地。

This geographical environment, which faces the sea on one side and on the other three sides is extremely inconvenient for land transportation outside the region, creates a relatively isolated state from the outside world. On the one hand, it hinders the cultural exchanges between China and the outside world, and on the other hand, it also helps Chinese culture to develop by its own laws. First of all, the relatively closed geographical environment created the psychological stereotype of Huaxia-centrism, taking Huaxia (an ancient name for China) as the center of the world, and the other surrounding countries are barbarians. This notion that the place of residence is the center of the world is mainly due to the lack of communication and understanding between the ancient Chinese and the outside world. Historically, ancient Greek and Mesopotamian civilizations had frequent exchanges through the Mediterranean. However, it is difficult to find records of other civilizations in early Chinese ancient books. Secondly, the geographical location of living isolated has formed the "protection response mechanism" of Chinese culture, which has made Chinese culture have extraordinary continuity and stability. The ancient civilizations of the Nile River Basin, Mesopotamia and Indus Basin civilizations, which are located at the same latitudes as China, have been interrupted in the course of their development. In the collision between Chinese culture and foreign cultures, although it has been impacted by heterogeneous cultures several times, it has shown great ability to contemplate heterogeneous cultures and finally integrate them into local culture. One of the important reasons is that although China is relatively isolated from the outside world, its territory is vast and its land is spacious enough to offer ample room for maneuvers.

（二）农耕经济特点 Farming economic characteristics

中国的地势西高东低，黄河、长江等大江大河由西向东奔流入海，所携带的泥沙积淀成辽阔肥沃的大平原。古代中原地区，黄河流域有很多支流，适宜于农业发展。从太平洋吹来的东南季风，给长江中下游地区带来了丰沛的降水，为农业文明的诞生和发展提供了有利的条件。以农立国的国策、农耕工具的改进和耕作技术的提高，大大促进了农业文明的发展。长江流域稻作经济的普及，以及朝廷移民开边屯田政策的推行，使中国的农耕区不断拓展。农耕经济是古代中国立国的基础，也是传统文化赖以发生和发展的经济基础。

The terrain of China is high in the west and low in the east. The Yellow River and the Yangtze River and other large rivers flow from west to east into the sea, and the sediment carried by them accumulates into a vast and fertile plain. In the ancient Central Plains, the Yellow River Basin had many tributaries, which was suitable for agricultural development. The southeast monsoon blowing from the Pacific Ocean brought abundant precipitation to the middle and lower reaches of the Yangtze River, and provided favorable conditions for the birth and development of agricultural civilization. The national policy of establishing the country by agriculture, the improvement of farming tools and techniques greatly promoted the development of agricultural civilization. The popularization of the rice farming economy in the Yangtze River Basin and the implementation of the policy of opening borders and farming fields by imperial immigrants enabled the continuous expansion of China's farming areas. Farming economy was the foundation of ancient China, and it was also the economic foundation on which traditional culture occured and developed.

以渔樵耕读为代表的农耕文明是千百年来中华民族生产生活的实践总结，是华夏儿女以不同形式延续下来的精华浓缩并传承至今的一种文化形态，和谐的理念已广播人心，所体现的哲学精髓正是传统文化核心价值观的重要精神资源。从思想观念方面来看，农耕文明所蕴含的精华思想和文化品格都是十分优秀的，例如培养和孕育出爱国主义、团结统一、独立自主、爱好和平、自强不息、集体至上、尊老爱幼、勤劳勇敢、吃苦耐劳、艰苦奋斗、勤俭节约、邻里相帮等文化传统和核心价值理念，值得充分肯定和借鉴。中国传统文化中理想的家庭模式是"耕读传家"，即既要有"耕"来维持家庭生活，又要有"读"来提高家庭的文化水平。这种培养式的农耕文明推崇自然和谐，契合中华文化对于人生最高修养的乐天知命原则，乐天是知晓宇宙的法则和规律，知命则是懂得生命的价值和真谛。崇尚耕读生活，提倡合作包容，而不是掠夺式利用自然资源，这符合今天的和谐发展理念。

The farming civilization represented by fishing, woodcutting, cultivating, and studying is a summary of the practice of the production and life of the Chinese nation for thousands of years. It is a cultural form that has been condensed and passed down to the present by the Chinese people in different forms. The concept of harmony has been broadcast to the hearts of the people, and the philosophical essence embodied is an important spiritual resource for the core values of traditional culture. From the perspective of ideological concepts, the core values of agricultural civilization and cultural characters are very good, such as cultivating and nurturing patriotism, unity, independence, peace-loving, self-improvement, collective supremacy, respecting the old and loving the young, diligence and bravery, hard work and frugality, and neighborhood help, worthy of full recognition and reference. The ideal family model in traditional Chinese culture is "farming and studying from generation to generation", that is, there must be both "farming" to maintain family life, and "studying" to improve the family's cultural level. This cultivated farming civilization respects natural harmony and conforms to the Chinese culture's principle of optimism and recognition of destiny for the highest level of cultivation. Optimism is to know the laws and rules of the universe, and recognition of destiny is to understand the value and true meaning of life. Advocating a career in farming and studying, advocating cooperation and tolerance, rather than predatory use of natural resources, this is in line with today's harmonious development concept.

农耕文明决定了中华文化的特征。中国的文化是有别于欧洲游牧文化的一种文化类型，农业在其中起着决定作用。欧洲文明掠夺式特征，诞生于此前的狩猎文化，与滥觞于种植的中国文明存在明显的差别。聚族而居、精耕细作的农业文明孕育了内敛式自给自足的生活方式、文化传统、农政思想、乡村管理制度等，与今天提倡的和谐、环保、低碳的理念不谋而合。历史上，游牧式的文明经常因为无法适应环境的变化，以致突然消失。而农耕文明的地域多样性、民族多元性、历史传承性和乡土民间性，不仅赋予中华文化重要特征，也是中华文化之所以绵延不断、长盛不衰的重要原因。

Farming civilization determines the characteristics of Chinese culture. Chinese culture is a type of culture different from European nomadic culture, and agriculture plays a decisive role in it. The predatory characteristics of European civilization were born in the previous hunting culture, which is obviously different from the Chinese civilization that originated in planting. The agricultural civilization that gathers together and cultivates intensively has nurtured introverted self-sufficient lifestyles, cultural traditions, agricultural policies, rural management systems, etc. , which coincides with the harmonious, environmentally friendly, and low-carbon concepts advocated today. Historically, nomadic civilizations often disappeared suddenly because they could not adapt to changes in the environment. The geographical diversity, ethnic diversity, historical heritage, and local folk nature of agricultural civilization not only endow Chinese culture with important characteristics, but also an important reason why Chinese culture continues to flourish.

（三）中国文化的基本特征 Basic characteristics of Chinese culture

不同民族的文化，产生并发展于不同的地理环境及经济和社会的土壤中，从而使不同民族的文化呈现出不同特征。就中国文化的总体面貌而言，其具有人文性、包容性、伦理性、和谐性、务实性等诸种特征。

The cultures of different nationalities are produced and developed in different geographical environments and economic and social soils, so that the cultures of different nationalities present different characteristics. As far as the overall appearance of Chinese culture is concerned, it has various characteristics such as humanity, inclusiveness, ethics, harmony, and pragmatism.

1. 人文性 Humanity

中国古代先哲不同于古希腊人专注于自然哲学的探究，着意探究宇宙的终极本体，把人与自然置于对立的两极，思考人怎样去认识自然、战胜自然。也不同于中东——印度地区的古典文化，对超自然的东西刻意关注，以探求人与神的关系。中国文化从思考人类自身的存在出发，以人为中心建构起自己的理论体系，强调人本位，将天、地、人三者并列，以人为宇宙的中心，认为人是"万物之本"，"最为天下贵"。

The ancient Chinese philosophers were different from the ancient Greeks who focused on the exploration of natural philosophy. They deliberately explored the ultimate ontology of the universe, placed man and nature at opposite poles, and thought about how people understand and defeat nature. It is also different from the classical culture of the Middle East—India, which deliberately pays attention to the supernatural in order to explore the relationship between man and god. Chinese culture starts from thinking about the existence of human beings, constructing its own theoretical system centered on human beings, emphasizing humanism, juxtaposing heaven, earth, and human beings, taking human as the center of the universe, and thinking that human beings are "the foundation of all things" "the most valuable in the world".

人文性的特征使中国文化具有鲜明的非宗教性倾向。自周代以来，神权在中国历史上从未占据统治地位，王权始终高于神权。周代统治者鉴于商朝灭亡的教训，已经认识到民意的重要，"重民轻神"的民本思潮开始兴起，殷商时代盛行一时的宗教意识得到抑制。重民轻神的传统随着以后儒学的勃兴又得到进一步发展。作为中国思想文化主流的儒学，其关注的是现世人生。这种重人道轻神道的思想，体现了人文性的特征。

The characteristics of humanity make Chinese culture have a distinct non-religious tendency. Since Zhou Dynasty, theocracy had never occupied a dominant position in Chinese history, and the royal power had always been higher than the theocracy. In view of the lessons from the demise of Shang Dynasty, the rulers of Zhou Dynasty had realized the importance of public opinion. The people-based thought of "valuing the people and despising the gods" began to rise, and the religious consciousness that prevailed during the Shang era was suppressed. The tradition of valuing the people and despising the gods has been further developed with the rise of Confucianism. As the mainstream of Chinese ideology and culture, Confucianism focuses on life in this world. This kind of thought of emphasizing humanity and despising Gods reflects the characteristics of humanity.

中国文化的人文性又体现在人生价值的自我实现。它不主张人去追求灵魂的不朽，而是要求人们关注现实人生，把内在的道德修养和外在的道德实践，即"内圣"和"外王"结合起来，努力地立德、立功、立言，从而实现理想人格。中国文化重视人生、关注现世的思想，在历史上曾经起过积极的作用。当欧洲文化笼罩在中世纪基督教神学之下而黯然失色时，中国人却在世界东方创造了高峰迭起的封建文化。当然，上述中国文化的人文性不同于现代意义上的人文精神，它所说的人并非具有独立性的个人，而是依附于宗法集团的人。

The humanity of Chinese culture is reflected in the self-realization of life value. It does not advocate that people pursue the immortality of the soul, but requires people to pay attention to the real life, to combine the inner moral cultivation with the outer moral practice, that is, "Inner Sageliness" and "Outer Kingliness", and strive to make a moral person, make achievement and make publication, so as to realize the ideal personality. Chinese culture values human life and pays attention to the thoughts of the present life, which has played an active role in history. While European culture was eclipsed by medieval Christian theology, the Chinese created a feudal culture with peaks in the east of the world. Of course, the humanity of the above-mentioned Chinese culture is different from the humanistic spirit in the modern sense. The people it refers to were not yet independent individuals, but attached to the patriarchal group.

2. 包容性 Inclusiveness

中国文化从来就不是一个自我封闭的僵死体系，中国文化的博大精深与绵延至今，在于它的兼容并包的宽容胸襟，在于对不同区域或民族文化的交汇与融合中，求得顽强的生存与发展。

Chinese culture has never been a self-enclosed rigid system. The breadth, depth and continuity of Chinese culture lies in its inclusiveness, in the convergence and integration of different regions or national cultures, to seek tenacious survival and development.

就汉民族内部而言，主要的区域文化有黄河流域的中原文化，以及长江流域的巴蜀文化、楚文化和吴越文化等。早在秦统一中国前，不同的区域文化之间就有着密切的交流。就汉族与境内其他少数民族的关系而言，民族间的文化在双向传播中互采各家之长。早在《尚书》中就提出"协和万邦"的理念，主张不同邦国和睦共处，彼此包容。周人灭商后，能吸纳殷商族群，在不同的诸侯国内，与当地土著民族共存同处。文化包容的传统有助于不同地域的文化融汇发展。

As far as the Han nationality is concerned, the main regional cultures include the Central Plains culture in the Yellow River basin, and the Bashu, Chu and Wuyue cultures in the Yangtze River basin. Long before Qin unified China, there were close exchanges between different regional cultures. As far as the relationship between the Han nationality and other ethnic minorities in the territory is concerned, the cultures between the nationalities adopt each other's strengths in two-way communication. As early as the King Yao, the concept of "coexistence of all in harmony" was put forward as early as in *The Book of Documents* which advocated the harmonious coexistence of different nations and mutual tolerance. After the Zhou people destroyed the Shang, they could absorb the Shang ethnic group, and coexisted with the local indigenous peoples in different vassal countries. The tradition of cultural inclusiveness is conducive to the development of cultural integration in different regions.

对于境外文化，中国文化多能以宽阔的胸怀去迎接挑战，并加以采撷、消化和吸纳，使之成为中华文化的有机组成部分。钱穆说："中国在世界上，是比较算得一个文化孤立的国家。但中国不断与其四邻异族相交通相接触。中国的对西交通，有西北的陆线与西南的海线两条大路。"

Regarding foreign cultures, Chinese culture can generally meet challenges with a broad mind, and collect, digest, and absorb them to make them an organic part of Chinese culture. Mr. Qian Mu (a famous scholar of Chinese culture) said: "China is a relatively culturally isolated country in the world. However, China is constantly in contact with its neighbors and other races. China's communication to the west has two main roads, a land line in the northwest and a sea line in the southwest. "

从中国文化的总体发展来看，其虽屡经内忧外患却一次又一次地表现出顽强的再生能力，历经数千年而从未中断，这一现象固然与农业宗法社会所具有的顽强的延续力有关，与半封闭的大陆环境所形成的隔离机制有关，同时，中国文化本身所具有的包容性特点也是重要原因之一。

From the perspective of the overall development of Chinese culture, despite repeated internal and external troubles, it has shown its tenacious regeneration ability time and time again. After thousands of years, it has never been interrupted. This phenomenon is certainly consistent with the tenacious continuity of the agricultural patriarchal society. It is related to the isolation mechanism formed by the semi-closed mainland environment. At the same time, the inclusive characteristics of Chinese culture itself is also one of the important reasons.

3. 伦理性 Ethics

中国文化具有鲜明的伦理道德倾向，偏重道德的价值取向在中国传统文化中处于亘古不变的核心地位。中国文化中的传统道德，正是为适应家国一体的宗法社会的需要而形成的。宗法制社会结构以血缘宗法组织为基石，家族或宗族的存在与巩固，离不开以血缘关系为纽带的长幼尊卑秩序，传统道德的重要功能之一，即是维护这种尊卑秩序。传统伦理道德的形成经历了长期而复杂的积淀过程，对铸造中国人的道德品质和民族精神产生过深远的影响。

Chinese culture has a distinct ethical and moral tendency, and the value orientation that emphasizes morality is in the everlasting core position in traditional Chinese culture. The traditional morality in Chinese culture was formed to meet the needs of a patriarchal society where family and country were unified. The social structure of the feudal clan system was based on the blood-related patriarchal organization. The existence and consolidation of a family or clan cannot be separated from the order of elders and children with kinship as the bond. One of the important functions of traditional morality is to maintain this order of the respectable and inferior. The formation of traditional ethics had gone through a long and complicated accumulation process, which had a profound impact on the moral character and national spirit of the Chinese people.

中国文化的伦理性特点有以下几方面的显著表现：首先，历代统治者视道德感化为政治统治的重要手段，将有助于统治稳固、社会有序的道德规范去"教化"民众，以规范社会成员的思想与行为，此即所谓"以德治国"；其次，强调个人的伦理义务，要求个人服从整体。中国传统文化不主张个人意志的高扬，而是强调个体与整体的融合，个体利益必须服从家庭、宗族乃至国家的利益，并以此为仁义道德之本；最后，强调个人自身的道德修养，视"修身"为立命之根本。

The ethical characteristics of Chinese culture are manifested in the following aspects: First, the rulers of the past dynasties regarded moral influence as an important means of political rule, to "educate" the people with moral norms to normalize the thoughts and behaviors of the people in order to keep stable governance and social order, which was called "ruling the country by virtue". Secondly, it emphasized the ethical obligations of individuals and required individuals to obey the whole. Chinese traditional culture did not advocate the promotion of individual will, but emphasized the integration of the individual and the whole. Individual interests must be subordinated to the interests of the family, clan and even the country, and this was the foundation of benevolence and morality. Lastly, Chinese culture emphasizes the individual's own moral cultivation, regards "self-cultivation" as the foundation of establishing oneself in the world.

中国传统的伦理性文化把上至天子、下及庶民都作为道德教育的对象，强调"为仁由己"，突出个人道德修养的自觉性和主动性，旨在塑造"至善"的人格，培养具有理想品德的"君子"。

The traditional Chinese ethical culture regarded the emperor, and the common people as the object of moral education, emphasized "readily practice benevolence and virtue", highlighted the self-consciousness and initiative of personal moral cultivation, and aimed to shape "the best" personality and cultivate a "gentleman" with ideal character.

4. 和谐性 Harmony

中国地理环境虽然相对封闭，但腹地辽阔，气候适宜，具有比较优越的农耕生产条件。生活在这片土地上的中华民族，与天地自然和睦相处，人要求与"天"合为一体的朴素愿望，随农业生产的发展而积淀为民族心理，也造就了中国文化的和谐精神。

Although China's geographical environment is relatively closed, its hinterland is vast, the climate is suitable, and it has relatively superior farming conditions. The Chinese people living on this land had a simple desire to live in harmony with the heaven and the earth, and to integrate with the "heaven", and the desire has accumulated as a national psychology with the development of agricultural production and also created the harmonious spirit of Chinese culture.

天人合一的思想强调人与自然要和谐相处，认为人与自然不是截然分离的对立物，人的存在与自然的存在是互相包含的。首先，天人合一思想肯定天地、万物、人是齐同的，同类相通，统一成一个整体。其次，人是"天地之心"。最后，人的活动要遵从自然的法则，与自然环境和谐交融。

The idea of harmony between man and nature emphasizes that man and nature should live in harmony. It believes that man and nature are not completely separate opposites, and that the existence of man and nature is mutually contained. First of all, the idea of the unity of nature and man affirms that the world, all things, and people are the same, or similar to each other, and unified into a whole. Secondly, man is the "center of heaven and earth". Thirdly, human activities must comply with the laws of nature and blend harmoniously with the natural environment.

情景合一是中华民族在创造美和鉴赏美时所追求的一种境界，其深层文化内核在于"天人合一"。它要求在追寻、创造美的过程中，执着于人的情感与自然、社会的"合一"，在再现自然之美、社会之真时渗透主体色彩，使审美客体成为被主体心灵所外化的客体，使"美"与"真"、"美"与"善"有机统一。在审美过程中，要求把人与自然、社会即审美主体与客体联系起来，强调客体与主体的和谐交融，这都体现了中国文化 "和谐性" 的特点。

The unity of sentiment and scene is a realm pursued by the Chinese nation when creating and appreciating beauty and its deep cultural core lies in "the unity of man and nature." It requires that in the process of pursuing and creating beauty, it is obsessed with the "unity" of human emotions, nature and society, and permeates the color of the subject while reproducing the beauty of nature and the truth of society, so that the aesthetic object becomes an object externalized by the subject's mind, thus "beauty" and "truth", "beauty" and "good" are organically unified. In the aesthetic process, it is required to connect human beings with nature, society, that is, the aesthetic subject and object, and it emphasizes the harmonious blending of the object and the subject. All above reflect the "harmonious" characteristics of Chinese culture.

总的来说，"合一" 就是让并存的不同事物在矛盾中求得统一，从而达到平衡协调，以推动事物的发展。"天人合一"、"知行合一" 和 "情景合一" 反映了中国文化重视平衡协调的理念，是古代中国人对天道运行规律的认识、追求人道政教的目标、建构 "美" 的思想构架。

In general, "unity" is to allow different coexisting things to seek unity in contradiction, so as to achieve balance and coordination, and to promote the development of things. "The unity of man and nature", "the unity of knowledge and action", and "the unity of sentiment and scene" reflect the concept of Chinese culture that emphasizes balance and coordination. It is the ancient Chinese understanding of the laws of the heavens, the pursuit of humanitarian, political and religious goals, and the construction of the thinking framework of "beauty".

5. 务实性 Pragmatism

务实性作为一种民族性格，植根于农耕经济的厚实土壤。历史上以农为本的中华民族在长期的生产实践中，形成 "一分耕耘一分收获" 的共识。

As a national character, pragmatism is rooted in the solid soil of farming economy. Historically, the agricultural-oriented Chinese nation has formed a consensus of "no pain, no gain" in long-term production practices.

中国文化的务实性，使之成为一种非宗教的、世俗的文化，其文化精神不在于力求构造彼岸世界和灵魂永存的幻象，也不去深究空疏世界的玄奥，而是告诫人们立足于此岸世界，把"立德、立功、立言"作为实现人生价值的目标。中国文化走的是"经世致用"的道路，儒家为人们指出一条影响深远的成己、成人的路径"修身、齐家、治国、平天下"。这里，"修身"是道德，"齐家、治国、平天下"是须躬身笃行的政治。"经世致用"所强调的正是关注现世的务实精神，所以，中国古代知识分子大体都是"入世"型的。所谓"致用"指的是学必有用，求知要与躬行结合起来。在民间，中国人历来视吃苦耐劳、勤俭节约、稳健务实为美德，满足于现世生活的幸福，相对于追求来世灵魂的不朽，更偏重于现世的实践理性。

The pragmatic spirit of Chinese culture has turned it into a non-religious but secular culture. Its cultural spirit does not lie in striving to construct the illusion of the everlasting soul in the other world or the other shore, nor does it delve into the mystery of the empty world, but warns people to stand on this shore. The world takes "make a moral person, make achievement, make publication" as the goal of realizing the value of life. Chinese culture is following the path where "study of ancient classics should meet present needs". Confucianism points out a far-reaching path for people to become oneself and a man, "cultivating oneself, managing the family, governing the country, and pacifying the world." Here, "cultivating" is morality, "governing the family, governing the country, and governing the world" are politics that must be practiced hard. "Study of ancient classics should meet present needs" emphasizes the pragmatic spirit of paying attention to the present world. Therefore, the intellectuals in ancient China were generally of the "living in the world" type. The so-called "use" means that learning must be useful, and seeking knowledge must be combined with practice. In daily life, the Chinese have usually considered hardworking, thrift, pragmatism as virtues. They are satisfied with the happiness of life in this world. Compared with pursuing the immortality of the soul in the next life, Chinese prefer practical rationality in this world.

务实精神使中国人在宗教方面未陷入迷狂，尽管中国本土产生有宗教，也输入了一些宗教，但历史上从未有哪种宗教成为国教。中国文化把人生价值的实现、精神和事业的"不朽"建立在实实在在的现实世界。实用理性的发达曾使古代中国在天文学、农学、医学、数学等应用科学领域长期处于领先的地位，但同时，重经验、重直觉、重实际应用的基本取向，导致对理论探讨和逻辑论证的相对忽视，这一旧有框架阻碍了传统科技的进一步发展。

The pragmatic spirit keeps the Chinese people from being crazy about religion. Although there are religions in China and some religions have been imported, no religion has ever become the state religion in history. Chinese culture establishes the realization of the value of life, the "immortality" of the spirit and career in the real world. The development of practical rationality once made ancient China a long-term leading position in applied disciplines such as astronomy, agriculture, medicine, and mathematics. Meanwhile, the basic orientation of emphasizing experience, intuition, and practical application led to the relative neglect of theoretical discussion and logical argumentation; as a result, the old framework hindered the further development of traditional technology in China.

＊ Culture means "The training, development, and refinement of mind, tastes, and manners; the condition of being thus trained and refined; the intellectual side of civilization"

中国的传统地理文化

一、中国地理的基本知识 Basic Knowledge of Chinese Geography

中国第一大岛是台湾岛。中国四大佛教名山指五台山、普陀山、九华山、峨眉山。中国山地面积约占全国总面积的 1/3。中国绝大部分地区具有大陆性气候特点，即夏雨冬干、气温年差较大。中国发生最频繁、影响最大的气象灾害是旱涝灾害。中国能源生产消费中最多的是煤。中国地势特点是西高东低，呈现三级阶梯。中国陆地边界全长 2.28 万公里。中国大陆基本轮廓形成时期，陆地上出现了大量的裸子植物。中国共有 14 个陆地邻国。中国最大的内陆咸水湖是青海湖。中国海洋气温最高值出现在 8 月。中国最热的地方在吐鲁番盆地。中国的大陆海岸线有 1.8 万公里。在中国，自古就有"天府之国"美誉的地区是四川盆地。中国最大的淡水湖是鄱阳湖。

The largest island in China is Taiwan Island. The four famous Buddhist mountains in China refer to Mount Wutai, Mount Putuo, Mount Jiuhua, and Mount E'mei. The mountain area accounts for about 1/3 of the total area in China. Most areas of China have the characteristics of continental climate, that is, in summer it rains and in winter it is dry, and the annual range of temperature is relatively big. The most frequent and most influential weather disasters in China are droughts and floods. Coal is the largest source of energy production and consumption in China. The terrain of China is characterized by the high west and the low east, forming a three-level ladder. The total length of China's land border is 22, 800 kilometers. When the basic mainland outline of China was formed, a large number of gymnosperms appeared on the land. China has 14 land neighbors. The largest inland saltwater lake in China is Qinghai Lake in Qinghai province. The highest ocean temperature in China occurs in August. The hottest place in China is in Turpan Basin. The maritime disaster that has the most severe impact on China is typhoon. China has 18, 000 kilometers of mainland coastline. In China, Sichuan Basin has been known as the "Land of Plenty" since ancient time. The largest freshwater lake in China is Poyang Lake.

二、中国传统文化与地理环境 Traditional Chinese Culture and Geographical Environment

中国传统文化诞生在中国这一特定的地理环境里，在发展的过程中形成了自己的独特性，地理环境对中国传统文化的特征产生了深远而持久的影响。

Traditional Chinese culture was born in this specific geographical environment of China and formed its own uniqueness in the process of development. The geographical environment has had a profound and lasting influence on the characteristics of traditional Chinese culture.

1. 优越的地理环境，形成了基于农耕文明的民族文化性格。首先，中国大部分地区处于亚热带和温带，非常适宜人的居住；其次，东部地势平坦，大多是冲积平原，土地肥沃，还有许多源远流长的大江大河和为数众多的湖泊，提供了农业灌溉和航运的便利；最后，气候雨热同期，降水和热量配合较好，大部分地区雨季与热季同时到来，为农作物的生长提供了非常好的条件，成为发展农业的理想地区，为中国传统文化的发展提供了重要的物质基础。

The superior geographical environment has formed a national cultural character based on farming civilization. First, most of China is in the subtropical and temperate zone, which is very suitable for people to live in. Second, the east is flat, mostly alluvial plains, fertile land, and there are many long rivers and numerous lakes, which provide agricultural irrigation and navigation. Third, the time of rain and heat is almost at the same period, thus precipitation and heat are well coordinated. In most areas, the rainy season and the hot season come at the same time, providing very good conditions for the growth of crops, and making China an ideal area for the development of agriculture, which provides an important material basis for the development of traditional Chinese culture.

中华民族在长期的农业生活中，形成了自己独特的民族文化性格。首先，求实入世的生活态度。传统的农业生产方式，使人们懂得"几分耕耘，几分收获"，"种瓜得瓜，种豆得豆"的道理，因此"重实际而黜玄想"。其次，对人与人、人与自然和谐一体的认识。文明早期艰苦的农业生活，导致人们对自然界的依赖并对其产生感恩戴德的心理。农业生活自然的季节密切相关，人们在生活中处处表现出对自然规律的顺应，在文化上表现为追寻一种"天人合一"的境界。

The Chinese nation has formed its own unique national cultural character in its long-term agricultural life. First of all, the life attitude is realistic and practical. The traditional methods of agricultural production enabled people to understand the principles of "little hard work, little harvest", "planting melons to get melons, sowing beans to get beans", and therefore "emphasizing reality and abandoning fantasy". Secondly, the understanding of harmony between man and man, man and nature. The arduous agricultural life in the early days of civilization led to people's dependence on the natural world and a feeling of gratitude for it. The seasons of nature are closely related, and people show compliance with the laws of nature in their lives, and culturally it is the pursuit of a realm of "unity of nature and man".

2. 复杂的地理环境，形成了具有多样性和包容性的、一体多元的传统文化。中国地域辽阔，地势西高东低，自西向东呈阶梯状逐级下降的态势，同时具备山地、高原、丘陵、盆地和平原五大基本地貌类型，其中又以山地和高原的面积最广。辽阔的地域，复杂的地形，往往形成了多样的气候，"十里不同天，百里不同日"的现象在中国十分普遍，具备了从热带到寒温带的各种气候类型。复杂的地形和多样的气候，形成了各具特色的地缘文化和区域思想观念。

The complex geographic environment has formed a diverse, inclusive, and integrated traditional culture. China has a vast territory, high in the west and low in the east, and descends step by step from west to east. At the same time, it has five basic landform types: mountains, plateaus, hills, basins and plains, among which mountains and plateaus cover the largest area. The vast area and complex topography often form diverse climates. The phenomenon of "ten miles bring different weathers, a hundred miles bring different days" is very common in China, with various climate types ranging from tropical to cold temperate. The complex terrain and diverse climate have formed distinctive geo-cultural and regional ideas.

中国早在先秦时代就形成了各具特色、对后世影响深远的齐鲁文化、燕赵文化、三秦文化、荆楚文化、吴越文化、巴蜀文化及岭南文化等。中原地区由于对农业的重视而养成安土重迁的观念；东南沿海一带由于耕地有限，重视海外贸易，思想观念开放；西北的绿洲地区因土地限制和地处交通要道，商业发展较早；北方游牧民族由于环境恶劣，不得不以频繁的迁徙和战争来对付环境的压力。中国的区域文化虽然表现出明显的差异，但又并存于中国传统文化之中，形成了中国传统文化的一体多元结构。随着中国农耕经济向周边的扩张，中国传统文化固有的包容性又促使区域文化相辅相成、渐趋合一。儒、道、佛三教的并行而立，盛唐时的胡汉交融，都充分地说明了这一点。正是由于这种多样性及包容性，中国传统文化始终保持着生机与活力。

As early as the pre-Qin era, Qilu (now Shandong Province) culture, Yanzhao (now Beijing and Hebei Province) culture, Three-Qin (now Shaanxi Province) culture, Jingchu (now Hubei Province) culture, Wuyue (now Zhejiang Province and Jiangsu Province) culture, Bashu (now Sichuan Province and Chongqing) culture and Lingnan (now Guangdong Province and Guangxi Province) culture were formed with their own characteristics and far-reaching influence on later generations. People living in the Central Plains region developed the sense of attachment to the land and unwillingness to more; the southeast coastal area has limited arable land and emphasizes international trade, and has an open mind. The oasis area in the northwest developed business and trade much earlier due to land restrictions but key transportation routes. Because of the harsh environment, the northern nomads had to resort to frequent migrations and wars to deal with environmental pressures. Although China's regional cultures show obvious differences, they coexist in Chinese traditional culture, forming an integrated and diverse structure of culture. With the expansion of China's farming economy to the periphery, the inherent inclusiveness of Chinese traditional culture has prompted regional cultures to complement each other and gradually become one. The three religions of Confucianism, Taoism and Buddhism stand side by side, and the blending of Hu (the minorities in the north and west of China) and Han nationalities in the flourishing Tang Dynasty fully illustrates this point. It is precisely because of this diversity and inclusiveness that traditional Chinese culture has maintained its vitality and vigour.

3. 完整而广阔的地理环境，形成了不曾中断、具有连续性的传统文化。中国有相对完整的地理环境。东部大多为平原、丘陵，西部大多为高原、山地，黄河、长江两大河流经中国的腹地。中国地域广阔，面积 960 万平方公里，与整个欧洲的面积差不多。完整而广阔的地理环境，为文化的生成和发展提供了广阔的空间和回旋余地。中国与古埃及、古巴比伦、古印度同为世界四大文明古国，但不同的是：中国文化的发展从一开始便依托黄河、长江两大流域，内部拥有广阔的回旋余地。

历史一再表明，当北方强悍的游牧民族挥师南下，中原王朝在失去黄河流域时，还可以以长江流域及珠江流域为依托延续着自己的文化。因而在中国历史上，西晋、北宋灭亡，随后还能在东南一隅分别建立了东晋、南宋，并且都延续一百多年。正是因为拥有这种回旋余地较大的空间，使得中国文化不像古埃及、古巴比伦、古印度等古文化在后来的历史进程中，或是被取代而中断，或是湮灭、消失了。在数千年的人类文明进程中，中国文化是唯一不曾中断的、具有连续性的文化，这是人类历史上的奇迹，在很大程度上不得不归功于中国拥有完整而广阔的地理环境。中国传统文化在对周边外来文化进行潜移默化中，始终保持着自己完整的风格和日趋完善的系统，长期绵延不绝，使中国文化具有较强的自信心和稳定的发展过程。

The complete and broad geographical environment has formed an uninterrupted and continuous traditional culture. China has a relatively complete geographical environment. The east is mostly plains and hills, and the west is mostly plateaus and mountains. The Yellow River and Yangtze River flow through the hinterland of China. China has a vast territory, covering an area of 9.6 million square kilometers, which is about the same size as the entire Europe. The complete and broad geographical environment provides a broad space and room for maneuver for the generation and development of culture. China, and ancient Egypt, Babylon, and ancient India, are the world's four major ancient civilizations, but what makes China so different is that the development of Chinese culture has relied on the Yellow River and the Yangtze River from the very beginning, and has a vast room for maneuver inside.

History has shown time and again that when the powerful northern nomads' marching south made Central Plains dynasties lose the Yellow River basin, they could still continue their own culture based on the Yangtze River Basin and the Pearl River Basin. Therefore, in Chinese history, the Western Jin and Northern Song dynasties were destroyed, and then the Eastern Jin and Southern Song dynasties were established in the southeast respectively, and both lasted for more than 100 years. It is precisely because of this large room for maneuver that Chinese culture is not like ancient Egyptian, Babylonian, ancient Indian and other ancient cultures that were replaced and interrupted, or even annihilated or disappeared in the later historical process. In the process of human civilization for thousands of years, Chinese culture is the only uninterrupted and continuous culture. This is a miracle in human history. To a large extent, it has to be attributed to China's complete and vast geographical environment. Chinese traditional culture has always maintained its own complete style and increasingly perfect system in the imperceptible influence of the surrounding foreign cultures, which lasts for a long time, giving Chinese culture a strong self-confidence and a stable development.

4. 相对封闭的地理环境，形成了较具保守性和封闭性的传统文化。中国文化是在三面陆地、一面临海，四周较为封闭的地域里发展起来的。东边是一望无际的太平洋，西南为难以跨越的青藏高原和横断山脉以及瘴疠弥漫的热带雨林，西北为茫茫无际的沙漠戈壁，北方为干旱的草原和西伯利亚针叶林。这些自然障碍将古代中国人与外界隔开，形成了相对封闭的地理环境；这与古代的地中海文化和近现代的大西洋文化的开放性地理环境形成了鲜明的对照。四周相对封闭的地理环境，很容易造成一种隔绝机制，阻断了中国同外部世界更多的交往。加上内部优越的自然条件，几乎完全可以自给自足，"万事不求人"，而且中国历史上的人口相对于辽阔的疆域来说一直不多。再加上早熟的农业文明，周边地区的相对落后，使一向以"天朝"自居的中国人更不愿主动与外部世界打交道。在中国历史上，虽有张骞开辟"丝绸之路"、郑和七下西洋的壮举，但大多数明清基本上都是奉行闭关自守的对外政策，与外部世界交往较少；到了近代更是采取愈发严重的闭关锁国。当 15 世纪哥伦布等西方人千方百计地寻找通往中国的航路时，中国的统治者却要禁止海上交通，连早已开辟的航道也弃之不用。由于中国传统文化的保守性及封闭性，中国在近代没能及时地吸收外来的优秀文化。

The relatively closed geographical environment has formed a more conservative and closed traditional culture. Chinese culture developed in a relatively closed area with three sides the land, one the sea. To the east is the endless Pacific Ocean, to the southwest are the insurmountable Qinghai-Tibet Plateau and Hengduan Mountains and tropical rain forests filled with miasma, to the northwest the boundless desert and Gobi, and to the north the arid grasslands and Siberian coniferous forests. These natural obstacles separated the ancient Chinese from the outside world and formed a relatively closed geographical environment; this is in sharp contrast with the open geographical environment of the ancient Mediterranean culture and the modern Atlantic culture. The relatively closed geographical environment can easily create an isolation mechanism, which blocks more exchanges between China and the outside world. Coupled with the superior natural conditions inside, it was almost completely self-sufficient, "asking no help for anything", and the population in China's history had been small compared to the vast territory. In addition, due to the premature agricultural civilization and the relative backwardness of the surrounding areas, the Chinese, who have usually regarded themselves as the people from "heavenly dynasty", are even more reluctant to deal with the outside world. In Chinese history, despite Zhang Qian's feats of pioneering the "Silk Road" and Zheng He's seven voyages to the Western Oceans, most dynasties basically pursued the closed-door policy and had less contact with the outside world; and even worse, no contact at all in modern times. When Westerners such as Columbus in the 15th century tried their best to find a route to China, the rulers of China banned maritime communication and even abandoned the already opened sea routes. Due to the conservative and closed nature of Chinese traditional culture, China has not been able to absorb outstanding foreign cultures in a timely manner in early modern times.

5. 中国传统文化呈现出由北向南迁移的趋势。文化中心迁移的基本动因，主要还是南北方自然条件的差异，特别是由此而形成的社会生产方式的差异及生产力的悬殊。江南地区，一是水、热资源丰富，生长期长，可满足一年两熟甚至三熟的需要，单位面积产量高。二是降水丰沛，灌溉便利，生产力水平高，因而南方对人口和文化的发展有较强的吸引力。

Traditional Chinese culture has shown a tendency to migrate from north to south. The basic motivation for the migration of cultural centers is mainly the differences in natural conditions between the north and the south, especially the resulting differences in social production methods and the disparity in productivity. The Jiangnan (the South of the Yangtze River) area is rich in water and heat resources, with a long growth period, which can meet the needs of two or even three crops a year, and the yield per unit area is high. On the other hand, abundant rainfall, convenient irrigation, and high productivity. Therefore, the South has a strong attraction for population and cultural development.

三、黄河、长江与中国传统文化 The Yellow River, Yangtze River and Traditional Chinese Culture

长江文化和黄河文化是中华文明最具代表性和影响力的两支主体文化。

The Yangtze River culture and the Yellow River culture are the two most representative and influential main cultures of Chinese civilization.

1. 黄河，中国北部大河，全长约 5464 公里，流域面积约 752 443 平方公里。世界第五大河，中国第二大河。黄河发源于青海省青藏高原，呈 "几" 字形，自西向东分别流经青海、四川、甘肃、宁夏、内蒙古、陕西、山西、河南及山东 9 个省（自治区），于山东东营最后流入渤海。

The Yellow River, a large river in northern China, has a total length of 5, 464 kilometers and a drainage area of 752, 443 square kilometers. It is the fifth largest river in the world and the second largest river in China. Originating from Qinghai-Tibet Plateau in Qinghai Province, the Yellow River is shaped like a "几" in Chinese character. It flows from west to east through 9 provinces (or autonomous regions), namely Qinghai, Sichuan, Gansu, Ningxia, Inner Mongolia, Shaanxi, Shanxi, Henan and Shandong, and finally flows into the Bohai Sea at Dongying, Shandong Province.

黄河中上游以山地为主，中下游以平原、丘陵为主。由于河流中段流经中国黄土高原地区，因此夹带了大量的泥沙，所以它也被称为世界上含沙量最多的河流。黄河是中华文明最主要的发源地，中国人称其为"母亲河"。黄河每年都会产生大量泥沙，形成冲积平原，有利于种植。

The middle and upper reaches of the Yellow River are dominated by mountains, and the middle and lower reaches are dominated by plains and hills. Since the middle section of the river flows through the Loess Plateau of China, it entrains a large amount of sediment and sand, so it is also known as the river with the most sediment and sand in the world. The Yellow River is the most important birthplace of Chinese civilization. Chinese call it the "Mother River". The Yellow River produces a large amount of sediment every year, forming an alluvial plain, which is conducive to planting.

黄河流域是中国开发最早的地区，形成了较为发达的农耕文明。大约在3500 年以前，以河南为中心的黄河两岸建立了中国历史上第二个王朝——商王朝。此后从秦汉到北宋相当长的历史时期内，黄河流域有中国的七大古都之四：西安、洛阳、开封、安阳。黄河是中华文明的摇篮：（1）夏、商、周三朝无不建都于黄河流域；（2）最早的文字出现在黄河流域；（3）最早的城市群出现在黄河流域。

The Yellow River Basin is the earliest cultivated region in China, and a relatively developed farming civilization has been formed. About 3, 500 years ago, the second dynasty in Chinese history, Shang Dynasty, was established on both sides of the Yellow River with Henan as the center. After a long historical period from Qin and Han Dynasties to the Northern Song Dynasty, the Yellow River Basin has accommodated four of the seven ancient capitals of China: Xi'an, Luoyang, Kaifeng, Anyang. The Yellow River is the cradle of Chinese civilization. （1）Xia, Shang, and Zhou dynasties were all built in the Yellow River Basin；（2）The earliest Chinese characters appeared in the Yellow River Basin；（3）The earliest cities appeared in the Yellow River Basin.

2. 长江发源于"世界屋脊"——青藏高原。干流流经青海省、西藏自治区、四川省、云南省、重庆市、湖北省、湖南省、江西省、安徽省、江苏省、上海市共 11 个省级行政区（八省二市一区），于崇明岛以东注入东海，全长约 6300 余公里，在世界大河中长度仅次于非洲的尼罗河和南美洲的亚马孙河，居世界第三位。

The Yangtze River originated from the "Roof of the World" ——Qinghai-Tibet Plateau. The main stream flows through Qinghai Province, Tibet Autonomous Region, Sichuan Province, Yunnan Province, Chongqing City, Hubei Province, Hunan Province, Jiangxi Province, Anhui Province, Jiangsu Province, and Shanghai City, a total of 11 provincial-level administrative regions (eight provinces, two cities and one autonomous region). It flows into East China Sea from east of Chongming Island, with a total length of more than 6,300 kilometers. It is second only to Nile River in Africa and Amazon River in South America among the major rivers of the world, ranking third in the world.

在长江流域发现的新旧石器时代的文化遗址仅次于黄河流域地区；长江中下游地区，以水稻为代表的水田农业文化是在中国文化中心逐渐南移的历史背景下发展起来的，催生了发达的商贸文化、丝织工艺文化、园艺文化和园林文化。

The cultural relics of the Paleolithic and Neolithic Ages discovered in the Yangtze River Basin are second only to the Yellow River Basin. In the middle and lower reaches of the Yangtze River, the paddy field agricultural culture represented by rice developed under the historical background of the gradual southward movement of the Chinese cultural center. Hence, developed business culture, silk weaving culture, horticulture and garden culture.

长江文化是一个时空交织的多层次、多维度的文化复合体。在文化体系上属中国南方文化体系。长江流域包括四川省、湖北省、湖南省、江西省、安徽省、江苏省、浙江省、上海市七省一市外，还包括云南省、贵州省、广西省、广东省、福建省等长江水系流经区。长江文化以巴蜀文化、楚文化、吴越文化为主体，聚合成一个共同的文化体——长江文化。

The Yangtze River culture is a multi-level and multi-dimensional cultural complex intertwined with time and space. Culturally it belongs to the cultural system of southern China. The Yangtze River Basin includes Sichuan, Hubei, Hunan, Jiangxi, Anhui, Jiangsu, Zhejiang, and Shanghai, as well as Yunnan, Guizhou, Guangxi, Guangdong, Fujian where the Yangtze River system flows through. The Yangtze River culture mainly consists of Bashu culture, Chu culture, and Wuyue culture which aggregate into a common cultural body—the Yangtze River culture.

中国文化的历史源头

一、两条大河 Two Rivers

在中国广袤的大地上，有两条横贯东西的大河——黄河与长江，把中华大地自然连成了两大块"文化哺育区"。在这里生活的原始人类，有足够的天地和自然资源可供栖息和生存。中国文化之所以数千年绵延不绝，中国文化的中心之所以能够回旋和转移，都和这个地理环境分不开。

On the vast land of China, there are two large rivers that traverse the east and the west-the Yellow River and the Yangtze River, which naturally connect the land of China into two large "cultural nurturing areas". The primitive humans living here had enough space and natural resources for habitation and survival. The reason why Chinese culture has lasted for thousands of years, and the reason why the center of Chinese culture can maneuver and shift, are inseparable from this geographical environment.

二、远古中国文化的发展 The Development of Ancient Chinese Culture

（一）三个直立猿人 Three Erect Apes/Homo Erectus/Pithecanthropus Erectus

"元谋猿人"，1965 年在云南省元谋发现（经过考古发掘），距今 170 万年；

"蓝田猿人"，1963 年到 1964 年间在陕西蓝田发现，距今 115 万到 70 万年以前；

"北京猿人"，1927 年在北京周口店发现，距今 69 万到 23 万年之间。

"Yuanmou Ape Man", discovered in Yuanmou, Yunnan Province in 1965 (after archaeological excavations), 1. 7 million years ago;

"Lantian Ape Man", discovered in Lantian, Shaanxi Province from 1963 to 1964, between 1. 15 million and 690, 000 years ago;

"Peking Man", discovered in Zhoukoudian, Beijing in 1927, between 700, 000 and 230, 000 years ago.

（二）八个智人 Eight Homo Sapiens

广东的马坝人，陕西的大荔人，湖北的长阳人，山西的丁村人，内蒙古的河套人，广西的柳江人，北京的山顶洞人，四川的资阳人。距今约 20 万年到 1 万年。

The Maba people of Guangdong, the Dali people of Shaanxi, the Changyang people of Hubei, the Dingcun people of Shanxi, the Hetao people of Inner Mongolia, the Liujiang people of Guangxi, the Upper Cave Man of Beijing, and the Ziyang people of Sichuan. About 200, 000 to 10, 000 years ago.

这时原始人群就进入了初期氏族公社的阶段，是氏族社会，即旧石器时代。

At this time, the primitive people entered the stage of the early clan communes. This period is identified as in clan society, i. e. the Paleolithic Age.

（三）两种文化 Two Cultures

1. "仰韶文化"，又称为"彩陶文化"，母系氏族公社文化的代表，因最早发现于河南省渑池县仰韶村而得名，广泛分布在黄河流域，属于距今 1 万年到 4000 年的新石器时代。

"Yangshao Culture", also known as "Painted Pottery Culture", is a representative of the matriarchal clan commune culture. It is named after it was first discovered in Yangshao Village, Mianchi County, Henan Province. It is widely distributed in the Yellow River Basin and existed during the Neolithic about 10, 000 to 4, 000 years ago.

2. "龙山文化"，又称"黑陶文化"，父系氏族社会文化的代表，因最早发现于山东省章丘龙山镇而得名，距今四五千年。父系氏族社会的文化遗址广泛分布在黄河流域和长江流域。

"Longshan Culture", also known as "Black Pottery Culture", is a representative of the social culture of the patrilineal clan, named after it was first discovered in Longshan Town, Zhangqiu, Shandong Province, about four to five thousand years ago. The cultural sites of the patrilineal clan society are widely distributed in the Yellow River Basin and the Yangtze River Basin.

三、四大文化区域 Four Major Cultural Areas

1. 黄河流域文化区，这是中国文明最重要的发祥地之一。在这个广大的区域内，先后发现了"裴李岗文化"（河南省新郑市），距今 8000 年左右；"仰韶文化"（河南省渑池县），距今 7000 年到 5000 年；"大汶口文化"（山东省泰安市），距今 5000 年左右；"龙山文化"（山东省济南市章丘区），距今四五千年；"马家窑文化"（甘肃省临洮县），距今四五千年；"齐家文化"（甘肃省广河县），距今 4000 年左右；"二里头文化"（河南省偃师市），距今 3500 年左右，约在新石器时代晚期、青铜时代初期。

The Yellow River Basin Cultural Area is one of the most important birthplaces of Chinese civilization. In this vast area, many cultures have been discovered successively. They are "Peiligang Culture" (Xinzheng City, Henan Province), about 8,000 years ago; "Yangshao Culture" (Mianchi County, Henan Province), 7,000 to 5,000 years ago; "Dawenkou Culture" (Taian City, Shandong Province), about 5,000 years ago; "Longshan Culture" (Zhangqiu District, Jinan City, Shandong Province), four to five thousand years ago; "Majiayao Culture" (Lintao County, Gansu Province), four to five thousand years ago; "Qijia Culture" (Guanghe County, Gansu Province), about 4,000 years ago; "Erlitou Culture" (Yanshi City, Henan Province), about 3,500 years ago, also about the late Neolithic period and early Bronze Age.

2. 长江流域文化区，包括江汉流域、太湖流域和巴蜀地区。已经发现的原始文化有"河姆渡文化"（浙江省余姚市），距今 7000 年左右；"马家浜文化"（浙江省嘉兴市），距今六七千年；"良渚文化"（浙江省杭州市余姚区），距今四五千年；"屈家岭文化"（湖北省京山县），距今四五千年。

The Yangtze River Basin Cultural Area includes Jianghan River Basin, Taihu Lake Basin and Bashu Region. The primitive cultures that have been discovered include "Hemudu Culture" (Yuyao City, Zhejiang Province), about seven thousand years ago; "Majiabang Culture" (Jiaxing City, Zhejiang Province), which is about six to seven thousand years ago; "Liangzhu Culture" (Yuyao District, Hangzhou City, Zhejiang Province), four to five thousand years ago; "Qujialing Culture" (Jingshan County, Hubei Province), four to five thousand years ago.

3. 珠江流域文化区，原始文化遗址主要有"石峡遗址"（广东省韶关市），距今已有四五千年。

The Pearl River Basin Cultural Area. The primitive cultural site mainly is the "Shixia Site" (Shaoguan City, Guangdong Province), which was about four to five thousand years ago.

4. 北方和东北文化区，代表性文化是"红山文化"（内蒙古自治区赤峰市），距今5000年左右，已有原始的宗教祭祀活动，出现了原始社会的国家的雏形。

The Northern and Northeastern Cultural Area. The representative culture is "Hongshan Culture" (Chifeng City, Inner Mongolia Autonomous Region). About 5,000 years ago, there had been primitive religious sacrificial activities, and the prototype of a primitive country emerged.

中国文明是在中国的土地上土生土长的，而不是从外域传来的；是多元融合的，而不是单一的。黄河流域的中原地区，原始文化比较发达，是中国文明起源的主要区域，约在5000年前已进入文明社会。其他地区的先民在5000年前至3000年前之间先后进入文明社会。

Chinese civilization was born and grew on Chinese soil, not from outside; it is a diversified fusion, not a single one. The Central Plains region in the Yellow River Basin had a relatively developed primitive culture and was the main region where Chinese civilization originated. It entered a civilized society about 5,000 years ago. The ancestors of other regions entered civilized society successively between 5,000 and 3,000 years ago.

四、"三皇五帝" Three Sovereigns and Five Kings

三皇：燧人、伏羲、神农

Three Sovereigns/Kings：Suiren（Flinting man），Fuxi（Fishing and Hunting Man），Shennong（God of Agriculture）

五帝：黄帝、颛顼、帝喾、尧、舜

Five Kings：Yellow King, King Zhuanxu, King Ku, King Yao, King Shun

据中国历史大系表记载，有巢氏生活在旧石器时代早期，开创了巢居文明。有巢氏被誉为华夏"第一人文始祖"和"文明的领航者"。

According to the records of Chinese history, a person surnamed Youchao （means there is a nest）lived in the early Paleolithic period and created the Tree Dwelling civilization. Youchao is hailed as the "first ancestor of human civilization" and "the pilot of civilization" in China.

前仰韶-大地湾文化时期（公元前4564~公元前4354年）

Former-Yangshao-Dadiwan Cultural Period（4564 BC~4354 BC）

燧人氏，又号燧皇，定都于燧明（今河南商丘），后迁都于河北省保定市（今河北保定南庄头遗址）。燧人氏为燧明国国君，为有巢氏之子、华胥氏之夫、伏羲氏与女娲氏之父。公元前4464~公元前4354年在位，燧人氏是中国迄今为止有史可考的第一位个体部落首领（非部落联盟首领）。燧皇陵位于河南省商丘市睢阳区境内，是中国历史上年代最为久远的帝王陵墓。

Suiren, also known as King Sui, had its capital in Suiming（now Shangqiu, Henan province），and later moved its capital to Baoding, Hebei Province（now Nanzhuangtou in Baoding, Hebei）. Suiren is the monarch of Suiming, a country, the son of Youchaoshi（the person surnamed Youchao），the husband of the person Huaxu, and the father of Fuxi and Nvwa. Reigned in 4464BC~4354 BC, Suiren is the first tribal leader（not-tribal alliance leader）in Chinese history. Located in Suiyang District, Shangqiu City, Henan Province, King Sui's Mausoleum is the oldest king's tomb in Chinese history.

仰韶文化时期（公元前 4354~公元前 3579 年）

Yangshao Cultural Period（4354 BC~3579 BC）

伏羲氏，又号羲皇、太昊、青帝。定都于汶上（今山东省汶上县），后迁都于宛丘（今河南淮阳），公元前 4354~公元前 4239 年在位。伏羲氏为燧人氏与华胥氏之子、女娲氏的兄长兼夫君。炎帝神农氏的外祖父。在燧人氏之后继位。一说伏羲即为天皇氏。传说太昊伏羲氏也是中国古代神话中的五方上帝之一。伏羲陵位于河南省周口市淮阳县城北 1.5 公里处。

Fuxi was also called King Xi, Taihao, and Green King. The capital was settled in Wenshang（now Wenshang County, Shandong Province）, and later moved to Wanqiu（now Huaiyang, Henan province）, reigned from 4354 BC to 4239 BC. Fuxi is the son of Suirenshi and Huaxushi, and the elder brother and husband of Nvwashi. The grandfather of King Yan−Shennongshi. Succeeded to the throne after Suiren. Legend has it that Taihao（Great Heaven）Fuxi is also one of the five gods in ancient Chinese mythology. Fuxi's Mausoleum is located 1.5 kilometers north of Huaiyang County, Zhoukou City, Henan Province.

神农氏，又号农皇、赤帝，公元前 4109~公元前 3579 年在位。神农氏是伏羲氏与女娲氏的外孙，女娲氏死后传位于他。神农氏首次统一中华民族。传说神农氏也是中国古代神话中的五方上帝之一。

Shennong（God of Agriculture）, also known as King of Agriculture, Red King, reigned from 4109 BC to 3579 BC. Shennong was the grandson of Fuxishi and Nvwashi, and Nvwashi passed the throne on to him at her death. The Chinese nation was unified under his government for the first time. Legend has it that Shennongshi was also one of the five gods in ancient Chinese mythology.

龙山文化时期（公元前 2697~公元前 2015 年）

Longshan Cultural Period（2697BC~2015BC）

有熊氏，即黄帝，又号轩辕。定都于有熊（今河南新郑）。陵墓位于河北涿鹿，其曾孙帝颛顼打败共工收复中原后迁葬于河南荆山。

Youxiong, the Yellow King, also nicknamed Xuanyuan. The mausoleum is located in Zhuolu, Hebei province. His great−grandson Zhuan Xu defeated Gonggong and recovered the Central Plains and was buried in Jingshan, Henan province.

高阳氏，即颛顼，又号黑帝、玄帝。公元前 2322~公元前 2245 年在位。

定都于穷桑、后迁都于商丘，打败共工氏之后定都于帝丘（今濮阳），并将黄帝陵墓由河北涿鹿迁至河南荆山。颛顼是黄帝的次子昌意的儿子。颛顼高阳氏也是中国古代神话中的五方上帝之一。陵墓位于河南省安阳市内黄县梁庄镇。

Gaoyang, Zhuanxu, also nicknamed as Black King, Reigned from 2322 BC to 2245 BC. The capital was settled in Qiongsang and later moved to Shangqiu. After defeating Gonggong, the capital was settled in Diqiu (now Puyang), and the tomb of Yellow King was moved from Zhuolu, Hebei province to Jingshan, Henan province. Zhuanxu was the son of Changyi, the second son of the Yellow King. Zhuanxu is also one of the five gods in ancient Chinese mythology. The mausoleum is located in Liangzhuang Town, Neihuang County, Anyang City, Henan Province.

高辛氏，即帝喾，公元前 2245~公元前 2176 年在位。定都于亳（今河南商丘）。帝喾乃白帝少昊之孙，颛顼高阳氏的堂兄。帝喾陵墓所在地位于商丘睢阳区高辛镇。

Gaoxin, namely King Ku, reigned from 2245 BC to 2176 BC. The capital was settled in Bo (now Shangqiu, Henan province) . King Ku is the grandson of the White King Shaohao and the cousin of King Zhuanxu. The tomb of King Ku is located in Gaoxin Town, Suiyang District, Shangqiu City.

陶唐氏，即尧，公元前 2168~公元前 2095 年在位。定都于北唐（今山西省太原市），后迁都平阳（今山西省临汾市）。帝尧为帝喾第四子。另外，鲧禹治水、后羿射日等传说就发生在陶唐氏时期。陵墓位于山东省菏泽市鄄城县富春乡谷林。

Taotang, namely King Yao, reigned from 2168 BC to 2095 BC. The capital was settled in North Tang (now Taiyuan City, Shanxi Province), and later moved to Pingyang (now Linfen City, Shanxi Province) . King Yao is the fourth son of King Ku. In addition, legends such as Gun and Yu's control of water and Houyi's shooting the suns occurred during the later Taotang Period. The mausoleum is located in Gulin, Fuchun Township, Heze City, Shandong Province.

有虞氏，即舜，分别于公元前 2095~公元前 2067 年、公元前 2064~公元前 2025 年在位。帝舜为黄帝裔孙。以孝闻名，是著名的 24 孝之首——"孝感动天"的主人公。继承陶唐氏之皇位。

Youyu, namely Shun, reigned in 2095BC~2067BC and 2064BC~2025BC respectively. King Shun was the descendant of Yellow King. Well-known for his filial piety, he is the protagonist of the most filial 24 persons- "filial piety touches heaven". Sun succeeded to the throne of Taotang, namely King Yao.

夏后氏，夏后禹，即大禹，定都阳城（今河南省登封市），后迁都于阳翟（河南禹州）。禹为黄帝嫡系子孙，是治水英雄夏后鲧的儿子，是夏朝的奠基人。

Xiahou, or Xiahou Yu, namely Yu the Great. His capital was first in Yangcheng (now Dengfeng City, Henan Province), later moved to Yangdi (Yuzhou, Henan). Yu the Great is the lineal descendant of Yellow King, the son of Xiahou Gun, the hero of water control, and the founder of Xia Dynasty.

大禹崩逝后，子夏后启继位，迁都于安邑（今山西省运城市夏县西）建立夏朝。古代中国部落联盟制时代结束。龙山文化时期告终，中国进入中央集权化奴隶制国家时期。

After the death of Yu the Great, his son Xiahou Qi succeeded to the throne and moved the capital to Anyi (now west of Xia County, Yuncheng City, Shanxi Province) to establish Xia Dynasty. Thus the era of ancient Chinese tribal alliance system ended and Longshan Cultural Period ended too, hence China entered the period of a centralized slavery state.

五、中国的王朝 Dynasties of China

中国的古代史，就是一部王朝史，由一个家族统治天下。据说这一制度由禹的儿子启开始。在启之前，部落联盟的首领是各个部落公推产生的，历史上称为"禅让制"，尧、舜、禹成为领袖，据称都是如此确定的，这可能就是原始社会的民主选举。公元前 21 世纪，启在中原地区建立了"夏"，实施最高权力由自己的子嗣继承的制度，开始了中国历史上的世袭制，史称"家天下"。"夏"成了中国历史上的第一个世袭制王朝。一直到 1911 年最后一个王朝清朝灭亡，中国的王朝历史足足有四千年之久，经历了奴隶制社会、封建制社会和半殖民地半封建社会三个历史阶段。

The ancient history of China is a history of dynasties, ruled by one family. It is said that this system was started by Yu's son Qi. Before Qi, the leaders of the tribal alliance were publicly recommended by various tribes. It was called the "Abdication System" in history, and it is said that Yao, Shun and Yu became leaders because of it. This may be the democratic election of primitive society. In the 21st century BC, Qi established "Xia" dynasty in the Central Plains and implemented a system where the supreme power was inherited by his own heirs, and started the hereditary system in Chinese history, known as "Family Country" in history, namely, the family was the country, the country belonged to the family. "Xia" became the first hereditary dynasty in Chinese history. Until the end of Qing Dynasty, the last dynasty, in 1911, China's dynasty had a history of four thousand years, and it had experienced three historical stages: slavery society, feudal society and semi-colonial and semi-feudal society.

有一段顺口溜说: "唐尧虞舜夏商周,

春秋战国乱悠悠。

两汉三国晋统一,

南朝北朝死对头。

隋唐五代又十国,

宋元明清帝王休。"

这把中国包括尧在内的王朝历史基本概括了。在四千年的王朝史上,一共约有大大小小、长长短短的王朝74个。其中,大多数王朝是由汉族人建立的,少数王朝是由不同的少数民族建立的;其中由蒙古族建立的元朝和满族建立的清朝,曾经长时间地统治中国全境。

A jingle said: "Tangyao, Yushun, Xia, Shang and Zhou;

Spring and Autumn, Warring States were in chaos.

Two Han Dynasties, Three Kingdoms, till Jin Dynasty as a whole,

but Southern and Northern Dynasties were foes.

Sui, Tang, Five Dynasties and Ten Kingdoms,

Dynasties of Song, Yuan, Ming, but Qing came to zero. "

That basically summarizes the history of the dynasties of China including Yao. In the four thousand years of dynasty history, there were about 74 dynasties, large and small, long and short. Among them, most dynasties were established by the Han people, and a few dynasties were established by different ethnic minorities; among them, Yuan Dynasty established by the Mongolians and Qing Dynasty established by the Manchus once ruled throughout China for a long time.

中国历史上最长的王朝是公元前 8 世纪建立的周朝，包括西周、东周（春秋战国）在内，一共 790 年。中国历史有确切的纪年，是从西周共和元年，即公元前 841 年开始的。历史最短的王朝是"大顺"，不足两年（公元 1644 年~公元 1645 年）。疆域最大的王朝是元朝，其领土面积最广时达 1400 万平方公里。

The longest dynasty in Chinese history is Zhou Dynasty established in the 8th century BC, including the Western Zhou Dynasty and the Eastern Zhou Dynasty (Spring and Autumn and Warring States), a total of 790 years. The definte chronology in Chinese history began in the first year of the Western Zhou Dynasty, that is, 841 BC. The dynasty with the shortest history is the "Great Shun", less than two years (1644~1645 AD). The dynasty with the largest territory is Yuan Dynasty, covering 14 million square kilometers at its widest.

历史上，有两个王朝对中国文化影响最大，差不多决定了中国文化的基本内核与品格，这就是汉朝（公元前 202 年~公元 220 年）与唐朝（公元 618 年~公元 907 年）。汉朝分"西汉"与"东汉"，前后延续了 420 来年。汉朝境内的人被称为"汉人"，后来演变成中原民族的专称"汉族"，把汉人所用的文字称为"汉字"，汉人使用的语言称为"汉语"，汉人的文化称为"汉文化"。

In history, there are two dynasties that have the greatest influence on Chinese culture, almost determining the basic core and character of Chinese culture. They are Han Dynasty (202 BC~220 AD) and Tang Dynasty (618~907 AD). Han Dynasty was divided into "Western Han" and "Eastern Han", which lasted over 420 years. People under Han dynasty were called "Han people", and later evolved into the term "Han nationality" referring to the Central Plains people. The characters used by the Han people are called "Han characters", the language used by the Han people is called "the Han Language", and the culture of the Han people is called "Han Culture".

唐朝的经济在当时的世界上极为发达，文化最为灿烂，社会最为开放，对外交流最为频繁，大大影响了周边国家的文化。唐朝的都城长安是当时世界上最大的城市，人口达 100 多万。这时的中国人以此缘故又被称为"唐人"，今天分布在世界各地的"唐人街"即由此而来。

The economy of Tang Dynasty was fairly developed in the world at that time, with the most splendid culture, the most open society, and the most frequent foreign exchanges, which greatly affected the culture of neighboring countries. The capital of Tang Dynasty, Chang'an, was the largest city in the world at that time, with a population of over 1 million. For this, the Chinese are also called "Tang Ren" meaning Tang People, and from that comes the "Tang Ren Street" referring to "China town" scattering over the world today.

中国王朝的生命延续依靠子嗣继承，代代相传，这就是所谓的"世袭制"。子嗣继承按照"嫡长子继承制"的原则进行。其来源是商朝末期、周朝初期形成的宗法制与分封制。所谓"宗法制"，就是按照血统与嫡庶来组织、维护社会秩序的制度，其核心是只有嫡妻（又称正妻，原配妻子）所生的长子才可以继承爵位。"嫡长子继承制"的内涵是"立嫡以长不以贤，立子以贵不以长"。

The continuation of the life of the Chinese dynasties depends on the inheritance of the children and passed on from generation to generation. This is the so-called "hereditary system." Heir inheritance is carried out in accordance with the principle of "the primogeniture inheritance system of the legitimate eldest son". Its origin is the feudal clan system and enforcement system formed in the late Shang Dynasty and the early Zhou Dynasty. The so-called "feudal clan system" is a system that organizes and maintains social order according to blood line and wife or concubine. The core is that only the eldest son born to a wife (also known as a true wife, original wife) can inherit the title. The connotation of "the primogeniture inheritance system of the legitimate eldest son" is "The eldest son of the Emperess be the heir to the crown."

六、中国的皇帝 Emperors in China

"皇帝"是中国历史上拥有最高权力的一个群体。"皇"的本义是"大"，意思是"煌煌盛美";"帝"本义是"德象天地",意思是"能行天道"。公元前221年,秦国国王嬴政消灭了其他六国,建立了秦王朝。他统一文字,统一货币,统一度量衡,推行"郡县制",自认为"德兼三皇,功高五帝",将"皇""帝"这两个最高的称呼结合起来,改"国王"为"皇帝",这就是著名的秦始皇,中国的第一个皇帝。从此,"皇帝"成为中国封建社会最高统治者的称号,延续时间长达两千余年。

"Emperors" are a group with the highest power in Chinese history. The original meaning of "Huang" is "big", which means "with bright and magnificent beauty"; the original meaning of "Di" is "Whose virtue is like heaven and earth", which means "can behave the way of heaven". In 221 BC, King Yingzheng of Qin eliminated the other six countries and established Qin Dynasty. He unified writing, currency, weights and measures, and promoted the "system of prefectures and counties". He considered himself as virtuous as the ancient "three sovereigns" and more meritable than "five kings", thus he combined the two highest titles of "Huang" and "Di" and changed "king" into "emperor", that is the famous Qin Shihuang (meaning the first emperor of Qin Dynasty), the first emperor of China. Since then, "emperor" has become the title of the supreme ruler of Chinese feudal society, which lasted for more than two thousand years.

七、中国历史的几个问题 Several Issues in Chinese History

(一) 战争与和平 War and peace

中国历史上的七大古都——西安、洛阳、开封、安阳、北京、南京、杭州,有五个在北方,因此围绕争夺中国最高统治权的战争绝大多数发生在中国的北方。中国古代一共发生了多少次战争? 据不完全统计,仅秦朝建立至清朝灭亡的2132年间,中国一共发生大大小小的战争有3134次,平均每一年就发生1.5次。可以说,中国历史几近一部战争史。

Of the seven ancient capitals in Chinese history-Xi'an, Luoyang, Kaifeng, Anyang, Beijing, Nanjing, and Hangzhou, five are in the north. Therefore, most of the wars surrounding the supremacy of China took place in the north of China. According to statistics, in the 2132 years from the establishment of Qin Dynasty to the demise of

Qing Dynasty, there were 3134 wars of various sizes in China, an average of 1.5 war per year. It can be said that Chinese history is almost a history of wars.

中国古代的战争，按其性质可以分为四种：第一种，中华本土不同民族之间的战争，其中多次是北部边疆的游牧民族武力南下，引发汉族抵御入侵的战争；第二种，统治集团之间的战争，其目的是争夺最高统治权；第三种，农民起义战争，中国自古以农业立国，农业经济关系国计民生，农民也因此成为国家的主体；第四种，海外异族的侵略战争，如英国发动的鸦片战争，西方八国联军的侵华战争。

Ancient Chinese wars can be divided into four types according to their nature: the first is wars between different ethnic groups in China, in which nomadic peoples from the northern frontier went south by force, hence wars by the Han people against invasion. The second is wars between ruling groups, the purpose of which is to fight for the supreme ruling power. The third is the peasant uprisings. China has been based on agriculture since ancient times, and the agricultural economy is related to the national economy and people's livelihood, and farmers have therefore become the main body of the country. The fourth is wars from overseas races, such as the Opium War launched by Britain and the war of aggression against China by the Western Eight-Power Allied Forces.

（二）融合与斗争 Integration and struggle

中国一直以来就是个多民族的国家。从民族的生存类型划分，以长城为界，古代中国的民族基本上可以分为北部边疆的游牧民族与中原地区的农耕民族，即汉族。在中国历史上，这两种类型的民族所创造的游牧文化与农耕文化之间，一直发生着冲突。一般来说，农耕民族居有定所，顺时守势，追求风调雨顺，期盼天下太平，本质上不具有进攻性；而游牧民族则居无定所，长于骑射，其攻击能力远大于农耕民族。但是，中原地区的农耕文化发展较早，与周边少数民族文化相比，一直处于高水平状态。进入中原地区的少数民族，都会自觉不自觉地仿效和吸收中原汉族文化，逐渐地与汉族融为一体，成为汉族的一个部分。我们现在所说的汉族，实际上是一个多民族的融合体。这也是中国文化具有巨大包容性的一个因素。

China has been a multi-ethnic country. From the classification of the ethnic groups, with the Great Wall as the boundary or demarcation, the ethnic groups in ancient China can basically be divided into the nomadic groups in the northern border and the farming groups in the Central Plains, namely the Han people. In Chinese history, there has been a conflict between the nomadic culture and the farming culture created by these two types of ethnic groups. Generally speaking, farming peoples live in a fixed place, follow the trend of the times, pursue good weather, and hope for peace in the world, and are not offensive in nature; while nomads live with no fixed place, are better at riding and shooting, and their offensive ability is much greater than that of farming nations. However, the agricultural culture in the Central Plains developed earlier, and compared with the surrounding ethnic minority cultures, it has been at a high level. The ethnic minorities entering the Central Plains would consciously or unconsciously imitate and absorb the culture of the Han nationality in the Central Plains, gradually integrated with the Han nationality and became a part of the Han nationality. The Han we call today is actually a multi-ethnic fusion. This is also a factor of the immense tolerance and inclusiveness of Chinese culture.

（三）统一与分裂 Unification and division

在中国历史上，尽管战争频发，割据纷呈，统一始终是历史发展的主流，分裂则是短暂的现象。这主要表现在：一是统一的时间呈逐步增长的趋势；二是统一的规模呈逐步扩大的趋势。统一之所以是中国历史发展的主流，或者说是中国历史发展的规律，其原因是多方面的。第一是处于疆域中心的中原地区，最先成为经济、政治、文化与科技中心，对周边民族与地区产生了强烈的吸引力和向心力。第二是中国古代哲学强调"中心与四方"的关系。第三是各民族交互杂居，相互通婚，形成了民族大融合。第四是文字的产生，使具有表意特征的汉字成为传递信息与沟通心灵的符号系统，它在民族统一的过程中发挥了强大的作用。第五是由先秦到汉代形成的"大一统"思想，对历代统一起了积极的促进作用，并且越来越深入人心，成为一种拥有凝聚力的哲学，一种容纳百川的胸怀和奋斗进取的精神。第六是中国的农耕文化是民心思定，祈盼"天下太平"，而只有统一，安定与太平才有相应的保证。"统一"因而成为中华民族的心理渴望与价值取向，这才是中国文化得以保持完整和绵延不绝的根本要素。

In the history of China, despite frequent wars and separate regimes, unification has been the mainstream of historical development, and division is a short-lived phenomenon. This is mainly manifested in: on the one hand, the unified time is gradually increasing; on the other hand, the unified scale is gradually expanding. There are many reasons why unification is the mainstream of China's historical development, or it is the law of China's historical development. The first is the Central Plains region, which is located in the center of the territory, the earliest to become the economic, political, cultural, and technological center, which produced a strong attraction and centripetal force for surrounding ethnic groups and regions. Second, ancient Chinese philosophy emphasized the relationship between the "center and the four directions". The third is that all ethnic groups live together and marry each other, forming a great ethnic integration. The fourth is the appearance of Han characters, making Chinese characters with ideographic characteristics a symbolic system that conveys information and communicates with each other. It has played a powerful role in the process of national unity. The fifth is the "Great Unification" thought formed from the pre-Qin to Han Dynasty, which played a positive role in promoting the unification of the past dynasties, became more and more deeply rooted in the minds of the Chinese people, a cohesive philosophy, a mind that accommodates hundreds of rivers and strives for progress. The sixth is that China's farming culture is based on the people's mind and wish for "the peaceful world". Only with unity, stability and peace can be guaranteed. "Unification" has thus become the psychological desire and value orientation of the Chinese nation. This is the fundamental element for Chinese culture to maintain its integrity and continuity.

中国的传统政治制度文化

一、中国的传统政治制度发展 The Development of China's Traditional Political System

中国传统的政治制度从夏朝（约公元前 21 世纪~约公元前 16 世纪，是中国史书中记载的第一个世袭制朝代）开始算起，夏商周时期中国政治制度的主要内容是宗法制（奴隶制宗法贵族君主制），这一时期政治制度的发展呈现以下三大特点：在王位和爵位的继承上实行世袭制；在地方管理上实行分封制；在王族内部实行以嫡长子继承制为特点的宗法制。中国的政治制度在不同的朝代有不同的规定，经历了不同的发展。

The traditional Chinese political system started from Xia Dynasty（about the 21st century BC-about the 16th century BC, it was the first hereditary dynasty recorded in Chinese history books）. The main content of the political system of China during Xia, Shang and Zhou Dynasties is the patriarchal clan system（slavery patriarchal aristocratic monarchy）. The development of the political system during this period showed the following characteristics: the implementation of hereditary system in the inheritance of the throne and knighthood; the system of enfeoffment in the local management; the implementation of the primogeniture inheritance system of the legitimate eldest son in the royal family. China's political system had different regulations in different dynasties and experienced different developments.

周朝：西周时期是奴隶制的顶峰时期，向心型政治结构的初建。为了巩固统治，在此基础上实行了分封制、宗法制、礼乐制、井田制。战国时期法家提出君主专制的中央集权制，商鞅变法建立县制。

Zhou Dynasty: The Western Zhou Dynasty was the peak period of slavery and the initial establishment of a centripetal political structure. In order to consolidate the rule, enfeoffment system, patriarchal clan system, rites and music system, and "井" field system (the "nine squares" system of land ownership) were implemented on this basis. During the Warring States period, legalists proposed a centralized system of monarchy, and Shang Yang established a county system with his reform.

秦朝：中央集权制度（封建君主专制）模式的确立，首创皇帝制度，在中央设置三公九卿制度，协助皇帝处理政务，在地方上推行郡县制度。秦朝所确立的封建中央集权的君主专制政体，延续了 2000 年之久。这种政体具有三个基本特征。第一，君权至上。国家的最高权力集中到皇帝一人，地方政府与中央各部门只是名义上的权力机构，一切政务的最高决定权掌握在皇帝手中。第二，皇权不可转移，皇位父死子继。皇帝一旦即位，便终身任职。第三，官僚系统庞大。

Qin Dynasty: The establishment of a centralized system (feudal monarchy) model, the first emperor system, the establishment of a system of three prime ministers and nine ministers in the center, assisted the emperor to handle government affairs, and promoted the county system in the local area. The feudal centralized monarchy established by Qin Dynasty lasted for 2000 years. This type of government has three basic characteristics. First, the sovereign is supreme. The supreme power of the country is concentrated in the emperor. The local governments and the central departments are only nominal institutions of power. The supreme decision-making power of all government affairs rests with the emperor. Second, the imperial power is not transferable, and the throne shall be inherited only by the first son of the lineal descents at the emperor's death. Once the emperor ascends the throne, he shall serve for life. Third, the bureaucracy is huge.

汉朝：汉武帝接受主父偃的意见实行推恩令，削弱王权。大大加强监察制度，中央设立司隶校尉，地方设置刺史。

Han Dynasty: Emperor Wu of Han Dynasty accepted the advice of Chancellor Zhufu Yan and implemented the Favor-expansion Act to weaken the royal power. The supervisory system was greatly strengthened. The central government set up a Colonel Director of Retainers, and the local government set up a provincial governor.

隋唐：中央设置三省六部制度，中书省负责起草诏令，门下省负责审核，尚书省负责执行，在尚书省下设六部，吏部、礼部、户部、刑部、兵部、工部。

Sui and Tang Dynasties: The central government set up a system of three provinces and six ministries. The Province of Imperial Secretary was responsible for drafting edicts, the Province of Assessment was responsible for reviewing edicts, and the Shangshu Sheng (Department of State Affairs) was responsible for enforcement. There were six ministries under the Shangshu Sheng, including Ministry of Personnel, Ministry of Rites, Ministry of Revenue, Ministry of Justice, Ministry of War, and Ministry of Works.

两宋：中央集中军权。赵匡胤通过"杯酒释兵权"，解除禁军将领的兵权；设置枢密院，主管全国军政，与将领互相牵制；实行"更戍法"，使得"兵无常帅，帅无常师"。中央分相权，设枢密使、参知政事、三司使分别分割宰相的军权、行政权、财政权。地方收权，派文臣出任州郡长官，设通判监督；设转运使把地方财富运到中央，解决中央财政危机。

Two Song Dynasties: Centralized military power. Emperor Zhao Kuangyin took over the military power from the forbidden army generals through the "glass wine releases military power"; set up a Privy Council to be in charge of the national military and administration, and to hold back each other with the generals; to implement the "Army Rotating", so that "the soldiers are without a fixed commander, and the commander is with no fixed soldiers". Division of the prime minister's power. To set up Privy Envoy, Assistant Minister of State Affairs, and Directors of the Highest Rank to respectively take charge of the military, administrative, and financial powers instead of the prime minister. Local power collection: To send civil officials to serve as head of prefects and counties, and to set up general supervisors; to set up transshipment agents to transport local wealth to the central government to solve the central financial crisis.

元朝：设立中书省作为中央的最高行政机构，总理全国政务，地方设置行中书省，简称行省。设置宣政院，掌管藏族及佛教事务。

Yuan Dynasty: the establishment of the Province of Imperial Secretary as the highest administrative body of the central government, in charge of national government affairs, and the establishment of the local Secretariat. To set up Bureau of Buddhist and Tibetan Affairs to take charge of Tibetan and Buddhist affairs.

明朝：废丞相，权分六部，尚书直接对皇帝负责。明成祖时期，设置内阁大学士，在各省设置三司，即承宣布政使司、提刑按察使司、都指挥使司，分掌行政、司法和军政，都直属中央。设置特务机构，明太祖设立锦衣卫，负责侦察、逮捕、审讯，直接听命于皇帝。明成祖设立东厂，明宪宗设立西厂，厂卫的设立是明朝封建专制主义统治加强的重要表现。明朝大学士张居正主持推行"一条鞭法"，把原来田赋、徭役、杂税合并，折成银两分摊在田亩上，按田亩多少收税。

Ming Dynasty: Abolished the prime minister, the power was divided into six parts, and the Imperial Enforcing Secretary was directly responsible to the emperor. During the Ming Chengzu period, the Grand Secretary of the cabinet was established, and three departments were set up in each province, namely, the Provincial Administration Commission, the Provincial Surveillance Commission, the Provincial Military Commission, respectively in charge of administration, justice, and military affairs, all directly under the Central Government. Set up a secret service agency, Ming Taizu set up Secret Service Guards, responsible for investigation, arrest, interrogation, directly under the emperor's orders. Ming Chengzu established the Dongchang (Eastern Depot), Ming Xianzong established the Xichang (Western Depot), and the establishment of such agencies was an important manifestation of the strengthening of the feudal despotism of Ming Dynasty. The Grand Secretary Zhang Juzheng presided over the implementation of the "one whip law", combining the original land tax, corvee, and miscellaneous taxes, converting them into silver, and sharing them on the fields, and collecting taxes according to the number of fields.

清朝：雍正时期设立军机处，军机大臣完全听命于皇帝，辅导皇帝政务，军机处的设置标志着中央集权制发展到顶峰。

Qing Dynasty: During the Emperor Yongzheng period, the Office of Military and Political Affairs was established. The Ministers of Military and Political Affairs were completely obedient to the emperor and helped the emperor with government affairs. The establishment of the Office of Military and Political Affairs marked the peak of the development of centralized power.

从历朝历代的政治制度，可以看出，历代在政治制度方面呈现一种不断加强中央集权的趋势，也正是此原因，在某种程度上导致明清的衰落。

From the political systems of the past dynasties, it can be seen that the past dynasties have shown a tendency to continuously strengthen the centralization of power in the political system. It was precisely this reason that led to the decline of Ming and Qing dynasties to some extent.

二、中国传统政治制度的基本特征 Basic Characteristics of Traditional Chinese Political System

中国古代政治制度的演变趋势，在中央表现为君主专制的不断强化，在地方表现为中央集权的不断强化，此间虽偶有反复，历经近 3000 年，其总体趋势从奴隶社会到封建社会变化不大。呈现出六个基本特征。

The evolution of the ancient Chinese political system is manifested in the continuous strengthening of the monarchy in the central government and the continuous strengthening of centralization in the localities. Although there had been occasional repetitions during almost 3,000 years, the overall trend changed little from the slave society to the feudal society. Six basic characteristics are presented.

第一，君主专制、个人集权与宗法血统关系、婚姻裙带关系贯穿在中国传统政治制度史的始终。

第二，政治与神权相结合，以神权作为政治合理性的依据，以政权和神权作为制定制度的标准。

第三，政治制度与伦理道德相结合，儒家思想长期影响中国的传统政治制度。

第四，贵族特权和官僚政治伴随着中国传统政治制度文化的始终，专制主义中央集权制度显示出传统政治制度的集权化、严密化和任意化的特点。

第五，在高度君主集权制度下，行政权力包揽一切，使中国传统政治制度出现人治的特点。

第六，政治制度公开承认不平等原则，肯定社会等级差别，承认特殊权力阶层，对不同的阶层采用不同的对待方法。

First, the autocratic monarchy, the centralization of individual power, the relationship between patriarchal lineage, and the relationship of marriage nepotism ran through the history of traditional Chinese political system.

Second, the combination of politics and theocracy, using theocracy as the basis for political rationality, and political power and theocracy as the standards for formulating systems.

Third, the combination of political system and ethics. Confucianism had influenced traditional Chinese political system for much long time.

Fourth, aristocratic privileges and bureaucratic politics accompanied the persistence of traditional Chinese political system and culture. The authoritarian centralized system showed the characteristics of centralization, strictness and arbitrariness in political systems.

Fifth, under a highly centralized monarchy system, administrative power took over everything, giving the traditional Chinese political system the characteristics of rule of man.

Sixth, the political system publicly recognized the principle of inequality, affirmed the classification of social classes, recognized some classes with special rights, and treated different classes differently.

三、中国传统政治文化的特征 Characteristics of Traditional Chinese Political Culture

中国传统政治文化，是指中国所特有的、在过去产生、经过了历史的社会化过程、至今仍然在政治生活中活着的东西，是相对稳定地积淀在中国民众心理层面上的政治态度和政治价值取向，是中国政治系统和政治运作层面的依托。中国政治文化来自中国传统的生产方式和生活方式。归纳起来，影响着中国政治文化的主要有四大因素：一是小农自然经济方式，二是宗法家族制的社会构造，三是国家意识形态化的儒家学说，四是国家制度和权力阶层的支配与匡约。它们结成互为依存、相互支持的政治生态系统，成为育化中国政治文化传统的土壤。

Traditional Chinese political culture refers to those that are unique to China, which were born in the past, have gone through the process of historical socialization, and are still alive in political life. It is the political attitudes and politics orientation that are relatively stable on the psychological level of the Chinese politics. Value orientation is the support of Chinese political system and political operation. Chinese political culture comes from traditional Chinese production methods and lifestyles. To sum up, there are four main factors affecting Chinese political culture. The first is the natural economic mode of small farming, the second is the social structure of the patriarchal system, and the third is the ideology of the country——Confucianism, the fourth is the domination and covenant of the state system and the power class. They form a mutually dependent and mutually supportive political ecosystem, and become the soil for cultivating Chinese political and cultural traditions.

可以说传统的中国政治制度文化属于依附型政治文化，积淀于国民心理层面的政治价值意识与行为习惯取向所展示的政治文化特征主要是：家长本位，权力崇拜，潜规则，以及均平取向。

It can be said that traditional Chinese Political System culture belongs to a dependent political culture. The political value consciousness and behavioral habits accumulated in the national psychological level show the main political and cultural characteristics: patriarchal system, power worship, unspoken rules, and equalization orientation.

家长制体现的是人们自上而下拥有绝对权力而无相应的义务，由下而上只有绝对的义务而无相应的权利。与家长制相映随形的，是中国特有的礼制秩序或伦理角色定位系统。五伦三纲既是一种礼制秩序，又是一种角色规范，从而固化了家长本位的政治文化。具体来说，家长制导致的权威主义人格主要表现为皇权崇拜意识、虚饰好伪倾向和奴性仆从习惯。

The patriarchal system embodies that people have absolute power from top to bottom without corresponding obligations, and from bottom to top there are only absolute obligations without corresponding rights. Contrasting with the patriarchal system is China's unique ritual order or ethical role positioning system. The Five Ethics and Three Guidelines are not only a kind of ritual order, but also a kind of role norms, which solidify the parent-based political culture. Specifically, the authoritarian personality caused by patriarchy is mainly manifested in the consciousness of imperial power worship, falsehood of hypocrisy and the habit of being servile and obedient.

权力崇拜作为一种社会价值取向，即是说国家与社会、政治与经济的一体化。这一点清楚体现于王权时代权力与特权、权力与土地、权力与工商、权力与读书等多重关系之中。以封建皇权为尖顶的金字塔型官僚体系按权力大小和官位高低进行社会资源分割的现实，成为对于社会成员的直感刺激，由此在社会成员中形成根深蒂固的权力崇拜意识。

As a kind of social value orientation, power worship refers to the integration of state and society, politics and economy. This is clearly embodied in the multiple relationships between power and privileges, power and land, power and industry and commerce, power and reading in the royal power era. The fact that the pyramidal bureaucratic system with feudal imperial power as its spire divides social resources according to the size of power and the level of official position has become an intuitive stimulus for members of society, thus forming a deep-rooted awareness of power worship among members of society.

潜规则这一提法是针对正式规则即由官方明文规定的法律法规规章条例以及种种文件而言的。相比之下，非正式规则虽然不成具文，却能深入人心，虽然不登台面，却是约定俗成。它是合情不合法的规矩，是意会而非言传的陋规，是当事者彼此的认可和期待。

The so-called unspoken rules are aimed at formal rules, namely, laws, regulations, rules and various documents stipulated by the government. In contrast, although informal rules are unwritten, they are deeply rooted in the minds of the people. Although they are not on the stage, they are established by convention. It is a rule that is sensible but illegal, a bad rule that will be understood rather than verbal, and it is the mutual recognition and expectation of the parties involved.

纵观几千年的中国从奴隶社会到封建社会的政治制度文化传统，在均平主义和家长政治、特权现象及无政府主义之间存有某种亲缘关系，它一碗水端平的实践不依市场调节而只能靠人为摆布，这就为实施人治、加固集权找到了一个合适的理由，其主张从来都是按照三纲五常角色将利益分配建立在均平旗帜掩盖下滋生的权力阶层。相对于平民大众的种种特权，均平主义中还潜伏着无政府主义，这不仅因为人们对均平的要求必然会由经济生活伸向政治和其它社会生活，而且还因为与均平共生的家长政治会制造社会反弹从而积蓄起反抗与无政府情绪。所以在均平主义高调存在的地方，人们完全有理由对集权、特权和无政府倾向保持足够警惕。

Throughout thousands of years of China's political system and cultural traditions from slave society to feudal society, there was a certain kind of kinship between egalitarianism and paternal politics, the phenomenon of privilege and anarchism. It is a well-balanced practice. It does not rely on market regulation but can only rely on human manipulation. This has found a suitable reason for the implementation of the rule of man and the reinforcement of centralization. Its proposition has been based on the role of Three Fundamental Bonds and Five Constant virtues to establish the distribution of benefits under the banner of egalitarianism. Among the various privileges of the public, there is anarchism lurking in egalitarianism. This is not only because people's requirements for equalization will inevitably extend from economic life to politics and other social life, but also because of the parental political association that coexists with egalitarianism. The social rebound has accumulated resistance and anarchy. So where egalitarianism is prominently present, people have every reason to be sufficiently vigilant against centralization, privilege, and anarchist tendencies.

中国传统政治文化从为君、为政、治国三个方面来说，又呈现着三大特征。

Traditional Chinese political culture presents three main characteristics in terms of the three aspects of the monarch, administration, and governance.

为君之方：亲贤远佞。中国古代政治思想家大多认同中央集权的君主专制体制，肯定君主的绝对统治。在儒家，从来就是把权力是否下移作为衡量国家治乱的重要标准。一切权力归君主，国家命运系于君主一人。这种政治体制非常强调人的作用，强调为君者要亲贤臣，远小人。

为政之道：倡导德治。儒家所倡导的"礼治""德治""王道""仁政"等理想模式，在中国政治思想史上长期占主导地位。德治主义将政治伦理化，其本质是人治。这是因为传统的德治以君臣父子基础之上的等级关系和身份制度为基础。传统德治包括三个层面的内容。第一，要求执政的官员注重道德修养，严于律己，以身作则，为民表率。第二，要求执政者以道德教化百姓，以礼规范百姓的行为。第三，道德教化是为政的重要手段，但不是唯一的手段。

治国之道：以民为本。封建中国是个以农立国的国度，土地是最重要的生产资料和社会财富，解决农民的土地问题，不仅关系到其生存，而且关系到封建政权的安危。百姓老有所养，幼有所教，就会出现安居乐业的局面，国家也就会稳定和富强。

For the emperor: being close to the virtuous and far away from the vicious. Most ancient Chinese political thinkers agreed with the centralized monarchy system and affirmed the absolute rule of the monarch. In Confucianism, the downward shift of power has always been an important criterion to measure whether the state is in orders or in chaos. All power belongs to the monarch, and the destiny of the country depends on the monarch. This kind of political system puts great emphasis on the role of human beings, and emphasizes that the ruler must be close to the virtuous ministers and be far from the vicious.

For administration: advocating the rule of virtue. The ideal models of "rule of the rite", "rule of virtue", "kingly way" and "benevolent governance" advocated by Confucianism have long dominated the history of traditional Chinese political thought. Rule of Virtue ethicizes politics, and its essence is rule of man. This is because the traditional rule of virtue is based on the hierarchical relationship and identity system based on the emperor and the subjects, fathers and sons. The traditional rule of virtue includes three levels of content. First, the ruling officials are required to pay attention to moral cultivation, be strict in self-discipline, lead by example, and set an example for the people. Second, the rulers are required to educate the people with morals and regulate their behavior with rite. Third, moral education is an important means of administration, but it is not the only means.

For governance: being people-oriented. Feudal China was a country based on agriculture. Land was the most important means of production and social wealth. Solving the peasants' land problem was not only related to their survival, but also related to the safety of the feudal regime. With the support of the elderly and the education of the young people, a situation of living and working in peace and contentment will emerge, and the country will be stable and prosperous.

四、中国古代官制的特点 Characteristics of the Official System in Ancient China

中国自秦统一全国到清朝灭亡，王朝帝国体制延续了 2000 余年。其间，完备的文官制度和庞大的官僚体系，对于君主专制集权的运作起了有效的作用；另一方面，君主集权专制又赋予了文官制度鲜明的特点。

China's dynasty and imperial system lasted for more than 2, 000 years from the time when Qin unified the country to the end of Qing Dynasty. During the period, a complete civil service system and a huge bureaucratic system played an effective role in the operation of the autocratic monarchy. On the other hand, the autocratic monarchy gave distinctive characteristics to the civilian system.

中国古代的文官制度，也就是官僚制度，形成于政府划分为文武职官和专制主义集权政治确立以后。中国古代文官制度的建立是和封建专制主义政治体制相适应的，并随着这一体制的发展而发展。经过战国时期的初创，至秦汉，随着皇帝制度的建立与专制主义中央集权制度的发展，中国古代文官制度也进入了奠基阶段。

The civil service system in ancient China, that is, the bureaucratic system, was formed after the government was divided into civil and military officials and the establishment of authoritarian centralization politics. The establishment of the civil service system in ancient China was compatible with the feudal despotic political system and developed with the development of this system. After the beginning of the Warring States period, to Qin and Han Dynasties, with the establishment of the emperor system and the development of the authoritarian centralization system, the ancient Chinese civil service system also entered the foundation-laying stage.

中国古代文官制度的内容十分广泛，除文官的组织系统与结构之外，还包括文官的任免、考课、监察、休致等一系列具体制度。中国古代的文官制度，受专制主义下权力争夺的支配，也在结构上形成了相互制衡的关系。封建王朝的皇帝虽然被神秘化、偶像化，握有垄断一切的法定大权，但皇权的行使需要通过百官。在封建专制制度下，虽然是以君为本位，但是，无限膨胀的皇权，必然大大地限制和削弱官僚机构的能动性和协调性，导致政治上的腐败。

The content of the civil service system in ancient China was very extensive. In addition to the organization system and structure of the civil service, it also included a series of specific systems such as the appointment and dismissal of the civil officials, their examination and supervision. The civil service system in ancient China, dominated by power struggles under authoritarianism, also formed a relationship of mutual checks and balances in structure. Although the emperors of the feudal dynasty were mystified and idolized, they had the legal power to monopolize everything, but the exercise of the imperial power needed to pass hundreds of officials. Under the feudal autocratic system, although the monarch was the priority, the unlimited expansion of imperial power would inevitably greatly restrict and weaken the initiative and coordination of the bureaucracy, leading to political corruption.

从文官选任的历史发展可以看出：（1）建立稳定的任官制度，有助于贯彻封建国家的政策，提高行政效率。（2）重才德不论门第，重实学不重资历，从布衣中破格选士为官，可以改善封建的吏治，缓和社会矛盾，为封建政府带来生气。（3）在任官制度上，保守与改革的斗争是统治阶级内部权力如何再分配的斗争。这个斗争或者发生在社会大变动之际，或者发生在国家统治出现危机之时。（4）储才养士是任官的基础，任何一个王朝教育不兴，文化衰敝，不可能从总体上提高文官的素质，改善政府的行政效能。

From the historical development of the selection and appointment of civil officials, it can be seen that: (1) Establishing a stable appointment system would help implement the policies of the feudal state and improve administrative efficiency. (2) Emphasizing talents and virtues regardless of the status, real learning but not seniority, and selecting the officials from the commoners, could improve the feudal government, alleviate social conflicts, and bring vitality to the feudal government. (3) In the official system, there are struggles between conservatives and reformers. It is the struggles of how to redistribute power within the ruling class. Such struggles occur either at the time of major social changes, or at the time of crisis of state governance. (4) Cultivating and reserving talents was the basis for official appointment. The failure of education in any dynasty and the decline of culture make it impossible to improve the quality of civil officials and the administrative efficiency of the government as a whole.

中国古代文官制度在漫长的发展过程中，形成了以下几个主要特点：

1. 文官制度的历史不仅悠久，而且连绵不绝，从未中断。尽管不同的时代各有发展变化，但是沿革清晰、源流可考，并在历代因革损益的基础上，经过几千年的积累，形成了功能完备、制度详审、独树一帜的文官系统与活动原则。

2. 文官制度的主宰和灵魂是皇帝，同时，文官机构又是支撑皇帝专制主义统治的重要支柱。

3. 制定文官法，用法律确认和调整文官组织和制度。中国自秦汉时起，便开始制订文官律。文官律是秦汉行政立法的重要内容，文官法成为中国古代法律体系的组成部分。

4. 文官制度的发展是在封闭的环境中进行的，很少受到外来的影响。因此，形成虽早，但却陈陈相因，充满了孤立性、保守性与专断性。

5. 文官制度的改革是在矛盾中进行的，它常发生在阶级矛盾、民族矛盾激化的时代，表现为统治阶级内部的权力再分配。因此，带有革故鼎新，自我完善的性质。此外，在文官制度改革中一个经常性的重要课题是任官唯亲还是任官唯贤。士家大族与高官显贵由于享有门第与恩荫的特权，总是坚持任人唯亲，而中小地主和开明的官吏为了登上政治舞台和刷新政治，一般主张任人唯贤。

During the long development of the ancient Chinese civil service system, the following main characteristics have been formed:

1. The history of the civil service system is not only long, but also uninterrupted. Although there have been developments and changes in different eras, the history is clear, the source can be checked, and on the basis of the addition and subtraction of the past dynasties, after thousands of years of accumulation, a fully functional, detailed system, and unique civil service system and activity principles have been formed.

2. The ruler and soul of the civil service system is the emperor. At the same time, the civil service system is an important pillar supporting the emperor's autocratic rule.

3. To formulate a civil service law, and use the law to confirm and adjust the civil service organization and system. Since Qin and Han Dynasties, China have

made civil service laws. Civil service law was an important part of the administrative legislation of Qin and Han Dynasties. Civil service laws have become an integral part of the ancient Chinese legal system.

4. The development of the civil service system is carried out in a closed environment and is rarely influenced by outsiders. Therefore, although formed early, it is full of isolation, conservativeness and arbitrariness.

5. The reform of the civil service system is carried out in contradictions. It often occurs in an era when class contradictions and ethnic contradictions are intensified, and it is manifested in the redistribution of power within the ruling class. Therefore, it has the nature of innovation and self-improvement. In addition, a frequent and important subject in the reform of the civil service system is whether to appoint officials by cronyism or meritocracy. Because of the privileges of family and grace, the noble families and high-ranking officials always insisted on nepotism, while small and medium landlords and enlightened officials generally advocated appointing people on their merits in order to enter the political arena and refresh politics.

五、中国的传统宗法制度 Traditional Chinese Patriarchal System

（一）中国宗法制度的缘起 The origin of Chinese patriarchal system

中国的宗法制度是由氏族社会父系家长制演变而来的，是王族贵族按血缘关系分配国家权力，以便建立世袭统治的一种制度。其特点是宗族组织和国家组织合二为一，宗法等级和政治等级完全一致。

Chinese patriarchal system evolved from the patriarchal system of the clan society. It is a system in which royal aristocrats distribute state power according to their blood relationship in order to establish hereditary rule. Its characteristic is that the clan organization and the state organization are combined into one, and the patriarchal hierarchy and political hierarchy are completely consistent.

此制度确立于夏朝，发展于商朝，完备于周朝，影响着后来的各封建王朝。按照周代的宗法制度，宗族中分为大宗和小宗。周王自称天子，称为天下的大宗；天子的除嫡长子以外的其他儿子被封为诸侯；诸侯对天子而言是小宗，但在他的封国内却是大宗；诸侯的其它儿子被分封为卿大夫，卿大夫对诸侯而言是小宗，但在他的采邑内却是大宗。从卿大夫到士也是如此。因此贵族的嫡长子总是不同等级的大宗（宗子）。大宗不仅享有对宗族成员的统治权，而且享有政治上的特权。后来，各王朝的统治者对宗法制度加以改造，逐渐建立了由政权、族权、神权、夫权组成的封建宗法制。

This system was established in Xia Dynasty, developed in Shang Dynasty, and completed in Zhou Dynasty, and influenced subsequent feudal dynasties. According to the patriarchal clan system of Zhou Dynasty, the clans were divided into major clans and minor clans. The king of Zhou called himself the Son of Heaven and was called the greatest sect of the country. The King's sons except the first son of the lineage were made vassals. The vassals are small sects to the King, but they are big sects in his feudal country. The other sons of the vassals were entitled as Qing Dafu (Ministers and Grand Masters) . The master is a small sect to the vassal, but he is a big sect in his fief. The same is true from masters to the senior ministerial class. Therefore, the noblest eldest sons of the nobles are always big sects at different levels. The big sect enjoys not only the right to rule over clan members, but also political privileges. Later, the rulers of various dynasties reformed the patriarchal system and gradually established a feudal clan system composed of political power, clan power, divine power, and husband power.

（二）中国宗法制度的社会影响 The social influence of Chinese patriarchal system

中国的宗法制对中国社会的影响长达几千年，即使是在今日中国的社会，仍然能感觉到其影响的存在。这些影响主要表现在三个方面。

Traditional Chinese patriarchal system has had an impact on Chinese society for thousands of years. Even in today's Chinese society, its influence can still be felt. These influences are mainly manifested in three aspects.

1. 宗法制导致中国父系单系世系原则的广泛实行

所谓父系单系指的是血缘集团在世系排列上完全排斥女性成员的地位，女性在继承方面没有权力。西周的家庭关系与宗法制度密切联系，突出地表现为"父权统制，男尊女卑"的观念及夫妻不平等。宗法理论及宗法社会有"出妇"之道，汉代统治者为加强家庭中丈夫的统治地位，还制造了"夫为妻纲"的理论，汉儒又总结了"妇女七去"，这七条都是因为违反了宗法原则。"嫁出去的女儿泼出去的水"，女人出嫁后连姓氏都要随夫。在某些专业技艺、技巧方面有家规行规，如"传子不传女，传媳不传女"。从政治权利方面看，则是不允许母系成员染指且也不传给女性的后代，因此，中国历史上唯一的女皇帝武则天，在历史上一直被看作不正统，遭到满朝官吏的非议，史家的谴责。

1. Patriarchal system has led to the widespread implementation of the principle of single patrilineal line in China

The so-called single patrilineal line means that the blood group completely excludes the status of female members in lineage, and women have no right in inheritance. The family relationship in the Western Zhou Dynasty was closely related to the patriarchal system, which was prominently manifested in the concept of "patriarchy, male superior, female inferior" and inequality between husband and wife. Patriarchal theory and patriarchal society have a way of "casting off the wife". In order to strengthen the dominance of husbands in the family, the rulers of Han Dynasty also created the theory of "husband as wife's master". Han Confucianism also summarized the "seven outs of women" which were all because of violating patriarchal principles. "the daughters who are married out are water thrown out." After a woman is married, even her surname must follow her husband. In some professional skills, there are family rules and regulations, such as "pass on to sons but not to daughters, and to daughters-in-law but not to daughters". From the perspective of political rights, it is not allowed for matrilineal members to intervene and not pass on to the offspring of women. Therefore, Wu Zetian, the only female emperor in Chinese history, was regarded as unorthodox, and criticized by ministers and officials and condemned by historians.

2. 宗法制造成家族制度的长盛不衰

宗法制明显体现宗族制度森严。封建社会，宗族主要以家族方式体现，家族长盛不衰的依据有祠堂、家谱、族权。祠堂主要供奉祖先的神主排位，对祖先的崇拜，是中国传统文化心理的一个重要特征。对祖先的祭祀是最重要、最严肃、最重的礼制，"礼有五经，莫重于祭"。祠堂也是宗族的祭祀场所，还是向宗族成员灌输家规、族规的场所，所以祠堂起到强化家族意识、维系家族团结，在精神上起到训导家族尊宗的作用。家谱是家庭的档案、经典、家族法规，主要起到防止因战乱、流动所导致的血缘关系紊乱，防止家族瓦解的作用，还是解决家族纠纷，惩戒不肖子孙的文字依据。家族制度长盛不衰的最主要标志是族权，族权对中国历史影响颇深。

2. The patriarchal system makes the family system prosperous

The patriarchal system clearly reflects the strict clan. In feudal society, clan was mainly embodied in the way of family, and the bases for the eternal prosperity of the family were ancestral hall, genealogy and clan authority. The ancestral hall mainly enshrines the ancestor's ranking of gods, and the worship of ancestors is an important feature of traditional Chinese cultural psychology. Sacrifice to ancestors is the most important, solemn, and severe ritual system. "There are five classics about rituals, and nothing is more important than sacrifice." The ancestral hall is also a place of worship for the clan, and it is also a place to instill family rules and clan rules into the clan members. Therefore, the ancestral hall strengthens family consciousness, maintains family unity, and spiritually teaches the family. Genealogy is the family's archives, classics, and family laws. It mainly plays a role in preventing blood relationship disorder caused by war chaos and mobility, preventing family disintegration, and is also a written basis for resolving family disputes and punishing unfilial children. The most important indicator of the prosperous family system is clan power. Clan power has a profound influence on Chinese history.

族权在宣传封建伦理，执行封建礼法上有独特的功能。族权凭借自己的血缘宗法制的特点，比政权赤裸裸的灌输显得更加有效、更容易起到管摄天下人心的作用。族权在强制执行封建礼法方面，其威力往往在地方官员之上。因为族长与家族成员有着血缘关系，所以他们比官吏更贴近家族成员，他们可以对家族成员毫无顾忌地施加教化，甚至对违规的成员实行处罚。

Clan rights had a unique function in propagating feudal ethics and implementing the law of feudal rites. Based on its own blood patriarchal system, clan power is more effective than the naked indoctrination of the regime by virtue of its own blood patriarchal system, and it is more likely to play a role in controlling people's minds in the world. In terms of enforcing feudal ritual laws, clan power was often more powerful than local officials, because of the blood relationship between the patriarchs and the family members, they are closer to the family members than the officials, they can impose their education on the family members without control, and even impose penalties on the members who have violated the rules.

族权在维护封建秩序、巩固封建统治方面，很大程度上承担了地方政权职能。

族权以血缘亲属关系掩盖阶级关系的优势，有效地粉饰封建政权阶级压迫的本质。如从东汉末到南北朝这段历史，中国出现了四分五裂的状态，这种状态显然与族权的强大有密切的关联：社会上出现了与朝廷分庭抗礼的宗主、壁主等族权组织形式，事实上形成了一个个独立的自治的乡土社会，就像古代所言"山高皇帝远，村落犹一国"。

Clan rights have largely assumed the functions of local power in maintaining feudal order and consolidating feudal rule.

Clan power concealed the advantages of class relations with blood kinship, effectively whitewashing the nature of class oppression by feudal regimes. For example, from the end of the Eastern Han Dynasty to the Southern and Northern Dynasties, China appeared to be divided. This state was obviously closely related to the strength of clan power: there were clan power organizations such as suzerain and wall lord who stood up to the court as an equal. In fact, independent and autonomous rural societies were formed, as an ancient saying goes, "High in the moutains, far from the emperor's reach, the village functions as its own kingdom."

3. 宗法制导致中国出现"家国同构"

家与国同一结构是宗法社会最鲜明的结构特征，这种宗法制结构的明显特点，在中国封建社会被长期保留下来。家庭或家族与国家在组织结构方面具有共同性，也就是说不论国家或家族、家庭，他们的组织系统和权力结构都是严格的父权家长制。家国同构的共同性具体表现为"家是小国，国是大家"。在家庭或家族内，父亲地位尊，权力最大；在国内，君主的地位至尊，权力至大。所以，家长在家庭中就像君主一样，即"家人有严君焉，父母之谓也"。而君主就是全国的严父，各级行政长官也被百姓视为父母，所谓"夫君者，民众父母也"。所以，家国同构可以看作父亲为一家之君，君为国父，君与父互为表里，国与家是彼此沟通的。因此，中国古语有"欲治其国者，先齐其家"的说法。这种结构表明宗法关系渗透到社会各个方面，它掩盖了阶级关系、等级关系，家国同构直接导致了家庭或家庭成员和国家子民品质的统一，这就是忠、孝同义，也即"求忠臣必于孝子之门"之说。忠的内容和孝一样都是对权力的绝对顺从，所不同的仅仅在于他们所顺从的对象不一样。忠和孝成为中国的道德本位和伦理本位。

3. The patriarchal system led to the emergence of "the same structure of family and country" in China

The same structure of family and country is the most distinctive structural feature of patriarchal society. The obvious characteristics of this patriarchal structure have been preserved for a long time in Chinese feudal society. Families have commonality with the country in terms of organizational structure, which means that regardless of the country, or family, their organizational system and power structure are strictly patriarchal. The commonality of the same structure of family and country is embodied as "a family is a small country, and a country is a big family." In a family or clan, the father is the highest and most powerful; in the country, the monarch is the highest and most powerful. Therefore, the father is like the monarch in the family, that is, "the family has strict monarch, and it refers to the father." The monarch is the named father of the nation, and chief executives at all levels are also regarded as parents by the people. The so-called "the emperor is also the father of the people." Therefore, the same structure of family and country can lead to the fact that the king of a country, the father of a family, the king and the father, and the country and the family are the same with each other. Therefore, there is an old Chinese saying that goes "to rule a country, one must first manage a family". This structure shows that the patriarchal relationship penetrates into all aspects of society. It conceals the class relationship and hierarchical relationship. The same structure of family and country directly leads to the unity of the quality of the family or family members and the people of the country, which is the synonym of loyalty and filial piety, that is "to seck a loyal subject at the gate of a filial family". The content of loyalty and filial piety is absolute obedience to power, the only difference is that the objects they are subject to are different. Loyalty and filial piety have become China's moral and ethical standards.

4. 宗法制对现代中国社会的影响

宗法制实际上是以种群为区分的缺乏自我存在意识的团体，这是一种原始的组织结构，但就是这种原始的结构至今还影响着现代中国包括社会、政治、文化等诸多层面，如果将这些碎片拼凑起来，就不难发现诸多所谓"中国特色"现象的精神根源。

4. The influence of patriarchal system on modern Chinese society

The patriarchal system is actually a group that lacks awareness of self - existence, which is divided into groups. This is a primitive organizational structure, but it is this primitive structure that still affects many aspects of modern China including society, politics, and culture. Putting these pieces together, it is not difficult to find the spiritual root of many so-called "Chinese characteristics" phenomena.

中华传统文化的君、臣、父、子，看似经纬万端其实就是一个"德"字，而这种"德"就始自于宗法制。宗法制习惯依托于道德去组织和管理族群，因为他们发现在对族群的管理中法律显然过于迂腐和呆板，但往往在道德的干预下，许多事情的处理不但能变得高效，而且更灵活且具备相当的延续性。因此"道德"成为宗族制度的首选管理方式。现代社会我们观察生活，依然不难找到这种道德标志和体系。

In traditional Chinese culture, monarchs, courtiers, fathers, and sons seem to be nothing more than the word "de" (morality), and this "de" originated from the patriarchal system. The patriarchal system was accustomed to organize and manage ethnic groups relying on morality, because it is found that law is obviously too pedantic and rigid in the management of ethnic groups. With the intervention of morality, the handling of many things can not only become efficient, but also more flexible and sustainable. Therefore, "morality" has become the preferred method of the patriarchal system. In modern society, if we observe life, it is still not difficult to find such moral signs and systems.

所以在此建制下繁衍出言谏制度，而言谏制度不以宗法，而以法律与仁义为首，下者可谏上，故有曰当仁不让，就算君臣，父子，师生当遇上违背之事，亦以律义当头，成为中国独有的制度。而言谏制度亦规范天子之谕，下臣可以当朝律例，阻止皇帝进行违反律法的行为。

Therefore, a system of remonstrance appeared under such an institutional system. In terms of the remonstrance system, it was not based on the patriarchal clan system, but with law and benevolence as the first thing. Taking the law and justice as the first important became a unique system in China, that's why the lower people could admonish the upper, and we say we don't decline to take the responsibility of remonstrance even before the emperor, father, or teacher when they violate the law and righteousness. In terms of the remonstrance system, it also regulated the emperor's decree, and his subordinates could act at court to prevent the emperor from violating the law.

中国的传统经济制度文化

一、中国古代的经济发展 The Economic Development in Ancient China

中国远古社会经济的发展，是中国社会经济发展历史长河的源头，旧石器时代经历了上百万年的漫长道路，新石器时代只有几千年，进入文明时期以后，各个王朝的更替不过数百年的时间。每一个时期的经济发展都有一定的特点，也都遵循着中国传统文化和农业经济的共同规律。

China's ancient social and economic development is the source of the long history of China's social and economic development. The Paleolithic era went through a long road of millions of years, and the Neolithic era had only a few thousand years. After entering the civilization period, the dynasties were changed only hundreds of years in between. The economic development of each period had certain characteristics, and it also followed the common laws of traditional Chinese culture and agricultural economy.

夏商西周时期代表新的生产力的文字、青铜器和城市已经在北方的辽河流域、长江以南地区纷纷出现，从而使中国的奴隶制王朝得以巩固和发展，成为东方世界的经济发展中心。

In the Xia, Shang, and Western Zhou periods, the characters, bronzes, and cities representing the new productive forces appeared in the Liao River Basin in the north and in the south of the Yangtze River, thus consolidated and developed the slavery dynasty in China, and China became the economic center of the Eastern world.

春秋战国时期生产力发展迅速，出现了先进的生铁冶铸技术，即出现了铸铁，促进了铁器的普遍使用，并由此推动了农业、手工业的发展，使中国在经济发展上走在了世界的前列。

During the Spring and Autumn and Warring States period, the productive forces developed rapidly, and advanced pig iron smelting and casting technology appeared, that is, cast iron appeared, which promoted the widespread use of ironware, thus pushed forward the development of agriculture and handicrafts, making China a world leader in economic development.

秦汉时期建立了统一的专制主义中央集权的封建国家，迫使封建统治集团对古代社会的自然经济状态进行干预，以使社会经济朝着有利于巩固封建统一的轨道运行，于是产生了封建经济的自然发展与封建国家经济制度的矛盾，也就是经济基础与上层建筑的矛盾。

During the Qin and Han dynasties, a unified despotism and centralized feudal state was established, forcing the feudal ruling group to intervene in the natural economic state of ancient society, so that the social economy moved towards the track conducive to the consolidation of feudal unity, thus forming the contradiction between the natural development of feudal economy and the economic system of a feudal country, which was the contradiction between the economic foundation and the superstructure.

魏晋南北朝是中国历史上专制集权较弱，政治上相对宽松的时代。因而对经济活动的控制也相对宽松，经济活动也比较活跃。

The Wei, Jin, Southern and Northern Dynasties were an era of weak authoritarianism and relatively loose politics in Chinese history. Therefore, the control of economic activities was relatively loose, and economic activities were correspondingly active.

隋唐时期的南北经济均有发展，更主要的是南方经济已逐渐成为中国中央政权的主要支柱。生产力有了巨大发展，新的技术给生产带来突破性变化。如造船、建筑、农田水利、造纸印刷术、瓷器、丝织都有创造性发明并向海外流传。与外国经济交流达到前所未有的程度，与非洲、西欧、中亚、西亚、东南亚、日本、朝鲜等国，都有贸易往来，陆上、海上丝绸之路畅通无阻。

The economy in both the North and South developed during Sui and Tang Dynasties. What's more, the southern economy gradually became the main pillar of China's central government. Productivity developed tremendously, and new technologies brought breakthrough changes to production. For example, shipbuilding, construction, farmland water conservancy, papermaking and printing, porcelain, silk weaving all had great inventions and spread overseas. Economic exchanges with foreign countries reached an unprecedented level. There were trade exchanges with Japan, Korea and countries from Africa, Western Europe, Central Asia, West Asia, Southeast Asia. The land silk road and sea silk road were unimpeded.

宋辽夏金时期以农业为主、以手工操作为基础的社会生产体系及其相应的制度保证体系已经趋于完善；从对资源开发的深度和广度而言，已经接近甚至几乎达到了古代的技术条件所能允许的最高水平。

During the Song, Liao, Xia and Jin periods, the agricultural-oriented and manual-based social production system and its corresponding institutional guarantee system tended to be perfect; in terms of the depth and breadth of resource development, it approached or almost reached the highest level that ancient technical conditions allowed.

元代经济历史提供的经验和教训在中华民族经济管理历史上占有极重要的地位。一代天骄成吉思汗卓越的军事、经济管理谋略运筹思维，忽必烈多元一体化的国民经济管理思想模式，对后世的经济巩固、各族人民的团结交往、封建社会后期经济的进步发展都有重要而深远的影响。

The experience and lessons provided by the economic history of Yuan Dynasty occupies an extremely important position in the history of the economic management of the Chinese nation. Genghis Khan's outstanding military and economic management and strategic thinking and Kublai Khan's diversified and integrated national economic management ideology were important and profound for the economic consolidation, the unity and communication of people of all ethnic groups, and the economic progress of the future generations and late feudal society.

明代中国经济领域发生了结构性的变化：白银成为主导货币、赋役体制中基于土地并以货币征收的赋税比例扩大、货币财政体制形成、国内和国际市场体系发展、人口大幅度增长。明朝政府经济干预的三个杠杆——赋税制度、政府财政支出、货币管理在明朝中期以后都有顺应市场经济的动向，但又都没有完全适应市场经济发展，原因主要在于帝制体系本身的僵化和明王朝自身进入衰败期之后的调整乏力。变化中形成的新的经济结构，可以容纳更大规模的商业繁荣，但是并不构成产业升级的直接基础，距离资本主义经济体制尚远，是一种帝制农商社会经济结构。

Structural changes took place in the economic field of China in Ming Dynasty: silver became the dominant currency, the proportion of land-based and currency-based taxes in the revenue system expanded, the monetary and fiscal system was formed, the domestic and international market systems developed, and the population increased significantly. The three levers of government's economic intervention——the taxation system, the government fiscal expenditure, and the currency management, had all adapted to the market economy since the middle of Ming Dynasty, but they were not fully suitable to the development of the market economy. The main reason was the rigidity of the imperial system itself and the weak adjustment when late Ming Dynasty entered a period of decline. The new economic structure formed during the change could accommodate larger-scale commercial prosperity, but it did not constitute a direct basis for industrial upgrading. It was still far from the capitalist economic system, and was a monarchy economic structure based on agricultural and commercial society.

清朝采取开垦荒地、移民边区及推广新作物以提高农业生产量；由于国内与国外的贸易提升，经济农业也相对发达。手工业方面改工匠的徭役制为代税役制，产业以纺织和瓷器业为重，棉织业超越丝织业。清朝商业发达，分成十大商帮。其中，占据金融领域的是晋商和徽商，闽商和潮商则专事海外贸易。货币方面采取银铜双本位制。

Qing Dynasty adopted policies of the wasteland reclamation, immigration to border areas and promotion of new crops to increase agricultural production. Due to the increase in domestic and foreign trade, economic agriculture was also relatively developed. In the handicraft industry, the servitude system of craftsmen was changed to the system of substitute taxation. The industry focused on textiles and porcelain, and the cotton weaving industry surpassed the silk weaving industry. Qing Dynasty developed commerce and there were ten major groups of merchants. Among them, Shanxi merchants and Huizhou merchants dominated China's financial industry, while Fujian merchants and Chaozhou merchants controlled overseas trade. The currency adopted a dual-standard system of silver and copper.

二、中国古代土地制度与经济结构 Ancient Chinese Land System and Economic Structure

（一） 中国传统的自然经济形态 Traditional Chinese natural economic form

自然经济是传统社会封建经济形态下主要的经济形式，指生产是为了直接满足生产者个人或经济单位的需要，而不是为了交换的经济形式。自然经济是商品经济的对立面，是私有制经济的一种表现。该种经济形态占统治地位的持续时间涵盖原始社会、封建社会以及早期的资本主义社会与半殖民地半封建社会。

Natural economy was the main economic form under the feudal economy of traditional society. It referred to the economic form in which production was directly to meet the needs of producers or economic units, not for exchange. The natural economy was the opposite of the commodity economy, a manifestation of the private economy. The duration of the dominance of this economic form covered primitive society, feudal society, early capitalist society, and semi-colonial and semi-feudal society.

在中国，自给自足的自然经济占主要地位，一直延续到近代，从而形成了几千年来稳定的生产格局和劳动组合方式。第一，一家一户为生产单位的小农生产格局。以一家一户为一个经济单位来从事生产，封建国家的财政收入来源，即是由无数个家庭提供的，一家一户的个体生产，构成了封建经济的基石。安土重迁、农恒为农、世不徙业、不思变革的自然经济形态，抑制了后来资本主义的萌芽。第二，男耕女织的生产格局和自给自足的生产目的。生产单位小规模，生产工具自备，家庭成员实行原始分工，通过勤于耕织，自给自足，解决生存所需的衣食。耕织结构构成中国农民赖以生存的最基本手段。

In China, the self-sufficient natural economy took the lead and continued into modern times, thus forming a stable production pattern and labor combination pattern for thousands of years. First, the production pattern of small farmers with one household as the production unit. One family is an economic unit to engage in production. The financial income source of a feudal country is provided by countless families. Individual production by one family constitutes the cornerstone of the feudal e-conomy. The natural economic form of being attached to the land and reluctant to move, farmers being farmers generation after generation, not changing their walks of life for generations, and not thinking about change, inhibited the budding of capital-ism. Second, the production pattern of male farming and female weaving, and the production purpose of self-sufficiency. The production unit is small-scale, the production tools are self-provided, and the family members implement primitive division of labor, and through diligent farming and weaving, self-sufficiency solves the needs for survival. The structure of farming and weaving constitutes the most basic means for Chinese farmers to survive.

（二）中国传统的土地所有制形式 Chinese Traditional land ownership

古代中国历来以农立国，农业是国家的经济命脉，而农业的基本生产资料是土地。因此，在中国，土地所有权成为农业生产中一切经济关系的基础。中国古代的土地制度主要有原始社会的土地氏族公社公有制、奴隶社会奴隶主贵族土地国有制（土地王有制）、封建社会的封建地主土地所有制等三种形式。

Ancient China had been based on agriculture, agriculture was the country's economic lifeline, and the basic production means of agriculture was land. Therefore, in China, land ownership became the basis of all economic relations in agricultural production. The land system in ancient China mainly had three forms: the public land ownership of clan commune in the primitive society, the state-owned land ownership by the slave owners and nobles in the slave society (king land ownership), and the feudal land ownership by landlords in the feudal society.

原始社会实行氏族公社土地公有制度。夏商周时期，实行土地国有制——井田制；春秋时期，井田制瓦解；战国时期，井田制被废除，封建土地所有制确立，一直延续了两千多年。曹魏时期曾经实行屯田制；北魏到唐朝中期，实行均田制；均田制是中国古代一项重要的土地制度。随着地主经济的发展壮大，土地兼并也随之日益严重，均田制形同虚设。到了唐代中叶，均田制终于退出历史舞台。

The primitive society implemented the public land ownership system of clan communes; during Xia, Shang and Zhou Dynasties, the state-owned land system——the "nine squares" system was implemented; in the Spring and Autumn Period, the "nine squares" system collapsed; during the Warring States period, the "nine squares" system was abolished and the feudal land ownership system was established, which lasted for more than two thousand years. During the Cao Cao period, the Tuntian system was practiced; from the Northern Wei Dynasty to the Mid-Tang Dynasty, the system of equalized land was implemented. The land equalization system was an important land system in ancient China. With the development and growth of the landlord economy, land annexations became increasingly serious, and the system of land equalization was ineffective. In the middle of Tang Dynasty, the system of land equalization finally withdrew from the stage of history.

三、中国传统的经济结构特点 Characteristics of Traditional Chinese Economic Structure

1. 传统中国农业经济的基本特点：以小农户个体经营为主，是古代中国农业经济的基本特点。小农经济以家庭为生产、生活单位，农业和家庭手工业相结合，是自给自足的自然经济，是中国封建社会农业生产的基本模式，是中国封建社会发展缓慢和长期延续的重要原因。在没有天灾、战乱和苛政干扰的情况下，"男耕女织" 式的小农经济可以使农民勉强自给自足。其狭小的生产规模和简单的性别分工，很难扩大再生产，阻碍了社会分工和交换经济的发展。到近代以后，它已经成为阻碍生产发展的因素。中国古代农业，世界闻名，中国古代的重大文明成就，都是在农业经济发展的基础上取得的。

The basic characteristics of traditional Chinese agricultural economy: It was the basic characteristics of ancient China's agricultural economy that small farmers were self-employed. The small farming economy was self-sufficient natural economy and the basic mode of agricultural production in Chinese feudal society, taking the family as the production and living unit, and combining agriculture and cottage industry, which was an important reason for the slow development and long-term continuation of Chinese feudal society. In the absence of natural disasters, wars, and harsh government interference, the small farming economy of "men farming and women weaving" style can make farmers barely self-sufficient. Its small production scale and simple gender division of labor make it difficult to expand reproduction, hindering the development of social division of labor and the exchange economy. In modern times, it had become a factor hindering the development of production. Traditional Chinese agriculture is well-known in the world, and the major achievements of ancient Chinese civilization were all made on the basis of agricultural economic development.

2. 传统中国手工业发展的特点：从春秋战国时期开始，官营手工业、民营手工业和家庭手工业就成为传统中国手工业的三种主要经营形态。在漫长的自给自足自然经济时代，家庭手工业占有相当的比重。家庭手工业生产对于稳定小农经济起到一定作用，但技术落后，生产分散，妨碍了市场发育。代表中国古代手工业水平的则是官营和专业的私营手工业生产。中国传统社会长期存在以农耕为主兼营副业的自给自足的手工业经济（田庄手工业）。

The characteristics of the development of traditional Chinese handicraft industry: Since the Spring and Autumn Period and the Warring States Period, the official handicraft industry, private handicraft industry and cottage handicraft industry have become the three main business forms of ancient Chinese handicraft industry. In the long era of self-sufficient natural economy, cottage industry occupies a considerable proportion. Household handicraft production played a certain role in stabilizing the small farming economy, but the backward technology and scattered production hindered the development of the market. What represented the level of traditional Chinese handicrafts was official and professional private handicraft production. The self-sufficient handicraft economy (farming handicraft industry) with farming as its mainstay and some sideline operations has long existed in traditional chinese society.

3. 传统中国商业发展的特点：中国人很早就学会经商，春秋战国时期，官府控制商业的局面被打破。古代中国的商业发展促进了经济的进步，因为商业的繁盛而兴起古代都会。农耕时代的中国商业和商人的命运，与政府的商业政策息息相关。

The characteristics of traditional commercial development in China: Chinese people learned to do business very early, and during the Spring and Autumn and Warring States period, the government's control of commerce was broken. The development of commerce in ancient China promoted economic progress, and the prosperity of commerce gave rise to ancient cities. The fate of Chinese commerce and businessmen in the agricultural era was closely related to the government's commercial policies.

4. "重农抑商"政策的影响：它是为了维护专制主义国家政权的经济基础，也有安定人心的政治文化方面的考虑。它使社会经济活力受到压抑，新的经济因素和生产方式的萌芽长期得不到正常发育，这是中国资本主义萌芽发展缓慢的重要原因。明清的"重农抑商"政策不仅阻碍工商业发展，而且强化了自然经济，使之迟迟难以瓦解，也使资本主义萌芽发展非常缓慢。明清时期的抑商政策，虽然不能完全遏制民间商品经济的发展，但它导致中国被远远甩在世界工业文明潮流的后面。

The influence of the policy of "emphasizing agriculture and restraining commerce": It is to maintain the economic foundation of authoritarian state power, and it also has political and cultural considerations to stabilize people's minds. It has suppressed the social and economic vitality, and the germination of new economic factors and production methods could not develop normally for a long time. This is an important reason for the slow growth of the germination of Chinese capitalism. The policies of "emphasizing agriculture and restraining commerce" in Ming and Qing dynasties not only hindered the development of industry and commerce, but also strengthened the natural economy, making it difficult to disintegrate, and making the germination of capitalism very slow. Although the anti-business policy in Ming and Qing Dynasties could not completely curb the development of the private commodity economy, it caused China to be far behind the trend of world industrial civilization.

5. 闭关锁国政策的影响：它不仅妨碍海外市场开拓，抑制资本的原始积累，阻碍资本主义萌芽滋长，而且使中国与世隔绝，从而阻断了中国学习西方的先进科学技术，使中国落后于世界潮流。它使中国失去了利用国际贸易的优势地位开辟海外市场、刺激资本扩张、推进工业化的契机。

The impact of the closed-door policy: It not only hindered the development of overseas markets, inhibited the primitive accumulation of capital, and hindered the germination and growth of capitalism, but also isolated China from the world, thus blocking China from learning advanced science and technology from the West, making China lag behind the world trend. It had made China lose the opportunity to use its dominant position in international trade to open up overseas markets, stimulate capital expansion, and promote industrialization.

四、中国传统经济制度的特点 Characteristics of Traditional Chinese Economic System

春秋战国时期，随着铁犁牛耕技术的出现和普及，封建土地所有制逐渐确立，以家庭为单位的小农经济产生，它是古代农业经济最主要的生产模式，使中华文明延绵不断，领先世界。中国传统经济制度经过不断发展完善，其主要特点有：农业是传统经济制度的重点；经济制度制定的宗旨是将农民束缚在土地上，以利于稳定社会秩序；以户籍制度作为制定经济制度的依据；封建土地所有制是传统经济制度的基础，地主土地所有制占主要地位，农民土地所有制虽不占支配地位，但却广泛而分散，是专制主义中央集权制度建立和长期存在的基础。经济制度既制约土地兼并，又受制于土地兼并。古代赋役制度是土地私有制的产物，起到确立私人对土地占有的作用，但又受制于大土地所有制。

During the Spring and Autumn and Warring States period, with the emergence and popularization of iron plow and cattle farming technology, the feudal land ownership system was gradually established, and the family-based small farming economy emerged. It was the main production mode of ancient agricultural economy, which enabled Chinese civilization to continue and lead the world. The traditional Chinese economic system continuously developed and improved, its main characteristics are: agriculture is the focus of the traditional economic system; the purpose of the economic system is to tie farmers to the land in order to stabilize the social order; the household registration system is used as the basis for the economic system; the feudal land ownership system is the traditional economic system. The landowner's land ownership system occupies the main position. Although the farmer land ownership system does not occupy a dominant position, it is extensive and scattered. It is the foundation for the establishment and long-term existence of the authoritarian centralized power system. The economic system not only restricts land mergers, but is also subject to land mergers. The ancient taxation system was a product of private land ownership, which played a role in establishing private ownership of land, but it was also subject to large land ownership.

土地和赋税、徭役制度构成古代经济制度的基本框架。中国封建社会前期，赋役制度与土地制度并存；后期独立存在，并逐渐与土地占有结合。

简而言之，中国的传统经济制度是农业经济，中国农业经济的特点可以概括为三点：（1）农业技术的主流是精耕细作；（2）以种植业为中心、农牧结合、综合经营的广大农区与以游牧为主的广大牧区同时并存和相互补充；（3）各地区各民族农业发展不平衡。中国不同地区、不同民族存在着不同类型的农业文化，中国传统农业是在这些不同类型的农业文化的相互交流和融汇中向前发展的。

Land, taxes, and corvee systems constituted the basic framework of the ancient economic system. In the early period of Chinese feudal society, the taxation system and the land system coexisted; in the later period, they existed independently and gradually integrated with land ownership.

In short, the traditional economic system in ancient China was the agricultural economy. The characteristics of Chinese agricultural economy can be summarized in three points: (1) The mainstream of agricultural technology is intensive farming; (2) Vast agricultural areas taking planting as the center, comprehensive management, agriculture and husbandry combined, and vast pastoral areas dominated by nomadism co-exist and complement each other at the same time; (3) The agricultural development of various regions and ethnic groups is not balanced. There are different types of agricultural cultures in different regions and different nationalities in China. Traditonal Chinese agriculture developed in the mutual exchange and integration of these different types of agricultural cultures.

五、中国传统的经济思想 Traditional Chinese Economic Thoughts

中国传统经济思想十分丰富，其中影响最为深远的是重本抑末、重义轻利思想。

Traditional Chinese economic thoughts are very rich, among which the most far-reaching influence is the thought of emphasizing the fundamental and restraining the end, and emphasizing righteousness and neglecting profit.

（一）重本抑末 Emphasizing the fundamental and restraining the end

重本：以根本大事为重。常指重视农田之事。抑末：指抑制商贾。在两千余年封建历史中，"农本商末"的观念是中国传统经济思想主调，由此形成"重农抑商"的政治方针，是中国古代统治者惯行的基本治国之策。其主张是重视农业，以农为本，限制工商业的发展。从李悝变法、商鞅变法规定的奖励耕作，到汉文帝的重农措施，直到清初恢复经济的调整，都是重农抑商政策的体现。

Emphasizing the fundamental: focus on the fundamental issues, often referring to things that attach importance to farmland. Restraining the end, referring to the control of merchants. In the feudal history of more than two thousand years, the concept of "farming is fundamental and business is trivial" was the main theme of traditional Chinese economic thought, which formed the political policy of "emphasizing agriculture and restraining business", which was the basic rule of the country taken by ancient Chinese rulers. Its proposition was to attach importance to agriculture, put agriculture first, and restrict the development of industry and commerce. From Li Di's Reform and Shang Yang's Reform to reward farming, to Emperor Wen's measures in Han Dynasty to emphasize agriculture, until the economic adjustment in early Qing Dynasty, they all embodied the policy of emphasizing agriculture and restraining business.

在封建社会中，形成的自然经济是以土地为基础，农业与手工业结合，以家庭为生产单位，具有自我封闭性、独立性，以满足自身需要为主的经济结构。这种经济结构中的关键生产资料大部分都掌握在地主手中，故而能够形成"地主剥削农民"的阶级关系。工商业的发展不利于其统治，统治者希望稳固自己的统治，因此需要抑制工商业。由于农民是赋税的主要承担者，农业的兴衰决定着国家的兴衰，因此重视农业。"重本抑末"政策对于社会的安定和经济的发展起到了积极的作用，在每个王朝的兴起阶段具有重要作用。但"重农抑商"政策导致地主官僚采取多种手段兼并土地，使土地高度集中，农民破产流亡，这不仅影响了农业生产的发展，且激化了阶级矛盾，造成农民起义不断爆发，还导致地主官僚集团因疯狂兼并土地而更加腐败。到了明清时期随着生产力的发展，商品经济的活跃，中国资本主义萌芽已经出现，而在这时统治阶级依然坚持"重农抑商"的政策，把商农发展对立起来，并在这一思想的指导下推行一系列不利于资本主义发展的措施，从而阻碍了资本主义萌芽的成长，违反了经济发展规律，使中国在清朝时落后于世界先进国家。

In the feudal society, the natural economy formed was based on land, combined with agriculture and handicrafts, and took the family as the production unit. It was self-enclosed and independent to meet its own needs. Most of the key production materials in this economic structure were in the hands of landlords, so a class relationship of "landlords exploiting farmers" was formed. The development of industry and commerce was not conducive to its rule. The ruler wanted to stabilize his rule and therefore needed to restrain industry and commerce. Since farmers were the main bearers of taxes, the rise and fall of agriculture determined the rise and fall of the country, so agriculture was attached much importance to. The policy of "emphasizing the fundamental and restraining the end" played a positive role in social stability and economic development, and played an important role in the rise of each dynasty. However, the policy of "emphasizing agriculture and restraining business" led landlords and bureaucrats to adopt various methods to merge land, which resulted in a high concentration of land and bankruptcy and the exile of farmers. This not only affected the development of agricultural production, but also intensified class contradictions and caused continuous outbreaks of peasant uprisings. As a result, the landlord bureaucracy became more corrupted due to frantic annexation of land. In Ming and Qing Dynasties, with the development of productivity and the active commodity economy, the budding of Chinese capitalism emerged. At this time, the ruling class still adhered to the policy of "emphasizing agriculture and restraining business", putting the development of business at the opposite side of agriculture. Under such guidance of ideology, a series of measures that were not conducive to the development of capitalism were implemented, which hindered the growth of the buds of capitalism, violated the laws of economic development, and made China lag behind the advanced countries in the world during Qing Dynasty.

（二）重义轻利 Emphasizing righteousness over profit

重义轻利是战国以后封建正统思想家对待社会伦理规范与人们物质利益之间关系的基本思想。其内容实质是以封建伦理道德制约人们追求物质利益的活动，限制人们追求物质利益。春秋末年，儒学创始人孔子将人们的逐利活动看作礼乐崩坏、天下动乱的根源。认为通晓义、追求义是社会上层人物的高尚美德，而好利、逐利则是下层小人的行为。

Emphasizing righteousness over profit was the basic idea of feudal orthodox thinkers on the relationship between social ethical norms and people's material interests after the Warring States period. The essence of its content is that feudal ethics restrict people's pursuit of material interests, degrade and restrict people's pursuit of material interests. At the end of the Spring and Autumn Period, Confucius, the founder of Confucianism, regarded people's profit-seeking activities as the root cause of the collapse of rite and music and the chaos of the world. It was believed that knowing righteousness and pursuing righteousness were the noble virtues of the upper-class people in society, while pro-profit and profit-seeking were the behaviors of the lower-class people.

传统的义利思想包含了先利后义、以利说义、先义后利三个层面。

The traditional thought of righteousness and profit includes three levels: profit first and righteousness later, righteousness persuasion with profit, and righteousness first and profit later.

（1）先利后义。古代中国哲学家认为要让老百姓讲道德礼义，首先要保证他们起码的物质利益，满足他们基本的物质生活需求。生存问题解决了，才会想如何体面的生存，做受人尊敬的讲礼义的人。

Profit first and righteousness later. Ancient Chinese philosophers believed that in order for ordinary people to observe morality and justice, they must first ensure their minimum material interests and satisfy their basic material needs. Once the survival problem is solved, only then will they think about how to survive decently and be a respectable person of courtesy and righteousness.

（2）以利说义。中国人传统上把义和利联系在一起，再三告诉人们只有按道义的原则做人行事，才能得到正当长远的利益。孟子游说诸侯、劝导民众的方式带有明显的功利色彩，讲仁义是因为它有用，大则可以得天下，小则可以满足个人的求利、求名、求自尊的欲望。"三代之得天下也以仁，其失天下也以不仁。""仁者爱人，有礼者敬人。爱人者人恒爱之，敬人者人恒敬之。"人都想求名利，求富贵，要达到这些目的，孟子认为只有义才是最正确、最宽敞、最稳妥的道路。

Righteousness persuasion with profit. Chinese traditionally associate righteousness with profit and have repeatedly told people that only by acting in accordance with moral principles can they obtain legitimate long－term profits. Mencius's method of lobbying the princes and persuading the people was obviously utilitarian. The focus on benevolence is just because it is useful. The big one can win the world, and the small one can satisfy the individual's desire for profit, fame, and self－esteem. "That within three generations they can win the world is owing to benevolence, and that within three generations they lose the world is due to malevolence. " "The benevolent love others, and the courteous respect others. Those who love others are always loved, and those who respect others are always respected. " People want fame, wealth and honor. To achieve these goals, Mencius holds that only righteousness is the widest, safest, and most correct way.

（3）先义后利。这种观点的代表人物是孟子。孟子是热衷于治国平天下的思想家，先义后利、重义轻利主要是作为一种治国策略提出来的。他认为当时"天下之人，唯利是求"，执政者行仁义的力度非常小。从宏观调控的角度看，就是利益驱动的力量过大而道德制约作用太小，物质文明与精神文明的发展严重失衡。面对这种形势，孟子觉得必须加大道德对人们求利行为的制约力度，强调以仁义治国，才能达到国泰民安的目的。因此孟子对诸侯讲治国之道，总是主张先义后利。儒家创始人孔子和孟子大概认识到人们追求物质利益的本性难以改变，但又不能不加以节制，他们竭力伸张道义，宣传仁爱。

Righteousness first and profit later. The representative holding this view is Mencius. Mencius was a thinker who was keen on governing the country and pacifying the world. First righteousness and then profit, emphasizing righteousness and neglecting profit was mainly put forward as a strategy of governing the country. He believed that at that time, "every man under the sky pursues nothing but profits", and those in power were very weak in benevolence and righteousness. From the perspective of macro-control, it was that the driving force of interests was too big and the role of moral restraint was too small. The development of material civilization and spiritual civilization was seriously out of balance. Faced with this situation, Mencius felt that it was necessary to increase morality's restriction on people's profit-seeking behavior and emphasize the rule of benevolence and justice in order to achieve the goal of national peace and security. Therefore, Mencius taught the princes to govern the country, by advocating righteousness first and profit later. The founders of Confucianism, Confucius and Mencius, probably realized that people's nature in pursuing material interests was difficult to change, but they must be restrained. They tried their best to uphold morality and promote benevolence.

中国传统的小农经济属于自然经济，它的特点一是分散，二是生产出来的产品都用来自己消费或绝大部分用来自己消费，而不是进行商品交换，是一种自给自足的自然经济。在整个中国传统社会，自然经济始终在中国封建经济中占主导地位。自然经济的牢固存在，是中国封建社会发展缓慢和长期延续的重要原因。

China's traditional small-scale farming economy was a natural economy. It is scattered; the products produced are all used for self-consumption or most of the products are used for self-consumption instead of commodity exchange. It is a self-sufficient natural economy. In the entire traditional Chinese society, the natural economy dominated the Chinese feudal economy. The solid existence of the natural economy was an important reason for the slow development and long-term continuation of Chinese feudal society.

中国的传统教育文化

一、中国古代的学校教育及其发展 School Education and Its Development in Ancient China

中国古代，把教育作为社会生存发展的命脉。早在 5000 年前，就设有学官，管理教育事务。商周时期，中国教育有了一定规模。当时出现了国学、乡学、大学、小学以及宫廷、幼儿家庭教育，教育内容以礼、乐、射、御、书、数"六艺"为主体。春秋战国时，孔子、墨子、孟子、荀子等一批民间私学大师，他们的教育思想流芳千古，他们不朽的著作《论语》《墨子》《孟子》《荀子》等记载了大量的教育思想和精华，对后世中国文化的影响全面而巨大。其中《学记》是世界上最早的古典教育学专著，为中国古代教育的发展奠定了基础。

In ancient China, education was regarded as the lifeblood of social survival and development. As early as 5, 000 years ago, there were academic officials to manage educational affairs. During Shang and Zhou Dynasties, Chinese education had a certain scale. At that time there appeared national schools, countryside schools, universities, elementary schools, court education, and infant family education. The education content was mainly based on the "six arts" of rite, music, shooting, driving, calligraphy, and mathematics. During the Spring and Autumn and Warring States period, a group of private school masters such as Confucius, Mozi, Mencius, and Xunzi, their educational thoughts survive forever. Their immortal works *The Analects*, *Mozi*, *Mencius*, and *Xunzi* recorded many educational thoughts. And the essence has a comprehensive and huge influence on Chinese culture of later generations. Among them,

"*Xueji*" is the world's earliest monograph on classical education, which laid the foundation for the development of ancient Chinese education.

　　两汉教育以儒学经典为教材，虽然各派讲授内容大相径庭，但对于教育的主张，却在"明经修行"这一点达成共识。汉代的教育设施、教育思想和汉代的选举制度相辅相成、相互统一。到了晋代，中央把学制分为国子学和太学。国子学招收富家贵族子弟，太学主要考虑平民子弟。唐朝时，继承了隋代的学校教育制度，在政治统一、经济繁荣、文化科学水平发达的基础上，经过百余年的发展，学校教育制度已相当完备，在中国和世界学校教育发展史上占有重要的地位，也是中国古代教育史和官制史上的重要转折点，同时，发展了唐朝学校教育和社会教育，促进了社会的进步。唐代留学生也是与日俱增。其中，日本、新罗、高丽等国最多，他们学习中国的经史、法律、礼制、文学和科技等文化知识。当时的国都长安成为东西方各国文化教育交流的中心，中国文化通过留学生传播到世界各国，促进了中国与世界各国的联系，为传播中国文化起到了桥梁纽带作用。宋朝时，出现了书院。宋代书院成为学者们收纳弟子、传道授业、培养人才的地方。选址多为山林名胜之地，建制有民办、官办、民办官助等形式，大都以功名为读书目的。清代学制沿袭明制，科举制沿袭宋元，分乡试、会试、殿试三种。

　　The education of Han Dynasty used Confucian classics as teaching materials. Although the teaching content of each school was quite different, the views on education reached a consensus on the point of "Understanding the Classics and Cultivating Oneself". The educational facilities and educational thoughts of Han Dynasty and the election system of Han Dynasty complemented each other and were unified. In Jin Dynasty, the central government divided the school system into Guozixue (Imperial College) and Taixue (Imperial Academy). Guozixue (Imperial College) recruited children of wealthy aristocrats, while Taixue (Imperial Academy) was mainly for the children of common people. In Tang Dynasty, it inherited the school education system of Sui Dynasty. On the basis of political unification, economic prosperity, and a developed cultural and scientific level, after more than a hundred years of development, the school education system was quite complete, and it played an important role in the history of school education in China and the world. The period was also an important turning point in the history of China's ancient education and official system. At the same time, it developed the Tang Dynasty school education and social education and promoted social progress. The number of international students in Tang Dynasty was also increasing day by day. Among them, Japan, Silla (now Thailand), and Korea sent the most. They studied Chinese cultural knowledge such as Chinese classics, history, law etiquette, literature and technology. The capital Chang'an at that time became the center of cultural and educational exchanges between the East and the West. Chinese culture was spread through international students. Traveling to countries around the world promoted the connection between China and other countries in the world, and played a role as a bridge and link to spread Chinese culture. During Song Dynasty, the academy appeared. The academy became a place for scholars to accept disciples, preach and teach students, and cultivate talents. The selected sites were mostly scenic spots, and the organizational system had the form of private, public, or both, and most of them were for the purpose of winning an official position. The educational system of Qing Dynasty followed Ming Dynasty system, and the imperial examination system followed Song and Yuan Dynasties. It was divided into three types: provincial examination, national examination and court examination.

二、中国传统教育文化的特征 Cultural Characteristics of Traditional Chinese Education

中国传统学校教育在人类文化史上，首创了建立在实用人文主义基础之上的"政治——伦理——教育"三位一体化的结构模式。这种结构模式的最大特点有三条：一是教育带有强烈的政治务实性。要求学校必须无条件地为社会现实服务，政治实用即为教育之本。二是具有浓厚的道德伦理性。要求把学校教育归结为单一的道德教育，而道德教育的核心又在于理想人格的培养。三是注重教育内容与手段的趋同性，把授业、传道、解惑与学业、受道、释惑之间的师承关系，看作是高于一切的东西。

In the history of human culture, traditional Chinese school education pioneered the three-in-one structural model of "politics-ethics-education" based on practical humanism. There are three main characteristics of this structural model: First, education is strongly politically pragmatic. Schools are required to serve social reality unconditionally, and political practicality is the foundation of education. The second is strong morality. It is required that school education be focused on a single and moral education, and the core of moral education lies in the cultivation of ideal personality. The third is to pay attention to the homogeneity of educational content and methods, and regard the teacher‑student relationship of teaching, preaching, solving puzzles, and learning, receiving, understanding as above all.

中国传统教育文化的特征：Characteristics of traditional Chinese education culture：

（1）政治务实性是中国传统学校教育的根本特征。两千多年的中国封建社会，一直实行的是君主专制制度。这就从根本上决定了中国传统学校教育的性质，只能是一种以维护封建统治为目的的文化工具。第一，强调教育理论同政治实践相结合，努力使学校教育与现实社会融为一体。第二，注重治国之道，把历史与现实紧密结合，致力于国家和社会发展模式的建构。社会的治乱兴衰，对中国人来讲是头等大事，尤其为读书人所重视。在强烈的忧患意识驱使下，中国传统知识分子把治国安邦的方法问题作为自己探讨的一项重要内容。

Political pragmatism was the fundamental feature of ancient Chinese school education. In the feudal society of China for more than two thousand years, the monarchy system had been practiced. This fundamentally determined the nature of ancient Chinese school education, which can only be a cultural tool aimed at maintaining feudal rule. First, it emphasized the combination of educational theory and political practice, and strived to integrate school education with the real society. Second, paying attention to the way of governing the country, closely integrating history and reality, and committing to the construction of the country and social development model. Whether the society is in the rise or fall, in order or chaos is a top priority for Chinese people, and is especially valued by intellectuals. Driven by a strong distress awareness, ancient Chinese intellectuals took the method of governing the country as an important content of their research.

（2）道德人格培养是中国古代学校教育的核心内容。中国古代教育文化，面向的基层面是人和以人为核心的社会生活组织。人与人之间、人与社会之间的相互关系，以及与人有关的诸如为人之理、成人之道和修身齐家治国平天下之类的问题，便成为教育首要关注的对象。他们都把人格价值理解为一种由低级向高级形态不断演化的、充满深刻内涵的动态结构；把遵从人伦之德作为人格价值的基本特征；把内圣外王之道当作人格价值的核心内容；把向内用功为主、内外修养相结合为辅作为人格价值实现的根本途径和方法。注重道德教育，强调心身的修养，突出实践理性和理想人格的作用，几乎成了几千年中国古代学校教育价值观的永恒主题。

Moral personality cultivation was the core content of ancient Chinese school education. The basic level of Chinese ancient education culture was people and the social organization centered on people. The interrelationships between man and man, man and society, as well as people-related issues such as the principles of how to behave, the way to be a man, and self-cultivation, managing the family, governing the country and pacifying the world, became the primary concern of education. They understood personality value as a dynamic structure full of profound connotations that evolved from low-level to high-level; they regarded obedience to human morality as the basic feature of personality value; they took the inner sageliness and outer kingliness as the core content of personality value. The fundamental approach and method to realize the value of personality was to work hard and combine internal and external cultivation as the main way and supplement. Emphasizing moral education, the cultivation of mind and body, and highlighting the role of practical reason and ideal personality almost became the eternal theme of ancient Chinese school education values for thousands of years.

（3）经学方法是中国古代学校教育的思维特征。以注释、阐发儒家经典为核心内容的经学方法，构成了中国古代学校教育文化的基本特征。中国传统思想文化，本质上属于一种"天人合一""王民相依""上下相维"的求同和谐型文化。中国古代的圣贤先哲，总是把承继传统当作生活的第一要义，认为传统是尽善尽美的，只可敬畏，不能超越，并且力图使每个人的思想与传统定势保持同一。

Confucian learning method was the thinking characteristic of ancient Chinese school education. The method of interpreting Confucian classics with annotations as the core content constituted the basic characteristics of ancient Chinese school education culture. Chinese traditional ideology and culture essentially belonged to a culture of seeking common ground and harmony which was "the unity of nature and man", "the king and the people depend on each other", and "the upper and lower are mutually dependent". The sages and philosophers of ancient China always regarded inheriting tradition as the first priority of life. They believed that tradition is perfect and can only be awe-inspired and cannot be surpassed, and they tried to keep everyone's thinking consistent with the tradition.

以儒家思想为主导的中国古代学校教育，实际上是一种建立在实用人文主义思想基础之上的、以政治教育和道德教育为核心的、以经学方法为思维特征的政治——道德型文化教育。

Ancient Chinese school education dominated by Confucianism was actually a political-moral culture based on practical humanism, centered on political education and moral education, and characterized by Confucianism education.

三、中国的传统教育思想 Traditional Chinese Educational Thoughts

中国古代教育有着悠久的历史，其间涌现出许多著名的教育家，他们丰富的教育思想，是中国传统文化的重要组成部分。概而言之，中国传统的教育思想呈现出五大特征。

Ancient Chinese education had a long history, during which many famous educators emerged. Their rich educational thoughts were an important part of Chinese traditional culture. In a nutshell, traditional Chinese educational thoughts presented five major characteristics.

一是伦理本位。中国古代教育家十分重视人文思想的传授和道德伦理的教化功能。主张以教育为手段，把一种完善的德性，通过人的自觉和自我完善逐步推广到民众，以构建理想的社会。他们认为教育的目的其一是培养英才，其二是社会教化。

The first was the ethical standard. Ancient Chinese educators attached great importance to the teaching of humanistic thought and the cultivation function of moral ethics. It was advocated to use education as a means to gradually extend a kind of perfect virtue to the people through human consciousness and self-improvement to build an ideal society. They believed that the purpose of education was to cultivate talents and moralize people.

二是因材施教。就是根据不同教育对象，选择符合实际的教育内容和教育方法，各尽其才。因材施教最早的实践者是孔子。因材施教的方法，被历史上许多教育家所采用。

The second was to teach students in accordance with their aptitude. It was to choose educational content and educational methods that were in line with the reality according to different educational objects, and each did its best. The earliest practitioner of teaching students in accordance with their aptitude was Confucius. Such method has been adopted by many educators in history.

三是启发诱导。启发诱导旨在调动学生学习的积极性，深受教育者欢迎。孔子是长于启发教学的大师。就教而言，当学生经思考不能透彻理解时，教师要启发引导学生；就学而言，则要求学生能举一反三，从已知的拓展到未知的。孟子也主张要引导学生积极思考，主动学习。朱熹根据自己多年的教学经验，认为培养学生的学习能力，应是教学的关键，教师的任务是将有效的学习方法传授给学生。

The third was to inspire and induce. Such method was aimed at motivating the enthusiasm of students in learning and was very popular among educators. Confucius was a master who was good at inspiring and inducing students. As far as teaching is concerned, when students cannot fully understand through thinking, teachers should inspire and guide them; as far as learning is concerned, students are required to draw inferences from one another and expand from the known to the unknown. Mencius also advocated guiding students to think and learn actively. Based on his teaching experience for years, Zhu Xi, a famous master of Neo-Confucianism believed that cultivating students' learning ability should be the key to teaching, and the task of teachers was to teach students effective learning methods.

四是学思结合。学思结合就是要将学习和思考密切联系起来，既重视学，又重视思。学思结合最早由孔子提出，由孟子继承并发展。学思并重，相互促进，以提高自己的认识、思考和辨析问题的能力。博学可以促进思考的深入，深入的思考又可以促进博学，这正是学思结合的精髓所在。

The fourth was the combination of learning and thinking. It was to closely link learning and thinking, which emphasized both learning and thinking. The combination of learning and thinking was first proposed by Confucius and inherited and developed by Mencius. Paying equal attention to learning and thinking and promoting each other to improve their ability to understand, think and analyze problems. Erudition can promote deep thinking, and deep thinking can promote erudition. This is the essence of the combination of learning and thinking.

五是教学相长。教学相长是指教和学之间存在相互制约、相互渗透、相互促进的对立统一关系。只有通过学习，才知道不足；只有通过教学，才能发现自己的困惑，知道不足与困惑，才能激励自己更加努力学习，奋发自强。教学活动不是单向的知识传授，而是师生都能受益的互动过程，在这一过程中，师生双方共同提高。教与学是辩证统一的关系。

The fifth was teaching is learning (education is a two-way proars), which means that there is a unity of opposites between teaching and learning, which restricts, penetrates and promotes each other. Only through learning can we know the shortcomings; only through teaching can we discover our own confusion, knowing the shortcomings and confusion, motivate ourselves to work harder and strive for self-improvement. Teaching is not a one-way knowledge transfer, but an interactive process that can benefit both teachers and students. In this process, both teachers and students can improve together. Teaching and learning is a dialectical and unified relationship.

四、中国古代的家庭教育 Family Education in Ancient China

中国古代由于学校教育不够发达，教育对象也多半限于官僚贵族子弟，大多数平民子弟很难获得官办学校学习的机会，在这种情况下，作为学校教育补充的家庭教育，在中国古代教育上具有很重要的作用。

In ancient China, due to the insufficient development of school education, the education objects were mostly limited to the children of officials and nobles. It was difficult for the children from average family to get the opportunity to study in government-run schools. In this case, family education as an important supplement to school education was used in ancient education in China.

(一) 中国传统家庭教育的基本内容 Basic content of traditional Chinese family education

从文献记载看，中国最早的家庭教育可以说始于西周。中国家庭教育的鼻祖应当是孔子，据《论语·季氏篇》记载，孔子明确要求其子孔鲤学诗学礼，以成为一个有用的人才。

According to the literature, the earliest family education in China can be said to have started in the Western Zhou Dynasty. The originator of family education in China should be Confucius. According to the "*Analects of Confucius：Ji Shi*", Confucius clearly required his son Kong Li to learn *Book of Songs* and *Book of Rites* in order to become a useful talent.

汉代以后，由于儒学逐渐在社会上占据了优势地位，家庭教育的基本内容相应地也以诗礼之教为主，以忠、孝、节、义为基本要求，封建社会的家庭教育逐渐规范化，并相继出现了一些专门讲述家庭教育的著作，比如著名的《颜氏家训》，作者为南北朝末年教育家颜之推。他从各个方面详细阐述了家庭教育的原则和方式，涉及封建家庭教育的方方面面，诸如尊老爱幼、为人正直、勤俭朴素、刻苦学习等内容。此外还有清代朱柏庐的《治家格言》，里面有许多关于家训的名言警句，加之语言精练，雅俗共赏，在社会上流传广泛，对中国的家庭教育产生了很大影响。

After Han Dynasty, as Confucianism gradually occupied a dominant position in society, the basic content of family education was correspondingly based on the teaching of *Book of Songs* and *Book of Rites*, with loyalty, filial piety, integrity and righteousness as the basic requirements, and family education in feudal society was gradually standardized. There have been some books dedicated to family education, such as the famous *Family Instructions for the Yan Clan* written by Yan Zhitui, an educator in the late Southern and Northern Dynasties. He elaborated the principles and methods of family education, involving many aspects of feudal family education, such as respecting the old and loving the young, being upright, diligent and frugal, and studying hard. In addition, there was Zhu Bailu's *Family Precepts* in Qing Dynasty, which contained many famous aphorisms about family precepts, coupled with concise language, elegant and popular, widely circulated in society, and had a great impact on Chinese family education.

中国古代家庭教育所使用的启蒙教材《三字经》《百家姓》《千字文》《幼学琼林》等，还有以后的四书五经等，都和当时学校所用教材基本一致，家庭教育可以直接服务于当时人才选拔制度。另外，由于中国古代的学校教育不够普及和发达，家庭教育可以说是古代教育制度的重要补充，并对培养当时社会所需的人才起到了很大作用。

The enlightening textbooks *San Zi Jing*（*Three Character Primer*），Handreds of Chinese Surnames，*Thousand-Character* and *For the Children to Learn By* used in ancient family education in China，as well as the Four Books and Five Classics，were basically the same as those used in schools at that time，so family education could directly serve the talent selection system. In addition，due to the insufficient popularization and development of school education in ancient China，family education could be said to be an important supplement to the ancient education system and played a great role in cultivating talents needed by society at that time.

（二）中国古代家庭教育的基本原则 Basic principles of family education in ancient China

中国古代家庭教育的基本原则有如下六点：

The basic principles of ancient Chinese family education were as follows：

教儿宜早：中国古代认为对孩子的教育越早越好，这不仅仅强调要对孩子早教，还强调要对孩子实行一以贯之的教育。

Teach children early：Ancient Chinese believed that the earlier the education of children，the better. This not only emphasized the need to teach children early，but also to implement consistent education for children.

教子义方：父母要从道义上，从做一个正派人的根本方向上，为子女指出道路。

To bring up one's children in accordance with truth and righteousness：parents should point out the way of being a decent person for their children from the moral and fundamental perspective .

信而勿诳：父母教育子女要以身作则，即要培养孩子什么品德，自己就要先具备什么品德。

Be faithful and don't lie：Parents must lead by example in educating their children, that is, what kind of character they want to cultivate their children, and what kind of character they must first have.

潜移默化：将家庭教育和社会环境结合起来，强调环境对儿童的教育意义。

Osmosis：Combine family education with social environment and emphasize the educational significance of environment to children.

量资循序：对儿童的教育不能求之过急，要根据儿童的才能，逐步将教育加深加宽，才符合循序渐进的教育原则。

Tailored progression：The education of children should not be rushed, but gradually deepened and widened according to children's talents. This is in line with the principle of step-by-step education.

有教有爱：家长对孩子的教育，既要爱又要教，既要慈又要严，爱与教结合，严慈相济，这样才能收到良好的效果。

Education and love：Parents must both love and teach their children, be kind and strict, combine love and education, so that good results can be achieved.

五、中国古代的书院教育 Ancient Chinese Academy Education

（一）书院的形成与发展 The formation and development of academies

书院的名称始于唐代。这时的书院是官办藏书校书的场所，实质上是国立图书馆。它们都不是真正的教育机关，不具备教育功能。至于真正具有聚徒讲学性质的书院到五代末期才基本形成。

The name of the academy began in Tang Dynasty. The academy at this time was a place where the government stored and proofread books, in essence, a national library. Academies were not real educational institutions and did not have educational functions. As for the academy with the nature of gathering students to give lectures, it was basically formed at the end of the Five Dynasties.

南唐皇帝李昇（公元 889 年~943 年），在江西庐山白鹿洞建立学馆，称"庐山国学"，也称"白鹿洞国庠"，后在此基础上发展成为著名的白鹿洞书院。庐山国学是由私人读书治学之所发展为聚徒讲学的书院的典型。

Emperor Li Sheng (889~943 AD) of the Southern Tang Dynasty established an academy in Bailu Cave (White Deer cave), Lushan Mountain, Jiangxi, called "Lushan Guoxue" (means Lushan National School), also known as "Bailudong Guoxiang", and later developed into the famous Bailudong Academy. Lushan Guoxue was a model academy that developed from a private scholarly place to an academy where disciples gathered to be taught.

到北宋时期，书院已经发展成为比较完备的书院制度。江西庐山的白鹿洞书院，河南商丘的应天府书院，湖南衡阳的石鼓书院，长沙的岳麓书院，号称"天下四大书院"。南宋是书院发展的极盛时期。书院数量之多，规模之大，组织之严密和制度之完善都是空前的。元代，政府对书院也采取奖励和支持的做法。各地纷纷设立书院，不仅文化荟萃的江南普遍兴建或复兴了书院，而且北方各地也相继建立了书院。明代，书院发展经历了由衰而兴的历程。江苏无锡的东林书院是明末影响最大的书院。它不仅是当地教育和学术中心，而且还是思想舆论和政治活动中心。师生积极参加当时的政治活动，因而名声大振。清朝取代明朝的统治，使书院的发展发生新的转折。统治者一方面抑制书院，另一方面又表示对书院的爱护和关心。直至雍正年代，开始积极利用和发展书院；到乾隆时期，进入清代书院的兴盛阶段。书院的经费、教学内容、教学人员、生徒等都要经官府审批，这样书院自由设立的时代从此告终。

By the Northern Song Dynasty, the academy had developed into a relatively complete academy system. Bailudong Academy in Lushan, Jiangxi, Yingtianfu Academy in Shangqiu, Henan, Shigu Academy in Hengyang, Hunan, and Yuelu Academy in Changsha, were known as the "Four Greatest Academies in the Country". The Southern Song Dynasty was the heyday of the development of academies. The number of academies, their scale, rigorous organization, and systems were unprecedented. In Yuan Dynasty, the government also adopted incentives to support the academies. Academies were established in various places. Not only had academies been built or revived in the south of the Yangtze River where the culture was rich, but also academies were established in various parts of the north. In Ming Dynasty, the development of the academy experienced a process from decline to prosperity. Donglin Academy in Wuxi, Jiangsu Province, was the most influential academy in the late

Ming Dynasty. It was not only the local education and academic center, but also the center of ideological public opinion and political activities. Teachers and students actively participated in political activities at that time, and thus became famous. Qing Dynasty replaced Ming Dynasty's rule, which brought a new turn in the development of the academy. On the one hand, the rulers restrained the academy, and on the other hand expressed their love and concern for the academy. Until Emperor Yongzheng period, The ruler began to actively use and develop the academy; in Emperor Qianlong period, it entered the prosperity stage of Qing Dynasty academy. The funds, teaching content, teaching staff, and students of academies must be approved by the government, so the era of free establishment of the academy came to an end.

（二）书院的组织管理 Organization and management of the academy

书院初创时，组织机构比较简单，主持人既是组织管理的负责者，又是日常教学工作的承担者。随着书院的发展，规模的扩大和生徒的增多，开始有了协助主持人管理和教学的辅助人员，组织机构也随着扩大，分工更细，责任更明确。书院的主持者有多种名称，"院长"，即书院之长；"教授"，即本为地方官学学官名称，有的主持人由地方官学教授兼任，仍用原称。书院对管理人员采用专兼职结合，学生中的优秀者可以兼职管理工作。这是书院，特别是宋代书院管理中的一个特色。

When the academy was founded, the organization was relatively simple. The host was not only the person in charge of the organization and management, but also the undertaker of daily teaching work. With the development of the academy, the expansion of the scale and the increase of students, there began to be auxiliary personnel to assist the host in management and teaching, and the organizational structure was also expanded, with more detailed division of labor and clearer responsibilities. The host of the academy had a variety of names, "dean", that was, the head of the academy; "professor", originally the name of the local government academic official, was concurrently served by the local government professor, still using the original name. The academy adopted a combination of full-time and part-time management for management personnel, and outstanding students could take part-time management. This was a characteristic of academies, especially in the management of academies in Song Dynasty.

书院的生源范围也较广。书院招收学生一般只有学问、品德的基本要求，没有出身、年龄、地域、学派、人数的严格限制，学生来去自由，流动性较大。但也有少数著名书院，其任务在于进一步提高学生修养，因此规定书院有一定的资格条件。到清代，随着书院官学化程度的提高，自由就学的传统也随之发生变化，书院的招生、考核等由官方控制。

The range of students in the academy was also wide. Generally speaking, with some basic requirements of knowledge and morality the academies enrolled students. There were no strict restrictions on birth, age, region, school, or number of students. Students came and went freely and had greater mobility. However, there were also a few well-known academies whose mission was to further improve students' accomplishments. Therefore, academies were required to have certain qualifications. In Qing Dynasty, as the degree of officialization of academies increased, the tradition of free education also changed, and the admissions and assessment of academies were controlled by the government.

书院的经费来源也不尽一致。不同的书院有不同筹集经费的渠道，大致有：个人提供、富有的家族提供、地方绅士捐资、奏请官府拨给等。书院虽然经济上是自给的，但为了保持稳定发展以至扩大社会影响，常通过地方政府申奏朝廷，朝廷给以赏赐（赐钱、赐物、赐田），有的地方政府为了对书院施加影响，也主动拨田、拨钱。

The sources of funding for the academies were not the same. Different academies had different channels for raising funds: personally provided, wealthy families provided, local gentlemen donated, the government allocated by application. Although the academy was economically self-sufficient, in order to maintain stable development and expand social influence, it often applied to the court through the local government. The court offered rewards (with money, gifts, and land), and some local governments wanted to exert influence on the academy, also actively allocated land and money.

书院的教学内容以儒家知识为主。宋代书院的主持者多数是理学家，以理学思想为指导来制定教学计划，安排教学内容。《诗》、《书》、《礼》、《易》、《春秋》和《大学》、《中庸》、《论语》、《孟子》为代表的"五经"及"四书"等儒家经典是书院基本和必修教材。除了重视儒家的知识之外，书院还十分重视对学生的品德教育，重视学生的身心修养。

The teaching content of academies was based on Confucian knowledge. The hosts of the academies in Song Dynasty were mostly Neo–Confucianists, who made teaching plans and arranged teaching content under the guidance of Neo–Confucianism. Confucian classics, represented by the "Five Classics" and "Four Books" of *The Book of Songs*, *The Book of Documents*, *The Book of Rites*, *The Book of Changes*, *The Spring and Autumn Annals*, and *The Great Learning*, *The Doctrine of the Mean*, *The Analects of Confucius*, and *The Book of Mencius*, were basic and required textbooks at academies. In addition to valuing the knowledge of Confucianism, academies also attached great importance to the moral education of students and the physical and mental cultivation.

（三）书院的教学特点 The teaching characteristics of the academy

（1）自学为主。以学生个人读书钻研为主，十分注重培养学生的自学能力。书院教学非常重视对学生进行指导、启发。许多名师都把指导学生自己学会读书作为教学的重要任务，他们往往根据自己的治学经验概括出不少读书的原则，帮助学生提高自学的能力和读书的效果。

Self–study. It focuses on students' personal study and research, and pays great attention to cultivating students' self–learning ability. Academy teaching attached great importance to guiding and enlightening students. Many famous masters regarded guiding students to learn to read as an important task of teaching. They often summarized many principles of reading based on their academic experience to help students improve their self–learning ability and the effect of reading.

（2）书院盛行"讲会"制度。允许不同学派进行会讲，开展争辩，书院中的学术讨论、辩论氛围很浓。这是书院区别于一般学校的一个重要标志。这种讲会，比之当时的官学，在学术思想上要活跃得多，既论学，又论政，突破了当时束缚知识分子思想的八股学风。

The "lecture" system prevailed in academies. Different schools of thought or philosophy were allowed to be lectured and debated. The academic discussion and debate in the academy were very heated. This was an important mark that distinguished the academy from ordinary schools. This kind of lecture was much more active in academic thinking than the official school at the time. It centered both on academic and political issues, breaking through the stereotypical style of study that restrained intellectuals at that time.

（3）教学实行"门户开放"，不受地域限制。

Teaching implemented "open-the-door" policy, not restricted by region.

（4）教研结合。这是书院的一个最突出的特点，学术研究是书院教学的基础，书院的教学又是学术成果得以传授和进一步发展的必要条件。

Combination of academic research and teaching. This was one of the most prominent features of the academy. Academic research was the foundation of the academy's teaching, and the academy's teaching was a necessary condition for the teaching and further development of academic achievements.

（5）感情融洽。书院内的师生关系比较融洽，师生之间的感情相当深厚。书院的名师不仅以渊博的学识教育学生，而且以自己的品德气节感染学生。

Teachers and students in the academy were rather harmonious and kind. The famous masters of the academy not only educated students with profound knowledge, but also effected students with their own moral integrity.

从书院产生到清末（公元 1898 年）书院改为学堂，书院经历了将近 1000 年的历史，各种书院共 2000 余所，对中国古代学术发展和人才培养做出了重大贡献。书院制度产生、发展于封建社会，随着封建社会政治、经济和文化的没落，书院制度被废除。

From the birth of the academy to the change to the school in late Qing Dynasty (1898 AD), the academy had experienced nearly 1, 000 years. There were more than 2, 000 various academies, and they made significant contributions to the academic development and talent cultivation of ancient China. The academy system was born and developed in the feudal society. With the decline of feudal society, politics, economy and culture, the academy system was abolished.

中国的传统饮食文化

中国饮食文化源远流长，形式与内容丰富多样。从食品资源的开发到加工保存，从烹饪技艺的精湛到食具的讲究，都称得上博大精深。人们在长期的生活实践中，不仅形成了具有地域特色的烹饪技艺，而且还传承着种种饮食习俗和饮食礼仪，反映了中国人的饮食观念。

Chinese food culture has a long history, rich in forms and contents. From the development of food resources to the processing and preservation, from the exquisite cooking skills to the exquisite food utensils, they are all broad and profound. In the long-term life practice, people have not only formed cooking skills with regional characteristics, but also inherited various dietary customs and dietary etiquette, reflecting the Chinese dietary concepts.

一、中国的饮食文化发展史 The History of Chinese Food Culture

说到饮食文化离不开历史的发展，不同的朝代有着不同的饮食文化。

Speaking of food culture is inseparable from the development of history, there are different food cultures in different dynasties.

最早的是有巢氏（旧石器时代）：积鸟兽之肉聚草木之实，但当时人们不懂人工取火和熟食。饮食状况是茹毛饮血，不属于饮食文化。

The earliest was the Youchao period (Paleolithic Age): To gather the flesh of birds and beasts, the fruits of trees and grasses, but people did not know how to make fire and cook food artificially. The diet situation was to eat animal raw flesh and drink its blood, so it did not belong to a diet culture.

燧人氏：钻木取火，从此吃熟食，进入石烹时代。

Sui-Ren Shi：Drilling wood to make fire, and then eating cooked food, entering the age of stone cooking.

主要烹调方法：Main cooking methods

①炮，即钻火使果肉而燔之；Burning, that is, drilling to make fire to burn the flesh；

②煲：用泥裹后烧；Potting, wrap in mud and burn；

③用石臼盛水、食，用烧红的石子烫熟食物；Use stone mortars to hold water and food, and scald the food with red stones；

④焙炒：把石片烧热，再把植物种子放在上面炒；Roasting：Heat the stone flakes, then put plant seeds on top and fry；

伏羲氏：在饮食上，结网以教捕鱼，养牺牲以充庖厨，有很大的进步。

Fuxi：In terms of diet, netting to teach people to fish, and breed animals to be used by the cook, which made great progress in food culture.

神农氏："耕而陶"，是中国农业的开创者，尝百草，开创古医药学，发明耒耜，教民稼穑。陶具使人们第一次拥有了炊具和容器，为制作发酵性食品提供了可能。

Shennong："Cultivation and pottery", was the pioneer of Chinese agriculture. He tasted herbs, pioneered ancient medicine, invented tilling tools, taught the people to harvest crops. Pottery made people own cooking utensils and containers for the first time. It was possible to make fermented food.

黄帝：此时中华民族的饮食状况又有了改善，黄帝作灶，始为灶神。集中火力可以节省燃料，使食物速熟。从此，人们不仅懂得了烹还懂得了调，有益人的健康。

Yellow King：At this time, the diet of the Chinese nation improved again. Yellow King made the stove and became the kitchen god. Concentrated firepower can save fuel and make food cooked quickly. Since then, people not only know how to cook, but also know how to flavor, which is good for people's health.

周秦时期：是中国饮食文化的成形时期，以谷物蔬菜为主食。春秋战国时期，自产的谷物菜蔬基本都有了，但结构与现在不尽相同。

Zhou& Qin Dynasties：It was the forming period of Chinese food culture, with cereals and vegetables as the main food. During the Spring and Autumn and Warring States Period, the self-produced cereals and vegetables were basically available, but the food structure was different from the present.

汉朝：中国饮食文化的丰富时期，归功于汉代中西（西域）饮食文化的交流，引进石榴、芝麻、葡萄、胡桃（即核桃）、西瓜、甜瓜、黄瓜、菠菜、胡萝卜、茴香、芹菜、胡豆、扁豆、苜蓿、莴笋、大葱、大蒜，还传入一些烹调方法，如炸油饼、胡饼（即芝麻烧饼）。西汉时期，淮南王刘安发明豆腐，使豆类的营养得到消化，物美价廉，可做出许多种菜肴。东汉还发明了植物油。在此以前都用动物油。南北朝以后，植物油的品种增加，价格也便宜。

Han Dynasty: the enriching period of Chinese food culture was attributed to the exchange of Chinese and Western food culture in Han Dynasty. The introduction of pomegranate, sesame, grape, walnut, watermelon, melon, cucumber, spinach, carrot, fennel, celery, beans, lentils, alfalfa, lettuce, green onions, garlic, but also introduced some cooking methods, such as fried oil cakes, sesame cakes. During the Western Han Dynasty, Huainan King Liu An invented tofu, which made people digest the nutrients of beans, and cook many kinds of dishes with good quality and low price. The Eastern Han Dynasty also invented vegetable oil. Before this, animal oil was used. After the Northern and Southern Dynasties, the variety of vegetable oils increased and the price was low.

唐宋：饮食文化的高峰，过分讲究。

Tang and Song Dynasties: the peak of food culture, too particular.

明清：饮食文化的又一高峰，是唐宋食俗的继续，同时又混入满蒙的特点，饮食结构有了很大变化，豆料不再作主食，成为菜肴。北方黄河流域小麦的比例大幅度增加，面成为宋以后北方的主食，明代又一次大规模引进。马铃薯、甘薯、蔬菜的种植达到较高水准，成为主要菜肴。人工畜养的畜禽成为肉食主要来源。满汉全席最能代表清代饮食高峰。

Ming and Qing Dynasties: Another peak of the food culture, were the continuation of the food customs in Tang and Song dynasties. At the same time, it was mixed with the characteristics of Manchuria. The diet structure changed a lot. Soybeans were no longer the staple food but became dishes. The proportion of wheat in the Yellow

River basin (North China) increased greatly, and flour became the staple food in the north after Song Dynasty, and it was introduced on a large scale again in Ming Dynasty. Potatoes, sweet potatoes, and vegetables were grown to a high level and became main dishes. Domesticated livestock and poultry became the main source of meat. The Manchu-Han Imperial Feast could best represent the peak of Qing Dynasty diet.

二、中国传统饮食结构与烹饪技艺 Traditional Chinese Diet Structure and Cooking Skills

中国在进入新石器时代以后，即从采集经济中逐渐产生了农业，开始步入以种植和养殖经济为主体的农业社会。从那时起，中国人形成了以谷物为主食，以肉类、蔬菜为副食的饮食结构，在以后的几千年中，这一饮食结构相沿未改。

After China entered the Neolithic Age, agriculture gradually developed from the gathering economy, and began to enter an agricultural society dominated by planting and breeding economy. Since then, Chinese have formed a diet consisting of cereals as their staple food and meat and vegetables as non-staple foods. In the following thousands of years, this kind of diet has remained unchanged.

（一）主食 Staple food

中国传统的主食是谷类，"谷"是禾本科粮作物的总称。主要的粮食作物是黍、稷、秫、稻、麻、大小豆、大小麦，这些粮食作物在先秦已大致齐备了。稷与粟名异实同，都是指小米；黍指黄米；秫即高粱米；粱是粟中精品；麻即芝麻；还有大豆、小豆、大麦、小麦。

The traditional staple food in China is cereals, and "grain" is the general term for gramineous crops. The main food crops are millet, rice, bast fibre crep, big and small beans, barley and wheat. These food crops were generally available in the pre-Qin Dynasty. The names of "sù" and "jì" are the same, both refer to millet; "shǔ" refers to yellow rice; "shú" refers to sorghum rice; "liáng" refers to fine millet; "má" refers to sesame; there are soybeans, adzuki beans, barley, and wheat.

秦代以前，主食的加工主要有做成干粮、饭和粥三种。汉代有了石磨，于是主食的加工又有了粉食。"饼"是各种面食的总称。到了晋代，由于掌握了发酵技术，于是出现了发面饼、馒头、包子等主食，当时还有了饺子和馄饨。点心花色之多，足以令人眼花缭乱。北宋皇家每至中秋食"宫饼"，中秋食月饼的习俗传承至今。

Before Qin Dynasty, the main staple foods were processed into dry food, rice and porridge. In Han Dynasty, there appeared a stone mill, so the processing of staple food also had powder food. "Bing" (cake) was the general term for all kinds of pasta. In Jin Dynasty, due to the mastery of fermentation technology, staple foods such as leavened pancake, steamed buns (mantou), and steamed stuffed buns (bao-zi) appeared. At that time, there were dumplings and wontons. The variety of refreshment was enough to dazzle. The royal family of the Northern Song Dynasty ate "imperial cakes" during Mid-Autumn Festival, and the custom of eating mooncakes in Mid-Autumn Festival has been passed down to this day.

（二）副食 Non-staple food

中国人饮食结构中的副食为菜肴。"菜"是蔬菜和可食野菜的总称，"肴"指鱼肉之类的荤菜，"馐"指美味的食品，"核"指梅、李、桃等各类的水果。

Non-staple food in the Chinese diet refers to vegetables and meat. "cài" is the general term for vegetables and edible wild vegetables. "yáo" refers to meat dishes such as fish meat, animal meat. "xiū" refers to delicious food, and "hé" refers to various fruits such as plums and peach.

肉类副食品有家畜类的马、牛、羊、鸡、狗、猪六畜。但人们不轻易食用马肉和牛肉，经常食用的是猪、狗、羊、鸡。除家畜、家禽外，古人又常食用野生动物。因受经济条件限制，古代下层庶民是吃不上肉的，因此把上层阶级称为肉食者，把庶民称为食菜者。蔬菜、水果在传统中国人的食物结构中占有十分重要的地位。

Non-staple meat food includes six domestic animals such as horses, cattle, sheep, chickens, dogs, and pigs. But people do not eat horse meat and beef easily, and often eat pigs, dogs, sheep, and chickens. In addition to livestock and poultry, the ancients often ate wild animals. Due to economic constraints, the lower class people could not eat meat in ancient times, so the upper class were called meat eaters and the common people were called vegetable eaters. Vegetables and fruits played a very important role in the traditional Chinese food structure.

三、中国传统饮食的特点 Characteristics of Traditional Chinese Diet

（一）中国人的传统饮食以植物性食料为主 The traditional Chinese diet is mainly plant-based foods

主食是五谷（因为吃粮食较多，淀粉较多，故中国人肠子较长），辅食是蔬菜，外加少量肉食。《黄帝内经》就有这样的句子"五谷为养，五果为助，五畜为益，五菜为充"。粮食被视为主食，而"果"（水果、干果）"畜"（肉类）"菜"是副食，而且主食的地位高于副食。形成这一习俗的主要原因是中原地区以农业生产为主要的经济生产方式。但在不同的阶层中，食物的配置比例不尽相同，古话曾有"肉食者鄙"。欧洲的饮食是游牧民族饮食文化的一种延续，因此他们对于肉类和奶类的摄入较多，而中国的饮食是农耕文明饮食文化的延续。中国人的日常饮食有主、副食之分，中国人大约65%的热量来自主食——五谷杂粮；在中国人的饮食中非常重视蔬菜的作用，古人讲"食不可无绿"，蔬菜中的叶酸、维生素等营养物质对于我们的健康是非常有好处的；主副食比例适当，保持酸碱平衡。中国人吃饭分主食副食，连食品店也分成"主食厨房""副食商店"。这一点在欧洲就不明显。饮食不仅有主副食之分，而且主食高贵，副食低贱（不是指价格，而是指地位），这是西方饮食文化中不能想象的。中国人非常重视豆类食品的保健功能，"可一日无肉，不可一日无豆"，而"青菜、豆腐保平安"更成了中国人几千年来不断传承的饮食"金科玉律"。随着国人饮食结构逐渐西化（吃肉增加），出现所谓"文明病"，又称"五病综合征"，就是以肥胖为核心，伴随高血压、高血脂、心脑血管病、糖尿病。

The staple food is grains (the Chinese have longer intestines because they eat more grains and starches), and the complementary food is vegetables, plus a small amount of meat. *The Yellow King's Inner Classic* has such a saying: "Five grains are for nourishment, five fruits are for help, five animals are for benefit, and five vegetables are for filling. " Grain is regarded as the staple food, while "fruit" (fruit, dried fruit), "livestock" (meat) and "vegetable" are non-staple foods, and the status of staple food is higher than non-staple food. The main reason for the formation of this custom is that agricultural production is the main economic production method in the Central Plains. But in different classes, the proportion of food allocation is not the same. There was an old saying that "meat eaters are despised". European food is a continuation of nomadic food culture, so they consume more meat and milk, while Chinese food is a continuation of farming civilization food culture. The daily diet of Chinese people is divided into staple food and non-staple food. About 65% of the calories of the Chinese come from the staple food——various grains; the role of vegetables is very important in the Chinese diet. The ancients said that "food must not have no green. " Nutrients such as folic acid and vitamins are very good for our health; the proportion of staple and non-staple food is appropriate to maintain pH balance. Chinese people eat staple food and non-staple food, and even food stores are divided into "staple food store" and "non-staple food store. " This is not obvious in Europe. Food is not only divided into staple and non-staple food, but also noble staple food and low non-staple food (not referring to price but status), which is unimaginable in Western food culture. Chinese people attach great importance to the health function of beans. "You can have no meat for a day, but not beans for a day. " And "green vegetables and tofu to ensure safety" has become the "golden rule" of Chinese people's diet for thousands of years. With the gradual westernization of the Chinese diet (increasing meat consumption), the so-called "disease of civilization", also known as the "five disease syndromes", is centered on obesity, accompanied by high blood pressure, hyperlipidemia, cardiovascular and cerebrovascular diseases, and diabetes.

（二）种类多样 Diverse in variety

在中国菜中，地球上生长的万物——花草树木、鸟兽虫鱼，只要是能食用的东西几乎都被用来作原料。由于中国人居住的这块土地上人口稠密，并伴有周期性天灾和战乱，中国人不得不广泛地开拓食源。西方人的祖先是游牧民族，他们吃肉喝奶，并无主副食之分。而中国人的祖先是农耕民族，很早就以粮食为主食，以蔬菜鱼肉为副食，菜是用来送饭的，为了好吃，就要求菜的味道好，久而久之就养成了追求美味的强烈愿望。中国人的"天人合一"的哲学观念，使中国人将人与天地万物视若一体，从来不以为某一物不可接触，这为中国人广泛地开辟食源扫清了障碍。而中国人又以极其开朗、极其大度的心态认同万物，随之便引申出"吃啥补啥"的观念。

In Chinese cuisine, everything that grows on the earth——flowers, trees, birds, beasts, insects and fish, as long as they are edible, are almost used as raw materials for food. Due to the dense population and periodic natural disasters and wars on the land where Chinese live, they have to explore food sources extensively. The ancestors of Westerners were nomads. They ate meat and drank milk, and they had no main and non-staple food. Chinese ancestors were farming people, and they used food as their staple food and vegetables and fish as non-staple food. Vegetables were used to deliver meals. In order to be delicious, they demanded that the dishes taste good. Over time, they developed a strong desire pursuing delicious food. The philosophical concept of "the unity of man and nature" makes Chinese regard man and the nature as one. They never think that something is inaccessible. Opening up food sources cleared away the obstacles; they identified everything with an extremely cheerful and generous mentality, and then extended the concept of "what to eat to replenish what".

（三）以热食、熟食为主 Mainly hot food and cooked food

这和中国文明开化较早和烹调技术的发达有关。中国人的烹饪，全是在水环境下完成的，而烹饪的水环境最高能达到 100 度，因此高温有效地避免了烹饪带来的食品安全隐患。

This is related to the earlier development of Chinese civilization and the development of cooking technology. Chinese cooking is all done in a water environment, and the maximum cooking water environmentcan can be up to 100 degrees, so high-temperature cooking effectively avoids the hidden dangers of food.

（四）饮食方式上，中国人也有自己的特点 In terms of eating ways, Chinese also have their own characteristics

（1）聚餐制。聚餐制的长期流传，是中国重视血缘亲属关系和家庭家族观念在饮食方式上的反映。围桌会食，既显得热烈，又显得隆重，彼此亲密无间。（2）用筷子进食。世界上的人，按进食方法的不同，可以分为三类：用手指、用刀叉、用筷子。用叉子进食的人主要分布在欧洲和北美洲，用筷子吃饭的人主要分布在东亚大部，而用手指抓食的人多是在非洲、中东、印度尼西亚及印度次大陆的许多地区。

One is the to-eat-together system. The long-term spread of the to-eat-together system is a reflection of China's emphasis on blood kinship and family concepts in diet. Sitting around the table and eating seems warm and solemn, and makes people feel close to each other. The other is to eat with chopsticks. People in the world can be divided into three categories according to different ways of eating: using fingers, using knives and forks, and using chopsticks. People who eat with knives and forks are mainly distributed in Europe and North America, those who eat with chopsticks are mainly distributed in most of East Asia, and those who eat with fingers are mostly in Africa, the Middle East, Indonesia and many parts of the Indian subcontinent.

（五）吃的艺术 Eating style is somehow a form of artistic

"王以民为天，民以食为天，食以味为主"。中国烹调术的核心是"五味调和"。所谓"五味"是指人类味觉神经最能感受的酸、甜、苦、辣、咸五种味道。而在这五种味道调和的过程中，有时还要添加一些特殊的调料、配料，使原有的美味升华至更高的境界，此一"画龙点睛"已超出了调味的范畴，因称为"提味"。如在烹制若干荤菜时要投入葱姜，出味后即取出，即北京人所谓"吃葱不见葱，吃姜不见姜"。中餐讲究"色、香、味"。食物的味道第一，满足味觉享受；食物的形与色，属于视觉享受，也需要讲究。中国菜肴注重色彩效果，讲究色彩搭配，一盘色形俱佳的菜肴，就像一幅好的美术作品，有很强的感染力。

"The king regards the people as heaven, the people regard food as heaven, and the food gives priority to taste." The core of Chinese cooking is "Five-Flavor Harmony". The so-called "five flavors" refer to sour, sweet, bitterness, spiciness and saltiness that human taste nerves can most sense. In the process of reconciling these five flavors, some special seasonings and ingredients are added to sublimate the original flavor to a higher level. This "finishing but inspiring touch" has gone beyond the scope of seasoning, so it is called "to enhance flavor". For example, when you are cooking some meat dishes, you need to add green onion and ginger, and take them out after the dishes are tasty. That is what Beijingers call "you can't see green onions when you eat green onions, and you don't see ginger when you eat ginger." Chinese food pays attention to "color, aroma and taste". The taste of food is the first to satisfy the taste enjoyment; the shape and color of the food belong to the visual enjoyment and need to be exquisite. Chinese cuisine pays attention to color effects and pays attention to color matching. A dish of good color and shape is like a good art work and has a strong appeal.

（六）菜系繁多 There are many types of dishes

通常说的八大菜系：鲁、川、粤、苏、湘、闽、徽、浙。

Often we say eight major cuisines: Shandong, Sichuan, Guangdong, Jiangsu, Hunan, Fujian, Huizhou, Zhejiang.

（七）寓医于食，膳药同功 Combine medicine with food; diet and medicine serve the same purpose

（八）讲究食礼 Pay attention to food etiquette/table manners

中国的传统酒文化

酒，对于中国人来说，是很特殊的一种东西。它不仅是一项饮食行为，更是最具中国特色的处事之道。酒渗透于整个中华五千年的文明史中，从文学创作、到传统民俗、再到人际社交等各方面在中国人生活中都占有重要的位置。酒从中国文化的血脉中延续到今天，给中国人的生活带来无限乐趣，推杯换盏之间，演绎多少风情，或许中国人的酒场生活就是中国人的酒文化。

Wine is a very special thing for Chinese people. Drinking liquor is not only a dietary behavior, but also the most Chinese way of life. Liquor permeates the 5,000-year history of Chinese civilization, from literary creation, traditional folk customs, to interpersonal social interaction, thus occupies an important position in Chinese life. Wine has flown in the blood of Chinese culture to the present day, bringing infinite joy to Chinese people's life. Between exchanging toasts, how much flavor is deduced, perhaps the Chinese drinking life is the Chinese drinking culture!

一、中国酒文化的缘起 The Origin of Chinese Drinking Culture

酒文化是中华民族饮食文化的一个重要组成部分。酒是人类最古老的食物之一，它的历史几乎是与人类文化史一道开始的。自从酒出现之后，作为一种物质文化，酒的形态多种多样，其发展历程与经济发展史同步，而酒又不仅仅是一种食物，它还具有精神文化价值。作为一种精神文化，酒体现在社会政治生活、文学艺术乃至人的人生态度、审美情趣等诸多方面。在这个意义上讲，饮酒不是就饮酒而饮酒，也是在饮文化。

Drinking culture is an important part of Chinese food culture. Wine is one of the oldest foods for mankind, and its history almost began with the history of human culture. Since the appearance of wine, as a material culture, wine has a variety of forms, and its development process is synchronized with the history of economic development; wine is not only a kind of food, it also has spiritual and cultural value. As a kind of spiritual culture, it is embodied in many aspects such as social and political life, literature and art, and even people's life attitude, aesthetic taste and so on. In this sense, drinking is not just drinking, it is also a culture.

（一）传统民俗与酒有关 Traditional folklore is related to wine

中国传统民俗中与酒有关的，除了节庆婚嫁要饮酒助兴外，其它饮酒的场合更是五花八门，各种会亲酒由此而生：小孩儿出生喝满月酒、百日酒；寿辰有祝寿酒；亲人团聚有团圆酒；办丧事也要喝丧酒；待客之道自然离不开迎宾酒；送客之时便有饯别酒；求师学艺有拜师酒、谢师酒、出师酒；立功报捷有庆功酒；中国人的生活因酒而饱满，中国人的好客于酒席上更是发挥得淋漓尽致。大事小事，事事不离酒，正所谓百态生活源于对酒的品味。

China's traditional folklore is related to wine. In addition to drinking at festivals and weddings, other relative-meeting drinking occasions are even more diverse, such as the full-moon celebration feast of a baby, 100th-day celebration drinking of a baby, birthday celebration drinking, reunion drinking, funeral drinking, welcome drinking, farewell drinking; apprenticeship drinking, graduation drinking, wine feast to thank the teachers, drinking to finish one's apprenticeship; a celebration drinking for success; the life of the Chinese is full of drinking, and the hospitality of the Chinese is fully displayed at the banquet. Whether there is something important or even not so, Chinese people are likely to resort to drinking wine. The so-called variety of life stems from the taste of wine.

（二）文人墨客离不开酒 Literati like drinking

文人墨客离不开酒，似乎酒能激发灵感，酒后吟诗作文，每有佳句华章。饮酒本身，也往往成为创作素材。一部中国文学史，几乎页页都散发出酒香。李白和杜甫，中国文人的杰出代表，都终生嗜酒。李白自称"酒仙"，杜甫因有一句"性豪业嗜酒"，被郭沫若先生谥之为"酒豪"。酒醉而成传世诗作，这样的例子在中国诗史中俯拾皆是。

Literati prefer wine, it seems that wine can inspire them to write good sentences and beautiful lines of poems. Drinking itself often becomes the subject matter of their literary works. It is not a stretch to say that almost every page of the Chinese history of literature exudes the fragrance of wine. Li Bai and Du Fu, both famous poets and outstanding representatives of Chinese literati in Chinese history, were addicted to alcohol all their lives. Li Bai called himself the "Wine Immortal", and Du Fu was called a "Wine Tycoon" by Guo Moruo, because he had a saying, "generous and alcohol-addicted." In drunkenness poets create famous works, and such examples are not few in the history of Chinese poetry.

"醉里从为客，诗成觉有神。"杜甫《独酌成诗》

A traveller I am while in drinking,

with help from god a poem finishing .

       — "Writing a poem while drinking alone" by Du Fu

"举杯邀明月，对影成三人。"李白《月下独酌》

Inviting the moon with cups of spirits,

Three persons now we are with the shadow.

       — "Drinking alone under the moon" by Li Bai

"俯仰各有态，得酒诗自成。"苏轼《和陶渊明〈饮酒〉》

All in the world have their shape,

With wine they can be a poem.

       — "Rhyming with Tao Yuanming's *Drinking*" by Su Shi

不仅为诗如是，在绘画和中国文化特有的艺术书法中，酒神的精灵更是活泼万端。"吴带当风"的画圣吴道子，作画前必酣饮大醉方可动笔，醉后为画，挥毫立就。"元四家"中的黄公望也是"酒不醉，不能画"。

Besides poetry, for painting and calligraphy which is unique to Chinese culture, the spirit of Bacchus is even more lively. The painting sage Wu Daozi famous for "the sashes in Wu's painting flutter as if in the wind", would have to drink before painting, and when he was almost drunk, he could finish his painting at once. Mr. Huang Gongwang, one of the "Four Masters of Yuan Dynasty" was also "no drinking, no painting".

（三）大宴小席不可无酒 A feast without wine is hard to enjoy

高兴的时候，比如逢年过节，要喝酒；不高兴的时候，比如失恋、失意，也要喝酒；文人雅士爱喝酒——"李白斗酒诗百篇"；帝王将相也爱喝酒——曹刘"煮酒论英雄"，宋太祖"杯酒释兵权"，一番惊心动魄在推杯换盏之中化为不动声色。至于贩夫走卒，寻常百姓一杯浊酒喜相逢，生活同样离不开酒的润滑。无论居庙堂之高，还是处江湖之远，酒，都是一种充满了无限可能性且刚柔并济、收放自如的媒介。令外国人惊讶与佩服的是，中国人还在不断刷新这项"博大精深"的酒桌礼仪。

When happy, such as on New Year's holidays or other festivals, drink; when unhappy, such as lovelorn or frustrated, drink; literati love to drink— "Li Bai wrote many poems after heavy drinking"; emperors and generals also liked to drink—Cao Cao and Liu Bei of the Three Kingdoms period "talking about heroes while boiling wine", Emperor Taizu of Song Dynasty "stripping military power over a cup of wine", the thrilling change turned into a calm expression while exchanging toasts. As for pedlars, menial servants, in a word, common people, they meet with a cup of wine, and their life is also inseparable from the lubrication of wine. For people of high or low positions, wine is a flexible medium that is full of infinite possibilities, both rigid and soft. To the surprise and admiration of foreigners, the Chinese are still refreshing this "extensive and profound" drinking etiquette.

"风萧萧兮易水寒，壮士一去兮不复还。"这句很激励豪情也壮胆的名句，出自刺客荆轲的大嘴。嚷这话前，他决定只身一人刺秦王，燕国太子丹率众在易水边摆酒送行，几杯浊酒壮起英雄胆，荆轲和挚友们的歌唱出心声。这样诙谐易懂的酒场典故，道出了中国酒文化的源远流长。

"The wind is strong the water is cold, and the warrior will never come back. " This very inspiring and courageous phrase came from the mouth of the assassin Jing Ke. Before shouting this, he decided to assassinate the King of Qin alone. Prince Dan of the Kingdom of Yan led the crowd to see him off by the side of Yishui River, a few cups of wine strengthened the hero's courage, and Jing Ke and his best friends sang their hearts. Such a witty and easy-to-understand drinking story tells the long history of Chinese drinking culture.

二、中国传统酒文化的基本特点 Basic Characteristics of Traditional Chinese Drinking Culture

中国人饮酒由来已久，中国又是喝酒者的乐土：地无分南北，人无分男女，族无分汉满蒙回藏，饮酒之风，历经数千年而不衰。中国更是酒文化的胜地，饮酒的意义远不止生理性消费，远不止口腹之乐；在许多场合，它都是作为一个文化符号，一种文化消费，用来表示一种礼仪，一种气氛，一种情趣，一种心境；酒与诗，从来就结下了不解之缘。

Chinese people have been drinking for a long time, and China is a paradise for drinkers: there is no distinction between north and south, no distinction between men and women, no distinction between nationalities, such as Han, Manchu, Mongol, Hui, or Tibetan. The spirit of drinking has lasted thousands of years. China is the land of drinking culture. The meaning of wine is far more than physiological consumption, far more than just appetite; on many occasions, it is used as a cultural symbol, a cultural consumption, and used to express an etiquette, an atmosphere, a taste, or a mood; wine and poetry have forged an indissoluble bond.

1. 特别注重喝酒的精神。中国人喝酒的酒神精神以道家哲学为源头。庄周主张，物我合一，天人合一，齐一生死。庄周高唱绝对自由之歌，倡导"乘物而游""游乎四海之外""无何有之乡"。庄子宁愿做自由的在烂泥塘里摇头摆尾的乌龟，而不做受人束缚的昂首阔步的千里马。追求绝对自由、忘却生死利禄及荣辱，是中国酒精神的精髓所在。

Chinese pay special attention to the spirit of drinking. The Chinese people's Bacchus spirit derived from Taoist philosophy. The Taoist philosopher Zhuang Zhou held that nature and man are one (the same), heaven and man are one, death and life are one. Zhuang Zhou sang the song of absolute freedom, advocating "following the laws of nature", "traveling beyond the seas", and "a land of nothing. " Zhuangzi would rather be a tortoise shaking his head and tail in a muddy puddle freely than a strutting one-thousand-li horse (meaning a swift horse) that is restrained by others. Pursuing absolute freedom, and forgetting life, death, profit, honor and disgrace is the essence of the Dionysian Spirit of Chinese.

2. 特别讲究饮酒的过程。"杯小乾坤大，壶中日月长"，中国人喝酒过程中特别注重酒趣。酒趣富于酒令之中，酒令则纯是以文化入酒的，是酒文化中的文化精粹。早在两千多年前的春秋战国时代，酒令就在黄河流域的宴席上出现了。酒令分俗令和雅令。猜拳是俗令的代表，雅令即文字令，通常是在具有较丰富文化知识的人士间流行。白居易曰："闲征雅令穷经史，醉听清吟胜管弦。"认为酒宴中的雅令要比乐曲佐酒更有意趣。文字令又包括字词令、谜语令、筹令等。

Chinese pay special attention to the process of drinking. "In drinking, the universe is expanding, and the time is lingering." Chinese people pay special attention to the interest of wine when drinking. The drinking interest is rich in the drinking game, and the drinking game is purely based on culture, which is the cultural essence of the drinking culture. As early as the Spring and Autumn Period and the Warring States Period more than two thousand years ago, drinking games appeared at banquets in the Yellow River Basin. Drinking games are divided into popular games and elegant games. Finger-guessing game is the representative of popular drinking games, and the elegant game is a Chinese character game, which is usually popular among the people with rich cultural knowledge. The poet Bai Juyi thought the elegant games at the banquet were more interesting than the music in drinking. The character game also includes the word game, the riddle game, and the chip game.

3. 特别注意饮酒的座次。中国人在喝酒的时候特别讲究礼节，注重长幼有序；也特别讲究敬酒的顺序：晚辈先敬长辈，下属先敬上级，平辈互敬。

Chinese pay special attention to the seating position for drinking. Chinese people pay special attention to etiquette when drinking, and the sequence according to the age; they also pay special attention to toasting: younger generations propose a toast to elders first, subordinates to superiors, and peers toast each other.

4. 特别看重饮酒的环境。中国人认为饮酒实际上是一种境界颇高的艺术享受，有许多学问。特别是在古代，人们不仅注重酒的质量和强调节制饮酒，而且还十分讲究饮酒的环境，如什么时候能饮、什么时候不宜饮、在什么地方饮酒、饮什么酒、如何饮酒等，都有许多规矩和讲究。中国古人饮酒时还有七大讲究：心情要好，温酒而喝，饮必小咽，切勿混饮，空腹勿饮，无需强饮，酒后少饮茶。

Chinese pay special attention to the drinking environment. Chinese people believe that drinking is actually a kind of artistic enjoyment of a high level, with much knowledge. Especially in ancient times, people not only paid attention to the quality of wine and the quantity of drinking, but also paid great attention to the drinking environment, such as when to drink, when not to drink, where to drink, what to drink and how to drink. There were many rules and particulars. The ancient Chinese people also had seven requirements when drinking: they should be in a good mood, drink warm wine, drink bit by bit, not drink various wines at one time, not drink on an empty stomach, not need to drink more than enough, and drink less tea after alcohol.

5. 特别表现饮酒的文化。中国古人喝酒不仅是喝酒，还会情景交融的吟诗作赋。仅仅是饮酒诗就可分为宴会酒、饯行酒、传统节日酒、独酌、闲饮、咏怀酒、边塞酒、军中酒、祭祀神灵酒、村社酒，还有展现社会不合理的酒诗。

Chinese pay special attention to show the culture of drinking. In ancient China, drinking was not only drinking, people created poems suitable to the situation. Only drinking poems can be divided into banquet drinking, farewell drinking, traditional festival drinking, drinking alone, leisurely drinking, expressing drinking, frontier drinking, military drinking, sacrificial drinking, drinking at merry-making village activities, and other drinking poems that reveal unreasonable social phenomena.

三、中国酒的种类 Types of Chinese Wine

酒是人类生活中的主要饮料之一。中国制酒源远流长，品种繁多，名酒荟萃，享誉中外。黄酒是世界上最古老的酒类之一，约在三千多年前，商周时代，中国人独创酒曲复式发酵法，开始大量酿制黄酒。约一千年前的宋代，中国人发明了蒸馏法，从此，白酒成为中国人饮用的主要酒类。酒渗透于整个中华五千年的文明史中，从文学艺术创作、文化娱乐到饮食烹饪、养生保健，在中国人生活中都占有重要的位置。

Wine is one of the main drinks in human life. Chinese wine has a long history and a wide variety, well-known at home and abroad. Yellow rice wine is one of the oldest wines in the world. About three thousand years ago, during Shang and Zhou dynasties, the Chinese created a method of double fermentation of distiller's yeast and began to make large quantities of yellow rice wine. About a thousand years ago, in Song Dynasty, the Chinese invented the distillation method. Since then, white liquor has become the main drink for the Chinese. Wine permeates the 5, 000 – year history of Chinese civilization. From literature and artistic creation, entertainment to diet cooking, and even to health preservation, wine occupies an important position in Chinese life.

中国酒品种繁多，分类的标准和方法不尽相同，有以原料进行分类的，有以酒精含量高低分类的，也有以酒的特性分类的。最为常见的分类方法有两种：一是生产厂家根据酿制工艺来分类，二是经营部门根据经营习惯来分类。习惯上大都采用经营部门的分类法，将中国酒分为白酒、黄酒、果酒、药酒和啤酒五类。

There are many varieties of Chinese wine, and the classification standards and methods are not the same. Some are classified by raw materials, some are classified by alcohol content, and some are classified by wine characteristics. There are two most common classification methods: one is that manufacturers classify them according to the brewing process, and the other is that business departments classify them according to their business habits. Traditionally, the classification method of the business department is adopted to divide Chinese wine into five categories: white wine (alcohol), yellow rice wine, fruit wine, medicinal wine and beer.

1. 白酒 Baijiu（White Liquor）

白酒是用粮食或其他含有淀粉的农作物为原料，以酒曲为糖化发酵剂，经发酵蒸馏而成。白酒的特点是无色透明，质地纯净，醇香浓郁，味感丰富，酒度在 30 度以上，刺激性较强。白酒根据其原料和生产工艺的不同，形成了不同的香型与风格，白酒的香型有以下五种：

White Liquor is made from grains or other crops containing starch as raw materials, using distiller's yeast as a saccharification starter, and fermentation and distillation. White Liquor is characterized by colorlessness and transparency, pure texture, rich aroma, rich taste, alcohol content above 30 degrees, and strong irritation. White Liquor has different fragrances and styles according to its raw materials and production process. There are five fragrances of white liquor:

（1）清香型 Qingxiang Xing（Mild Flavour）

清香型的特点是酒气清香芬芳，醇厚绵软，甘润爽口，酒味纯净。以山西杏花村的汾酒为代表，故又有汾香型之称。

Mild flavour is characterized by fragrant aroma, mellowness and softness, sweetness and refreshingness, and pureness in taste. It is represented by Fenjiu from Xinghua Village in Shanxi province, so it is also known as Fen Flavour.

（2）浓香型 Nongxiang Xing（Strong Flavour）

浓香型的特点是饮时芳香浓郁，甘绵适口，饮后尤香，回味悠长，可概括为"香、甜、浓、净"四个字。以四川泸州老窖特曲为代表，故又有泸香型之称。

Strong Flavour is characterized by thick aroma, sweetness and palatableness, especially fragrant after drinking, with a long aftertaste, which can be summarized as "fragrant, sweet, thick, clean". It is represented by Luzhou Laojiao Special Yeast Liquor in Sichuan province, so it is also called Luxiang（Lu Flavour）.

（3）酱香型 Jiang-Flavour

酱香型的特点是香而不艳，低而不淡，香气幽雅，回味绵长，杯空香气犹存。以贵州茅台酒为代表，故又有茅台香型之称。

The characteristic of the jiang-flavour is that it is fragrant but not strong, low but not weak, the aroma is elegant, the aftertaste is long, and the aroma is still there even when the cup is empty. It is represented by Kweichow Moutai, so it is also called Moutai Flavour.

（4）米香型 Rice-Flavour

米香型的特点是蜜香清柔，幽雅纯净，入口绵甜，回味怡畅。以桂林的三花酒和全州的湘山酒为代表。

The characteristic of rice flavour is honey fragrance, soft, elegant and pure, sweet in the mouth, and pleasant aftertaste. It is represented by Guilin's Sanhua Wine and Quanzhou's Xiangshan Wine.

（5）复香型 Compound Flavour

兼有两种以上主体香型的白酒为复香型，也称兼香型或混香型。这种酒的闻香、回香和回味香各有不同，具有一酒多香的特点。贵州董酒是复香型的代表，还有湖南的白沙液、辽宁的凌川白酒等。

White liquor with two or more main flavours is compound flavour, also called mixed flavour. The smell and aftertaste of this wine are different, and it has the characteristics of one wine with multiple flavours. Dongjiu from Guizhou province is the representative of compound flavour, as well as Baishaye from Hunan province and Lingchuan Liquor from Liaoning province.

白酒中生产得最多的是浓香型白酒，清香型白酒次之，酱香型、米香型、复香型等较少。白酒质量的高低是以其色泽、香气和滋味 3 个方面，通过专家的感官鉴定和理化鉴定得出的。一种质量优良的白酒，在色泽上应是无色透明，瓶内无悬浮物、无沉淀现象。在香气上应有其本身特有的酒味和醇香，其香气又可分为溢香、喷香和留香等。在滋味上应是酒味纯正，各味协调，无强烈的刺激性。白酒是中国酒品生产中很重要的组成部分。随着人们饮酒习惯的逐步改变，许多名酒的生产厂家都相继研制出中度白酒，以适合出口和国内广大消费者的需要。

Strong flavour white liquor is the most produced liquor, followed by mild flavour liquor, and then jiang-flavour, rice-flavour, and compound flavour liquors. The quality of white liquor is based on the three aspects of color, aroma and taste, through the sensory appraisal and physical and chemical appraisal of experts. Good liquor should be colorless and transparent, with no suspended matter in the bottle and no precipitation. The aroma should have its own unique taste and frarance, and its aroma can be divided into spilling fragrances, spraying fragrance and retention fragrance. In terms of taste, it should be pure, with coordinated tastes, but without strong irritation. White liquor is a very important part of the wine in China. With the gradual changes in people's drinking habits, many famous wine manufacturers have successively developed medium-grade spirits to suit the needs of export and domestic consumers.

2. 黄酒 Yellow rice wine

黄酒是中国生产历史悠久的传统酒品，因其颜色黄亮而得名。以糯米、黍米和大米为原料，经酒药、麵曲发酵压榨而成。酒性醇和，适于长期贮存，有越陈越香的特点，属低度发酵的原汁酒。酒度一般在 8 度~20 度之间。黄酒的特点是酒质醇厚幽香，味感谐和鲜美，有一定的营养价值。黄酒除饮用外，还可作为中药的"药引子"。在烹饪菜肴时，它又是一种调料，对于鱼、肉等荤腥菜肴有去腥提味的作用。黄酒是中国南方和一些亚洲国家人民喜爱的酒品。黄酒根据其原料、酿造工艺和风味特点的不同，可以划分成以下3种类型：

Yellow rice wine is a traditional wine with a long history of production in China, and it is named for its bright yellow color. Using glutinous rice, millet rice and rice as raw materials, it is fermented and squeezed by liquor medicine and flour yeast. The wine is mellow, suitable for long-term storage, and has the characteristics of "More Time, more fragrance". It is a low-fermented raw wine. The alcohol content is generally between 8 degrees and 20 degrees. Yellow rice wine is characterized by its mellow and delicate flavor, harmonious taste, and certain nutritional value. In addition to drinking, rice wine can also be used as a "medicine primer" for traditional Chinese medicine. When cooking any dishes, people take it as another kind of seasoning, which has the effect of removing the gaminess such as fish and meat. Yellow rice wine is a favorite wine for the people in southern China and some Asian countries. Yellow rice wine can be divided into the following three types according to its raw materials, brewing technology and flavor characteristics：

（1）江南糯米黄酒 Jiangnan（South of the Yangtze River）Yellow Rice Wine

江南黄酒产在江南地区，以浙江绍兴黄酒为代表，生产历史悠久。它是以糯米为原料，以酒药和麸曲为糖化发酵剂酿制而成。其酒质醇厚，色、香、味都高于一般黄酒。存放时间越长越好。由于原料的配比不同，加上酿造工艺的变化，形成了各种风格的优良品种，主要品种有状元红、加饭酒、花雕酒、善酿酒、香雪酒、竹叶青酒等。酒度在 13 度~20 度之间。

Jiangnan（South of the Yangtze River）Yellow Rice Wine is produced in Jiangnan region, represented by Shaoxing Yellow rice wine in Zhejiang Province, with a long production history. It is brewed with glutinous rice as raw material, and wine medicine and flour yeast as saccharification starter. Its color, aroma and taste are higher than those of ordinary Yellow Rice Wine. The longer the storage time, the better. Due to the different ratios of raw materials and the changes in the brewing process, excellent varieties have been formed. The main varieties are Champion Red, Rice Wine, Huadiao Wine, Good Brewing Wine, Xiangxue Wine, Bamboo Leaf Green Wine. The ABV is between 13 and 20 percent.

（2）福建红曲黄酒 Fujian red yeast Yellow Rice Wine

福建红曲黄酒以糯米、粳米为原料，以红曲为糖化发酵剂酿制而成。其代表品种是福建老酒和龙岩沉缸酒，具有酒味芬芳，醇和柔润的特点。酒度在 15 度左右。

Fujian red yeast Yellow Rice Wine is made with glutinous rice and japonica rice as raw materials, and red yeast is used as a saccharification starter. Its representative varieties are Fujian Old Wine and Longyan Chen Gang Yellow Rice Wine, which have the characteristics of fragrance, mellowness and softness. The ABV is around 15 percent.

（3）山东黍米黄酒 Shandong millet Yellow Rice Wine

黍米黄酒是中国北方黄酒的主要品种，最早创于山东即墨，现在北方各地已有广泛生产。以黍米为原料，以米曲霉制成的麸曲为糖化剂酿制而成。具有酒液浓郁，清香爽口的特点，在黄酒中独具一格。即墨黄酒还可分为清酒、老酒、兰陵美酒等品种。酒度在 12 度左右。

Millet rice wine is the main variety of yellow rice wine in northern China. It was first created in Jimo, Shandong province, and is now widely produced throughout the north. It is brewed with millet rice as raw material and rice yeast made from Aspergillus oryzae as saccharifying agent. It has the characteristics of rich liquor and refreshing fragrance, which is unique among rice wines. Jimo rice wine can also be divided into pure wine, old wine, Lanling wine. The ABV is around 12 percent.

黄酒质量的高低也是按其色、香、味 3 个方面进行评定的，色泽以浅黄澄清（即墨黄酒除外）、无沉淀物者为优，香气以浓郁者为优，味道以醇厚稍甜、无酸涩味者为优。黄酒大多采用陶质坛装，泥土封口，以助酯化，故越陈越香。保存的环境要凉爽，温度要平稳。由于黄酒是低度酒，开坛后要及时使用，时间久了，易被污染而变质。

The quality of rice wine is also evaluated according to its color, aroma and taste. The color is light yellow, clear (except Jimo rice wine), and no sediment, better; the aroma is thick, better; and the taste is mellow, slightly sweet, no sour taste, better. Most rice wines are packed in pottery jars and sealed with soil to aid esterification, so the more it ages, the more fragrant it is. The storage environment should be cool and the temperature should be stable. Because rice wine is a low-alcohol wine, it must be used in time after the jar is opened. If a long time, it is easy to be contaminated and deteriorated.

3. 果酒 Fruit Wine

凡是用水果、浆果为原料直接发酵酿造的酒都可以称为果酒，品种繁多，酒度在 15 度左右。各种果酒大都以果实名称命名。果酒因选用的果实原料不同而风味各异，但都具有其原料果实的芳香，并具有令人喜爱的天然色泽和醇美滋味。果酒中含有较多的营养成分如糖类、矿物质和维生素等。由于人们更喜欢用葡萄来酿造酒，所以果酒可以分成葡萄酒类和其他果酒类。其他果酒有苹果酒、山楂酒、杨梅酒、广柑酒、菠萝酒等多种。果酒除葡萄酒外，其他果酒的产量是比较少的。

Any wine that is directly fermented with fruits and berries as raw materials can be called fruit wine. There are many varieties and the ABV is about 15 percent. Most fruit wines are named after the fruit. Fruit wines have different flavors due to different fruit materials, but they all have the aroma of the raw materials, and have a natural color and mellow taste. Fruit wine contains more nutrients such as sugars, minerals and vitamins. Since people prefer to use grapes to make wine, fruit wines can be divided into grape wines and other fruit wines. Other fruit wines include cider, hawthorn wine, bayberry wine, Tangor wine, pineapple wine and so on. In addition to grape wine, the output of other fruit wines is relatively small.

4. 药酒 Medicinal wine

药酒是以成品酒（大多用白酒）为酒基，配各种中药材和糖料，经过酿造或浸泡制成，具有不同作用的酒品。药酒可以分为两大类：一类是滋补酒，它既是一种饮料酒，又有滋补作用，如竹叶青酒、五味子酒、男士专用酒、女士美容酒；另一类是利用酒精提取中药材中的有效成分，以提高药物的疗效，此种酒是真正的药酒，大都在中药店出售。

Medicinal wine is based on finished wine (mostly white liquor), mixed with various Chinese medicinal materials and sugars, brewed or soaked, and has different effects. Medicinal wine can be divided into two categories: one is tonic wine, which is a kind of beverage wine and has nourishing effects, such as green bamboo leaf wine, schisandra wine, special wine for men, and beauty wine for women; the other is to use alcohol to extract active ingredients from Chinese herbs to improve the efficacy of the medicine. This kind of wine is a real medicinal wine and is mostly sold in Chinese medicine stores.

5. 啤酒 Beer

啤酒是以大麦为原料，啤酒花为香料，经过发芽、糖化、发酵而制成的一种低酒精含量的原汁酒，通常人们把它看成为一种清凉饮料。其酒精含量在2度~5度之间。啤酒的特点是有显著的麦芽和啤酒花的清香，味道纯正爽口。啤酒含有大量的二氧化碳和丰富的营养成分，能帮助消化，促进食欲，有清凉舒适之感，所以深受人们的喜爱。啤酒中含有11种维生素和17种氨基酸。1升啤酒经消化后产生的热量，相当于10个鸡蛋或500克瘦肉或200毫升牛奶所生产的热量，故有"液体面包"之称。啤酒分类有以下几种：

Beer uses barley as raw material and hops as spice. It is a kind of low-alcohol raw wine made through sprouting, saccharification and fermentation. People usually regard it as a refreshing drink. Its alcohol content is between 2 to 5 degrees. The beer is characterized by the distinctive aroma of malt and hops, and the taste is pure and refreshing. Beer contains a lot of carbon dioxide and rich nutrients, can help digestion, promote appetite, and has a cool and comfortable feeling, so it is deeply loved by people. Beer contains 11 vitamins and 17 amino acids. The heat produced by 1 liter of beer after digestion is equivalent to the heat produced by 10 eggs, or 500 grams of lean meat, or 200 ml of milk, so it is called "liquid bread". There are several types of beer:

（1）根据啤酒是否经过灭菌处理，可将其分为鲜啤酒和熟啤酒两种。鲜啤酒又称生啤酒，没有经过杀菌处理，因此保存期较短，在15℃以下保存期是3~7天，但口味鲜美，目前深受消费者欢迎的"扎啤"就是鲜啤酒。熟啤酒是经过杀菌处理的啤酒，所以稳定性好，保存时间长，一般可保存3个月，但口感及营养不如鲜啤酒。

According to whether the beer has been sterilized or not, it can be divided into fresh beer and cooked beer. Fresh beer, also known as draft beer, has not undergone sterilization treatment, so it has a short shelf life. The shelf life is 3~7 days below 15℃, but it tastes delicious. The "draft beer" that is currently popular among consumers is fresh beer. Ripe beer is a beer that has been sterilized, so it has good stability and long storage time. Generally, it can be stored for 3 months, but the taste and nutrition are not as good as fresh beer.

（2）根据啤酒中麦芽汁的浓度，可将其分为低浓度啤酒、中浓度啤酒和高浓度啤酒三种。低浓度啤酒麦芽汁的浓度在 6 度~8 度之间，中浓度啤酒麦芽汁的浓度在 10 度~12 度之间，高浓度啤酒麦芽汁的浓度在 14 度~20 度之间。啤酒中的酒精量含量，也是随麦芽汁的浓度增加而增加的，低浓度啤酒的酒精量含量在 2%左右，中浓度啤酒的酒精量含量在 3.1%~3.8%之间，高浓度啤酒的酒精含量在 4%~5%之间。

According to the concentration of wort in beer, it can be divided into low-concentration beer, medium-concentration beer and high-concentration beer. The concentration of low-concentration beer wort is between 6 percent and 8 percent, the concentration of medium-concentration beer wort is between 10 percent and 12 percent, and the concentration of high-concentration beer wort is between 14 percent and 20 percent. The ABV in beer also increases with the increase in the concentration of wort. The ABV of low-concentration beer is about 2%, the ABV of medium-concentration beer is between 3.1% and 3.8%, and the ABV of high-concentration beer is between 4% and 5%.

（3）根据啤酒的颜色，可将啤酒分为黄色啤酒、黑色啤酒和白色啤酒 3 种。黄色啤酒又称淡色啤酒，口味淡雅，目前中国生产的啤酒大多属于此类，其颜色的深浅各地不完全一致。黑色啤酒又称浓色啤酒，酒液呈咖啡色，有光泽、口味浓厚，并带有焦香味，产量较少，仅在北京、青岛有生产。白色啤酒是以白色为主色的啤酒，其酒精含量很低，中国已有生产，适合不善饮酒的人饮用。

According to the color of beer, beer can be divided into three types: yellow beer, black beer and white beer. Yellow beer, also known as pale beer, has a light taste. At present, most of the beers produced in China belong to this category, and the color depth is not exactly the same in different places. Black beer is also called strong beer. The liquid is brown, shiny, strong in taste, and has a burnt aroma. The output is small, and it is only produced in Beijing and Qingdao. White beer is a beer with white as its main color and has a low alcohol content. It has been produced in China and is suitable for people who are not good at drinking.

（4）根据啤酒中有无酒精含量，可将其划分为含酒精啤酒和无酒精啤酒两种。无酒精啤酒是近年来啤酒酿造技术的一个突破，它的特点是保持了啤酒的原有味道，但又不含酒精，受到广泛的好评。

According to the alcohol content of beer, it can be divided into two types: alcoholic beer and non-alcoholic beer. Non-alcoholic beer is a breakthrough in beer brewing technology in recent years. It is characterized by maintaining the original taste of beer, but without alcohol, and has been widely praised.

啤酒的鉴定是从透明度、色泽、泡沫、香气、滋味等方面来检查的，质量优良的啤酒，应是酒液透明有光泽，色泽深浅因品种而异，泡沫洁白细腻、持久挂杯，有强烈的麦芽香气和酒花苦而爽口的口感。

The identification of beer is checked from the aspects of transparency, color, foam, aroma, and taste. The beer of good quality should be transparent and shiny, and the color depth varies from type to type. The foam is white and delicate, long-lasting, and the fragrance is strong with aroma of malt, and the taste is bitter and refreshing from hops.

中国的传统茶文化

一、中国茶文化的缘起 The Origin of Chinese Tea Culture

茶，是中国人开门七件事（柴米油盐酱醋茶）之一，不言而喻，它在人们生活中所处的位置很重要。饮茶在古代中国是非常普遍的。中国茶文化源远流长，博大精深，不但包含物质文化层面，还包含深厚的精神文明层次。唐代茶圣陆羽的《茶经》在历史上吹响了中华茶文化的号角。从此茶的精神渗透了宫廷和社会，深入中国的诗词、绘画、书法、宗教、医学。几千年来中国不但积累了大量关于茶叶种植、生产的物质文化，更积累了丰富的有关茶的精神文化，这就是中国特有的茶文化。

Tea is one of the seven things for Chinese people in daily life (firewood, rice, oil, salt, sauce, vinegar and tea). It goes without saying that its place in people's lives is very important. Tea drinking was very common in ancient China. Chinese tea culture has a long history and is broad and profound. It contains not only the material level, but also the profound spiritual level. *The Tea Classic* by Lu Yu, a tea sage in Tang Dynasty, sounded the clarion call of Chinese tea culture in history. Since then, the spirit of tea has penetrated the court and society, and has permeated into Chinese poetry, painting, calligraphy, religion, and medicine. For thousands of years, China has not only accumulated a large amount of material culture about tea planting and production, but also a rich spiritual culture about tea. This is the unique tea culture of China.

中国是茶的故乡，是世界上最早发现茶树、利用茶叶和栽培茶树的国家。茶树的起源至少已有六七万年的历史。茶被人类发现和利用，大约有四五千年的历史。茶有健身、治疾之药物疗效，又富欣赏情趣，可陶冶情操。品茶待客是中国人高雅的娱乐和社交活动，坐茶馆、茶话会则是中国人社会性群体茶艺活动。中国茶艺在世界享有盛誉，在唐代就传入日本。

China is the hometown of tea and the first country in the world to discover, use and cultivate tea trees. The origin of the tea tree has a history of at least 60, 000 to 70, 000 years. Tea was discovered and used by humans, with a history of about four to five thousand years. Tea has the therapeutic effects of fitness and disease treatment, and it is also full of human appreciation and can cultivate sentiment. Offering guests with tea is an elegant entertainment and social activity for Chinese people, while sitting in tea houses and taking part in tea parties are Chinese social group tea activities. Chinese tea art enjoys a high reputation in the world and was introduced to Japan in Tang Dynasty.

饮茶始于中国。茶叶冲以煮沸的清水，顺乎自然，清饮雅尝，寻求茶的固有之味，重在意境，这是中式品茶的特点。同样质量的茶叶，如用水不同、茶具不同或冲泡技术不一，泡出的茶汤会有不同的效果。中国自古以来就十分讲究茶的冲泡，积累了丰富的经验。泡好茶，要了解各类茶叶的特点，掌握科学的冲泡技术，使茶叶的固有品质能充分地表现出来。

Tea drinking began in China. Tea leaves are brewed with boiled water, which is natural, clear and elegant, seeking the inherent taste of tea, focusing on the artistic conception, which are the characteristics of Chinese tea tasting. The same quality of tea, with different water, different tea sets or different brewing techniques, the tea soup will have different effects. China has been very particular about tea brewing since ancient times and has accumulated rich experience. To make good tea, you'd better understand the characteristics of various types of tea and master scientific brewing techniques to fully express the inherent qualities of tea.

二、中国传统茶文化特点 The Characteristics of Traditional Chinese Tea Culture

中国茶文化反映出中华民族悠久的文明和礼仪。

Chinese tea culture reflects the long‐standing civilization and etiquette of the

Chinese nation.

茶文化意为饮茶活动过程中形成的文化特征，包括茶道、茶德、茶精神、茶联、茶书、茶具、茶画、茶学、茶故事、茶艺等。茶文化起源地为中国，中国是茶的故乡，中国人饮茶，据说始于神农时代，少说也有 4700 多年了。直到现在，中华同胞还有以茶代礼的风俗。

Tea culture means the cultural characteristics formed during tea drinking activities, including tea ceremony, tea virtue, tea spirit, tea couplets, tea books, tea sets, tea paintings, tea studies, tea stories, tea art, etc. The origin of tea culture is China. China is the hometown of tea. It is said that Chinese people started drinking tea in the Shennong（God of Agriculture）era, or at least 4,700 years. Until now, Chinese compatriots still have the custom of using tea in lieu of gifts.

中国茶文化的内容主要是茶在中国精神文化中的体现，这比"茶风俗""茶道"的范畴深广得多，也是中国茶文化之所以与欧美或日本的茶文化区别很大的原因。

The content of Chinese tea culture is mainly the embodiment of tea in Chinese spiritual culture, which is much deeper and broader than "tea customs" and "tea ceremony". It is also the reason why Chinese tea culture is very different from European, American or Japanese tea culture.

茶道最早起源于中国。中国人至少在唐或唐以前，就在世界上首先将茶饮作为一种修身养性之道。在唐宋年间，人们对饮茶的环境、礼节、操作方式等饮茶仪程都很讲究，有了一些约定俗成的规矩和仪式，茶宴已有宫廷茶宴、寺院茶宴、文人茶宴之分。

The tea ceremony originated in China. At least in or even before Tang Dynasty, Chinese first took tea as a way of self-cultivation in the world. During the Tang and Song Dynasty, people were very particular about the environment, etiquette, operation methods and other tea-drinking rituals. There were some conventions and rituals that were commonly recognized. Tea banquets included palace tea banquets, temple tea banquets, and literati tea banquets.

中国的茶道早于日本数百年甚至上千年，中国的茶道可以说是重精神而轻形式，在各历史阶段也有不同的表现，各种茶也不尽相同，百花齐放，但都体现了"清、敬、怡、真"的茶文化精神。什么是茶道？就是"把茶视为珍贵、高尚的饮料，因茶是一种精神上的享受，是一种艺术，或是一种修身养性的手段。"茶道是一种通过饮茶的方式，对人民进行礼法教育、道德修养的一种仪式。中国茶道包含茶艺、茶德、茶礼、茶理、茶情、茶学说、茶道引导七种义理，中国茶道精神的核心是"和"。

The tea ceremony in China predates Japan for hundreds or even thousands of years. It can be said that the tea ceremony in China emphasizes the spirit and neglects the form. It has different performances in various historical stages. The types of tea are various. The spirit of tea culture "purity, reverence, serenity and sincerity". What is the tea ceremony? It means "to treat tea as a precious and noble beverage, because tea is a spiritual enjoyment, an art, or a means of self-cultivation." The tea ceremony is a way to educate people in ethics and morality. Chinese tea ceremony includes seven principles: tea art, tea virtue, tea etiquette, tea philosophy, tea sentiment, tea theory, and tea ceremony guidance. The core spirit of Chinese tea ceremony is "harmony".

中国人饮茶，注重一个"品"字。"品茶"不但是鉴别茶的优劣，也带有神思遐想和领略饮茶情趣之意。在百忙之中泡上一壶浓茶，择雅静之处，自斟自饮，可以消除疲劳、涤烦益思、振奋精神，也可以细啜慢饮，达到美的享受，使精神世界升华到高尚的艺术境界。品茶的环境一般由建筑物、园林、摆设、茶具等因素组成。饮茶要求安静、清新、舒适、干净。中国园林世界闻名，山水风景更是不可胜数。利用园林或自然山水间，用木头做亭子、凳子，搭设茶室，给人一种诗情画意。供人们小憩，不由意趣盎然。

The Chinese drink tea and pay attention to the word "tasting". "Tasting tea" not only distinguishes the pros and cons of tea, but also implies reverie and taste of tea. Make a pot of strong tea in the midst of busy schedule, choose an elegant and quiet place, and drink it by oneself. It can relieve fatigue, clear up troubles, refresh our mind and our spirit. We can also sip and drink slowly to achieve the enjoyment of beauty and sublime the spiritual world to the noble state of art. The environment for tasting tea is generally composed of factors such as buildings, gardens, furnishings, and tea sets. Tea drinking requires quiet, fresh, comfortable and clean environment. Chinese gardens are world-famous, and the landscapes are innumerable. Use gardens or natural landscapes, use wood to make pavilions, stools, and set up tea rooms to give people a poetic and picturesque mood, where people can take a rest full of fun.

献茶是中国人的待客之道。中国是文明古国，礼仪之邦，很重礼节。凡来了客人，沏茶、敬茶的礼仪是必不可少的。当有客来访，可征求意见，选用最合来客口味的茶具待客。以茶敬客时，对茶叶适当拼配也是必要的。主人在陪伴客人饮茶时，要注意客人杯、壶中的茶水残留量，一般用茶杯泡茶，如已喝去一半，就要添加开水，随喝随添，使茶水浓度基本保持前后一致，水温适宜。在饮茶时也可适当佐以茶食、糖果、菜肴等，达到调节口味之功效。

Offering tea is the Chinese way of hospitality. China is a country with an ancient civilization, a country of etiquette. When guests come, the etiquette of making tea and offering tea is essential. When a visitor comes, you can seek advice and choose the best tea set that suits the visitor's taste. When serving customers with tea, it is also necessary to mix tea properly. When the host accompanies the guests to drink tea, we should pay attention to the residual amount of tea in the cups and pots of the guests. Generally, the tea cup is used to make tea. If half of the tea has been drunk, boiling water should be added with the drink, so that the tea concentration is generally consistent and the water temperature is suitable. When drinking tea, it can also be accompanied by tea, candies, dishes, etc. to achieve the effect of adjusting taste.

三、中国茶的种类 Types of Chinese Tea

中国茶叶按照制作方法分为绿茶、红茶、青茶（乌龙茶）、黑茶、白茶、黄茶等几大类，各类茶中又包括许多品种。

According to production method, Chinese tea can be divided into green tea, black tea, oolong tea, dark tea, white tea and yellow tea, with each type having various subtypes.

1. 绿茶 Green tea
绿茶，属"不发酵茶"，品质特征为清扬绿叶、形美、色香、味醇。

Green tea belongs to "non-fermented tea", and its quality is characterized by clear green leaves, beautiful shape, fragrance and mellow taste.

著名的绿茶品种有杭州西湖龙井茶、江苏碧螺春茶、贵州的绿宝石茶、河南信阳市的信阳毛尖、安徽黄山的毛峰茶和产于安徽六安市一带的六安瓜片茶。

The famous green teas include Hangzhou West Lake Longjing tea; Jiangsu Biluochun tea; Guizhou green gem tea, Xinyang Maojian tea from Xinyang, Henan province; Maofeng tea from Huangshan Mountains, Anhui province; Lu'an Guapian tea from Lu'an, Anhui province.

2. 红茶 Black tea

红茶是经过"全发酵"的茶，品质特点是红汤红叶、香甜味醇。世界红茶的产地主要有中国、斯里兰卡、印度、肯尼亚等。

Black tea is a "fully fermented" tea, and its quality is characterized by red soup and red leaves, sweet and mellow. The main producing areas of black tea in the world are China, Sri Lanka, India, and Kenya.

红茶与绿茶不同，绿茶随着时间的流逝会陈化失去味道，而红茶能够保存相当长的时间，这样能适应长途运输，适合出口。但红茶创制时被称为"乌茶"，所以英语称之为"Black Tea"，而非"Red Tea"。

Black tea is different from green tea. Green tea will age and lose its flavor over time, while black tea can be stored for a long time, so that it can adapt to long-distance transportation and is suitable for export. But when created, it was called "wū tea", so it is called "Black Tea" in English instead of "Red Tea".

中国著名的红茶有武夷山正山小种、金骏眉，安徽的祁门红茶，云南的滇红茶和国内巅作的单丛红茶。

The famous black teas in China include Lapsang Souchong Black tea, Jin Junmei Black tea from Wuyi Mountain, Qimen black tea in Anhui province, Yunnan black tea in Yunnan province.

3. 青茶 Oolong tea

青茶也称乌龙茶，属"半发酵茶"，乌龙茶介于绿茶和红茶之间，是具有两种茶特征的一种茶叶。青茶外形条索粗壮，色泽青灰有光，茶汤金黄，香气馥郁芬芳，花香明显，叶底绿叶红镶边。

Green tea is also called oolong tea, which belongs to "semi-fermented tea". Oolong tea is between green tea and black tea. It is a kind of tea with two tea characteristics. The leaf form of green tea is strong, the color is brightly blue and gray, the tea soup is golden, the aroma is rich and fragrant, the floral fragrance is obvious, and the bottom of the leaf is green and red.

凤凰单丛在乌龙茶家族中是最浓酽又比较高香的高品质茶叶，铁观音和大红袍全国知名。

Fenghuang Dancong produced in Guangdong Province is the strongest and relatively high-quality tea in the oolong tea family. Tie Guanyin, and Dahongpao from Fujian province are very famous across China.

4. 黑茶 Dark tea

黑茶属"后发酵茶"，是中国特有的茶类，主要产于云南、湖南、湖北、四川、广西等地，其中云南的普洱茶古今中外久负盛名。黑茶色泽黑褐，粗老，气味较重，常作紧压茶的原料。由于黑茶属于后发酵茶，存放的时间越久，其味道越醇厚。汤色橙黄至暗褐色，有松烟香。

Dark tea is a kind of "post-fermented tea", which is unique to China. It is mainly produced in Yunnan, Hunan, Hubei, Sichuan, and Guangxi provinces. Among them, Pu'er tea in Yunnan has long been famous both at home and abroad. Dark tea is dark brown, thick and old in color, and has a strong smell. It is often used as a raw material for pressed tea. Since dark tea is a post-fermented tea, the longer it is stored, the more mellow it will taste. The soup is from orange-yellow to dark brown, with pine smoke fragrance.

5. 白茶 White tea

白茶是一种表面满披白色茸毛的"轻微发酵茶"，是中国茶类中的特殊珍品，主要产于福建的福鼎、政和、松溪和建阳等地。白茶有"一年是茶，三年是药，七年是宝"之说。

White tea is a kind of "lightly fermented tea" covered with white hairs. It is a special treasure among the teas in China. It is mainly produced in Fuding, Zhenghe, Songxi and Jianyang in Fujian province. White tea has the saying "White tea of one year is tea, white tea of three years is medicine, and white tea of seven years is treasure".

白茶因茶树品种、原料（鲜叶）采摘的标准不同，有芽茶和叶茶之分：单芽制成的称为"银针"，叶片制成的称为"寿眉"，芽叶全采的称为"白牡丹"。其毫色银白，芽头肥壮，汤色黄亮，滋味鲜醇，叶底嫩匀。

White tea is divided into bud tea and leaf tea due to different tea trees varieties and raw materials (fresh leaves) picking standards: the one made from a single bud is called "Silver Needle", the one made from leaves is called "Shoumei" (the brow of God of Longevity), and the one made from both bud and leaf is called "White Peony". Its color is silvery white, the buds are fat and strong, the soup is yellow and bright, the taste is mellow, and the bottom of the leaves is tender and even.

6. 黄茶 Yellow tea

黄茶属"轻微发酵茶"，由于运用特殊的"闷黄"工艺制作，造就了其"黄汤黄叶"的特点。黄茶的产量很少，主要在湖南君山、安徽金寨、四川蒙山、浙江平阳等地生产。黄茶多数芽叶细嫩，显毫。

Yellow tea is a kind of "lightly fermented tea", and its characteristics of "yellow soup and yellow leaves" are created due to the special "supple yellow" process used in its production. Yellow tea is produced in few places, mainly in Junshan, Hunan Province; Jinzhai, Anhui Province; Mengshan, Sichuan Province; and Pingyang, Zhejiang Province. Most yellow tea buds and leaves are delicate and bright.

7. 花茶 Scented tea

花茶，又名窨花茶、香片茶等，是一种茶叶和花香进行拼和窨制，使茶叶吸收花香而制成的再加工茶类。花茶因窨制所用的香花不同，可分为茉莉花茶、珠兰花茶、玉兰花茶、玫瑰花茶等。

Scented tea, also known as fragrant sliced tea, is a reprocessed tea made by blending and scenting tea to make the tea absorb the fragrance of flowers. Scented tea can be divided into jasmine tea, pearl orchid tea, magnolia tea, and rose tea because of the different fragrant flowers used in scenting.

花茶的分类：窨制花茶——以红茶、绿茶或乌龙茶等作为茶杯，配以能够吐香的鲜花作为原料，采用窨制工艺制作而成的茶叶，比如茉莉花茶、桂花茶等，其中以茉莉花茶最具代表性。

The classification of scented tea: (1) Scented tea, including black tea, green tea, or oolong tea, is used as raw tea, with flowers that can spit fragrance as ingredients, and the scenting process is used to make tea, such as jasmine tea, and osmanthus tea. Jasmine tea is the most representative.

工艺花茶——用茶叶和干花手工捆制造型后干燥制成的造型花茶，其最大的特点就是沸水冲泡后，如盛开的花朵，千姿百态，灵动娇美，非常美观。

（2）Crafty scented tea, a shaped scented tea made by hand-bundled tea leaves and dried flowers, and then dried again. Its biggest feature is that after boiling water, it looks like a blooming flower in various postures, delicate and agile, and very charming.

四、中国民间的茶俗文化 Chinese Folk Tea Culture

随着中华民族传统文化的积淀，茶事活动的兴起，茶俗逐渐成了我国民间风俗的一种，成为人们文化生活的一部分，且内容丰富，各呈风采。

With the accumulation of the Chinese nation's traditional culture and the rise of tea activities, tea customs have gradually become a kind of folk customs in our country, and have become part of people's cultural life, with rich contents and various styles.

（一）大碗茶 Big Bowl tea

大家熟悉的大碗茶流行于北京和山东等地。因用大号碗盛茶而得名。多为"忙人解渴"，旧时专门有卖大碗茶的茶水摊，因价廉物美，去暑解渴，很受大众欢迎。有一首很有名的歌就叫"前门情思大碗茶"。

The familiar Big Bowl Tea is popular in Beijing, Shandong. It is named after serving tea in a large bowl. Mostly for "busy people to quench their thirst." In the old days, there were tea stalls selling large bowls of tea. The large bowls of tea were very much popular because they helped people to relieve summer heat and quench their thirst with inexpensive price and good quality. There is a famous song about this "Affection on the Big Bowl Tea at the Front Gate".

（二）功夫茶 Kungfu Tea

功夫茶源于清代的富豪人家，后成为汉族民间的传统茶艺。流行于广东潮汕和福建漳州、泉州等东南沿海地区，后又传到香港、台湾地区和东南亚。茶盖大部分采用陶瓷材料，冲泡时间比较短，茶味高扬。

Kungfu tea originated from wealthy families in Qing Dynasty and later became a traditional tea art among the Han people. It is popular in the southeast coastal areas such as Chaozhou and Shantou in Guangdong province, Zhangzhou and Quanzhou in Fujian province, and then spread to Hong Kong, Taiwan region, and Southeast Asia. tea is mostly made of ceramic materials, the brewing time is relatively short, the tea taste is strong.

（三）打油茶 Dayoucha（Making Oil Tea）

打油茶亦称"吃豆茶"，瑶族、侗族传统待客食品，流行于广西、湖南、贵州等地区，尤其以广西恭城的侗族最为普遍。主要用于家常饮料和待客。用油炸糯米花、炒花生或浸泡的黄豆、玉米、炒米和新茶配制而成。

Dayoucha is also known as "eating bean tea". It is a traditional hospitality food of the Yao and Dong nationalities. It is popular in Guangxi province, Hunan province, and Guizhou province, especially for the Dong nationality in Gongcheng, Guangxi province. Mainly used for home-cooked drinks and hospitality. It is made with fried glutinous rice, fried peanuts or soaked soybeans, corn, fried rice and new tea.

中国的传统建筑文化

一、中国传统建筑的历史文脉 The Historical Development of Traditional Chinese Architecture

原始社会时期的人们要么是栖身天然洞窟，要么挖土为穴，构木为巢；穴居是原始社会时期非常重要的"住宅"形式之一，是原始人类对自我的一种重要保护屏障。原始的、极其简陋的巢居、穴居，并非真正的建筑，但为其后中国传统建筑的发展奠定了基础，成为中国建筑的两大源头。到了新石器时代的河姆渡文化和仰韶文化阶段，真正的建筑才诞生。河姆渡人的建筑是在地上架空的建筑，这是最早的"干栏式建筑"。"仰韶文化"的房屋属于"木骨泥墙"建筑。

People in primitive society either lived in natural caves, or digged into caves and built wood into nests; cave living was one of the most important forms of "housing" in primitive society, and it was an important element of primitive humans to protect themselves as a barrier. The primitive and extremely simple nesting and cave dwellings are not real buildings, but they have laid the foundation for the development of traditional Chinese architecture and become the two major sources of Chinese architecture. It was at the Hemudu and Yangshao cultural stages of the Neolithic Age that real architecture was born. The buildings of the Hemudu people were raised above the ground, which was the earliest "pile-dwelling building". The houses of "Yangshao Culture" belong to the "wood bone and mud wall" architecture.

夏代已基本有了宫室、民居、墓葬等建筑类别，甚至还有了较正规意义上的城市。商代的城市周围大多有壕沟和城墙，周代建筑的类型则更为丰富，建筑与营造的范围也更为广阔，对后世影响最为深远的是周代的都城。春秋时期的建筑施工已逐渐形成专业分工，鲁班就是一位著名的建筑木工，被后代奉为建筑工匠的祖师；建筑装修的发展，又促成了彩绘和雕刻的专业化。西周出现了最早的相当严整的四合院式建筑。

In Xia Dynasty, there were basically palaces, houses, tombs, and even cities in a more formal sense. Most cities in Shang Dynasty were surrounded by trenches and city walls. The types of buildings in Zhou Dynasty were more abundant, and the scope of construction was broader. The capital of Zhou Dynasty had the most profound impact on later generations. During the Spring and Autumn Period, the construction gradually formed a professional division of labor. Lu Ban was a famous construction carpenter who was regarded as the forefather of construction craftsmen by later generations; the development of construction decoration also contributed to the specialization of painting and carving. The earliest fairly neat quadrangle courtyards appeared in the Western Zhou Dynasty.

战国时期开始兴建大规模宫室和高台建筑，大城市出现，瓦的技术得到发展，开始制作砖块。宫殿建筑是中国建筑史中成就最高、规模最大的建筑类型，强烈凸显了帝王的无上权威，秦代宫殿在这方面表现尤其突出；始皇陵是中国帝王陵发展史上的重要转折，对后世皇陵影响很大，被誉为"世界第八大奇迹"。汉朝建筑的一个重大成就就是砖石拱券技术的提高。汉代与秦代一样，供帝王田猎游弋的离宫园囿非常盛行，因此对相关建筑、景观的营造也非常多，比较著名的有上林苑等。

During the Warring States period, large-scale palaces and high-rise buildings began to be built, big cities appeared, tile technology was developed, and bricks were now made. The palace building is the most accomplished and largest building type in the history of Chinese architecture. It strongly highlights the supreme authority of the emperor. The palaces of Qin Dynasty were particularly prominent in this aspect. The imperial tomb of the first Qin Emperor is very influential and is known as the "eighth wonder of the world". A major achievement of the Han Dynasty architecture is the improvement of the masonry arch technology. In Han Dynasty, as in Qin dynasty, the imperial palace gardens for hunting and cruising in the emperor's fields were very popular, so there were many related buildings and landscapes. The most famous was Shanglin Imperial Park.

汉代是中国传统建筑的第一个高峰。此时高台建筑减少，多屋楼阁大量增加，庭院式的布局已基本定型，并和当时的政治、经济、宗法、礼制等制度密切结合，中国建筑体系已大致形成。

Han Dynasty was the first peak of traditional Chinese architecture. At this time, the number of high-rise buildings decreased, and the number of multi-house pavilions increased. The courtyard-style layout was basically finalized, and was closely integrated with the political, economic, patriarchal, and ritual systems of the time. The Chinese architectural system was roughly formed.

魏晋南北朝时期的建筑，随着民族融合以及在文化上的交流，也有了不少新的发展，其中最重要的就是佛教建筑的兴盛，佛寺、佛塔和石窟是这个时期最突出的建筑类型。

The architecture of the Wei, Jin, Southern and Northern Dynasties, along with ethnic integration and cultural exchanges, also saw many new developments, the most important of which was the prosperity of Buddhist architecture. Buddhist temples, pagodas and grottoes were the most prominent architectural types of this period.

唐代是中国封建社会经济文化发展的高潮时期。唐代的建筑发展到了一个成熟的时期，形成了一个完整的建筑体系。城市和宫殿的建设在唐代成就最为突出，唐代皇家园林的最大特点就是规模宏大，私家园林发展也极为繁盛。

Tang Dynasty was the climax of the economic and cultural development of Chinese feudal society. The architecture of Tang Dynasty developed to a mature period and formed a complete architectural system. The construction of cities and palaces was the most prominent in Tang Dynasty. The biggest feature of Tang Dynasty imperial gardens was its grand scale, and the development of private gardens was extremely popular.

宋代建筑发展的最重要的特点是模数化与定型化，《营造法式》是中国第一部有关建筑设计及技术经验总结的完整巨著。两宋的私家园林在北方以洛阳为代表，南方以苏州为代表。重礼强制使宋代成为中国历史上礼仪制度发展的最鼎盛时期，与此相应，宋代的礼制建筑业有长足的发展。配合各种祭祀活动都有相应的礼制建筑。宋代的礼制建筑主要有两大类：一是祭坛，一是祠庙。

The most important feature of the development of architecture in Song Dynasty was modularization and stereotypes. *Yingzao Fashi* (*Treatise on Architecture Methods*) was China's first complete masterpiece on architectural design and technical experience. The private gardens of Song Dynasty were represented by Luoyang city in the north and Suzhou city in the south. The emphasis on rituals made Song Dynasty the most prosperous period of the development of ritual buildings in Chinese history. Correspondingly, the ritual construction industry in Song Dynasty made considerable progress. Corresponding ritual architectures were available for various sacrificial activities. There were two main types of ritual architecture in Song Dynasty: one was the altar and the other was the ancestral temple.

元代兴建北京城，使其成为全中国的政治、经济和文化中心，并延续到明、清两代。观星台是中国现存最古老的天文建筑，也是世界上一座著名的天文科学古迹，它反映了中国古代天文学发展的卓越成就。明清建筑继汉、唐建筑之后，成为中国封建社会的最后一个高潮。明清建筑的最大成就是在园林领域，明代的江南私家园林和清代北方的皇家园林都是最具艺术性的传统建筑群。明清建筑还大量使用砖石，促进了砖石结构的发展。

The city of Beijing was built in Yuan Dynasty, making it the political, economic and cultural center of China, and it lasted into Ming and Qing dynasties. The Observatory is the oldest existing astronomical building in China and a famous astronomical monument in the world. It reflects the outstanding achievements of the development of ancient Chinese astronomy. The Ming and Qing architecture became the last climax of Chinese feudal society after the Han and Tang architecture. The greatest achievement of the Ming and Qing architecture was in the field of gardens. The private gardens in the south of the Yangtze River in Ming Dynasty and the royal gardens in the north of Qing Dynasty were the most artistic traditional architectural complexes. The buildings of Ming and Qing Dynasties also used a lot of masonry, which promoted the development of masonry structure.

二、中国传统建筑的主要特征 Main Features of Traditional Chinese Architecture

中国传统建筑是中国传统文化在居住方式上的反映，主要具有五大特征。

Traditional Chinese architecture is a reflection of traditional Chinese culture in the way of living, and it has five major characteristics.

1. 以木料为主要构材。古代中国是木建筑的王国，祖先对木材情有独钟并非因为森林资源丰富，而是受民族文化心理影响——现世为重，不求永恒。木结构建筑在节省材料、劳动力和施工时间方面显示出优越性。

Wood as the main construction material. Ancient China was a kingdom of wood architecture. The ancestors' special liking for wood was not because of their rich forest resources, but because of the psychological influence of the nation's culture——this life was more important than eternity. Wood structure buildings showed superiority in saving materials, labor and construction time.

2. 以斗拱为结构之关键。巧妙而科学的框架结构是中国传统建筑在建筑结构上最重要的一个特征。

Brackets as the key structure. Ingenious and scientific frame structure is the most important feature of traditional Chinese architecture in terms of architectural structure.

3. 庭院式的组群布局，审美上追求平稳、整齐、对称。

The courtyard-like group in layout. The traditional Chinese architecture pursues stability, neatness and symmetry aesthetically.

4. 丰富多彩的艺术形象。

Colorful artistic images.

5. 诗情画意的自然式园林。园林成为中国传统建筑的精华。从某种意义上说，园林已成了中国人精神上的归宿，中国古典园林崇尚自然，对自然的模仿达到极高的境界，反映了中国古人寄情山水、崇尚自然的生活情趣。

Poetic and picturesque natural gardens. The garden has become the essence of traditional Chinese architecture. In a sense, gardens have become the spiritual home of the Chinese. Classical Chinese gardens advocate nature and imitate nature to a very high level, reflecting the traditional Chinese people's love for landscape and nature.

三、中国传统建筑的人文意蕴 The Humanistic Implications of Traditional Chinese Architecture

1. 中国传统建筑追求"天人合一"观念的体现。春秋时代的老子就提出了"人法地，地法天，天法道，道法自然"的观点。这正是中国古代的朴素唯物主义者对人与自然关系的看法，指明了人与自然有共同的根源，这正是对"天人合一"思想的明确表述。中国古代的建筑设计者秉承这一思想，在建筑中融入人们对自然的认识，使建筑成为不只是人们生活活动的空间，还成为自然的象征。

Traditional Chinese architecture pursues the embodiment of the concept of "Unity of Man and Nature". In the Spring and Autumn Period, Lao Tzu put forward the view that "man follows the laws of the earth, earth follows the laws of the universe, the universe follows the laws of the Tao, the law of the Tao is in being what it is". This is the view of the simple materialists in ancient China on the relationship between man and nature, and it points out that man and nature have a common root. This is a clear expression of the idea of "the unity of man and nature". Traditional Chinese architects upheld this idea and integrated people's knowledge of nature in architecture, making architecture not only a space for people's living activities, but also a symbol of nature.

2. 中国自古即有"天圆地方"的观点。人们将这一观点用在了建筑上，就出现了一些方圆套用的建筑形式。以北京国子监辟雍为例，方形的辟雍殿建在环形河水之中，正是"天圆地方"思想融入建筑的一个典型代表。

Since ancient times, China has had a view of "Round Sky and Square Earth". When people apply this view to architecture, some architectural forms appear squares and circles together. Take Biyong in Beijing Imperial College as an example. The square Biyong Palace is built within the circular river, which is a typical example of the idea of "Round Sky and Square Earth" in architecture.

3. 中国传统建筑的"以人为本"。中国传统建筑的创作以现实生活为依据，没有高不可攀的尺度，没有逻辑不清的结构，没有节奏模糊的序列和不可理喻的装饰，不以孤高蛮霸来震慑人，却用博大精深的气势来震撼人心。

The "people-orientedness" of traditional Chinese architecture. The creation of traditional Chinese architecture was based on real life, there was no unattainable scale, no illogical structure, no unrhythmic sequence and unreasonable decoration, no proud or potency to intimidate people, but with a broad and profound aura to attract people.

4. 中国传统建筑文化的宇宙观念。中国传统建筑的审美强调单体建筑融于群体序列和自然环境的宇宙观念，即不仅在乎局部个性趣味，更在乎整体精神气质；不仅重视标新立异的创作，更重视秩序井然的维护；如人在中央，四方有四神明：青龙（东）、白虎（西）、朱雀（南）、玄武（北）。四神是保护人的神灵，同时它又代表着四种物质的宇宙态：木、金、火、水，加上中间人所处的土，于是形成"五行"。

The concept of the universe in traditional Chinese architectural culture. The aesthetics of traditional Chinese architecture emphasizes the cosmic concept of single buildings blending with the group sequence and the natural environment, that is, not only the local individuality and interest, but also the overall spiritual temperament; not only the unconventional creation, but also the maintenance of order; like people in the center, there were four gods in the four directions: Blue Dragon (East), White Tiger (West), Rosefinch (South), Black Tortoise (North). The four gods were the deities that protected people, and at the same time they represented the four cosmic states of matter: wood, gold, fire, water, and earth in the center where man was located, forming the "five elements".

五行的这五种物质与建筑关系密切，东为木，西为金，这是两种实物；南为火，北为水，这是两种虚物。所以大多数中国传统建筑东、西向多用实的山墙，南北向多用虚的门窗。

The five elements are closely related to architecture. The east is wood and the west is gold. These are two physical objects; the south is fire and the north is water. These are two virtual objects. Therefore, most traditional Chinese buildings used solid gables in the east and west, and virtual doors and windows in the north and south.

5. 艺术效果主要依靠群体序列来表现。传统建筑的单座造型比较简单，大部分是定型化的式样，任何一座孤立的建筑都不能构成完整的艺术形象。中国传统建筑结构有统一的数学比例关系。中国古代建筑广泛运用数的等差关系，以表现不同建筑等级的差别。屋脊走兽以十一为至多，依次递减至二个；斗拱挑出的层数有三、五、七、九、十一之分。

The effect of architectural art mainly depends on the group sequence. The single model of traditional buildings is relatively simple, and most of them are stereo-typed. Any isolated building cannot constitute a complete artistic image. There was a unified mathematical proportional relationship in Chinese traditional building struc-ture. The arithmetic relationship of numbers was widely used in traditional Chinese architecture to express the differences of different architectural levels. The number of beasts on the roof ridge was at most eleven, descending to two sequentially; the number of layers standing out by the brackets was three, five, seven, nine, and e-leven.

四、中国园林的美学特征 The Aesthetic Characteristics of Chinese Gardens

中国古典园林作为一个园林体系，若与世界上的其他体系相比较，它所具有的个性是鲜明的，而它的各个类型之间，又有着许多相同的共性。

As a garden system, classical Chinese gardens have distinct personalities com-pared with other systems in the world, and there are many similarities among its vari-ous types.

1. 本于自然，高于自然。山、水、植物乃是构成自然风景的基本要素，也是风景式园林的构景要素（建筑、山、水、植物）的三个方面。中国古典园林表现的是一个精炼概括的自然，典型化的自然。这就是中国古典园林的一个最主要特点。本于自然、高于自然是中国古典园林创作的主旨。目的在于求得一个概括、精炼典型而又不是自然生态的山水环境。它是感性的、主观的写意，侧重于表现主体对物像的审美感受和因之而引起的审美感情。这样的创作又必须合乎自然之理，方能获致天成之趣。

Based on nature but above nature. Mountains, water, and plants are the basic elements that make up the natural scenery, as well as the three aspects of the compo-sition elements of landscape gardens (buildings, mountains, water, plants). Clas-sical Chinese gardens express a refined, generalized, and typical nature. This is one of the most important features of classical Chinese gardens. Being based on nature but above nature, is the main theme of classical Chinese garden creation. The purpose is to obtain a general, refined and typical landscape environment that is not natural ecology. It is a perceptual and subjective freehand brushwork, focusing on the subject's aesthetic feelings towards objects and the aesthetic feelings caused by it. This kind of creation must conform to the principles of nature in order to gain natural interest.

2. 建筑美与自然美的融糅。中国古典园林的建筑无论多寡，也无论其性质、功能如何，都力求将山、水、花木这三个造园的要素有机地组织在一系列风景画中，突出彼此协调、互相补充的积极的一面，达到一种人工与自然高度协调的境界——天人谐和的境界。

The blend of architectural beauty and natural beauty. Regardless of the number of buildings in classical Chinese gardens, or regardless of their nature and functions, they strive to organize the three garden elements of mountains, water, and flowers and trees in a series of landscape paintings, highlighting the positive coordination and complement of one another. It achieves a realm of harmony between man power and natural force—the realm of harmony between man and nature.

3. 诗画的情趣。中国古典园林的创作，能充分地融诗画艺术于园林艺术，使得园林从总体到局部都包含着浓郁的诗画情趣。这就是通常所谓的"诗情画意"。

The taste of poetry and painting. The creation of classical Chinese gardens can fully integrate the art of poetry and painting with the art of gardening, making the gardens a poem and painting from the overall to the part. This is what is usually referred to as "poetic and picturesque".

4. 意境的涵蕴。简单说来，意即主观的理念、感情，境即客观的生活、景物。意境产生于艺术创作中两者的结合，即创作者把自己的感情、理念熔铸客观生活、景物之中，从而引发类似的情感激动和理念联想。

The implications of artistic conception. Simply put, conception means subjective ideas and feelings, and environment means objective life and scenery. Artistic conception arises from the combination of the two in artistic creation, that is, the creator casts his own feelings and ideas into objective life and scenery, thereby triggering similar emotional excitement and conceptual associations.

中国园林与中国文化的底蕴一致，作为一种文化信息载体，中国园林的发展包含了心灵深层次的文体审美信息。沈复在《浮生六记》中说："大中见小，小中见大，虚中有实，实中有虚，或藏或露，或浅或深，不仅在周回曲折四字也。"这就是中国园林美学的最大特点。

Chinese gardens are consistent with Chinese culture. As a kind of cultural information carrier, the development of Chinese gardens contains profound spiritual and aesthetic information. Shen Fu said in *Six Chapters of a Floating Life*："The big can be seen in the small, the small in the big; the empty has the real, the real has the empty; sometimes hidden sometimes exposed, either shallow or deep, not just expressed by the four Chinese characters of round, back, curve, and zigzag." This is the major feature of Chinese garden aesthetics.

五、中国的传统民居 Traditional Chinese Houses

1. 羌族碉楼。羌族民居为石片砌成的平顶房，呈方形，多数为 3 层，每层高 3 米多。房顶平台的最下面是木板或石板，伸出墙外成屋檐。木板或石板上密覆树丫或竹枝，再压盖黄土和鸡粪夯实，有洞槽引水，不漏雨雪，冬暖夏凉。房顶平台是脱粒、晒粮、做针线活及孩子老人游戏休憩的场地。走进每个羌寨，可以看到各家各户的房顶上都有白石英石，那是羌民敬奉的白石神。羌寨中最具特色的莫过于碉楼，已经有 2000 多年的历史，羌碉有 30 米高，共有 9 层。

Qiang Diaolou (watchtowers of the Qiang people). The dwellings of the Qiang nationality are flat-roofed houses made of slabs of stone, which are square in shape, mostly with three floors, each with a height of more than 3 meters. The bottom of the roof platform is a wooden or stone slab, which extends out of the wall to form an eave. The planks or stone slabs are densely covered with tree or bamboo branches, and then covered with loess and chicken manure to ram, with holes for diversion, not leaking rain or snow, warm in winter and cool in summer. The roof platform is a place for threshing, drying grain, needlework and games for children and the elderly. Walking into each Qiang village, you can see white quartz stone on the roof of each household, which is the god of white stone worshipped by the Qiang people. The most distinctive of Qiang Village is the Diaolou, which has a history of more than 2, 000 years. The Qiang Diaolou is 30 meters high and has 9 floors.

2. 藏族碉房。在青藏高原，碉房是藏族普遍使用的一种民居建筑形式，是用乱石垒砌而成的房子，高二至四层，外观很像碉堡，所以被称为"碉房"。由于藏族信仰藏传佛教，诵经拜佛的经堂占有重要位置，神位上方不能住人或堆放杂物，以示对佛的尊敬，所以经堂都设在房屋的顶层，这是一家中最神圣、最庄严的地方。

Tibetan blockhouses. On Qinghai – Tibet Plateau, blockhouses are commonly used by Tibetans. They are houses built of various stones. They are two to four storeys high and look like blockhouses, so they are called "blockhouses". As Tibetans believe in Tibetan Buddhism, the scripture hall for chanting and worshiping the Buddha occupies an important position. No people or piles of debris can be placed above the god to show respect to the Buddha. Therefore, the scripture hall is set up on the top floor of the house. This is the most sacred and the most solemn place in the house.

3. 徽州民居。徽州民居的外部造型非常简洁，建筑的四面都是白色墙壁，很少开窗子。徽州民居的大门由石库门和门楼两部分组成，内部造型为楼房形式，正房（厅堂）是人字形屋顶，大多是三开间，中间开间的楼上、楼下都是不带门窗的敞厅形式。所有屋顶都向院内倾斜，没有向外倾斜的屋顶，一旦下雨，雨水都流到自家的院子里面。徽州人崇尚自然美，追求人与自然高度的和谐和统一。这就集中体现在徽州建筑的风水美。在徽州古民居建筑中，儒家严格的等级制度，以及尊卑有别、男女有别、长幼有序的封建道德观表现得也十分明显。实用性与艺术性的完美统一，是徽州民居的又一典型特点。

Huizhou folk dwelling. The exterior shape of Huizhou residential buildings is very simple, with white walls on all sides of the building and few windows. The gate of Huizhou folk house consists of two parts: Shikumen (Stone – framed door) and gate tower. The internal shape is in the form of a building. The main room (hall) has a gable roof, mostly three – bay. The upper and lower floors of the middle bay are open without doors and windows. All roofs are sloping toward the courtyard, and there is no roof sloping outwards. Once it rains, rainwater flows into the courtyard of the house. Huizhou people advocate natural beauty and pursue a high degree of harmony and unity between man and nature. This is concentrated in the geomantic beauty of Huizhou architecture. In Huizhou ancient residential buildings, the strict hierarchy of Confucianism and the feudal ethics of distinction between superiority and inferiority, distinction between man and women, and respect for seniority were also very obvious. The perfect unity of practicality and artistry is another typical feature of Huizhou residential buildings.

4. 江南水乡民居。密如蛛网的水道交通网络，贯穿整个城镇与乡村，形成特有的水乡景色。家家临水，户户通舟；水巷小桥多，人家尽枕河；民居多古朴，住宅尽清幽。

Jiangnan Watertown Folk Houses. The dense cobweb-like waterway traffic network runs through the entire town and village, forming unique water village scenery. Every family is close to the water, and every family can go on boats; there are many alleys and small bridges, and people rest on the river; the houses are more primitive and quiet.

5. 客家土楼。土楼是以土作墙而建造起来的大型集体建筑，呈圆形、半圆形、方形、四角形、五角形等，各具特色，其中以圆形最引人注目，当地人称之为圆楼或圆寨。圆楼是当地土楼群中最具特色的建筑，一般它以一个圆心出发，依不同的半径，一层层向外展开，非常壮观。其最中心处为家族祠院，最外一环住人。

Hakka Tulou (earth building). Tulou is a large-scale collective building built with earth as walls. It is round, semicircular, square, quadrangular, or pentagonal, each with its own characteristics. Among them, the round one is the most eye-catching, and the locals call it the round building, or Yuanzhai (means round village). The round building is the most distinctive building in the local tulou group. Generally, it starts from a center and spreads out layer by layer according to different radii, which is very spectacular. The most central part is the family shrine, and the outermost ring live people.

6. 窑洞。窑洞是中国西北黄土高原上居民的古老居住形式，这一"穴居式"民居的历史可以追溯到4000多年前。窑洞一般窑壁用石灰涂抹，显得白晃晃的，干爽亮堂。窑洞内一侧有锅和灶台，在炕的一头都连着灶台，由于灶火的烟道通过炕底，冬天炕上很暖和。窑洞防火，防噪音，冬暖夏凉，既节省土地，又经济省工，确是因地制宜的完美建筑形式。

Cave dwelling. Cave dwellings are an ancient form of residence for residents on the Loess Plateau in northwest China. The history of this "cavern-style" dwelling can be traced back to more than 4, 000 years ago. Generally, the walls of the cave dwellings are painted with lime, which looks white, dry and bright. There are pots and stoves on one side of the cave, and the stove is connected to one end of the kang (a heatable brick bed). Because the flue of the stove passes through the bottom of the kang, it is very warm on the kang in winter. The cave dwelling is fireproof, noiseproof, warm in winter and cool in summer. It saves land and is economical and labor-saving. It is indeed a perfect building form adapted to local conditions.

7. 四合院，又称四合房，是中国的一种传统合院式建筑，其格局为一个院子四面建有房屋，从四面将庭院合围在中间，故名四合院。四合院就是三合院前面又加门房的屋舍来封闭。若呈"口"字形的称为一进院落；"日"字形的称为二进院落；"目"字形的称为三进院落。一般而言，大宅院中，第一进为门屋，第二进是厅堂，第三进或后进为私室或闺房，是妇女或眷属的活动空间，一般人不得随意进入，难怪古人有诗云："庭院深深深几许"。庭院越深，越不得窥其堂奥。四合院至少有3000多年的历史，在中国各地有多种类型，其中以北京四合院为典型。四合院通常为大家庭所居住，提供了对外界比较隐秘的庭院空间，其建筑和格局体现了中国传统的尊卑等级思想以及阴阳五行学说。

Siheyuan (Quadrangle Courtyard), also known as Sihefang (Quadrangle house), is a traditional courtyard-style building in China. Its layout is a courtyard with houses on all sides, enclosing the courtyard from all sides in the middle, hence the name Siheyuan. Siheyuan is a house with a gatehouse in the front. If it is in the shape of "口", it is called a house with one courtyard; those with a shape of "日" are called a house with two courtyards; those with a shape of "目" are called a house with three courtyards. Generally speaking, in large houses, the first courtyard is the gatehouse, the second courtyard is the hall, and the third or last courtyard is the private rooms or boudoirs, which is the living space for women or family members. Most people are not allowed to enter at will. No wonder the ancients said: "The courtyard is deep and deep". The deeper the courtyard is, the less you can see its secrets. Siheyuan has a history of at least 3, 000 years, and there are many types throughout China, among which Beijing Siheyuan is a typical example. Siheyuan is usually inhabited by large families and provides a courtyard space that is relatively secret to the outside world. Its architecture and layout reflect traditional Chinese thought of superiority and inferiority and the theory of Yin and Yang and Five Elements.

中国的传统绘画文化

一、中国传统绘画的起源 The Origin of Traditional Chinese Painting

中国画画龄以千年计，形成了笔法、构图法、皴法等一套固定的模式，所以具有此种风格的国画称为传统绘画。

The age of Chinese painting has been thousands of years, and it has formed a set of fixed patterns such as brushwork, composition, and wrinkle method, so Chinese paintings with this style are called traditional paintings.

有关中国绘画的起源问题，像有关中国历史的起源一样，令人不可捉摸。究竟中国的绘画开始于何时？何地？是何人所创造？这一谜团千年以来一直萦绕在历代美术史研究者的思绪中。唐代的张彦远在他的开创性著作《历代名画记》中，将中国绘画的起源追溯到传说时代，指出那时的象形文字便是书写与绘画的统一。而在他看来，图形与文字的脱离，才使得绘画成为一门专门的艺术，探讨绘画技巧的工作则晚至秦汉才开始，魏晋时名家的出现，才标志着绘画臻于成熟。这1000多年前提出的有关早期中国绘画发展的理论至今仍基本成立。所不同的是现代考古发掘出土了大量的史前和历史早期绘画形象的实物，不断增加着我们对早期绘画艺术的了解。中国新石器时代的造型艺术，在彩陶及绘画、陶塑和雕刻方面，均有一定的成就。中国画这一艺术形式之所以能在世界绘画史上占有极其重要的地位，是因为它代表了东方民族特殊的艺术审美观念。纵观中国绘画史，从隋代的展子虔到清代"四僧"再到近代的黄宾虹、齐白石、徐悲鸿等，对中国的传统绘画都有不同的贡献。

The question of the origin of Chinese painting is as unpredictable as the origin of Chinese history. When did Chinese painting begin? Where? Who created it? This mystery has been haunting the minds of art history researchers of the past thousands of years. Zhang Yanyuan of Tang Dynasty traced the origin of Chinese painting back to the legendary era in his seminal book *Famous Paintings in Past Dynasties*, pointing out that the hieroglyphics at that time were the unity of writing and painting. In his view, the separation of graphics and text made painting a specialized art. The work of exploring painting techniques did not begin until Qin and Han Dynasties. The appearance of famous artists during Wei and Jin Dynasties marked the maturity of painting. The theory about the development of early Chinese painting that was put forward more than 1, 000 years ago is still generally established. The difference is that modern archaeological excavations have unearthed a large number of real objects of prehistoric and early historical painting images, which continue to increase our understanding of early painting art. The plastic arts of the Neolithic Age in China have made certain achievements in painted pottery, painting and sculpture. The reason why the art form of Chinese painting can occupy an extremely important position in the history of world painting is that it represents the special artistic aesthetic concept of the Eastern nations. Throughout the history of Chinese painting, from Zhan Ziqian in Sui Dynasty to the "Four Monks" in Qing Dynasty to modern Huang Binhong, Qi Baishi and Xu Beihong, they all have different contributions to traditional Chinese painting.

我们习惯上把从公元前 21 世纪建立的夏朝开始，经过商、西周直到春秋、战国的这一时间段统称为先秦。由于铜器和铁器的相继发明和推广，加上社会分工的进一步扩大，社会生产力显著提高，各种手工业得到了迅速发展。除了为礼教服务的青铜艺术、商周的玉石雕刻及战国的彩漆木雕以外，寓有兴废之诚的庙堂壁画及人物肖像画，受到了先秦统治者的普遍重视。

We are accustomed to refer to the period from Xia Dynasty established in the 21st century BC to the period from Shang Dynasty and the Western Zhou Dynasty to the Spring and Autumn Period and the Warring States Period as the pre-Qin period. Due to the successive invention and promotion of bronze and ironware, as well as the further expansion of social division of labor, social productivity increased significantly, and various handicraft industries developed rapidly. In addition to the bronze art that served ethics and rites, the jade carvings of Shang and Zhou Dynasties, and the color lacquered wood carvings of the Warring States, temple murals and portrait paintings containing the commandments of rise and fall were generally valued by pre-Qin rulers.

二、中国传统绘画的特点 Characteristics of Traditional Chinese Painting

用笔和用墨，是中国画造型的重要部分。用笔讲求粗细、疾徐、顿挫、转折、方圆等变化，以表现物体的质感。一般来说，起笔和止笔都要用力，力腕宜挺，中间气不可断，住笔不可轻挑。用笔时力轻则浮，力重则钝，疾运则滑，徐运则滞，偏用则薄，正用则板。要做到曲行如弓，直行如尺，这都是用笔之意。古人总结有勾线十八描，可以说是中国画用笔的经验总结。而对于用墨，则讲求皴、擦、点、染交互为用，干、湿、浓、淡合理调配，以塑造型体，烘染气氛。一般说来，中国画的用墨之妙，在于浓淡相生，全浓全淡都没有精神，必须有浓有淡，浓处须精彩而不滞，淡处须灵秀而不晦。用墨亦如用色，古有墨分五彩之经验，亦有惜墨如金的画风。用墨还要有浓淡相生相融，做到浓中有淡，淡中有浓；浓要有最浓与次浓，淡要有稍淡与更淡，这都是中国画的灵活用笔之法。由于中国画与书法在工具及运笔方面有许多共同之处，二者结下了不解之缘，古人早有"书画同源"之说。但是二者也存在着差异，书法运笔变化多端，尤其是草书，要胜过绘画，而绘画的用墨丰富多彩，又超过书法。笔墨二字被当做中国画技法的总称，它不仅仅是塑造形象的手段，本身还具有独立的审美价值。

How to use paint brush and ink is an important part of Chinese painting modeling. It emphasizes changes in thickness, rapidity, pause, turning, and squareness to express the texture of the object. Generally speaking, we must use force when starting and stopping the paint brush. The wrist should be straight. The breath should not be broken in the middle. Don't hold the pen lightly. When we use the paint brush, the painting will be buoyant if we use light force, but if we are heavy, the painting will be blunt; rapidly, slippery; slowly, sluggish; partially, thin; impartially, rigid. To behave like a bow and straight like a ruler, this is the gist of using paintbrush. The ancients summed up with eighteen methods on the line drawing, which can be said to be a summary of the experience of Chinese painting in how to use paintbrush. As for the ink, it emphasizes the interaction of dipping, rubbing, dotting, and dyeing, and the dryness, wetness, thickness and lightness are properly mixed to shape the body and foil the atmosphere. Generally, the beauty of using ink in Chinese painting lies in the combination of lightness and darkness. There must be no spirit in all thickness and lightness. There must be thickness and lightness alternately, the thickness/density must be wonderful but not stagnant, and the lightness must be delicate but not obscure. Using ink is like using color. In ancient times, there was the experience of dividing ink into five colors, and there was also a painting style that cherished ink like gold. In the use of ink, there must be a blend of thickness and lightness, so that the thickness within the lightness, the lightness within the thickness; the thickness should have the thickest and the second thickest, and the lightness should have lightness and the slight lightness. This is the flexible use of Chinese paintbrush. Since Chinese painting and calligraphy have many things in common in tools and brushstrokes, the two have forged an indissoluble bond. The ancients said that "calligraphy and painting have the same origin". However, there are also differences between the two. There are many variations in calligraphy, especially in cursive script, which is better than painting, and the use of ink in painting is richer and more colorful than calligraphy. The two Chinese characters of brush and ink are regarded as the general term of Chinese painting techniques. They are not only a means to shape the image, but also have an independent aesthetic value.

中国画在敷色方面也有自己的讲究，所用颜料多为天然矿物质或动物外壳的粉末，耐风吹日晒，经久不变。敷色方法多为平涂，追求物体固有色的效果，很少有光影的变化。

Chinese paintings also have their own particulars in applying colors. The pigments used are mostly natural minerals or powder from animal shells, which are resistant to wind and sun and remain unchanged for a long time. The color application method is mostly flat coating, pursuing the effect of the inherent color of the object, with little light and shadow changes.

三、中国传统绘画的基本原则 Basic Principles of Traditional Chinese Painting

什么是中国画的传统？根据中国画发展的特点，主要有以下五点：

What is the tradition of Chinese painting? According to the characteristics of the development of Chinese painting, there are mainly the following five points:

1. 以形写神、形神兼备。中国画讲究气韵、追求意境。一个画家应具备"画得像"的功夫。但如果作品有形无神，那么即使画得再像也不是中国画所要达到的目的。有形无神的画是存在的，而有神无形的画是不存在的。写形是为了传神、为了畅神。形可在"似与不似之间"。我们知道，"以形写神"的最终目的是"达意"。中国画历来要求以"形"这个支架表现"神"。这个"神"指的是客观对象的生命力、生动气韵和本质特征。"形"是次要的，而"神"是主要的。也就是说，画得太像就太俗了；画得一点儿也不像，更不是中国画。所谓"意象造型"就是这个道理。

Conveying spirit through form and having both form and spirit. Chinese painting pays attention to charm and artistic conception. A painter should have the skill to "paint alike". But if the work is tangible and spiritless, then even if it looks quite alike it is not the goal of Chinese painting. There are tangible and spiritless paintings, but there are no paintings with spirit but no form. The form painted is for expressiveness and vividness. The shape can be between "alike and unlike". We know that the ultimate goal of "conveying spirit through form" is to "express the meaning." Chinese painting has always required the use of "shape" to express "spirit". This "spirit" refers to the vitality, vivacity and essence of the object. "Shape" is secondary, while "spirit" is primary. In other words, it is too vulgar to paint too much alike; it is no Chinese painting if not alike at all. That is the meaning of the so-called "imagery modeling".

2. 以线、墨为主，讲究笔法。中国画追求"笔精墨妙"的艺术效果，讲究骨法用笔。这些都是对笔墨内涵的要求。"骨法"又作"骨力"，指书写点画中蕴蓄的笔力。它是构成点画与形体的支柱，也是表现神情的依凭。画家以挺劲的笔法将自己的感情倾注到形象中，使其更具有生命力。在造型过程中，画家的感情就一直和笔力融在一起。笔所到之处，留下的尽为画家感情活动的痕迹。

Mainly based on line and ink, paying attention to brushwork. Traditional Chinese painting pursues the artistic effect of "exquisite brushwork and ink", and especially in brushwork. These are all requirements for the connotation of brush and ink. "Structural Technique" is also referred to as "Structural Strength", which refers to the brush power accumulated in writing and painting. It is the pillar that constitutes the stippling and the body, and it is also the basis for expressing the look. The painter pours his feelings into the image with a vigorous brushwork, making it more vital. In the forming process, the artist's feelings have been blended with the brushwork. Wherever the brush goes, it leaves all traces of the artist's emotional activities.

3. 以墨为主，"尚纯而戒驳"。中国画虽也讲究随类赋彩，但最重要的是画面整体效果。为了整体的需要，对象的色彩可以做大的变动。在中国画中，无论是平涂的重色，还是晕染的轻色，都"尚纯而戒驳"。墨是中国画必不可少的基本色。强调"墨分五色"。墨分为焦墨、浓墨、重墨、淡墨、清墨五种，每一种墨色若运用得巧妙、适当，则会呈现丰富的变化。

Mainly use the ink, emphasizing "Pure but not heterogeneous ink". Although Chinese painting also pays attention to color according to the category, the most important thing is the overall effect of the picture. For the overall needs, the color of the object can be greatly changed. In Chinese paintings, whether it is the heavy color of flat painting or the light color of shading, they are "pure and far from heterogeneity". Ink is an indispensable basic color for Chinese painting. Ink can be divided into five types: burnt ink, thick ink, heavy ink, light ink and clear ink. If each ink color is used ingeniously and appropriately, it will present rich changes.

4. 构图讲究气势，不受透视规律束缚。画家取景时，要步步移、面面观；要善于利用纸的空白，做到疏中有物、密而不闷。"画意"是画家精神感受的传达。构思"画意"是创作的开始。它是理性与非理性的统一。"画意"在构思之后并不是不可变化，而是可根据需要在作画过程中不断调整。画家边作画边改变自己的"画意"，在逐步完善绘画中寻找创作的乐趣。因此，作品的"画意"产生于作画前，完善于创作中。

The composition emphasizes momentum and is not bound by the laws of perspective. When framing the scene, the painter must move step by step and look at different aspects; he must make good use of the blank space of the paper, so that there are objects in the sparse, dense but not stuffy. "Picture" is the conveyance of the artist's spiritual feelings. The idea of "painting" is the beginning of creation. It is the unity of rationality and irrationality. "Painting meaning" is not unchangeable after being conceived, but can be adjusted continuously during the painting process as needed. The painter changes his "painting intention" while painting, seeking the joy of creation while gradually improving his painting. Therefore, the "painting meaning" of the work is produced before painting and is perfected in the creation.

构图是因得势而称尽善的，是因所欲得之势不同而变化的。构图、布势有两种，一张一敛。张的力量是向外扩散，呈辐射状，能给人一种画外有画的感觉；敛的力量是向内集结，能给人一种画中有画的感觉。一张一敛以求其变、求其势。

The composition is perfect because of gaining power, and it changes because of the different desired power. There are two kinds of composition and posture, tension and convergence. The tension power spreads outwards, radiating, which can give people a feeling of painting outside the painting; the power of convergence is gathering inward, giving people a feeling of painting within the painting. Tension and convergence are to seek its change and its momentum.

5. 强调宏观把握世界，"以大观小"。中国绘画主张用历史的眼光、全局的眼光、发展的眼光来观察世界。中国画创作可以超越复杂的时空关系，对复杂的客观世界，作概括的自由描绘。以"写意"为特点的中国艺术观、以线为主的中国笔墨观和以"程式"为主的高度意匠等构成中国传统绘画的特点。

Emphasizing the macro-control of the world, "viewing the small from the big". Chinese painting advocates observing the world from a historical perspective, an overall perspective, and a development perspective. The creation of Chinese painting can transcend the complicated time-space relationship and make a general free description of the complex objective world. The Chinese art viewpoint characterized by "freehand brushwork", the Chinese brush and ink viewpoint based on lines, and the artistic conception based on "pattern", constitute the characteristics of traditional Chinese painting.

四、中国传统绘画的分类 Classification of Traditional Chinese Painting

1. 中国传统绘画形式是国画，是一种以水为媒介调和颜料在纸上、绢上或墙上的绘画。从艺术的分科来看，中国画可分为山水、花鸟、人物三大画科，它主要是以描绘对象的不同来划分的。而中国画中的畜兽、鞍马、昆虫、蔬果等画可分别归入此三类。

The traditional Chinese painting form is national Chinese painting, which is a kind of painting on paper, silk or wall using water as a medium to blend paint. From the perspective of art divisions, traditional Chinese painting can be divided into three major painting divisions: landscapes, flowers and birds, and portraits, which are mainly based on different painting objects. The paintings of animals, horses, insects, fruits and vegetables in Chinese paintings can be classified into these three categories.

山水画：欣赏中国山水画，先要了解国画制作者的胸襟意象。画家把名山大川的特色，先储于心，再形于手，所以不以"肖形"为佳，而以"通意"为主。一树一石、一台一亭，皆可代表画家的意境。不必斤斤计较透视、比例等显示的问题。

花鸟画：动物种类繁多，大小不一，狮、虎、猫、犬可称为走兽，各种鱼类可称为游鱼，蝉、蝶、蜻蜓称为草虫，各种雀鸟称为翎毛。动物画可以归到花鸟画一类。

人物画：可分为道释人物、仕女、肖像三大类。道释人物多绘仙佛鬼怪，仕女专指女性题材，肖像则重写生传神。因人物需刻画动作神态，故为画科中精深者。

Landscape painting. To appreciate Chinese landscape painting, we must first understand the mind and image of the maker of the Chinese painting. The painter first stores the characteristics of famous mountains and rivers in his mind and then forms them in his hands. Therefore, it is not better to paint "alike" but to "express". One tree, one stone, one platform, one pavilion can all represent the artist's mood. Don't worry about display issues such as perspective ratio.

Flower and bird painting. There are many kinds of animals of different sizes. Lions, tigers, cats, and dogs can be called beasts, all kinds of fish can be called swimming fish, cicadas, butterflies, and dragonflies are called insects, and all kinds of birds are called feathers. Animal painting can be classified as flower and bird painting.

Figure Painting: Traditionally categorized into three major types: Taoist and Buddhist figures, court ladies, and portraiture. Taoist and Buddhist figures predominantly depict immortals, buddhas, and mythical beings; court ladies focus on feminine themes, while portraiture emphasizes lifelike representation and spiritual essence. As figure painting requires the meticulous portrayal of gestures and facial expressions, it stands as one of the most technically demanding disciplines in Chinese painting.

2. 根据制作技巧、笔法，国画还可以分为工笔、写意和兼工带写。

工笔画：用细致的笔法制作。工笔画着重线条美，一丝不苟，是工笔画的特色。

写意画：以心驱笔、意存笔先，谓之意笔。写意画不囿于形似线条，更重笔墨意趣，与工笔的工整形成对照，而气韵灵动尤具独特表现力。

According to painting skills and brushwork, traditional Chinese painting can also be divided into elaborate-style brushwork, freehand brushwork, and elaborate-style with freehand brushwork.

Elaborate-style painting (Gong bi painting). It is produced with meticulous brushwork. Elaborate-style painting emphasizes the beauty of lines and that painting is meticulous, which is the characteristic of elaborate-style painting.

Freehand-style Painting (Xieyi): Guided by the dictum "the heart commands the brush, with intent preceding the stroke", this style is termed yibi (conceptual brushwork). Freehand painting transcends rigid adherence to formal resemblance in lines, prioritizing instead the expressive interplay of brush and ink. In contrast to the precision of meticulous-style (gongbi) painting, it exhibits a unique expressive power through dynamic spiritual resonance.

五、中国传统绘画与西洋画的比较 Comparison of Traditional Chinese Painting and Western Painting

相对西洋画来说，中国画有着自己鲜明的特征。传统的中国画不采用焦点透视，不强调自然界对于物体的光色变化，不拘泥于物体外表的肖似，而多强调抒发作者的主观情趣。中国画讲求"以形写神"，追求一种"妙在似与不似之间"的感觉。而西洋画则讲求"以形写形"，当然，创作的过程中，也注重"神"的表现。但它非常讲究画面的整体、概括。有人说，西洋画是"再现"的艺术，中国画是"表现"的艺术，这是不无道理的。

Compared with western painting, traditional Chinese painting has its own distinct characteristics. Traditional Chinese painting does not emphasize the focus perspective, the light and color change of the object in nature, and the resemblance of the object, but the subjective interest of the painter. Traditional Chinese painting emphasizes "conveying spirit through form" and pursues a feeling of "the beauty lies between the like and the unlike". The western painting emphasizes "expressing forms in form". Of course, in the process of creation, western painters also pay attention to the expression of "spirit". But western painting is very particular about the overall and generalization of the picture. It's said that western painting is the art of "reproduction" while Chinese painting is the art of "expression". This is not unreasonable.

中国画与西洋画相比有着自己独有的特征，还表现在其艺术手法、艺术分科、构图、用笔、用墨、敷色等多个方面。按照艺术的手法来分，中国画可分为工笔、写意和兼工带写三种形式。工笔就是用画笔工整细致，敷色层层渲染，细节明彻入微，用极其细腻的笔触描绘物象，故称"工笔"。而写意呢？相对"工笔"而言，用豪放简练的笔墨描绘物象的形神抒发作者的感情。它要有高度的概括能力，要有以少胜多的含蓄意境，落笔要准确，运笔要熟练，要能得心应手，意到笔到。兼工带写的形式则是把工笔和写意这两种方法进行综合的运用。

Compared with western painting, traditional Chinese painting has its own unique characteristics, which are also expressed in its artistic techniques, artistic division, composition, brush, ink, and color application. According to the artistic techniques,

Chinese painting can be divided into three forms: elaborate-style brushwork, free-hand brushwork, and both. Elaborate brushwork is to use brushes neatly and meticulously, with layers of color applied to render, with clear details, and extremely delicate brushstrokes to depict objects, so it is called "elaborate-style brushwork". How about freehand brushwork? Compared with "elaborate-style brushwork", the bold and concise brush and ink are used to describe the shape and spirit of the object and express the painter's feelings. It requires a high degree of generalization ability, the implicit mood of winning more with less. The brush must be used accurately, proficiently handled. Elaborate and freehand brushwork is a comprehensive application of the two methods.

中国画在构图、用笔、用墨、敷色等方面，也都有自己的特点。中国画的构图一般不遵循西洋画的黄金律，而是或作长卷，或作立轴，长宽比例是"失调"的。但它能够很好表现特殊的意境和画者的主观情趣。同时，在透视的方法上，中国画与西洋画也是不一样的。透视就是在作画的时候，把一切物体正确地在平面上表现出来，使之有远近高低的空间感和立体感，这种方法就叫透视。因透视的现象是近大远小，所以也常常称作"远近法"。西洋画一般是用焦点透视，这就像照相一样，固定在一个立脚点，受到空间的局限，摄入镜头的就如实照下来，否则就照不下来。中国画就不一定固定在一个立脚点作画，也不受固定视域的局限，它可以根据画者的感受和需要，使立脚点移动作画，把见得到的和见不到的景物统统摄入自己的画面。这种透视的方法，叫做散点透视或多点透视，如著名的北宋名画、张择端的《清明上河图》，用的就是散点透视法。《清明上河图》反映的是北宋都城汴梁内外丰富复杂、气象万千的景象。它以汴河为中心，从远处的郊野画到热闹的"虹桥"；观者既能看到城内，又可看到郊野；既看得到桥上的行人，又看得到桥下的船；既看得到近处的楼台树木，又看得到远处纵深的街道与河港。而且无论站在哪一段看，景物的比例都是相近的，如果按照西洋画焦点透视的方法去画，许多地方是根本无法画出来的。这是中国的古代画家们根据内容和艺术表现的需要而创造出来的独特的透视方法。

Traditional Chinese painting also has its own characteristics in terms of composition, brush, ink and color. The composition of traditional Chinese paintings generally does not follow the golden rule of western paintings. Instead, they are painted on long scrolls or vertical scrolls, and the ratio of length to width is "out of balance". But such paintings can well express the special mood and subjective interest of the painter. At the same time, in the method of perspective, traditional Chinese painting and western painting are also different. Perspective is to say when painting, all objects are correctly expressed on a plane, so that they have a sense of space and three-dimensionality. This method is called perspective. Because the phenomenon of perspective is near large and far small, it is often called "far-near method". Western paintings generally use focus perspective, which is like a picture fixed on a standpoint. Due to the limitation of space, what is taken in the lens will be taken as real, otherwise it will not be taken. Chinese painting is not necessarily fixed at a standpoint for painting, nor is it limited by a fixed horizon. It can move the standpoint to paint according to the painter's feelings and needs, and incorporate all the sights and unseen scenes into their own pictures. This method of perspective is called cavalier perspective or multipoint perspective. For example, the famous paintings by Zhang Zeduan of the Northern Song Dynasty Along the River During the Qingming Festival, cavalier perspective is used Along the River During the Qingming Festival reflects the rich, complex and varied scenes inside and outside the capital of Bianliang in the Northern Song Dynasty. It is centered on Bianhe River, from the remote countryside to the lively "Rainbow Bridge"; the viewer can see both the city and the countryside; both the pedestrians on the bridge and the boats under the bridge; We can see not only the trees near the terraces, but also the deep streets and river ports in the distance. No matter which part we look at, the proportions of the scenes are similar. If we paint according to the method of the focus perspective of western painting, many places cannot be drawn at all. This is a unique perspective method created by ancient Chinese painters based on the content and artistic expression needs.

六、中国传统绘画著名画家 Famous Traditional Chinese Painters

中华古代具有里程碑意义的画家有：顾恺之、吴道子、王维、荆浩、李唐、赵孟頫、倪瓒、董其昌、朱耷、石涛等。他们的画潇洒飘逸，深入人心。

时而是对景物的深厚情感，时而是对时势的不满，时而又表现出自己内心的凄凉。

Pivotal artists in ancient Chinese painting history include Gu Kaizhi, Wu Daozi, Wang Wei, Jing Hao, Li Tang, Zhao Mengfu, Ni Zan, Dong Qichang, Zhu Da, and Shi Tao. Their paintings are chic and elegant, deeply rooted in the hearts of the people. Sometimes it's the deep feelings for the scenery, sometimes it's the dissatisfaction with the current situation, and sometimes it shows one's bleakness at heart.

1. 顾恺之

中华绘画史上，魏晋南北朝（公元 220 年~公元 581 年）是一个非常重要的历史时期。东晋顾恺之（公元 348 年~公元 409 年）字长康，汉族，晋陵无锡（今江苏无锡）人。顾恺之博学有才气，工诗赋、书法，尤善绘画。精于人像、佛像、禽兽、山水等，时人称之为三绝：画绝、文绝和痴绝。谢安深重之，以为苍生以来未之有，为中华传统绘画的发展奠定了基础。

In the history of traditional Chinese painting, Wei, Jin, Southern and Northern Dynasties (220~581 AD) were a very important historical period. In the Eastern Jin Dynasty, Gu Kaizhi (348~409 AD), also named Changkang, was of Han nationality and born in Wuxi, Jinling (now Wuxi, Jiangsu province). Gu Kaizhi was erudite and talented, good at poetry, calligraphy, and especially at painting. He was proficient in portraits, buddhas, animals, landscapes, etc., entitled three excellences in painting, writing, and infatuation. The poet Xie An valued him so much that such a person had never been born ever before. Gu Kaizhi laid a foundation for the development of traditional Chinese painting.

2. 吴道子

吴道子（约公元 680 年~公元 759 年），唐代画家，画史尊称吴生，又名道玄。汉族，阳翟（今河南禹州）人。被尊称为"画圣"的人，非天纵奇才不能获如此殊荣，吴道子也确实厉害，他的许多发明创造是中华画史中的最亮点，诸如高度的写实技巧、笔法的解放、推动水墨山水萌芽等，皆是肇始于吴道子。吴道子对中华绘画的贡献是划时代的，如果没有他，中华画的发展不会如现在我们所见，历史也会随之改弦易辙。

Wu Daozi (approximately 680~759 AD) was a Tang Dynasty painter. In the history of painting he is called Master Wu, also known as Daoxuan, Han nationality, from Yangzhai (now Yuzhou, Henan province). He who is honoured as "Painting Sage" cannot be awarded such honors without outstanding talents. Wu Daozi was indeed excellent. Many of his inventions and creations are the highlights in the history of traditional Chinese painting, such as high - level realistic skills, liberation of brushwork, and Pioneered the embryonic development of ink-wash landscape painting, all beginning with him. Wu Daozi's contribution to traditional Chinese painting is epoch-making. Without him, the development of Chinese painting would not be as what we see now, and history might change the course.

3. 王维

王维（公元701年~公元761年），字摩诘，汉族，祖籍山西祁县，唐朝诗人，外号"诗佛"。他的画喜用雪景剑阁栈道等题材，其画最重要的特色是诗和画的有机结合，创造了诗情画意的境界。他首创了中国山水画中优美独特的禅境表现，在山水画中真正实现了天人合一的审美境界。后人推其为南宗山水画之祖。

Wang Wei (701~761 AD), named Mojie, Han nationality, ancestral home in Qixian County, Shanxi province, a Tang Dynasty poet, nicknamed "Poetry Buddha". He liked to use snow scenes, sword pavilions, boardwalks as subject matters in his paintings. The most important feature of his paintings was the organic combination of poetry and painting, creating the poetic and picturesque realms. He pioneered the beautiful and unique expression of zen in Chinese landscape painting, and truly realized the aesthetic realm of the unity of nature and man in his paintings. He was honored as forefather of southern landscape painting.

4. 荆浩

荆浩，字浩然，沁水（今属山西）人，生于唐朝末年，中华五代后梁画家，博通经史，并长于文章。现在人可以随意用程式在画室里做"造山运动"，但千万别忘了前人的伟大创造，是他们让绘画——这个巨大的困难——变得相对容易，荆浩就是这样伟大的画家。荆浩创造了全景山水的基本模式，这个创造为中国人表现自己崇高理想，提供了一个切实可行的路径。

Jing Hao, a painter of the later Liang Dynasty of China, was a master of classics and history, and good at writing. He was a native of Qinshui (in present-day Shanxi province), born in last years of of Tang Dynasty. Nowadays, people can do "mountain-making" in the studio at will, but please don't forget the great creations of the predecessors. They made painting mountains—this huge difficulty—relatively easy. Jing Hao was such a great painter who created the basic model of panoramic landscape. This creation provides a truly feasible path for the Chinese to express their lofty ideals.

5. 李唐

李唐（公元 1066 年~公元 1150 年），字晞古，河阳三城（今河南孟州）人。宋朝画家，精于山水画和人物画。传言李唐在八十岁的时候，仍然在杭州摆地摊，谁都可以想象他的内心一定充满矛盾，但是生命的动荡没有影响画家对艺术品质的要求，他的作品精致华丽又大气磅礴，虽然意气使然却又坚持理性。后人如果凭借笔墨挥洒情绪，仍然可以借鉴李唐之作，他的创造是放纵和节制结合的完美典范。

Li Tang (1066~1150 AD), also named Xi Gu, was born in Heyang Sancheng (now Meng County, Henan Province), a painter of Song Dynasty, specializing in landscape painting and portrait. Rumors suggest that Li Tang was still selling paintings on the streets of Hangzhou at the age of eighty. It can be imagined that his mind must be full of contradictions, but the turmoil of life did not affect the painter's requirements for artistic quality. His works are exquisite, gorgeous and majestic. However, he insisted on being rational. If later generations use their brush and ink to express their emotions, they can still learn from Li Tang. His creation is a perfect example of the combination of indulgence and temperance.

6. 赵孟頫

赵孟頫（公元 1254 年~公元 1322 年），字子昂，号松雪道人，汉族，吴兴（今浙江湖州）人。元代著名画家，楷书四大家之一。赵孟頫博学多才，能诗善文，擅金石，通律吕，懂经济，解鉴赏。特别是书法和绘画成就最高，被称为"元人冠冕"。赵孟頫对中华艺术最重要的贡献，就是一个字——雅。他创造了中华书画的雅文化。看赵孟頫的作品，就是品一杯香茗，听一段丝竹，享受一种心灵安静的状态。赵孟頫的影响力如此之大，以至于在他之后，南方的娟秀文化渐渐成为中华画家心目中的文化主流。

Zhao Mengfu (1254~1322 AD), also named Zi'ang, nicknamed Songxue, Taoist, Han nationality, native to Wuxing (now Huzhou, Zhejiang Province), a famous painter of Yuan Dynasty, one of the four masters of regular script. Zhao Mengfu was erudite and talented, good at poetry, tablet inscription and music, understanding economy and appreciation. Particularly in calligraphy and painting he had the highest achievements, called "the crown of Yuan Dynasty". Zhao Mengfu's most important contribution to Chinese art, in one word—elegance. He created the elegant culture of Chinese calligraphy and painting. Reading Zhao Mengfu's works is to savor a cup of tea, listen to a piece of music, and enjoy a state of peace of mind. Zhao Mengfu's influence was so great that after him, the graceful culture of the south gradually became the cultural mainstream in the minds of traditional Chinese painters.

7. 倪瓒

倪瓒（公元 1301 年~公元 1374 年），元代画家、诗人，初名珽。倪瓒自古是"逸品"的代表，他不隐也不仕，漂泊江湖，别人都不了解他，他也不想被人了解，但仍然可以在精神上向往出尘境界。倪瓒的诗歌语言自然秀拔，清隽淡雅，不雕琢，散文也一样。他的绘画理想，或者说人性的光芒，成为中华文人的精神彼岸。他的许多力作给后来的明清绘画以巨大的影响，使其成为元四大画家之一。

Ni Zan (1301~1374 AD), a Yuan Dynasty painter and poet, Initially named Ting. Ni Zan has been a representative of "graceful works with a transcendent quelity" ever since. He was neither reclusive nor official. He wandered in the world. Others did not understand him, and he did not want to be understood, but he could still yearn for the unearthly world in spirit. Ni Zan's poetry language is natural, clear and elegant, and it is not refined, so is with his proses. His painting ideals, or his light of human nature, have become the spiritual side of Chinese literati. Many of his masterpieces had a huge influence on the later paintings of Ming and Qing Dynasties and he became one of the four major painters in Yuan Dynasty.

8. 董其昌

董其昌（公元 1555 年~公元 1636 年），明代后期著名画家、书法家、书画理论家、书画鉴赏家，"华亭派"的主要代表。董其昌的魅力，不单在他书画的美轮美奂、"南北宗"理论的巨大影响，还在于他的为人处世，虽仕途险恶，却成就一份书画大事业，他的人格魅力是历史中罕有的。董其昌的综合素质无人可比，他是一位可以被多方位挖掘的伟大人物。

Dong Qichang (1555~1636 AD), a famous painter, calligrapher, calligraphy and painting theorist, calligraphy and painting connoisseur in the late Ming Dynasty, and the main representative of "Huating School". Dong Qichang's charm lies not only in the beauty of his calligraphy and painting, and the great influence of the "North and South School" theory, but also in his lifestyle. Although his official career was not without its twists and turns, he achieved a great career in calligraphy and painting. His personality charm is rare in history. Of the comprehensive qualities, Dong Qichang is unmatched, and he is a great man who can be explored in many ways.

9. 朱耷

朱耷（约公元 1626 年~约公元 1705 年），八大山人，明末清初著名画家，江西南昌人，清初画坛"四僧"之一。其画笔墨简朴豪放、苍劲率意、淋漓酣畅，构图疏简、奇险，风格雄奇朴茂。八大山人证明了一个道理，就是绘画天才和疯子只有一线之隔。许多常人不可能做到的事情，在八大山人的笔下得以实现。八大山人的绘画给人的感觉是如释重负后的意犹未尽，是给人思考而不仅仅限于观看的，他的作品代表着中华画的真谛。

Zhu Da (about 1626 ~ about 1705 AD), nicknamed Badashanren. A famous painter in the late Ming and early Qing dynasties, was born in Nanchang, Jiangxi province and one of the "Four Monks" in the painting circle in the early Qing Dynasty. His painting brush is simple and bold, vigorous and forthright, and dripping and hearty, and his composition is simple, strange and eccentric, and his style is majestic and simple. Badashanren proved a truth, that there is only a thin line between the painting genius and the lunatic. Many things that could not be done by ordinary people have been realized in the writings of Badashanren. The paintings of Badashanren give people the feeling that they are still unfinished after being relieved. They are for people to think and not just to watch. His works represent the true essence of Chinese painting.

10. 石涛

石涛（公元 1642 年~公元 1707 年），清代画家，"清初四僧"之一。作画构图新奇。中华画发展到石涛，已经到了变幻无穷的境地，他尤其善用

"截取法"以特写之景传达深邃之境，他的理论对清代以至现当代的中华绘画发展产生了极为深远的影响。《苦瓜和尚画语录》成为在世界范围内畅销的中华画理论著作。

Shi Tao (1642 ~ 1707 AD), a painter in Qing Dynasty. He was one of the "Four Monks in the Early Qing Dynasty" and was known for the novelty in his painting composition. The development of Chinese painting up to Shi Tao has reached an endlessly changing situation. He especially used the "intercepting method" to convey the profound realm with close-up views. His theories had a profound impact on the development of Chinese painting in Qing Dynasty and even in modern times. *Discourse on Landscape Painting* became the best-selling Chinese painting theoretic work in the world.

七、中国古典十大名画 Top Ten Classical Chinese Paintings

中国自古以来出现了许多名画，中国十大名画如下：

There have been many famous paintings in China since ancient times, and the top ten famous paintings in China are as follows.

1.《洛神赋图》，是东晋顾恺之的画作，原《洛神赋图》卷为设色绢本，是由多个故事情节组成的类似连环画而又融会贯通的长卷，现已失。

Nymph of the Luo River is a painting by Gu Kaizhi in the Eastern Jin Dynasty. The original one was ink and color on silk. It was a long scroll similar to comic strips composed of stories, but it has been lost.

2.《清明上河图》，为北宋风俗画，北宋画家张择端仅见的存世精品，属国宝级文物，现藏于北京故宫博物院。

Along the River on Qingming Festival is a genre painting of the Northern Song Dynasty. It is the only extant masterpiece of the Northern Song Dynasty painter Zhang Zeduan. It is a national treasure and now in the Palace Museum in Beijing.

3.《富春山居图》，是元代画家黄公望创作的纸本绘画，画家黄公望为师弟郑樗（无用师）所绘，1350 年绘制完成。

Dwelling in the Fuchun Mountains is a paper painting created by Yuan Dynasty painter Huang Gongwang. The painter Huang Gongwang painted it for his junior

Zheng Chu (Useless master), and the painting was completed in 1350 AD.

4. 《汉宫春晓图》，是明代画家仇英创作的一幅绢本重彩仕女画，现收藏于台北故宫博物院。这一人物长卷画，生动地再现了汉代宫女的生活情景。亦被誉为中国"重彩仕女第一长卷"。

Han Palace Spring Morning, is a heavy-color painting of ladies on silk created by Ming Dynasty painter Qiu Ying, which is now in the collection of the National Palace Museum in Taipei. The portrait scrolls vividly reproduce the life of the court ladies in Han Dynasty. It is also known as China's "First Long Scroll of Ladies with Colors".

5. 《百骏图》，是意大利籍清代宫廷画家郎世宁创作的绘画作品。此图稿本为纸质，原作分别收藏于美国纽约大都会博物馆（纸质稿本）和中国台北故宫博物院（绢本）。

One Hundred Horses is a painting created by the Italian court painter Lang Shining (Giuseppe Castiglione, 1688~1766 AD) of Qing Dynasty. This artwork is on paper. The original works are collected in the Metropolitan Museum of New York (paper manuscript) and the Palace Museum, Taipei, China (silk version).

6. 《步辇图》，是唐朝画家阎立本的名作之一。现藏于北京故宫博物院。作品设色典雅绚丽，线条流畅圆劲，构图错落富有变化，为唐代绘画的代表性作品。

Emperor Taizong Receiving the Tibetan Envoy is one of the masterpieces of Tang Dynasty painter Yan Liben. It is in the Palace Museum in Beijing. It is elegant and gorgeous in color, smooth and round in lines, and varied in composition. It is a representative work of the Tang Dynasty paintings.

7. 《唐宫仕女图》，是一幅中国画作，作者是唐代张萱、周昉，该画描述了唐代美女众生相。主要表现唐代贵族妇女的生活情调，成为唐代仕女画的主要艺术特征。唐代作为封建社会最为辉煌的时代，也是仕女画的繁荣兴盛阶段。

Noble Ladies in Tang Dynasty is a traditional Chinese painting created by Zhang Xuan and Zhou Fang in Tang Dynasty. The painting depicts the beauties in Tang Dynasty. It mainly expresses the life sentiments of noble women in Tang Dynasty, which becomes the main artistic feature of the paintings of ladies in Tang Dynasty. As the most glorious era of feudal society, Tang Dynasty was also the stage of prosperity for paintings of ladies.

8.《五牛图》，是唐朝韩滉创作的黄麻纸本设色画，又名《唐韩滉五牛图》，该作品现藏于北京故宫博物院。《五牛图》中的五头牛从左至右一字排开，各具状貌，姿态互异。

Five Oxen is a color painting on jute paper created by Han Huang of Tang Dynasty, also known as *Five Oxen of Han Huang of Tang Dynasty*, now in the collection of the Palace Museum in Beijing. The five bulls in the painting are lined up from left to right, each with its special appearance and posture.

9.《韩熙载夜宴图》，是五代十国时期南唐画家顾闳中的绘画作品，现存宋摹本，绢本设色，现藏于北京故宫博物院。《韩熙载夜宴图》描绘了官员韩熙载家设夜宴载歌行乐的场面。

The Night Revels of Han Xizai is a painting by the Southern Tang painter Gu Hongzhong during the Five Dynasties and Ten Kingdoms period. An extant copy of this painting, on silk and color, is currently in the collection of the Palace Museum in Beijing. *The Night Revels of Han Xizai* depicts the scene of official Han Xizai holding a night banquet in his house with singing and dancing.

10.《千里江山图》，是北宋王希孟创作的绢本画卷作品，收藏于北京故宫博物院。该作品以长卷形式，立足传统，画面细致入微，烟波浩渺的江河、层峦起伏的群山构成了一幅美妙的江南山水图，渔村野市、水榭亭台、茅庵草舍、水磨长桥等静景穿插捕鱼、驶船、游玩等动景，动静结合恰到好处。

A Thousand Li of Rivers and Mountains, is a silk scroll work created by Wang Ximeng of the Northern Song Dynasty, collected in the Palace Museum in Beijing. The work is in the form of a long scroll, based on tradition, and the picture is meticulous. The vast smoky rivers and undulating mountains constitute a beautiful landscape of the south of the Yangtze River. The fishing villages, the waterside pavilions, the grass houses, the water mill, long bridges are quiet. Static scenes are interspersed with dynamic scenes such as fishing, sailing, playing, and the combination of dynamic and static scenes is rightly to the point.

还有赵芾的《江山万里图》卷，是这类题材作品中风格独具、别开生面的一幅佳作。展开画卷，云遮雾掩，崇山连绵，数尺之后方现曲折的江岸，三两旅人沿路缓行，航船数只待客于山脚渡口。随之则是"惊涛拍岸，卷起千堆雪"，继而孤岭突起，峰回路转，茅舍村屋，行旅往来。最后用茫茫无际的大海终结画面，水天一色，气势磅礴。从图中的绘画技法不难看出，赵芾是师从宋代画家李唐，又广采博学，别具一格。山石用笔挺劲，先用淡墨勾皴，再以浓墨、重墨细绘局部轮廓，墨色的浓淡轻重相得益彰。波浪主要用淡墨勾出，复用淡墨染深，以现出惊涛穿空之势，可谓"前无古人"，堪称南宋绘画的杰作。

Another to be mentioned is Zhao Fu's *Ten Thousands of Li of Rivers and Mountains*, which is a unique and miraculous picture. Unfolding the picture scroll, the clouds cover the mist, the mountains are continuous, and a few feet later, there is a tortuous river bank. Some travelers walk slowly along the road, and a few boats wait for passengers at the foot of the mountain ferry. Then there is the "sweeping waves hitting the shore, rolling up a thousand piles of snow", and then lonely ridges protrude, the peaks turn around, the cottages, the village houses, coming back and forth. Finally, the picture is ended with the boundless sea, the water and the sky merge in one color magnificently. From the painting techniques in the picture, it is not difficult to see that Zhao Fu studied under Li Tang, a painter of Song Dynasty, and he also learned from others and formed his unique style. The mountain rocks are brushed very vigorously and stiffly, first using light ink to outline them, and then using the thick and heavy ink to draw the partial outlines. The light and intense ink complement each other. The waves are mainly drawn with light ink, and dyed deep with light ink to show the tendency of the storm to penetrate the sky. It can be described as "unprecedented" and can be called a masterpiece of the Southern Song paintings.

中国的传统书法文化

一、中国传统书法艺术的起源 The Origin of Traditional Chinese Calligraphy

中国书法是一门古老的艺术，它从发展到演变，起到了思想交流和文化传承的重要作用。它是中国人民智慧的体现，更是中华文化的重要瑰宝之一。

Chinese calligraphy is an ancient art. From development to evolution, it has played an important role in the exchange of ideas and cultural heritage. It is a manifestation of the wisdom of the Chinese people and one of the important treasures of Chinese culture.

中国书法从最初的甲骨文、金文，然后再演变成大篆、小篆、隶书，到了东汉、魏、晋转向草书、楷书、行书，一直散发着艺术的魅力。据考古研究，距今约七千年的黄河中游"仰韶文化时期"，已出现具有记事功能的刻画符号，此为汉字雏形。

Chinese calligraphy evolved from oracle-bone inscriptions and bronze inscriptions, and then into large seal script, small seal script, and clerical script. In the Eastern Han Dynasty, Wei and Jin, turned to cursive script, regular script, and semi-cursive script, which has always exuded the charm of art. According to archaeological research, carved symbols with rudimentary record-keeping functions, dating back approximately 7, 000 years to the Yangshao Culture period in the middle reaches of the Yellow River, have been discovered, representing the earliest embryonic forms of Chinese characters.

世界文字体系大致分为表意文字、表音文字和意音文字三类。中国的汉字，从图画、符号到创造、定型，由古文大篆到小篆，由篆而隶、楷、行、草，各种形体逐渐形成。在书写应用汉字的过程中，逐渐产生了世界各民族文字中唯一的、独立门类的书法艺术。

The world's writing systems are broadly categorized into three types: logographic, phonetic, and semanto-phonetic. Chinese characters are ideographic words developed from pictographic words, from pictures and symbols to creation and finalization of words, from the large seal to the small seal, and on to the clerical script, the regular script, cursive script, and semi-cursive script. In the process of writing and applying Chinese characters, the unique and independent calligraphy art among all ethnic languages in the world gradually emerged.

最初的时候，文字还是以一种图画的形式出现的，一般被刻在陶瓷上面，只能描述一个大概的意思。距今七千多年前，在黄河流域，在手制陶瓷上有许多的符号。这种符号，就是交际、记录事情的标记。这些虽不是真正的汉字，但确是汉字的雏形。

At the beginning, the words still appeared in the form of a picture, usually printed on the ceramics, it could only describe a general meaning. More than 7,000 years ago, in the Yellow River Basin, there were many symbols on hand-made ceramics. The symbols were the marks for people's communication and recording things. Although these were not real Chinese characters, they were indeed the embryonic forms of Chinese characters.

紧接着在仰韶文化的半坡遗址，出土了一些类似文字的简单刻画的彩陶。这些符号已区别于花纹图案，把汉文字的发展又向前推进了一步。这被认为是中国文字的雏形。接着有二里头文化和二里岗文化。二里头文化考古发掘中发现有刻画记号的陶片，其记号共有二十四种，有的类似殷墟甲骨文字，都是单个独立的字。最后，甲骨文经过商周，经过春秋战国，到秦汉王朝至今不断的演变，才有了我们今天的文字书法。

Immediately in the Banpo site of Yangshao Culture, some simple painted potteries with similar characters were unearthed. These symbols were different from floral patterns, and advanced the development of Chinese characters one step further. This is considered the embryonic form of Chinese writing. Then there were Erlitou Culture and Erligang Culture. In the archaeological excavations of Erlitou culture, there are 24 kinds of pottery tablets with marks. Some of them are similar to the Yinxu oracle-

bone inscriptions of Shang Dynasty, which are all single and independent charac-
ters. In the end, Oracle-bone inscriptions have undergone continuous evolution from
Shang and Zhou dynasties, through the Spring and Autumn and Warring States, from
Qin and Han Dynasties to today, and then we have today's words and calligraphy.

二、中国传统书法艺术的特点 Characteristics of Traditional Chinese Calligraphy Art

中国的传统书法艺术综合起来说，有三大特点：

Taken together, the traditional Chinese calligraphy art has three characteris-
tics：

1. 整体形态美。中国字的基本形态是方形的，但是通过点画的伸缩、轴线的扭动，也可以形成各种不同的动人形态，从而组合成优美的书法作品。结构形态，主要受两方面因素影响，一是书法意趣的表现需要；二是书法表现的形式因素。就后者而言，主要体现在三个方面：一为书体的影响，如篆体取竖长方形；二为字形的影响，有的字是扁方形，而有的字是长方形；三为章法影响。因此，只有在上述两类因素的支配下，进行积极的形态创造，才能创作出美的结构形态。

Beauty of the overall shape. The basic form of Chinese characters is square, but
through the expansion and contraction of the stippling and the twisting of the axis,
various different moving forms can be formed, which can be combined into beautiful
calligraphy works. The form of the structure is mainly affected by two factors, one is
the need for the expression of calligraphy interest; the other is the form factor of the
expression of calligraphy. As far as the latter is concerned, it is mainly reflected in
three aspects: one is the influence of the script, such as the seal type taking a vertical rectangle; another is the influence of the font, some characters are flat and some
are rectangular; the third is the composition influences. Therefore, only under the
control of the above-mentioned two types of factors and with active form creation can
we create a beautiful structure of characters.

2. 点画结构美。点画结构美的构建方式主要有两种，一是指各种点画按一定的组合方式，直接组合成各种美的独体字和偏旁部首。二是指通过将各种部首，再按一定的方式组合成各种字形。中国字的部首组合方式无非是左右式、左中右式、上下式、上中下式、包围式、半包围式等几种。这些组合原则主要是比例原则、均衡原则、韵律原则、节奏原则、简洁原则等。我们特别要提的就是比例原则，其中黄金分割比又是一个非常重要的比例，对点画结构美非常重要。

Beauty of the structure of strokes and dots. There are two main ways to construct the structural beauty of the strokes and dots. First, various strokes and dots are directly combined in certain ways to form a variety of beautiful single characters and radicals. Second, these radicals are further combined in certain ways to create different characters. The radical combinations of Chinese characters are nothing more than left–right, left–middle–right, upper–lower, upper–middle–lower, enclosed, and semi–enclosed structure. These combination principles are mainly the principle of proportionality, the principle of balance, the principle of rhythm, and the principle of simplicity. What's to be mentioned here is the principle of proportionality, particularly the golden ratio, is very important for the beauty of the structure of strokes and dots.

3. 墨色组合美。墨色组合的艺术性，主要是指其组合的秩序性。作为艺术的书法，它的各种色彩不能再是杂乱无章的，而应是非常有秩序的。这里也有些共同的美学原则，要求书者予以遵守。如重点原则、渐变原则、均衡原则等。书法结体的墨色组合，主要涉及两个方面：一是对背景底色的分割组合。人们常说的"计白当黑"，就是这方面的内容。二是点画结构的墨色组合。从作品的整体效果来看，不但要注意点画墨色的平面结构，还要注意点画墨色的分层效果，从而增强书法的表现深度。

Beauty of the combination of ink and color. The artistry of the combination of ink and color mainly refers to the order of their combination. As an artistic calligraphy, its various colors can no longer be chaotic, but rather orderly. There are also some common aesthetic principles, which the calligraphers are required to observe, such as the principle of key points, the principle of gradual change, and the principle of equilibrium. The ink and color combination of the calligraphy structure mainly involves two aspects: one is the segmentation and combination of the background color. What people often say "reckon blank as inked" refers to that. The other is the ink and color combination of the structure of the strokes and dots. From the perspective of the overall effect of the work, not only the plane structure of the stippling ink should be paid attention to, but also the layering effect of the stippling ink to enhance the depth of the calligraphy.

三、中国传统书法十大名家 Ten Most Famous Traditional Chinese Calligraphers

1. 王羲之（公元 303 年~公元 361 年），中国东晋书法家，字逸少，号澹斋，汉族，祖籍琅琊临沂，后迁会稽，晚年隐居剡县金庭，有书圣之称。后为会稽内史，领右军将军，人称"王右军""王会稽"。其子王献之书法亦佳，世人合称为"二王"。此后历代王氏家族书法人才辈出。王羲之的兰亭序被后人称为"天下第一行书。"其祖籍地现存纪念性故居于山东临沂兰山区洗砚池街。受其影响命名了洗砚池街，且王羲之故居就在洗砚池街上。

Wang Xizhi, （303~361 AD）, Chinese calligrapher of Eastern Jin Dynasty, also named Yishao, nicknamed Danzhai, Han nationality, ancestral home in Linyi, Langya, then moved to Kuaiji later, and lived in seclusion in Jinting, Yan County (also in Zhejiang Province) in his later years, honored as Calligraphy Sage. Later he was the Internal Historian of Kuaiji County, entitled the right general, known as "Wang Youjun" and "Wang Kuaiji". His son Wang Xianzhi's calligraphy was also very excellent, and the people called them "two Wangs". Since then, calligraphy talents of the Wang family have appeared in large numbers. *The Preface of the Orchid Pavilion* by Wang Xizhi was called "the No. 1 semi-cursive script in the world. " A commemorative former residence in his ancestral hometown is located on Xiyanchi Street, Lanshan District, Linyi City, Shandong Province. And Xiyanchi (Washing Inkstone Pool) Street was named after him. Wang Xizhi's former residence is on the Street.

2. 欧阳询（公元 557 年~公元 641 年），字信本，汉族，唐朝潭州临湘（今湖南长沙）人。欧阳询与同代的虞世南、褚遂良、薛稷三位并称初唐楷书四大家。因其子欧阳通亦善书法，故又称其"大欧"。他与虞世南并称"欧虞"，后人以其书于平正中见险绝，最便于初学者，号为"欧体"。

Ouyang Xun (557~641 AD), bynamed Xinben, Han nationality, from Linxiang in Tanzhou (now Changsha, Hunan Province) in Tang Dynasty, a famous calligrapher. Ouyang Xun, together with Yu Shinan, Chu Suiliang, and Xue Ji, was honoured as the four greatest masters of calligraphy in the early Tang Dynasty. Because his son Ouyang Tong was also good at calligraphy, he was called "Da Ou" (Ou the Senior). He and Yu Shinan were both experted at regular script also called "Ou Yu". Later generations entitled his calligraphy as "Ou style" because his calligraphy shows precipitousness in flatness, which is easy for beginners to learn.

3. 颜真卿（公元709年~公元784年），字清臣，京兆万年人，祖籍琅琊临沂。唐代名臣、书法家。颜真卿书法精妙，擅长行、楷。初学褚遂良，后师从张旭，得其笔法。其正楷端庄雄伟，行书气势遒劲，创"颜体"楷书，对后世影响很大。与赵孟頫、柳公权、欧阳询并称为"楷书四大家"。又与柳公权并称"颜柳"，被称为"颜筋柳骨"。又善诗文，宋人辑有《颜鲁公集》。

Yan Zhenqing (709~784 AD), by names Qingchen, was born in Wannian (Today Xi'an), Capital of Jingzhao, from Linyi, Langya (Shandong Province), a famous minister and calligrapher in Tang Dynasty. Yan Zhenqing was exquisite in calligraphy, and good at semi-cursive and regular scripts. He first learned from Chu Suiliang and later from Zhang Xu. His regular scripts are dignified and majestic, and his semi-cursive script is vigorous and powerful, creating a "Yan style" regular script, which has a great influence on future generations. Together with Zhao Mengfu, Liu Gongquan, and Ouyang Xun, they are called the "Four Masters of Regular Script". He and Lin Gongquan are also called "Yan Liu" together, and they enjoy the reputation of "Yan's Tendon and Liu's Bone". He is also good at poetry and essays, which were compiled into *Anthology of Yanlngong* by people in the Song Dynasty.

4. 柳公权（公元778年~公元865年），字诚悬，汉族，唐朝京兆华原（今陕西耀州区）人，著名书法家。柳公权幼年好学，善辞赋，懂韵律。柳公权是颜真卿的后继者，但唯悬瘦笔法，自成一格；后世以"颜柳"并称，成为历代书法楷模。他一生作品很多，主要有《大唐回元观钟楼铭》。

Liu Gongquan (778~865 AD), by names Chengxuan, Han nationality, was born in Huayuan, Jingzhao (now Yaozhou District, Shaanxi Province) in Tang Dynasty, and a famous calligrapher. Liu Gongquan was studious when he was young, good at poetry and music. Liu Gongquan was the successor of Yan Zhenqing, but his suspending and thin brushwork is a unique style; later generations call them "Yan Liu" and their calligraphic works become a model of calligraphy for future generations. He had many works throughout his life, mainly including the *Inscription on the Bell Tower of Huiyuan Abbey of the great Tang Dynasty*.

5. 赵孟頫（公元 1254 年~公元 1322 年），字子昂，汉族，浙江吴兴人。南宋末至元初著名书法家、画家、诗人，宋太祖赵匡胤十一世孙。赵孟頫博学多才，能诗善文，懂经济，工书法，精绘艺，擅金石，解鉴赏。尤其以书法和绘画成就最高。在绘画上，他开创元代新画风，被称为 "元人冠冕"；赵孟頫亦善篆、隶、行、草书，尤以楷、行书著称于世。其书风遒媚、秀逸，结体严整、笔法圆熟，创 "赵体" 书，与欧阳询、颜真卿、柳公权并称 "楷书四大家"。

Zhao Mengfu (1254~1322 AD), by names Zi'ang, Han nationality, was from Wuxing, Zhejiang province, a famous calligrapher, painter, and poet from the end of the Southern Song Dynasty to the beginning of Yuan Dynasty, the eleventh grandson of Zhao Kuangyin, the first emperor of Song dynasty. Zhao Mengfu was erudite and talented, good at poetry, economics, calligraphy, painting, especially good at seals, and appreciation of music. His achievement lay especially in calligraphy and painting. In painting, he created a new style in Yuan Dynasty, honoured as "the crown of Yuan Dynasty"; Zhao Mengfu was also good at seal, clerical script, semi-cursive script and cursive script, especially well known for his regular script and semi-cursive script. His calligraphy style is charming and beautiful, with strict structure and well-rounded brushwork, he created the "Zhao style" calligraphy, and is also called the "Four Masters of Regular Scripts" together with Ouyang Xun, Yan Zhenqing and Liu Gongquan.

6. 文徵明（公元 1470 年~公元 1559 年），初名壁，字徵明，长洲（今江苏苏州）人，祖籍衡山，故号衡山居士。文徵明的绘画兼善山水、兰竹、人物、花卉诸科，尤精山水；绘画承沈周之法，又与沈周、唐寅、仇英并称 "吴门四家"；书法上与祝允明、王宠并誉为 "吴中三家"。

Wen Zhengming (1470 ~ 1559 AD), originally named Bi with the byname

Zhengming, was born in Changzhou（now Suzhou, Jiangsu Province）, native from Hengshan（Hunan Province）, hence the name Hengshan Lay. Wen Zhengming's paintings covered landscapes, orchids, bamboos, protraits, and flowers, especially outstanding in landscapes. In painting, he followed the methods of Shen Zhou, and also called the "Four Masters of Wu School" with Shen Zhou, Tang Yin and Qiu Ying; in calligraphy, together with Zhu Yunming and Wang Chong, they are also known as the "Three Masters of Central Wu".

7. 董其昌（公元 1555 年~公元 1636 年），字玄宰，松江华亭（今上海闵行区马桥）人，明代书画家。万历十七年进士，授翰林院编修，官至南京礼部尚书。董其昌擅画山水，师法董源、巨然、黄公望、倪瓒，笔致清秀中和，恬静疏旷；用墨明洁隽朗，温敦淡荡；青绿设色，古朴典雅。以佛家禅宗喻画，倡"南北宗"论，为"华亭画派"杰出代表，兼有"颜骨赵姿"之美。其画及画论对明末清初画坛影响甚大。书法出入晋唐，自成一格，能诗文。

Dong Qichang（1555~1636 AD）, by names Xuanzai, was born in Huating, Songjiang（now Maqiao, Minhang District, Shanghai）, a calligrapher and painter of Ming Dynasty. In the seventeenth year of Emperor Wanli, he was awarded the editor of Hanlin Academy, and he went to Nanjing as Imperial Secretary of Ritual Department. Dong Qichang was good at painting landscapes, and he learned from Dong Yuan, Ju Ran, Huang Gongwang, and Ni Zan. His brushwork was delicate and neutral, quiet and open; the ink was bright and clear, warm and gentle; the blue and green colors were simple and elegant. Taking Buddhist Zen as a metaphor for painting and advocating the theory of "Southern and Northern Buddhism", he was an outstanding representative of the "Huating School" and had the beauty of "Yan's Bone and Zhao's Posture". His paintings and painting theory had a great influence on the painting circles in the late Ming and early Qing dynasties. His calligraphy came from the Jin and Tang dynasties, and had his own style, capable of poetry and proses.

8. 怀素（公元 725 年~公元 785 年），唐书法家，字藏真，出家为僧，僧名怀素，长沙人，另一说零陵人。精勤学书，以善狂草出名，是书法史上领一代风骚的草书家，他的草书称为"狂草"，用笔圆劲有力，使转如环，奔放流畅，一气呵成，与唐代另一草书家张旭齐名，人称"张颠素狂"或"颠张醉素"。他的书法虽率意飘逸，千变万化，而法度具备。怀素与张旭形成唐代书法双峰并峙的局面，也是中国草书史上两座高峰。怀素代表作品有《自叙帖》《苦笋帖》《食鱼帖》等。

Huaisu（725~785 AD）, a Tang calligrapher, by names Zangzhen, later became a monk named Huaisu, from Changsha, or from Lingling, Hunan Province. He worked assiduously with calligraphy and was famous for his cursive calligraphy. He was the leading cursive calligrapher in the history of calligraphy. His cursive calligraphy was called "crazy cursive". His brush was round and vigorous, making it turn like a circle, unrestrained and smooth. Zhang Xu had the same reputation, and they were called "Zhang Lunatic and Su Crazy" or "The Crazy Zhang and The Drunk Su". Although his calligraphy was freewheeling and unconstrained, infinitely varied, but he possessed his own method. Huai Su and Zhang Xu formed a situation where the two peaks of calligraphy in Tang Dynasty stood side by side, and they were also two peaks in the history of Chinese cursive script. Huai Su's representative works include "Autobiography", "Bitter Bamboo Shoots Copybook", and "Eating Fish Copybook".

9. 王铎（公元 1592 年~公元 1652 年），明末清初书画家，河南孟津人。他的书法与董其昌齐名，有"南董北王"之称。明天启二年，即 1622 年中进士，受考官袁可立提携，入翰林院庶吉士，累擢礼部尚书，崇祯十六年，即 1643 年，王铎为东阁大学士。1644 年满清入关后被授予礼部尚书，1652 年病逝故里。享年六十一岁，葬于河南巩义洛河边。

Wang Duo（1592~1652 AD）, was a calligrapher and painter at the end of Ming Dynasty and the beginning of Qing Dynasty, born in Mengjin, Henan Province. He was as famous as Dong Qichang in calligraphy, well-known as "South Dong and North Wang". In the second year of Emperor Tianqi of Ming Dynasty, namely 1622, he won the title of Jinshi（meaning winner in the imperial examination）, was promoted by the examiner Yuan Keli, and entered the Imperial Academy as an official scholar, later as Imperial Secretary of Ministry of Rites. In the 16th year of Emperor Chongzhen, that is, in 1643, Wang Duo was a Master of the Eastern Pavilion. In 1644, he was awarded as Imperial Secretary of Ministry of Rites in Qing Dynasty, and he died sixty-one years old at his hometown in 1652, and was buried by River Luo in Gongyi, Henan Province.

10. 何绍基（公元 1799 年~公元 1873 年），字子贞，号东洲，别号东洲居士，晚清诗人、画家、书法家。湖南道州，今道县人。道光十六年（1836）进士。通经史，精小学金石碑版。书法初学颜真卿，又融汉魏而自成一家，尤长草书。何绍基出身于书香门第，其父何凌汉曾任户部尚书，是知名的书法家、教育家、学者、藏书家。何绍基兄弟四人均习文善书，人称"何氏四杰"。

He Shaoji （1799 ~ 1873 AD）, a poet, painter and calligrapher in the late Qing Dynasty, by names Zizhen, nicknamed Dongzhou, and known as Dongzhou lay Buddhist. A native of Daozhou （1836）, Hunan province. A winner in the imperial examination in the 16th year of Emperor Daoguang. He was an expert in classics and history and skillful in inscription. He first learned from Yan Zhenqing in calligraphy, merged with those of the Han and Wei Dynasties to form his own style, especially excellent at cursive script. He Shaoji was born in a scholarly family. His father, He Linghan, used to be Imperial Secretary of Ministry of Revenue, was a well-known calligrapher, educator, scholar, and bibliophile. He Shaoji and his three brothers were all good at literature and calligraphy, known as the "Four Masters of the He Family".

四、中国古代十大书法作品 Top Ten Calligraphy Works in History

1. 苏轼《前后赤壁赋》Su Shi's *Former and Latter Ode to the Red Cliff*

北宋大文豪苏轼写过两篇《赤壁赋》，后人称之为《前赤壁赋》和《后赤壁赋》，都是中国古代文学史上的名篇，同时也是著名的书法作品。苏轼被贬为黄州（今湖北黄冈）团练副使的 1082 年秋、冬，先后两次游览了黄州附近的赤壁，写下这两篇赋。他的前后赤壁赋反映了这时的思想情感。

Su Shi, a great writer in the Northern Song Dynasty, wrote two *Ode to the Red Cliff*, later known as *Former Ode to the Red Cliff* and *Latter Ode to the Red Cliff*, both are famous in the history of traditional Chinese literature and calligraphy works. In the autumn and winter of 1082, when Su Shi was demoted to Huangzhou （now Huanggang, Hubei） regimental deputy envoy, he visited Chibi （the Red Cliff） near Huangzhou twice and wrote these two odes. His Odes reflect his thoughts and emotions at this time.

2. 颜真卿《祭侄文稿》Yan Zhenqing's *Draft of a Requiem to My Nephew*

颜真卿书法墨迹《祭侄文稿》，全名《祭侄赠赞善大夫季明文》。原作纸本，纵 28.8 厘米，横 75.5 厘米，共 234 字（另有涂抹字 30 余个）。现藏台北故宫博物院。因为此稿是在极度悲愤的情绪下书写，顾不得笔墨的工拙，故字随书家情绪起伏，纯是精神和平时工力的自然流露。这在整个书法史上都是不多见的。被誉为"天下第二草书"，《祭侄文稿》是极具史料价值和艺术价值的墨迹原作之一，至为宝贵。

Yan Zhenqing's calligraphy *Draft of a Requiem to My Nephew*, the full name is *Memorial to Nephew and to give to Prince's Secretary Ji Mingwen*. The original is paper version, 28.8 cm in length, 75.5 cm wide and contains 234 characters (more than 30 smeared characters), now in the collection of the Taipei Palace Museum. Because this manuscript was written in extreme grief and indignation, without regard for the tidiness of the brush and ink, but for the emotional ups and downs in the calligrapher, which was purely a natural expression of the spirit and daily practices. This is rare in the entire history of calligraphy, honored as "the second cursive script in the world", *Draft of a Requiem to My Nephew* is one of the original calligraphy works with great historical and artistic value, and is extremely precious.

3. 米芾《蜀素帖》Mifu's *Shu Silk Copybook*

为北宋书法家米芾的墨宝。写于北宋哲宗元祐三年（1088 年），以行书写成。今藏于台北故宫博物院。《蜀素帖》纵长 29.7 厘米，横长 284.3 厘米。"蜀素"指的是这卷仁宗庆历四年（1044 年）在四川东方所织造的名贵绢。卷上的乌丝栏也是织出来的，可见是专供书写用的。被后人誉为中华第一美帖，天下十大行书之一。

Shu Silk Copybook is the calligraphy of the calligrapher Mi Fu of the Northern Song Dynasty. Written in the third year of Yuanyou of Emperor Zhezong of the Northern Song Dynasty (1088), written in semi-cursive script. It is now stored in the National Palace Museum, Taipei. *Shu Silk Copybook* is 29.7 cm vertically and 284.3 cm horizontally. "Shu Silk" refers to the precious silk woven in the east of Sichuan province in the fourth year of Qingli of Emperor Renzong (1044). The silk column on the roll is also woven, which shows that it was exclusively for writing. It was hailed as the number one beautiful copybook in China and one of the top ten semi-cursive scripts in the world.

4. 王珣《伯远帖》 Wang Xun's *Boyuantie*

是东晋著名书法家王珣书写的一封信，纸本，行书，共 5 行 47 字，纵 25.1 厘米，横 17.2 厘米。现藏于北京故宫博物院。《伯远帖》是东晋时十分难得的名人书法真迹，且是东晋王氏家族存世的唯一真迹，一直被书法家、收藏家、鉴赏家视为稀世瑰宝，称为天下十大行书之一，排第四。

Boyuantie is a letter written by the famous calligrapher Wang Xun of the Eastern Jin Dynasty. It is on paper and in semi-cursive script. It has 47 characters in 5 lines, 25.1 cm in length and 17.2 cm in width. It is now in the Palace Museum, Beijing. *Boyuantie* is a very rare authentic book of celebrities in the Eastern Jin Dynasty, the only authentic work of the Eastern Jin Dynasty Wang family. It has been regarded as a rare treasure by calligraphers, collectors, and connoisseurs, and it is called one of the ten greatest semi-cursive scripts in the world, ranking the fourth.

5. 祝允明《草书诗帖》 Zhu Yunming's *Poems in Cursive Script*

被誉为明代奇才草书绝品，系中华十大传世名帖之一。现藏台北故宫博物院纸本，纵 36.1 厘米，横 1147.5 厘米，书曹植《乐府》四首。是祝允明草书成就的最杰出代表。作品狂而不乱，情浓势足，激跃奔发，气度不凡。其将字中妍媚和巧丽的笔画起收动作幅度缩短，增加行笔过程中的饱满度和厚实感。

Known as the masterpiece of cursive script of a prodigy of Ming Dynasty, it is one of the top ten famous copybooks in China, now in the collection of the National Palace Museum in Taipei, paper version, 36.1 cm vertically and 1147.5 cm horizontally, writing four pieces of *Yuefu* (namely, *Department of Folk Songs and Ballads* by Poet Cao Zhi. It is the most outstanding representative of Zhu Yunming's cursive achievements. The work is wildly scribbled but not chaotic, full of emotion and passion, with extraordinary bearing. It shortens the lifting and retracting motion range of the beautiful and fanciful strokes in the characters, and increases the fullness and thickness of the strokes.

6. 欧阳询《仲尼梦奠帖》 Ouyang Xun's *Dream of Confucius at the Alta*

《仲尼梦奠帖》是中华十大传世名帖之一，纸本，纵 25.5 厘米，横 33.6

厘米，为唐著名书法家欧阳询所作，是欧阳询现存的四件墨迹之一。现藏于辽宁省博物馆。《仲尼梦奠帖》行书，九行，每行九字，共七十八字。

Dream of Confucius at the Alta is one of the top ten famous copybooks in China. It is on paper, 25. 5 cm in length and 33. 6 cm in width. It was written by the famous Tang calligrapher Ouyang Xun. It is one of the four existing calligraphies by Ouyang Xun. It is now in Liaoning Provincial Museum. *Dream of Confucius at the Alta*, semi-cursive script, nine lines, each line of nine characters, a total of 78 characters.

7. 王羲之《快雪时晴帖》Wang Xizhi's *Timely Clearing After Snowfall*

《快雪时晴帖》传为东晋王羲之书札唐摹本，以行书写成，纸本墨迹。纵 23 厘米，横 14.8 厘米，4 行，28 字。《快雪时晴帖》是一封书札，其内容是作者写他在大雪初晴时的愉快心情及对亲朋的问候。收藏于台北故宫博物院。

The Kuai Xue Shi Qing Tie is traditionally attributed to a Tang Dynasty copy of a letter by Wang Xizhi of the Eastern Jin Dynasty, written in running script and in ink on paper. The length is 23 cm, the width 14. 8 cm, 4 rows, 28 characters. *Timely Clearing After Snowfall* is a letter, its content is that the author expressed his happy mood and greetings to his relatives and friends when the sun shone just after the heavy snow. It's collected in Taipei Palace Museum.

8. 王献之《中秋帖》Wang Xianzhi's *Mid-Autumn Copybook*

《中秋帖》为晋代王献之所书纸本手卷，纵 27 厘米，横 11.9 厘米。《中秋帖》是著名的古代书法作品，曾被清高宗弘历（乾隆皇帝）誉为"三希"之一，意即稀世珍宝，现藏故宫博物院。草书 5 行，共 22 字。

Mid-Autumn Copybook is a hand-scrolled paper version written by Wang Xianzhi of Jin Dynasty, 27 cm in length and 11. 9 cm in width. *Mid-Autumn Copybook* is a famous ancient calligraphy work. It was once hailed as one of the "Three Rarities" by Emperor Hongli (Emperor Qianlong) of Qing Dynasty, meaning a rare treasure, and is now in the Palace Museum. 5 lines of cursive script, 22 characters in total.

9. 怀素《自叙帖》Huai Su's *Autobiography*

怀素书于公元 777 年（唐大历十二年）。大草（狂草）书，凡一百二十六行，首六行早损，由宋代苏舜钦补成。《自叙帖》乃怀素草书的巨制，活泼飞动，笔下生风，"心手相师势转奇，诡形怪状翻合宜"，实在是一篇情愫奔腾激荡，"泼墨大写意"般的抒情之作。

Huai Su wrote it in 777 AD (the twelfth year of Dali of Tang Dynasty). Cursive style, consisting of one hundred and twenty-six lines, the first six lines were damaged early and later made up by Su Shunqin of Song Dynasty. *Autobiography* is the masterpiece of Huai Su's cursive scripts, lively and flying, and the brush is gone with the wind. "The mind and hands turn queer and the strange shapes go proper." It is really a lyrical work full of passion and emotion, "splashing freehand brush-work".

10. 王羲之《兰亭集序》Wang Xizhi's *Preface to the Poems Collected from the Orchid Pavillion*

王羲之是东晋的书法家，被后人尊为"书圣"，与儿子王献之合称"二王"。《兰亭集序》是最出名的作品之一，被誉为"天下第一行书"。现存版本出自唐代书法家冯承素之手，传说真迹在唐太宗李世民逝世后作为陪葬品下葬。

Wang Xizhi was a calligrapher in the Eastern Jin Dynasty and was revered as the "Calligraphy Sage" by later generations. He and his son Wang Xianzhi were co-called "Two Wangs". *Preface to the Poems Collected from the Orchid Pavillion* is one of the most famous works, known as "the No. 1 semi-cursive script in the world". The existing version is a simulation by the calligrapher Feng Chengsu of Tang Dynasty. It is said that the original one was buried as a sacrificial object after the death of the second Emperor Li Shimin of Tang Dynasty.

中国的传统舞蹈文化

一、中国传统舞蹈文化的起源 The Origin of Traditional Chinese Dance Culture

中华民族的舞蹈文化源远流长，上下五千年，记录中华民族舞蹈发展轨迹的文物图像和文字，连绵不断，这在世界文化史上也是罕见的。距今五、六千年前的新石器时代舞蹈纹陶盆的出土，向世人展示了原始舞蹈整齐的队势及其群体性、自娱性的特点。远古传说："帝俊有子八人，始为歌舞"，说明了歌舞的创造者是群体。可以说，中国有多少年的文明，就有多少年的舞蹈史。从最蒙昧的上古时代开始，中国传统舞蹈经过了多个阶段的发展和演变，逐渐形成了颇具中国独特形态和神韵的东方舞蹈艺术。

The dance culture of the Chinese nation has a long history, up to five thousand years, and the cultural relics of images and texts that record the development of the Chinese nation's dances are continuous, which is also rare in the history of world culture. The unearthed Neolithic pottery pots with dance patterns dating back five or six thousand years ago showed the world the primitive dances had a neat team and characteristics of group and self-entertainment. From ancient times, there went the legend "King Jun had eight sons and they began to sing and dance", which showed that the creators of singing and dancing were a group. It can be said that as many years of civilization as China has, there are as many years of dance history. Starting from the most obscure ancient times, traditional Chinese dance has gone through multiple stages of development and evolution, and gradually formed an oriental dance art with a unique Chinese form and charm.

二、中国传统舞蹈文化的发展 The Development of Traditional Chinese Dance Culture

(一) 夏商周时期 Xia, Shang and Zhou Dynasties

这时舞蹈从氏族部落的仪式性群体舞蹈，逐步分化为贵族礼乐与巫祭乐舞的双重体系，部分地进入表演艺术领域，并且出现了最早的专业舞人——乐舞奴隶；还出现了求神媚神、求神降神的巫舞。神权统治的殷商时代，巫是神的代言人，社会地位高，甚至可以左右国王的行动及国家政事。自春秋战国以后，由于社会的变革与思想的进步，人们对巫术的迷信程度渐减，巫舞由娱神向娱人的方向转化发展。

At this time, dance gradually differentiated from the ceremonial group dance of clan tribes into a dual system of aristocratic ritual music and shamanic music dance, partially entering the field of performing arts, and the earliest professional dancers emerged——music and dance slaves appeared; and there appeared witch dances praying for God, pleased God, and invited God to befall. Shang Dynasty was under theocratic rule, and witches were the spokespersons of gods and had a high social status. They could even influence the actions of kings and state affairs. Since the Spring and Autumn and Warring States period, due to social changes and ideological progress, people's degree of superstition in witchcraft gradually decreased, and "Witch Dance" transformed and developed from entertaining gods to entertaining people.

西周初年制礼作乐，汇集整理了从远古到周初歌颂对推动人类进步有贡献的领袖的乐舞。分文舞、武舞两大类。周代将这些乐舞用于礼仪祭祀。各种不同等级的人，用不同规模的乐舞，等级严明，不容僭越。周朝建立了中国第一个宫廷雅乐体系。雅乐，即中国古代祭祀天地、祖先、神灵以及祝祷风调、雨顺、丰收等典礼时所演奏的音乐形式，它体现在当时的宫廷郊社、庙宇宗堂或政治军事等各方面。例如最为西周统治者推崇的，便是被后来的儒家奉为典范的"六代之乐"。

The rite and music were made in the early years of the Western Zhou Dynasty. Dances with musical accompaniment were collected and compiled from ancient times to the beginning of the Western Zhou Dynasty that praised leaders who contributed to the advancement of mankind. They were divided into two categories: literary dance and martial dance. Zhou Dynasty used these dances for ritual sacrifices. People of all different levels used different scales of dance, with strict difference and no arrogance. Zhou Dynasty established China's first court music system Yayue. Yayue (Elegant music) was a form of music performed in ancient Chinese ceremonies such as offering sacrifices to heaven and earth, ancestors, and gods, as well as prayers for good weathers and harvests. It was embodied in various aspects such as palace and commune activities, ancestral temples, politics and military at that time. For example, it was most highly regarded by the rulers of Western Zhou Dynasty as the "Six Classic Dances" as a model by later Confucianists.

进入东周的春秋战国时代（公元前 770～前 221 年）。由于铁器的发明，生产力的提高，社会发生巨大变革，封建制度稳固确立。西周初年建立的雅乐体系，在短时期的辉煌后，出现了"礼崩乐坏"的局面。千姿百态的民间舞蓬勃兴起，《诗经》中描绘各地风情的诗歌，极生动地反映了民间舞的活动情景。周代是中国舞蹈发展史上第一个集大成的时代。

History entered the Spring and Autumn Period and the Warring States Period of Eastern Zhou Dynasty (770 BC~221 BC). Due to the invention of ironware and the improvement of productivity, great changes took place in society, and the feudal system was firmly established. After a short period of brilliance, the Yayue (Elegant Music) system established in the early years of Western Zhou Dynasty showed a situation of "disintegration of ritual and music". Folk dances in various forms were flourishing. The poems depicting local customs in the *Book of Songs* vividly reflect the activities of folk dance. Zhou Dynasty was the first agglomeration era in the history of Chinese dance development.

春秋战国时期的孔子、墨子、老子的音乐思想，对中国后世的音乐美学理论产生了不可估量的影响。孔子不仅追求完美的人生境界，而且在音乐上也立志"尽善尽美"。孔子以为，"善"是指乐舞的内容，其中包含了社会道德的内涵；"美"是乐舞的形式，就是指审美的标准。因此，孔子听《韶》乐并给予了极高评价，即"尽善尽美"，以至到了"三月不知肉味"的地步。与孔子持相反论调的，最典型的是墨家"非乐"（即否定音乐）之说。由于墨子十分强调勤俭节约，因此反对儒家"礼乐"制度的奢华。他批评儒家

"好乐而淫人，不可使亲治""儒之道，足以丧天下"。这种思想是站在平民百姓的立场阐发的，墨子认为由于贵族们放纵的音乐行为，使百姓不堪负荷。还有道家的"大音希声"之说。如老子音乐思想的哲学基础是"道法自然"。在他看来，"道"是无形、无象、无任何规定的性质。音乐的"道"，乃是"听之不闻名为希"，其中，"希"属于"道"的自然本性。所谓的"大音希声"，就是指具有"道"的属性的音乐。

The music thoughts of Confucius, Mozi and Laozi (Lao Tzu) in the Spring and Autumn Period and Warring States Period had an immeasurable influence on the music aesthetics theory of Chinese later generations. Confucius not only pursued the perfect state of life, but also determined to "perfect perfection" in music. Confucius believed that "goodness" refers to the content of musical dances, which contains the connotation of social morality; "beauty" is the form of musical dances, which refers to the standard of aesthetics. Therefore, Confucius listened to the *Shao* music to give a very high evaluation, that is, "reach the acme of perfection", and even to the point of "I don't know the taste of meat for three months". Contrary to Confucius, the most typical one was the Mohist's theory of "non-music" (that is, say no to music). Because Mozi emphasized diligence and thrift, he opposed the extravagance of the Confucian "rite and music" system. He criticized Confucians for their "preferring music and puzzling others", "not to be governed directly by them" and "the way of Confucianism is enough to destroy the world." This kind of thought was elucidated from the standpoint of the common people, and Mozi believed that the indulgence of music by the nobles made the people overburdened. There was also the Taoist theory of music "Da Yin Xi Sheng" (the loudest and most beautiful music is no music at all). For example, the philosophical foundation of Laozi's music thought was "the Tao (Way) follows nature". In his view, "Tao" is with no form, image, or regulation. The "Tao" of music is "Xi" that means "one has listened to music but heard nothing" which belongs to the innate nature of "Tao". The so-called "Da Yin Xi Sheng" refers to music with the attribute of "Tao".

（二）秦汉时期 Qin and Han Dynasty

汉代盛行的"百戏"，是多种民间技艺的串演，包括杂技、武术、幻术、滑稽表演、音乐演奏、舞蹈等，深受人民的喜爱。汉代舞蹈的特点是博采众长，技艺向高难度发展，结合了舞蹈与杂技的《盘鼓舞》就是一个典型例子。此外，以长袖为特征的《袖舞》，双手执长巾而舞的《巾舞》，也是汉代著名的舞蹈。以董仲舒为代表的汉儒在继承了孔孟精神的同时，又将"天人感应"和"君权神授"的观念汇入其中并加以发挥。

Baixi (All Performing Arts) was popular in Han Dynasty. It was a stringed performance of a variety of folk arts, including acrobatics, martial arts, illusion, burlesque, music performance, dance, etc. and was deeply affected by the people. The characteristics of the dance of Han Dynasty was that it learned from others' strengths, and its skills developed to high levels of difficulty. The *Plate and Drum Dance*, in which people combined dance and acrobatics, was a typical example. In addition, *Sleeve Dance* characterized by long sleeves and *Scarf Dance*, which danced with a long scarf with both hands, were also famous dances in Han Dynasty. Han Confucianism, represented by Dong Zhongshu, inherited the spirit of Confucius and Mencius, and at the same time incorporated and brought into play the concepts of "interaction between nature and man" and "divine right of kings".

（三）魏晋南北朝时期 Wei, Jin, Southern and Northern Dynasties

魏晋南北朝时期，由于民族迁徙杂居，文化交流频繁，出现了各民族乐舞的大交流。随着西北地少数民族内迁，大量西域乐舞传入中原，如影响颇大的龟兹（今新疆库车一带）乐舞，大约是在公元 384 年传入中原的。由于其欢快的调子、鲜明的节奏，非常适于伴奏舞蹈，深受人们欢迎，因而北周和隋唐时代的多种舞曲都加以采用。此外，其他如天竺（今印度）、高丽（今朝鲜半岛）等地的乐舞，也是这个时候传入中国的。

During Wei, Jin, Southern and Northern Dynasties, due to ethnic migration and frequent cultural exchanges, an era of great exchanges in musical dance between various ethnic groups appeared. With the inland migration of ethnic minorities from the northwest, a large number of Western musical dances were introduced into the Central Plains. For example, the influential musical dance (now Kuqa area in Xinjiang) was introduced to the Central Plains in 384 AD. Because of its cheerful tune and bright rhythm, it was very suitable for accompaniment dance and popular among people. Therefore, many dances and much music from the Northern Zhou Dynasty and Sui and Tang Dynasties were adopted. In addition, musical dance from other places such as Tianzhu (now India) and Goryeo (now Korean Peninsula) were also introduced to China at this time.

魏晋南北朝的文人，始终求索着精神的家园和思想的空间。他们将道家与儒家思想相会通，意图用"玄学"的方式来解放精神的困境。以嵇康、阮籍、阮咸、向秀、山涛、王戎和刘伶为代表的"竹林七贤"，将他们的思想困惑以狂放不羁的行为释放出来，以示对司马氏统治的不满情绪。在音乐方面，也出现了以嵇康为代表的、寄情于古琴的音乐家和经世古琴音乐作品。

The literati in Wei, Jin, Southern and Northern Dynasties often sought a spiritual home and a space for thought. They connected Taoism and Confucianism, and intended to use "metaphysics" to liberate the spiritual predicament. The "seven sages of the bamboo grove" of Ji Kang, Ruan Ji, Ruan Xian, Xiang Xiu, Shan Tao, Wang Rong, and Liu Ling released their ideological confusion through wild and unruly behaviors to show their dissatisfaction with the rule of the Sima family . In terms of music, there had also appeared musicians of Chinese zither and classic music works of Chinese zither represented by Ji Kang.

（四）隋唐五代时期 Sui, Tang and Five Dynasties

公元 581 年，隋代统一中国，结束了长期战乱的局面。隋文帝为了显示自己统一国家的功绩和国力强盛，于开皇初年（公元 581~585 年）集中整理了南北朝各族及部分外国乐舞，制定《七部乐》，后来发展成《九部乐》，使宫廷宴乐得到空前发展。唐代是中国文化蓬勃发展的时期，唐代的舞蹈艺术也得到高度的发展。唐代宫廷设置的各种乐舞机构，如教坊、梨园、太常寺，集中了大批各民族的民间艺人，使唐代舞蹈、音乐成为吸收异族文化精华的载体，反映出唐人自信而又宽怀的恢宏气量。这些宫廷宴乐，都是吸收了各民族乐舞而创制的新型乐舞节目，在内容上则都是歌功颂德的。

In 581 AD, Sui Dynasty unified China and ended the long-term wars. In order to show his achievements in reunifying the country and the strength of his country, Emperor Wen of Sui Dynasty organized the Southern and Northern Dynasties and some foreign musical dances in the early years from 581 to 585 AD, and formulated the "Seven Music", which later developed into the "Nine Music", the palace Yanyue (Banquet music) achieved unprecedented development. Tang Dynasty was a period of vigorous development of Chinese culture, and the dance art of Tang Dynasty was also highly developed. The various musical dance institutions were set up by the court, such as Jiaofang (Imperial music office), Liyuan (the operatic circle), and Taichangsi (Court of Imperial Sacrifices), gathered a large number of folk artists from various nationalities, and made Tang Dynasty dance and music a carrier for absorbing the essence of foreign cultures, reflecting the self-confidence and broadness of the Tang people. These pieces of court banquet music and dances were all new types created by absorbing the music and dance of various nationalities, and they were all eulogizing in content.

"大曲" 是音乐、舞蹈、诗歌三者相结合的多段歌舞曲。开始是一段节奏自由的乐器演奏，叫 "散序"；接着是行板的歌唱（有时插入舞蹈），叫 "中序"；最后是节奏急促，起伏变化的舞曲，叫 "入破"。《霓裳羽衣舞》是唐代著名的歌舞大曲，是唐玄宗李隆基部分地吸收了西凉节度使杨敬述所献印度《婆罗门曲》编创的。作者力图描绘虚幻中的仙境。刘禹锡诗有："三乡陌上望仙山，归作霓裳羽衣曲"。此外，也有唐明皇游月宫作《霓裳羽衣》的传说。

"Daqu" (Big music) was a combination of music, dance, and poetry. It started with a free-rhythm musical instrument performance called "Scattered prelude"; followed by Andante singing (sometimes inserted in dance), called "Middle prelude quence"; finally, there was a dance with rapid rhythm and fluctuations called "Into". *Rainbow Skirt and Feather Garment Dance* was a famous big music in Tang Dynasty. It was composed by Emperor Li Longji (7th emperor) of Tang Dynasty, who partly absorbed the Indian *Brahman music* presented by Yang Jingshu of the Western Liang (Now Gansu province) governor. The author tried to depict the fairyland in the illusion. Poet Liu Yuxi's poem said: "Look upon the fairy mountain from the farmland, when back Rainbow Skirt and Feather Garment Dance is made. " In addition, there was also a legend that Emperor Li Longji traveled to the moon palace and then made *Rainbow Skirt and Feather Garment Dance*.

唐代著名 "健舞"（指那些舞蹈动作风格健朗、豪爽的乐舞）——《剑器》，舞姿健美，气势磅礴。唐代的《剑器》舞继承了前代的剑术。今日武术、戏曲、舞蹈中舞剑的各种技法，更是从古代剑舞发展而来。

The famous "Jian Wu" in Tang Dynasty (referring to those dance moves with vigorous and bold style) —— "Sword Dance", danced with a strong and powerful posture. The "Sword Dance" of Tang Dynasty inherited the swordsmanship of the previous generations. Today, various techniques of sword dancing in martial arts, opera and dance are developed from the ancient sword dance.

（五）宋代时期 Song Dynasty

宋代是中国乐舞文化史上一个重要的转折阶段。这一时期，开封、临安等大城市商业繁华，交通畅达，促进了城市文娱生活的兴盛，民间文学、艺术有很大发展，乐舞文化亦出现新的生机。在大城市中，有许多叫"瓦子"的地方，瓦子内栏成一个个的圈子叫"勾栏"，是专门表演各种技艺的固定场所，表演项目包括杂技、说书、皮影、傀儡戏、舞剑、舞砍刀，以及舞旋等。当中的民间舞蹈及舞蹈性较强的歌舞节目，深受市民欢迎，在中国舞蹈史上占有一席之地。此外，宋代民间舞队也十分兴盛，每逢农历新年、元宵或清明，各地都会举行庆祝活动，各村、各社（城市内各行各业的行会组织）都有自己的民间舞队，即是综合性的街头游行表演队伍。这些舞队所表演的节目，不少至今仍在民间各地流传。

Song Dynasty was an important turning point in the history of Chinese musical dance culture. During this period, large cities such as Kaifeng and Lin'an were prosperous with commerce and communication, which promoted the prosperity of urban cultural and entertainment life. Folk literature and art developed greatly, and musical dance culture also showed new vitality. In big cities, there were many places called "Wazi" (tile market). The inner bars of Wazi were called "Goulan" (Circular Rail for play). They were fixed places dedicated to performing various skills. Performance items included acrobatics, storytelling, shadow play, puppet shows, sword dance, machete dance, and whirling dance. Among them, folk dances and dance performances with strong choreography were well received by the public and occupied a place in the history of Chinese dance. In addition, folk dance teams in Song Dynasty were also very prosperous. Every Lunar New Year, Lantern Festival or Qingming Festival, celebrations were held in various places, and each village and community (guild organizations from all walks of life in the city) had their own folk dance teams, which were the comprehensive street parade performance teams. Many of the perform-ances performed by these dance teams are still circulated among the countrysides.

（六）明清时期 Ming and Qing Dynasty

明代中叶以后，资本主义萌芽已在中国出现。舞蹈，作为独立的表演艺术，在明清两代，有逐渐衰落的趋势，社会上没有专业的舞蹈表演团体，只有极少专业的舞蹈艺人。但是，作为节庆时群众娱乐活动的民间歌舞却呈现出繁盛的局面，表演者多是业余或半业余的民间艺人。宗教活动中的舞蹈，依然由专职的巫师代代传习。

After the middle Ming Dynasty, the sprout of capitalism appeared in China. Dance, as an independent performing art, had a gradual decline in Ming and Qing Dynasties. There were no professional dance performance groups and very few profes-sional dance artists. However, folk songs and dances, as mass entertainment activities during festivals, shew a prosperous situation. The performers were mostly amateur or semi-amateur folk artists. Dances in religious activities were still passed on from gen-eration to generation by full-time wizards.

明清两代广泛流传的汉族民间歌舞，大多在正月十五灯节时演出。明代的社火，清代的走会，就是将多种民间娱乐或技艺，如音乐、舞蹈、杂技、武术等组织在一起，形成综合性的游行表演队伍。在这种队伍中，舞蹈如秧歌、跑旱船、跑竹马、大头和尚、狮子舞、龙舞、霸王鞭、高跷等表演占有重要地位。通过社火、走会的活动，这些舞蹈得以流传至今。

The folk songs and dances of the Han nationality that were widely spread in Ming and Qing Dynasties were mostly performed during the Lantern Festival on the 15th of the first lunar month. The Shehuo (literally Community Fire, a kind of Chinese folk carnival) in Ming Dynasty and the Zouhui (literally Walking Meeting, also a kind of Chinese folk carnival) in Qing Dynasty organized a variety of folk entertainment or skills, such as music, dance, acrobatics, and martial arts, to form a comprehen-sive parade. In this kind of team, dances such as Yangge, the row-boat dana, bam-boo horse dance, big head monk, lion dance, dragon dance, Ba Wang whip, and stilts occupied an important position. These dances have been passed down to this day through activities such as Shehuo and Zouhui.

这一时期中国少数民族地区保存了许多相当古老的传统舞蹈，中国各民族人民在民间歌舞中唱述历史、祭祀祖先、教育后代、祈祝丰收、倾诉爱情、赞美家乡，歌舞是中国各族劳动人民生活中必不可少的组成部分。明清时期，戏曲已成为最受群众欢迎的重要艺术形式，而舞蹈，是戏曲表演的重要组成部分。戏曲舞蹈，直接继承了唐宋歌舞大曲和古代传统舞蹈艺术，经过历代戏曲艺人的加工创造，已形成一套完整的训练体系和表演方法。在明清戏曲剧目中，保存了相当丰富的舞蹈遗产。清代乾隆、嘉庆年间（1736~1820），各地在民间歌舞的基础上形成了众多的丰富多彩的地方戏，如花鼓戏是在民间歌舞花鼓的基础上形成的，采茶戏是在采茶基础上形成的，五音戏剧则吸收了秧歌、花鼓灯的营养，花灯戏是从花灯等发展而来，台湾的歌仔戏是由从福建传到台湾的锦歌、采茶、车鼓弄发展而来的。戏曲舞蹈在清代已经具有程式严格、表现力强、技艺高超的特点。

During this period, many ancient traditional dances were preserved in China's ethnic minority areas. People of all ethnic groups in China sang history, sacrificed ancestors, educated descendants, prayed for a good harvest, talked about love, and praised their hometown in folk songs and dances. Song and dance are an indispensable part of people's lives. During Ming and Qing Dynasties, opera became an important art form most popular with the masses, and dance was an important part of opera performance. The opera dance directly inherited Tang and Song big music and the ancient traditional dance art. After the processing and creation of opera artists of the past dynasties, a complete training system and performance methods have been formed. In the opera repertoire of Ming and Qing Dynasties, quite rich dance heritage was preserved. During Qianlong and Jiaqing reigns (1736~1820) of Qing Dynasty, many colorful local operas were formed on the basis of folk songs and dances. For example, the flower drum opera was formed on the basis of folk song and dance flower drum, and the tea picking opera was formed on the basis of tea picking. The five-tone opera absorbed the nutrition of Yangge (a popular folk dance) and Huagudeng (Flower Drum Lantern). The flower lantern festival show was developed from the flower lantern. Taiwanese opera was developed from the brocade song, tea-picking, and cart drum dance spread from Fujian to Taiwan. In Qing Dynasty, opera dances already had strict formulas, strong expressiveness and superb skills.

三、中国传统舞蹈的特征 Characteristics of Traditional Chinese Dance

作为古老文明的多民族国家，中国舞蹈的发展有着悠久的历史。中国舞蹈以人类社会之初的原始社会为滥觞，其生成和发展经历了从图腾舞蹈文化到巫术舞蹈文化、百戏舞蹈文化，再到独立的舞蹈艺术文化几个不同的历史阶段。中国舞蹈作为一种中国文化的表现形式，在不同的历史发展阶段过程中，呈现出一些特征。

As a multi-ethnic country with ancient civilizations, the development of Chinese dance has a long history. Chinese dance was from the primitive society at the beginning of human society. Its generation and development have experienced several different historical stages of dance culture: from totem dance culture to witchcraft dance culture, from Bai xi culture to independent dance art culture. As a form of expression of Chinese culture, Chinese dance has shown some characteristics in different historical development stages.

（一）中国舞蹈早期的"娱神"特征

The "Entertaining God" Characteristics of Early Chinese Dance

中国戏曲最初的形态就具备"娱人"与"娱神"的双重功能，而中国舞蹈最初的形态倾向于"娱神"的功能，其原形结构则为原始的"宗教礼俗"。这些特征从中国目前发现的古代崖画舞蹈图中可以略见一斑。

Chinese opera has the dual functions of "entertaining people" and "entertaining gods" in its original form, while the original form of Chinese dance tended towards the function of entertaining the gods, and the original structure was primitive "religious etiquette". These characteristics can be seen in the ancient cliff painting dances currently found in China.

原始社会时期，舞蹈是原始人生活中的一部分，但那时并不是出于审美的目的，而是出于原始生活的需要。那时的舞蹈主要表现在"图腾崇拜""祭祀祈神""生殖崇拜""狩猎仪式"等领域。中国各民族之所以有众多的模拟鸟兽的舞蹈，与原始图腾崇拜的文化基因是密切联系的。中国民族民间舞蹈也是从这里开始起步的，从这里可以寻求到其文化原形结构。

In the primitive society, dance was part of the life of primitive people, but at that time it was not for aesthetic purposes, but for the needs of primitive life. At that time, dance was mainly manifested in "totem worship", "sacrifice to gods", "fertility worship", and "hunting rituals". The reason why there are so many dances simulating bird and beast among all ethnic groups in China is closely related to the cultural genes of primitive totem worship. The Chinese folk dance also started from here, from here we can find its original cultural structure.

（二）诗、乐、舞三位一体的综合性形态特征

The comprehensive morphological characteristics of the trinity of poetry, music and dance

远古时期，音乐和舞蹈是相伴而生、相辅相成、并肩发展的，乐和舞密不可分，乐时必有舞，舞时必奏乐。在《诗经》时代，随着民间诗歌的兴起，乐、舞又和诗歌紧密结合起来，形成了诗、乐、舞三位一体的文化特征和文化传统。这类中国舞蹈题材发展到唐代以至顶峰。表现了先民们对丰收的祈求、对天地祖先的崇拜以及对人类的赞美。

In ancient times, music and dance came together, complemented each other, and developed side by side. Music and dance were inseparable. There must be "dance" when "playing music", and "music" must be played when "dancing". In the era of "Book of Songs", with the rise of folk poetry, music, dance and poetry were closely integrated, forming the trinity of cultural characteristics and cultural traditions of poetry, music and dance. For the theme of this type of Chinese dance, it developed to its peak in Tang Dynasty, showing the ancestors' prayers for a good harvest, their worship of the heaven, earth, ancestors, and their praise of mankind.

（三）既"娱神"又"娱人"的双重发展特征

The dual development characteristics of both "entertaining gods" and "entertaining people"

随着人类社会历史的不断前进，奴隶社会制度和封建社会制度的相继建立，舞蹈也逐渐地告别了它的原始形态。如果说原始社会先民们的最初舞蹈

是生命形态的原始记录的话，那么到了奴隶社会，先民们不自觉地从原始时期的那种神秘崇高的生命形态中走出来，舞蹈也从全民性的活动逐渐演变为一部分人的艺术活动和宗教政治活动。至此，中国舞蹈就在"娱神"与"娱人"中双重纵深发展。这类舞蹈主要表现在周代的巫术舞蹈、傩舞蹈和汉代的百戏类舞蹈。在汉代，"百戏"是一种包含音乐、舞蹈、杂技、武术、滑稽戏等多种民间技艺的综合性的演出形式，民间舞蹈成为宫廷乐舞的主要内容，舞蹈通常融于"百戏"中表演。舞蹈过程中的以舞说戏、依戏作舞的表演，成为中国早期戏曲艺术形式的源头。

With the continuous advancement of human social history and the successive establishment of the slave social system and the feudal social system, dance gradually bid farewell to its primitive form. If the original dance of the ancestors of primitive society was the primitive record of life forms, then in the slave society, the ancestors unconsciously stepped out of the mysterious and noble life forms of the primitive period, and gradually evolved from the activities of the whole people to the artistic activities and religious and political activities of some people. So far, Chinese dance developed in the dual depth of "entertaining gods" and "entertaining the folk". This kind of dance was mainly manifested in the witchcraft dance, Nuo dance (Exorcising) of Zhou Dynasty, and Baixi (All Performing Arts) of Han Dynasty. In Han Dynasty, "Baixi" was a comprehensive form of performances that included various folk skills such as music, dance, acrobatics, martial arts, and burlesque. Folk dance became the main content of court music and dance, and dance was usually integrated into "Baixi" performance. In the process of dancing, the performance of telling stories through dance and performing dances based on the stories became the source of the early Chinese opera art form.

（四）舞蹈发展的程式性与专业性特征

The programmatic and professional characteristics of dance development

唐代舞蹈在整个中国古代舞蹈发展史中具有很高的历史成就，以其宏大的演出规模，容纳多国、多民族的舞蹈演出模式，以及雅俗共赏的姿态赢得了世人的喜爱，从宫廷的最高统治者到民间的老百姓无不好之，达到了顶峰时代。宋代舞蹈在历史的转折面前，独辟蹊径，以其独特的方式创造出新的舞蹈的划时代历史，那就是具有程式性特征的"队舞"，绘制了一个新的舞蹈形式。由于明清时期戏曲艺术的发展，舞蹈作为戏曲艺术表现的手段之一，戏曲表演的程式性特征决定了舞蹈表现的舞姿身段的固定性，形成了宋代戏曲舞蹈的高度程式性和综合性的美学特点。

The dance of Tang Dynasty made a high historical achievement in the entire history of ancient Chinese dance development. With its grand performance scale, the dance performance mode including various nations and ethnics, and the state of being enjoyed by both the elegant and the popular, it won the love of the people. From the highest rulers of the palace to the people in the folks, they all liked dances, and dances reached a peak era. At the historical turning point, Song Dynasty dances pioneered a unique way to create a new epoch-making history of dance, that is, the "team dance" with stylized characteristics, showing a new dance form. Due to the development of opera art in Ming and Qing Dynasties, dance was one of the means of opera performance. The stylistic characteristics of opera performance determined the stability of the dance performance and figure, which formed the highly programmatic and comprehensive aesthetics of opera dance in Song Dynasty.

概而言之，中国传统舞蹈自先秦以来，历经几千年的变化，先后经历了先秦诗乐舞三位一体的女乐舞蹈和雅舞、汉代的道具舞、唐代的宴乐舞蹈、宋代的"队舞"、明清时期的戏曲舞蹈、当代的专业舞蹈和舞蹈教育。所有这些在表现形式的演变上，都是一个渐次演进、符合艺术发展规律的过程。

To sum up, traditional Chinese dance has undergone thousands of years of changes since the pre-Qin Dynasties. It has experienced female dance and elegant dance with the trinity of poetry, music and dance in the pre-Qin Dynasties, prop dance in Han Dynasty, Yanyue (banquet dance) in Tang Dynasty, and "team dance" in Song Dynasty. Opera dance in the Ming and Qing Dynasties, contemporary professional dance and dance education. All these are a process of gradual evolution and in conformity to the law of artistic development in the evolution of expression forms.

四、中国传统著名舞蹈家 Famous Traditional Chinese Dancers

中国古代流传下来的著名舞蹈家可谓群星灿烂，各个时期有各个时期的翘楚。最著名的是如下四位。

The famous dancers handed down in ancient China could be said to be shining stars, and there were top dancers in different periods. The following four were the most famous.

1. 西施

是春秋时代著名的宫廷舞人。越王勾践为向吴国复仇使美人计，把西施送给昏庸好色的吴王夫差。夫差得西施后，终日沉溺在歌舞和酒色之中，不理朝政。据记载，为了西施表演《响屐舞》，夫差在御花园的一条长廊中，命人把廊挖空，放进大缸，上面铺木板，取名"响屐廊"。西施脚穿木屐，裙系小铃，在婀娜优美舞姿中，木屐踏在木板上时，沉重的"铮铮嗒嗒"回声和裙上小铃清脆欢快的"叮叮当当"声相互交织，别有一番迷人的风味。吴王为西施所迷，荒废了政务，民不聊生，怨声载道。越王勾践趁机发兵打败了吴国，夫差被迫自杀。

Xi Shi. She was a famous court dancer in the Spring and Autumn Period. In order to avenge the state of Wu, Goujian (King of the state of Yue) sent Xi Shi to the mediocre and lustful Fuchai, King of Wu. After Fuchai got Xishi, he indulged in singing, dancing and drinking all day long, ignoring government affairs. According to records, for Xi Shi to perform *Xiangji Dance* (*Chinese Clog Dance*), Fu Chai ordered to build a long corridor in the Imperial Garden. He ordered people to hollow out the corridor and put in large tanks instead, and then pave it with wooden boards, named "Sound Clogs Corridor". Xi Shi wore clogs on her feet and small bells on her skirt. In the graceful and charming dance, the clogs stepped on the wooden board, making a heavy "clank clank dada" echo and the crisp and cheerful "ding ding dang dang" sound of the little bells on the skirt intertwined. Ah, charming flavor. The King was fascinated by Xi Shi and abandoned government affairs. King Goujian took the opportunity to send troops to defeat Fuchai, the king of Wu, and he was forced to commit suicide.

2. 赵飞燕

原名宜主，汉代的著名舞人。为阳阿公主家的婢女，她聪明伶俐、身材窈窕，学习歌舞时精心、刻苦，所以出人头地。由于她的舞姿特别轻盈，故人称"赵飞燕"。后被汉成帝看中，召入宫中，封为"婕妤"（女官名），数年后立为皇后。

Zhao Feiyan (flying swallow) . Formerly known as Yizhu, a famous dancer in Han Dynasty. As the maid of Princess Yang's family, she was smart, slender, and meticulous and hardworking in singing and dancing, so she stood out. Because of her very light dance, she was called "Zhao Feiyan". Later, she was favored by Emperor Cheng, summoned into the palace, and was named "Jieyu" (female official), and became queen a few years later.

赵飞燕, 身轻若燕, 能作掌上舞。相传汉成帝为赵飞燕造了一个水晶盘, 令宫人用手托盘, 赵飞燕则在水晶盘上潇洒自如地舞蹈, 由此可见其舞蹈的功力。还有一个传说: 赵飞燕穿着南越进贡的云英紫裙, 表演歌舞——《归风送远之曲》, 成帝以文簪敲击玉瓯打拍子, 冯无方吹笙伴奏。歌舞正酣, 忽然起了大风, 飞燕随风扬袖飘舞, 好像要乘风飞去。成帝急忙叫冯无方拉住赵飞燕。一会儿, 风停了, 赵飞燕的裙子也被抓皱了。从此宫中就流行一种折叠有皱的裙子叫"留仙裙"。

Zhao Feiyan was as light as a swallow and could dance on the palm. According to legend, Emperor Cheng of Han Dynasty made a crystal plate for Zhao Feiyan, which was held by the palace staff, and Zhao Feiyan danced freely on the crystal plate. This shew her dancing skills. There was another legend: Zhao Feiyan wore a purple dress as a tribute from South Vietnam, and performed singing and dancing——*The Music of Gone with the Wind*. Emperor Cheng used the hairpin to beat the jade cup, and Feng Wufang played the Sheng (a Chinese wind instrument) as accompaniment. The singing and dancing were vigorous, and suddenly there was a strong wind, and Feiyan fluttered with the wind and raised her sleeves, as if to fly away with the wind. Emperor Cheng hurriedly asked Feng Wufang to hold Zhao Feiyan. After a while, the wind stopped and Zhao Feiyan's skirt was also creased. Since then, a kind of skirt was popular in the palace called "Liuxian skirt" (Keeping the fairy).

3. 杨玉环

唐代著名的舞蹈家, 她生得丰满艳丽, 是盛唐典型的美人。她音乐素养很好, 会演奏多种乐器, 歌舞尤为出色。据传她除了擅长表演《霓裳羽衣舞》外, 她跳的《胡旋舞》也有很高的舞蹈技艺。唐代大诗人白居易所写《霓裳羽衣歌》记述了这个舞蹈给予他的深刻印象。天宝四年（745 年），唐玄宗封杨玉环为贵妃，自此对她宠爱到极点，她的全家也都当上了大官，他们自由出入宫廷，十分专横跋扈。天宝十五年（756 年），"安史之乱"起，唐玄宗逃往四川，杨贵妃同行。当时潼关失守，人们对唐玄宗穷奢极欲引起的战乱非常愤慨，路过陕西马嵬坡时，六军不发，逼迫唐玄宗下诏令将杨贵妃缢死。

Yang Yuhuan. A famous dancer in Tang Dynasty, she grew up plump and gorgeous, and she was a typical beauty in the prosperous Tang Dynasty. She had a good musical accomplishment and could play a variety of instruments, especially was good at singing and dancing. It is said that in addition to performing *Rainbow Skirt and Feather Garment Dance*, she was also skilled at *Huxuan Dance*. *The Song of Rainbow Skirt and Feather Garment* written by Bai Juyi, a great poet of Tang Dynasty, described the deep impression that this dance made on him. In the fourth year of Tianbao (745 AD), Emperor Xuanzong of Tang Dynasty named Yang Yuhuan a noble concubine. Since then, the emperor had been extremely doted on her, and her whole family also became high officials. They were free to enter and leave the court and were very domineering. In the fifteenth year of Tianbao (756 AD), when the "An-Shi Rebellion" began, Tang Xuanzong fled to Sichuan, accompanied by Concubine Yang. At that time, Tongguan Pass fell, and people were very angry at the war caused by Tang Xuanzong's extravagance and lust. When passing by Maweipo, Shaanxi, the Six Armies did not set off by order, forcing Tang Xuanzong to order the concubine Yang to be hanged to death.

4. 公孙大娘

公孙大娘是开元盛世时唐宫的第一舞人。善舞剑器，舞姿惊动天下。以舞《剑器》而闻名于世。她在民间献艺，观者如山，应邀到宫廷表演，无人能比。她的《剑器》舞风靡一时。她在继承传统剑舞的基础上，创造了多种《剑器》舞。世事浮云，以公孙娘子盛唐第一的技艺，最终结局却是流落江湖，寂寞而终。然而，她的盖世技艺是与中国历史上的两座文化高峰联系在一起的。正是因为她，我们才有幸看到了草圣张旭的一卷绝妙丹青，才有幸读到了诗圣杜甫的一首慷慨悲凉的《观公孙大娘弟子舞剑器行》，就连画圣吴道子也曾通过观赏公孙大娘舞剑，体会用笔之道。公孙大娘成就三圣之道，这位绝代佳人当再不寂寞。

Aunt Gongsun was the best dancer in the Tang Palace in the prosperous period of Kaiyuan. Good at sword dance, her dancing posture shocked the world. She was famous for her dancing *Sword Dance*. She performed in folk art, and the audience were as many as a mountain, and she was invited to perform at the court, which no one could compare. Her *Sword Dance* was all the rage. On the basis of inheriting the traditional sword dance, she created a variety of "sword" dances. The world was full of clouds, with the best skill in the flourishing of Tang Dynasty, her ending was to live homelessly and lonely. However, her outstanding skills were connected with the two cultural peaks in Chinese history. It is precisely because of her that we are fortunate enough to see a volume of exquisite calligraphy by Zhang Xu, the sage of cursive script, and a generous and desolate poem *A Song of Sword Dancing to A Girl-Pupil of Lady Gongsun* by Du Fu, a poet sage, or the poet of poets. Even the painting sage Wu Daozi understood the way of using brush through his once watching her sword dances. Lady Gongsun's achievement in helping the three sages, this peerless beauty should never be lonely again.

中国的传统戏曲文化

一、中国传统戏曲艺术的起源 The Origin of Traditional Chinese Opera Art

中国和西方戏剧都是源自民间，与祭祀敬神的宗教仪式有关。西方戏剧主要起源于祭酒神的颂歌，带有浓厚的宗教色彩，神秘的、幻想的、悲剧性的基因多，从歌舞逐渐演变为戏剧表演。而中国戏剧虽然也和一定的宗教仪式有关，但主要为娱乐性活动，现实的、技艺的、喜剧性的基因多；是多源的、复杂的、交织的戏剧表演。

The origins of Chinese and Western dramas came from the folk and were related to religious rituals to worship the gods. Western dramas mainly originated from the ode to Dionysus, or God of Wine, with a strong religious color and a mysterious, fantastic and tragic genes, and later gradually evolved from singing and dancing to drama performance. Although Chinese dramas were also related to certain religious rituals, they were mainly entertainment activities, with many genes that were realistic, technical, and comedic; they were multi-source, complex, and intertwined drama performances.

若追溯源头，中国戏曲萌芽得非常早，从先秦时期的巫师祭祀，历经汉代俳优、百戏，唐代歌舞戏、参军戏等，一直停留在歌舞和滑稽戏的表演层面，没能形成真正意义上的戏曲。直到宋、金时期，宋杂剧兴盛，大型说唱艺术——诸宫调也日渐成熟，中国戏曲才真正开始形成。

If we go back to the source, Chinese opera sprouted very early. From the Shamanic Sacrificial Rites in the pre-Qin period, through Han Dynasty Paiyou (Comedian), Baixi (All Performing Arts), Tang Dynasty musical dance drama, Canjun opera（a kind of farce）, it stayed at the performance level of song, dance and bur-lesque, and it was not formed in the true sense of drama. It was not until Song and Jin Dynasties that Zaju（a Poetic Drama set to music）flourished in Song Dynasty, and the large-scale rap art, Zhugong Diao（Song-speech Drama）, also matured, that Chinese operas really began to take shape.

二、中国传统戏曲艺术的发展 The Development of Traditional Chinese Opera Art

中国传统的戏曲，是一种高度综合性的艺术，从 2000 多年前的秦汉时期孕育，到南宋时期成熟，距今已有七八百年的历史。秦汉时期以歌唱、舞蹈、说笑、杂耍以及滑稽表演为主，或操乐器歌唱表演动作。到了唐代，出现演员角色分工，一个叫"参军"，一个叫"苍鹘"，由这两个演员在台上作滑稽对话或即兴表演逗笑。唐玄宗在宫廷里集中艺人排练歌舞节目的地点叫"梨园"。从此，人们便称戏班为"梨园"，称戏曲演员为"梨园子弟"。

Traditional Chinese opera is a highly comprehensive art. It was conceived in Qin and Han dynasties more than 2000 years ago and matured in the Southern Song Dy-nasty. It has a history of 700 to 800 years. During Qin and Han dynasties, singing, dancing, jokes, juggling and burlesque were the mainstays, sometimes singing and performing actions with musical instruments. In Tang Dynasty, there was a division of roles of actors, one called "Canjun"（act as an officer）and the other called "Cang-hu"（act as a clown）. These two actors made funny dialogues or impromptu perform-ances on stage to make laughs. The place where emperor Tang Xuanzong gathered artists to rehearse singing and dancing shows in the palace was called Liyuan or "Pear Garden"（means the operatic circle）. Since then, people have called the opera troupe "Liyuan" and opera actors as "Liyuan children".

后来又不断发展，出现京剧等戏曲班子。不同宫调、曲牌的音乐组合到一起，唱白相间，具备了以音乐来歌唱讲述故事的功能，宋杂剧的角色体制要比此前的滑稽戏更丰富多样，这两种形式慢慢融合，从说唱的第三人称叙事体逐渐转变成了表演的第一人称代言体。到了元代，元杂剧形成，标志着中国传统戏曲成熟了。元杂剧《西厢记》便是从《西厢记诸宫调》发展而来。元杂剧体制是一本四折，只由一人主唱，其他角色只有说白。这种体制也是受说唱艺术的影响。事实上，元代的戏曲有南北之分。由于宋金时期，南北分治，南方的民间歌谣小调与说唱艺术结合，逐渐形成了南戏，南戏偏于俚俗，各个角色均可演唱，不像北杂剧有严格规范的体制，当时虽不受文人士大夫重视，但却颇受下层民众喜爱，流行于东南沿海。北方的北杂剧主要是宫廷、寺庙、民间音乐结合而成，以大都为中心，发展势头较猛。关汉卿便是活跃在大都的杂剧家，其《窦娥冤》便是家喻户晓的代表性作品。

Later, it continued to develop, and opera groups such as Peking Opera. Gongdiao (Modes of ancient Chinese music or Tunes) combined music of different tunes and different names of tunes together, singing and speaking alternately, and had the function of singing and telling stories with music. The role system of Zaju in Song Dynasty was richer and more diverse than the previous burlesques. These two forms were gradually integrated. The third-person narrative of rap gradually transformed into the first-person endorsement of performance. In Yuan Dynasty, Zaju (a poetic drama) was formed, marking the maturity of traditional Chinese opera. The Zaju *West Chamber* was developed from *West Chamber Tunes*. The Zaju system in Yuan Dynasty was a four-fold book, with only one leading singer, and the other characters only speaking plainly. This system was also influenced by the art of rap. In fact, the operas of Yuan Dynasty were divided into north and south. Due to the division of the North and the South during Song and Jin Dynasties, the Southern folk songs and the art of rap were combined, and the South-China folk Opera was gradually formed. The Southern Opera preferred slangs and could be sung by all roles. Unlike the Northern Zaju, which had a strict and standardized system, the Southern Opera was not valued by literati or scholar-officials at the time but was loved by lower classes and was popular in Southeast coastal areas. Northern Zaju (poetic drama) in the north was mainly a combination of music from palaces, temples, and countryside. The great playwright Guan Hanqing was an active dramatist in Big Capital (now Beijing), and his *Dou E's Injustice* was a well-known work.

戏曲发展到明清时期，北杂剧衰落，南戏发展起来，中国戏曲又逐渐打破了元杂剧这种一本四折只由一人主唱的体制，发展成了更为自由的传奇戏。传奇戏不受一本四折的限制，可长可短，且剧中不再是一人主唱，各个角色均可演唱。最初的南戏流行在南方的不同地区，形成了具有地方特色的不同声腔，主要有海盐腔、弋阳腔、昆山腔、余姚腔等。后来，明代魏良辅改良昆山腔，将南北音乐加以融合，创造出了格调新颖、字正腔圆、流利悠扬、细腻婉转的"水磨调"——昆曲，并加入了更丰富多样的伴奏乐器，使之更具有感染力。自此，昆曲便迅速流传开来，受到了上层的喜爱和重视，渐渐发展成了"官腔""雅部"，其他声腔被贬为"花部"遭到压制。于是，明清大量的传奇戏剧本都是昆曲剧本，比如《牡丹亭》《桃花扇》《长生殿》等。清代中后期，在民间发展的地方戏再次勃兴，地方诸腔又与昆曲再较短长。直到乾隆末年四大徽班进京，南腔北调汇集一城，各大声腔之间相互竞争和学习。以唱吹腔、二黄为主的徽班，集各家所长，吸收秦腔、汉调、昆曲等声腔最终衍生了京剧这一新的大剧种，其他地方戏也在各自基础上发展。

Traditional opera developed into Ming and Qing Dynasties, the northern opera declined, and the southern opera developed. Chinese opera gradually broke the system of Zaju in Yuan Dynasty, which had a four-fold book with only one leading singer, and developed into a more free legendary opera. The legendary play was not limited by a four-fold book, it can be long or short, and there was no longer a single lead singer in the play, and all roles can sing. The original South opera was popular in different regions of the south, and different tunes with local characteristics were formed, mainly including Haiyan, Yiyang, Kunshan, and Yuyao. Later, the musician Wei Liangfu of Ming Dynasty improved the Kunshan accent and merged the north and south music to create a new style, clear and articulate, fluent and melodious, delicate and tactile "water milling tune" ——Kun Tune, and added a richer variety of accompaniment instruments to make it more infectious and impressive. Since then, Kunqu Opera spread quickly and was loved and valued by the upper class. It gradually developed into "official tunes" and "yabu" (elegant opera). Other tunes were relegated to "huabu" (folk opera) and suppressed. As a result, a large number of legendary plays in Ming and Qing Dynasties were all Kunqu opera scripts, such as *Peony Pavilion*, *Peach Blossom Fan* and *Eternal Palace*. In the middle and late Qing Dynasty, the local operas developed by the people flourished again, and the local tunes were competitive with Kunqu opera. Until the last years of Emperor Qianlong, the four major opera troupes from Anhui province entered Peking, and the Southern and

Northern Tunes gathered in one city, and different tunes competed and learned from each other. The Anhui Troupes, which focused on singing and blowing tunes and Erhuang Melodies, gathered the advantages of various schools and absorbed the tunes of Qin Tune, Han Tune, and Kun Tune, which eventually gave birth to the new big opera genre, Peking Opera. Other local operas still developed on their own basis.

京剧是中华民族传统戏曲的主要剧种之一。它是在 19 世纪中叶从北京开始形成和发展起来的，故称"京剧"。京剧的前身叫"皮黄戏"，在中国大约有近 200 年的历史。京剧是综合当时流行的湖北省戏班的西皮调唱腔和安徽省徽戏二簧调等重要地方戏曲的特色，并吸收当时流行宫廷和民间的秦腔、弋腔和昆曲等戏剧的精华，逐步具有自己独特的风格。它的最大特点是唱、做、念、打的节奏特别鲜明。到清朝同治、光绪年间（公元 1862 年~公元 1908 年）京剧便盛行全中国。

Peking opera is one of the main types of traditional Chinese opera. It was formed and developed from Peking (now Beijing) in the mid 19th century, so it was called "Peking Opera". The predecessor of Peking Opera was called "Pihuang Opera", which has a history of nearly 200 years in China. Peking opera was a synthesis of the characteristics of important local operas such as the Xipi tune of opera troupe from Hubei Province and Erhuang Tune from Hui Opera of Anhui Province. It absorbed the essence of the popular court and folk operas such as Qin Opera, Yi Opera and Kun Opera, and gradually had its own unique style. Its striking feature is that the rhythm of singing, acting, reciting, and fighting is particularly distinct. In the Emperor Tongzhi and Emperor Guangxu reigns (1862~1908 AD) of Qing Dynasty, Peking Opera became very much popular throughout China.

总之，中国戏曲的形成，最早可以追溯到秦汉时代。但形成过程相当漫长，到了宋元之际才得成型。成熟的戏曲要从元杂剧算起，历经明、清的不断发展成熟而进入现代，历八百多年繁盛不败，如今有 360 多个剧种。中国古典戏曲在其漫长的发展过程中，曾先后出现了宋元南戏、元代杂剧、明清传奇、清代地方戏及近、现代戏曲等几种基本形式。

In short, the formation of Chinese opera can be traced back to Qin and Han Dynasties. But the formation process was quite long, and it was not formed until Song and Yuan Dynasties. The maturity of the genre of opera should be counted from the

Zaju of Yuan Dynasty, and entered the modern era through the continuous development and maturity of Ming and Qing Dynasties. It has been prosperous for more than 800 years. There are now more than 360 types of opera. In the long development process of Chinese opera, there have been several basic genres, including South-China folk Operas in the Song and Yuan Dynasties, Zaju Operas in Yuan Dynasties, Ming and Qing Legends, Qing Dynasty Local Operas and Modern Opera.

三、中国传统戏曲艺术的特点 Features of Traditional Chinese Opera Culture

1. 始于离者，终于和 Begin with separation, and end in harmony

中国戏曲的特点是将众多艺术形式，以一种标准聚合在一起，在共同具有的性质中体现其各自的个性，即和。这些形式主要包括：诗、乐、舞。诗指其文学，乐指其音乐伴奏，舞指其表演。此外还包括舞台美术、服装、化妆等方面。而这些艺术因素在戏曲中都为了一个目的，即演故事；都遵循一个原则，即美。

The characteristic of traditional Chinese opera is to bring together many art forms with one standard, and to embody their respective personalities in the common nature, that is harmony. These forms mainly include: poetry, music, and dance. Poetry refers to its literature, music refers to its musical accompaniment, and dance refers to its performance. It also includes stage art, costumes and makeup. These artistic factors all serve one purpose in opera, that is, to act out stories; they all follow one principle, that is, beauty.

2. 戏曲者，谓以歌舞演故事也 Operas act out stories with songs and dances

中国传统戏曲之特点，一言以蔽之，"谓以歌舞演故事也"。戏曲与话剧，均为戏剧之属，都要通过演员扮演人物，运用对话和动作去表现一定长度的故事情节。所不同者，戏曲是运用音乐化的对话和舞蹈化的动作去表现现实生活的，即歌舞的手段，也即人们所熟知的"唱、念、做、打"。

The characteristics of traditional Chinese opera can be summed up in a word, that is, "to act out stories with songs and dances." Chinese opera and drama are both varieties of play. In both categories actors play characters and use dialogues and actions to express a certain length of story. The difference is that Chinese opera uses musical dialogue and dance actions to express real life, that is, the means of singing and dancing. It is also known as "singing, reciting, acting and fighting".

3. 离形而取意，得意而忘形 Get to the point without considering the form

中国传统戏曲的表现生活，运用了一种"取其意而弃其形"的方式，如中国画之写意山水，用纵横的笔势去体现生活中一切美好的事物。所以，戏曲舞台上才有了红脸的关羽，白脸的曹操；有了长歌当哭，长袖善舞；有了无花木之春色，无波涛之江河。

The expression of life in traditional Chinese opera uses a way of "taking what it means and discarding its shape", just like the freehand brushwork of traditional Chinese painting, using vertical and horizontal strokes to reflect the good things in life. Therefore, the red-faced General Guan Yu and the white-faced Governor Cao Cao are present on the opera stage; and sing for crying, long sleeves for dance; there is a spring without flowers and trees, and a river without waves.

4. 舞台小天地，天地大舞台 The stage is a small world, and the world is a big stage

中国戏曲作为一种舞台艺术，需要面对一个舞台之狭小与生活之博大的矛盾。戏曲并没有像话剧那样用"三一律"的原则对生活进行挤压以便于表现。而是运用虚拟的手段，制造弹性的时空，又借助于演员生动的表演和观众的想象与理解，来完成对广大天地的描画。

As a stage art, traditional Chinese opera needs to face the contradiction between the narrowness of the stage and the vastness of life. Opera does not squeeze life with the principle of "trinity" as in drama to facilitate the expression. Instead, it uses virtual means to create flexible time and space, and draws on the vivid performances of actors and the imagination and understanding of the audience to complete the depiction of the vast world.

四、中国传统戏曲著名曲目 Famous Repertoires of Chinese Opera

1. 京剧：玉堂春、贵妃醉酒、长坂坡、群英会、打金枝、搜孤救孤、秦香莲、空城计、霸王别姬等。

Peking Opera: The Story of Su San, Drunken Noble Concubine, The Battle of Changban, The Gathering of Heroes, The Admonishment of the Princess, The Orphan of Zhao, The Forsaken Wife Qin Xianglian, Strategy of an Empty Town, Farewell to My Concubine, etc.

2. 昆曲：鸣凤记、牡丹亭、紫钗记、邯郸记、南柯记、义侠记、游园惊梦、阳关、三醉等。

Kun Opera: The Story of Crying Phoenixes, The Peony Pavilion, The Story of Purple Hairpin, The Story of Handan, A Dream Under the Southern Bough, The Story of Righteous Hero, Peony Pavillion: Wandering in the Garden Waking from a Dream, Yangguan, Three Times Drunks.

3. 越剧：梁山伯与祝英台、王老虎抢亲、红楼梦、西厢记、白蛇传、孟丽君、柳毅传书、孔雀东南飞等。

Yue Opera: Liang Shanbo and Zhu Yingtai (Chinese Romeo and Juliet), Tiger Wang's Force Marriage, Dream of the Red Chamber, Romance of the West Bower, The Story of White Snake, The Story of Miss Meng Lijun, Mr. Liuyi Delivers the Letter, The Peacock Flies Southeast.

4. 豫剧：对花枪、三上轿、宇宙锋、地塘板、铡美案、十二寡妇征西、春秋配等。

Yu Opera: Spear Fighting, Three Times on Sedan Chairs, The Sword Yuzhoufeng, Ditang ban, The Case of Chen Shimei, Twelve Widows Conquering the West, The Matching of Chunhua and Qinlian.

5. 黄梅戏：天仙配、牛郎织女、槐荫记、女驸马等。

Huangmei Opera: Marriage of the Fairy Princess, The Cowherd and the Weaver Girl, Love Under the Scholar-Tree, Emperor's Female Son-in-law.

6. 评剧：花为媒、樊梨花斩子、拜月记、无双传、白蛇传、樱花恋、喜神等。

Ping Opera: Flower is a Matchmaker, Ms. Fan Lihua Kills Her Son, Moon Worship, The Story of Miss Wushuang, The Story of White Snake, Sakura Love, God of Joy.

五、中国戏曲著名表演艺术家 Famous Performing Artists of Chinese Operas

京剧：梅兰芳、尚小云、程砚秋、荀慧生、马连良、谭富英、杨宝森、奚啸伯、周信芳、裘盛戎、袁世海、言菊朋、叶少兰……

Peking Opera：Mei Lanfang, Shang Xiaoyun, Cheng Yanqiu, Xun Huisheng; Ma Lianliang, Tan Fuying, Yang Baosen, Xi Xiaobo, Zhou Xinfang, Qiu Shengrong, Yuan Shihai, Yan Jupeng, Ye Shaolan. . .

评剧：新凤霞。

Ping Opera：Xinfengxia.

越剧：袁雪芬、戚雅仙；黄梅戏：严凤英；河北梆子：裴艳玲；豫剧：常香玉……

Yue Opera：Yuan Xuefen, Qi Yaxian；Huangmei Opera：Yan Fengying；Hebei Bangzi：Pei Yanling；Yu Opera：Chang Xiangyu. . .

京剧有四大名旦，四大须生，都是很著名的艺术家。

There were four male actors acted as female characters and four Elderly Male Characters in Peking Opera, they were all very famous artists.

黄梅戏有严凤英和王少舫，剧目有《天仙配》《女驸马》《牛郎织女》。

There were Miss Yan Fengying and Mr. Wang Shaofang in Huangmei Opera, the famous plays were *Marriage of the Fairy Princess*, *Emperor's Female Son-in-law*, *The Cowherd and The Weaver Girl*.

豫剧有常香玉和马金凤，常有《花木兰》《红娘》；马有《花枪缘》《穆桂英挂帅》《花打朝》。

Yu opera included Ms. Chang Xiangyu and Ms. Ma Jinfeng, and Ms. Chang was famous for *Mulan* and *The Matchmaker*；Ms. Ma had *Romance of the Spear*, *Ms. Mu Guiying Takes Command* and *The Seventh Grandma*.

越剧有徐玉兰、王文娟，最著名的就是《红楼梦》；还有袁雪芬《祥林嫂》、梁祝的《许九妹》；还有尹桂芳，最著名的是《何文秀》。

Yue opera included Ms. Xu Yulan and Ms. Wang Wenjuan, their most famous work was *Dream of the Red Chamber*；Ms. Yuan Xuefen's *Sister Xianglin* and Liang Zhu's *The Ninth Younger Sister Xu*；and Ms. Yin Guifang, the most famous being

Ms. He Wenxiu.

粤剧有红线女，最著名的是《关汉卿》。

Cantonese opera had Hung Sin-nui, the most famous one was *Guan Hanqing*.

还有昆曲的俞振飞和言慧珠（是梅兰芳的徒弟，京昆都佳），最著名的有《墙头马上》和《李白脱靴》。

There were also Kun Opera actors Mr. Yu Zhenfei and Ms. Yan Huizhu（Mei Lanfang's student, good at Peking Opera and Kun Opera）, the most famous were *On the Wall and Horse* and *Li Bai Takes Off Boots*.

第十五章

中国的传统音乐文化

一、中国传统音乐文化的起源 The Origin of Traditional Chinese Music Culture

中国音乐，文献一般追溯到黄帝时代。据考古发现，中国音乐可追溯至9000多年前，中华民族在几千年的历史长河中，创造了丰富的音乐文化。中国音乐曾经对中国周边地区的音乐产生了深远的影响。

Chinese music documents generally date back to the time of Yellow King. According to archaeological discoveries, Chinese music can be traced back to more than 9, 000 years ago. The Chinese nation has created a rich music culture over thousands of years. Chinese music has had a profound influence on the music of China's surrounding areas.

从孔子传六艺到唐代的胡琴再到近代的西方音乐，中国音乐在吸收外来音乐要素的过程中不断充实发展。中国素号"礼乐之邦"，传统音乐在人格养成、文化生活和国家礼仪方面有着很重要的作用和地位。孔子曾提出"兴于诗，立于礼，成于乐"的学习步骤。

From the Six Arts of Confucius to the Northern minority lyre in Tang Dynasty and then to modern Western music, Chinese music has continued to develop in the process of absorbing foreign music elements. China has long been known as "the country of rite and music", in which traditional music plays an important role and status in its personality formation, cultural life and national etiquette. Confucius once said, "It is by the Book of Songs that the mind is aroused. It is by the Rituals that the character is established. It is from the Music that the finish is received."

二、中国传统音乐文化的发展历程 The Development Process of Traditional Chinese Music Culture

根据文献记载，夏商两代为奴隶制社会早期。从古典文献记载来看，这时的乐舞已经渐渐脱离原始氏族乐舞为氏族共有的特点，它们更多地为高等阶级所占有。

西周是中国奴隶制的成熟时期，东周是奴隶制社会由盛到衰、君主统治因素日趋增长的历史时期。西周时期宫廷首先建立了完备的礼乐制度。

According to the historical documents, Xia and Shang Dynasties were the early days of slavery society. Based on the records of classical literature, the musical dances at this time gradually deviated from the characteristics shared by the primitive clan musical dances, and they were more enjoyed by the higher classes.

The Western Zhou Dynasty was the mature period of Chinese slavery, and the Eastern Zhou Dynasty slavery society went from prosperity to decline, and was the historical period of the monarch's rule increasing. In the Western Zhou Dynasty, the royal court first established a complete system of rite and music.

秦汉时开始出现"乐府"。它继承了周代的采风制度，搜集、整理、改编民间音乐，也集中了大量乐工在宴享、郊祀、朝贺等场合演奏。这些用作演唱的歌词，被称为乐府诗。乐府，后来又被引申为泛指各种入乐或不入乐的歌词，甚至一些戏曲和器乐也都称之为乐府。

由相和歌发展起来的清商乐在北方得到曹魏政权的重视，设置清商署。两晋之交的战乱，使清商乐流入南方，与南方的吴歌、西曲融合。在北魏时，这种南北融合的清商乐又回到北方，从而成为流传全国的重要乐种。

"Yuefu" (originally literally meant "Music Bureau") began to appear in Qin and Han Dynasties. It inherited the folk collection system of Zhou Dynasty, collected, sorted, and adapted folk music, and also concentrated a large number of musicians to perform on occasions such as banquets, rites and ceremonies. These lyrics used for singing were called Yuefu poems. Yuefu was later extended to refer to all kinds of lyrics that were either written into music or not. Even some operas and instrumental music were also called Yuefu.

The Qingshang music developed by mutual response songs received the attention of the Cao's regime in the north, and the Qingshang Office was set up. The wars at the turn of Jin Dynasty caused Qingshang Music to flow into the south and merge with Wu songs and Western Music in the south. In the Northern Wei Dynasty, this kind of north-south integration of Qingshang music returned to the north and became an important music type spread throughout the country.

汉代以来，随着丝绸之路的畅通，西域诸国的歌曲开始传入内地。北凉时吕光将在隋唐宴会中占有重要位置的龟兹（今新疆库车）乐带到内地。由此可见当时各族人民在音乐上的交流已经十分普及了。

隋唐两代，政权统一，特别是唐代，政治稳定，经济兴旺，统治者奉行开放政策，不断吸收他方文化，加上以魏晋以来已经孕育着的各族音乐文化融合为基础，终于爆发了以歌舞音乐为主要标志的音乐艺术的全面发展的高峰。

Since Han Dynasty, with the smooth flow of the Silk Road, songs from the Western Regions began to spread to the inland. During the Northern Liang Dynasty, Lü Guang brought Qiuci (now Kuqa, Xinjiang) music to the inland, which played an important role in the Banquet music in Sui and Tang Dynasties, to the inland. It can be seen that the exchange of music among people of all ethnic groups was very popular.

During Sui and Tang Dynasties, the regime was unified, especially in Tang Dynasty, with political stability and economic prosperity. The rulers pursued an open-policy and continuously absorbed other cultures. In addition, the integration of music and culture of various ethnic groups that had been bred since the Wei and Jin dynasties lay the foundation. Song, dance and music were the main symbols of the peak of the all-round development of the music art.

宋、金、元时代音乐文化的发展以市民音乐的勃兴为重要标志，较隋唐音乐得到更为深入的发展。随着都市商品经济的繁荣，适应市民阶层文化生活的游艺场"瓦舍""勾栏"应运而生。在"瓦舍""勾栏"中人们可以听到叫声、嘌唱、小唱、唱赚等艺术歌曲的演唱；也可以看到说唱类音乐种类的表演；可谓争奇斗艳、百花齐放。而鼓子词则影响到后世的说唱音乐鼓词。诸宫调是这一时期成熟起来的大型说唱曲种，其中歌唱占了较重的分量。

The development of music culture in Song, Jin, and Yuan Dynasties was marked by the prosperity of civilian music, which was more in-depth development than the music of Sui and Tang Dynasties. With the prosperity of the city commodity economy, the entertainment venues "Washe" (tile-roofed houses) and "Goulan" (Circular Rail for play) that adapted to the cultural life of the civilian class emerged. In "Washe" and "Goulan", people could hear the singing of songs such as shouting, pursing, slang song, and cyclical song; we could also see different rap music types; It could be said they were contending with each other, and a hundred flowers of music bloomed. The Drum Rap affected later generations in drum rap music. Zhugong Diao (Song-Speech Drama) matured during this period was a large-scale rap opera in which singing occupied a main part.

由于明清社会已经出现资本主义经济因素的萌芽，市民阶层日益壮大，音乐文化的发展更具有世俗化的特点。明代的民间小曲内容丰富，虽然良莠不齐，但其影响之广，已经达到"不问男女，人人习之"的程度。由此，私人收集编辑刊刻小曲成风，而且从民歌小曲到唱本、戏文、琴曲均有私人刊本问世。如冯梦龙编辑的《山歌》，朱权编辑的最早的琴曲《神奇秘谱》等。朱载堉的《乐律全书》对传统文化的最大贡献是他创建了十二平均律。这是音乐学和音乐物理学的一大革命，也是世界科学史上的一大发明。

As the society of the Ming and Qing Dynasties had the budding of capitalist economic factors, the citizen class was growing day by day, and the development of music culture became more secular. The popular tunes (ditties) of Ming Dynasty were rich in content. Although some were good and some were bad, their influence reached the level of "regardless of men and women, everyone learns them". As a result, private collection and editing, publishing and engraving of ditties became popular, and private publications came out from ditties to songbooks, operas, and lyre music. For example, *Folk Songs* edited by Feng Menglong, and *Mysterious Secret Music*, the earliest lyre music, edited by Zhu Quan. The greatest contribution of Zhu Zaiyu's *Musical Rules* to traditional culture was that he created the twelve equal temperaments. This was a revolution in musicology and music physics, and a major invention in the history of world science.

16 世纪晚明时期，西洋音乐通过传教士传到中国。在利玛窦进京呈现给万历皇帝的礼品单中，有西琴一张，据考这是一架古钢琴。清初，传教士徐日升教授康熙皇帝西方乐理，并著有《律吕正义》一书。五线谱也在这个时候传入中国。乾隆皇帝的时候，在宫中还组建了一支西洋乐队，乐器有小提琴、大提琴、木管乐器、风琴，演奏时戴西洋假发。

During the late Ming Dynasty in the 16th century, Western music was spread to China through missionaries. In the gift list presented by Matteo Ricci to Emperor Wanli when he came to Beijing, there was a western musical instrument. According to research, it was an ancient piano. In the early Qing Dynasty, the missionary Xu Risheng taught Emperor Kangxi western music theory and authored the book Treatise on Musical Temperament. The stave was also introduced to China at this time. At the time of Emperor Qianlong, a Western orchestra was formed in the palace. The musical instruments included violin, cello, woodwind, organ. When playing, they wore Western wigs.

三、中华传统十大名曲 Top Ten Pieces of Traditional Music in China

中华传统音乐，向有十大名曲一说。这十大古代名曲分别为《高山流水》、《广陵散》、《平沙落雁》、《梅花三弄》、《十面埋伏》、《夕阳箫鼓》、《渔樵问答》、《胡笳十八拍》、《汉宫秋月》和《阳春白雪》。据专家考证，这些古代名曲的原始乐谱大都失传，今天流传的不少谱本都是后人伪托之作。这些乐曲被历代乐师冠以十大古曲名，以历史典故为旁衬，从而借古人之旧事以壮声势。

For traditional Chinese music, there has always been a saying of "the ten famous pieces". They were *High Mountain and Flowing Water*, *Guanglin Folk Strains*, *Wild Geese Descending on the Snadbank*, *Three Variations of the Plum Blossoms*, *Ambush on All Sides*, *Flute and Drum at Sunset*, *Questions and Answers between Fisherman and Woodcutter*, *Eighteen Songs of a Nomad Flute*, *Autumn Moon in the Han Palace* and *White Snow on A Warm Spring Day*. According to expert textual investigation, most of the original scores of these music pieces have been lost, and many of the scores circulated today are fake works by later generations. These music pieces were named the top ten pieces of traditional Chinese music by musicians of the past generations, and they were supplemented by historical allusions, so as to take advantage of the old stories of the ancients.

1.《高山流水》——被善意无限夸大了的友谊

High Mountain and Flowing Water: Friendship infinitely exaggerated by kindness

早在公元前四世纪的春秋战国时代，郑国人列御寇记载，"伯牙善鼓琴，钟子期善听。伯牙鼓琴，志在高山，钟子期曰：'善哉，峨峨兮若泰山。'志在流水，钟子期曰：'善哉，洋洋兮若江河。'……"。《高山流水》蕴涵天地之浩远、山水之灵韵，诚可谓中国古乐主题表现的最高境界。《高山流水》之所以能被春秋战国的诸子典籍多次记录转载，与当时"士文化"的背景是分不开的。先秦时代百家争鸣，人才鼎盛。很多士人国家观念淡薄，并不忠于所在的诸侯国。这些恃才之士在各国间流动频繁，他们莫不企盼明主知遇。他们希望能遇见像知音一般理解自己的诸侯王公，从而一展胸中所学，这几乎是几千年来所有读书人的梦想。然而能达到此目标的毕竟是少数，更多的人一生怀才不遇而汲汲无名，有的或隐身市肆，有的则终老山林。由此可见，《高山流水》在先秦时代就广为流传，是因为这个故事背后的寓意是人生遇合的美妙及怀才不遇的缺憾，所以千百年来引起无数人的共鸣就在情理之中。

As early as the Spring and Autumn Period and the Warring States Period in the 4th century BC, Lieyu Kou from Kingdom Zheng recorded "Boya is good at playing lyre, Zhong Ziqi is good at listening. When Boya played lyre, aiming at the high mountain, Zhong Ziqi said: 'Great, as high as Mount Tai.' When Boya's ambition is in the flowing water, and Zhong Ziqi said: 'Great, as vast as the river' …" *High Mountain and Flowing Water* contains the vastness of the world and the charm of the mountains and rivers, and it can be seen as the highest level of thematic expression of traditional Chinese music. The reason why *High Mountain and Flowing Water* was recorded and reproduced many times in the classics of the Spring and Autumn Period and the Warring States period was inseparable from the background of the "literati culture" at that time. In the pre-Qin era, a hundred schools of thought contended and talented people flourished. Many scholars had a weak conception of the country and were not loyal to their vassal state. These talented people moved frequently between countries, and they all hoped that the Lord would know what happened. They hoped to meet the kings and princes who understood them like their friends, so that they could make themselves. This is almost the dream of all scholars for thousands of years. However, only a few can achieve this goal. More people have never had a chance to show their talents in their lifetimes and are obscure. Some may hide themselves in the society, and some may end up in the mountains and forests. It can be seen that "High Mountain and Flowing Water" was widely circulated in the pre-Qin era, because the implication behind this story was the wonderfulness of talents shown off and the pity of talents unsatisfied. So it's reasonable to cause countless people's resonance for thousands of years.

2.《广陵散》: 刺客的高义，名士的绝响

Guanglin Folk Strains: The righteousness of the assassin, the last of a celebrity

《广陵散》，又名《广陵止息》，是一首曲调较为激昂的古琴曲。《广陵散》大约产生于东汉后期。据说，《广陵散》这一旷世名曲，因聂政刺韩王而缘起，因嵇康受大辟刑而绝世。因而古曲《广陵散》的背后，实际上包含了聂政和嵇康的两个典故。《广陵散》虽"声调绝伦"，但历来有人批评《广陵散》"最不和平"，"愤怒躁急"。想必嵇康当时在刑场上以此曲来抒臆积郁于胸中的不平。曾著有《声无哀乐论》的嵇康，一向主张音声源于自然的本质，而与喜怒哀乐等主观情感无关。嵇康临刑时，神气不变，但曲为心声。不知嵇康面对大辟之刑时如何在"怫郁慷慨"处，表现出"雷霆风雨"和"戈矛纵横"的气势，从而以此曲作为对强权的最后反抗？

Guanglin Folk Strains, also known as "Guangling Stops Breathing", is a Chinese lyre piece with a more exciting tune. *Guanglin Folk Strains* was produced approximately in the late Eastern Han Dynasty. It was said that the famous *Guanglin Folk Strains* was caused by Nie Zheng's assassination of the King of the state Han, and it came to the end because of Ji Kang's capital punishment. Therefore, the ancient *Guanglin Folk Strains* actually contained two allusions of Nie Zheng and Ji Kang. Although *Guanglin Folk Strains* had an "excellent tune", it was often criticized as "the most unpeaceful" and "angry and impatient". Presumably, Ji Kang used this music on the execution ground to express the injustices he had accumulated in his chest. Ji Kang, the author of *Music Without Sadness and Joy*, argued that music originated from the essence of nature and had nothing to do with subjective emotions such as happiness, anger, sorrow, and joy. When Ji Kang was on the verge of punishment, his expression remained unchanged, but his voice became his heart's voice. We wonder: how Ji Kang showed the momentum of "thunder and rain" and "dagger-axes and spears" in the "depression and generosity" when facing the punishment of death, so that he could use this music as the final resistance to the power?

3. 《平沙落雁》：逸士胸怀鸿鹄之志

Wild Geese Desceding on the Sandbank：The hermit has a great ambition

《平沙落雁》所表现的 "逸士心胸" 中的逸士，虽身处隐逸之地，犹胸怀 "鸿鹄之志"，应属于儒之隐和仕前隐。真正做到彻底的隐逸，谈何容易。自古以来，像陶渊明、谢灵运一样纯正的逸士少之又少。古代大多数的逸士，或为世情所困，或因言获罪，最终归隐山林，潜居幽庐，也许不过是为世人做出的一种姿态而已。他们表面上超脱，但内心里也许从未平静过。从这个角度来看，《平沙落雁》的曲中之音和曲外之意，包含了对怀才不遇而欲取功名者的励志，和对因言获罪而退隐山林者的慰藉。

The hermit in the "heart of a hermit" shown in *Wild Geese Descending on the Sandbank*, although in a secluded place, still had the "great ambition" in mind, which belonged to the hermit of Confucianism and the hermit of officialdom. It is not easy to say that it is truly a complete seclusion. Since ancient times, there have been very few people as pure as Tao Yuanming and Xie Lingyun (both former senior officials). Most hermits in ancient times were either troubled by the world's conditions, or convicted of words, eventually returned to the mountains and forests, hiding in secluded cottages, all of which might just be a gesture shown to the world. They were detached on the surface, but they may never be at peace in their hearts. From this point of view, the melody and meaning outside the music of *Wild Geese Descending on the Sandbank* contain inspiration for those whose talents are not recognized, and comfort for those who have retired to the forest because of their words.

4. 《梅花三弄》——桓伊横笛作三弄

Three Variations of the Plum Blossoms：Huanyi played three times with flute

《梅花三弄》是笛曲或箫曲，后被改编为琴曲。"三弄" 是指同一段曲调反复演奏三次。这种反复的处理旨在喻梅花在寒风中次第绽放的英姿、不屈的个性和节节向上的气概。《梅花三弄》的历史典故是东晋大将桓伊为狂士王徽之演奏梅花 《三调》 的故事。

Three Variations of the Plum Blossoms was originally flute or Sheng music, and was later adapted into lyre music. "Three Times" means that the same tune is played three times repeatedly. This repetitive treatment aims to illustrate the heroic image, unyielding personality and steadfast spirit of plum blossoms in the cold wind. The historical allusion of *Three Variations of the Plum Blossoms* was the story of the Eastern Jin Dynasty general Huanyi playing the "Three Tunes" of plum blossoms for the self-conceited scholar Wang Huizhi.

5. 《十面埋伏》——力拔山兮，虞姬奈何兮

Ambush on All Sides: Powerful enough to pull a mountain, but what to do with my concubine Yuji?

项羽具有不可一世的胆识和气势，古今少有。他是一个顶天立地的英雄。勇猛之余，项羽残暴的一面也相当惊人。打碎了旧王朝后，他却不能建立一个新王朝。而刘邦，以一地位低微的亭长出身，与他的平民追随者们一道，打败了强大的项羽，缔造了一个新的大一统帝国，在当时也算得上是前无古人了。在《十面埋伏》高昂的曲调中，传来的不仅仅是胜利者的欢快的号角，还有失败者非凡的气概。

Xiang Yu, a very strong general, possessed unparalleled courage and aura, which is rare in ancient and modern times. He was an indomitable hero. In addition to being brave, Xiang Yu's brutality was also quite shocking. After breaking the old dynasty, he could not establish a new one. Liu Bang, born as a low-ranking pavilion chief, together with his civilian followers, defeated the powerful Xiang Yu and created a new unified empire, which was unprecedented at the time. In the high-pitched tune of *Ambush on All Sides*, not only the cheerful horn of the winner, but also the extraordinary spirit of the loser could be heard and felt.

6. 《夕阳箫鼓》——江月何年初照人

Flute and Drum at Sunset: When did the riverside moon begin to illuminate people?

《夕阳箫鼓》是一首琵琶名曲。有人认为《夕阳箫鼓》的立意来自白居易的《琵琶行》，也有人认为《夕阳箫鼓》的音乐内容和其展示的意境来自张若虚的《春江花月夜》一诗。《夕阳箫鼓》的曲情基本来自《春江花月夜》的诗情。《春江花月夜》是初唐向盛唐过渡的标志性诗作，兼具初唐气度和盛

唐气象。博大、进取、宽容、唯美，已经成为唐朝的一种"时代气质"。《春江花月夜》只有一首，唐朝只有一个。《夕阳箫鼓》的琵琶声阵阵传来，绘声绘影，《春江花月夜》所描述的那种画韵诗境尽现于眼前，使人有如梦回唐朝，进而无限感怀大唐盛世之万千气象。

Flute and Drum at Sunset is famous Pipa music. Some people think that the idea of *Flute and Drum at Sunset* comes from the famous poet Bai Juyi's *Pipa Xing*（a poem which can be sung）. Others in history believed that the music content and the artistic conception of *Flute and Drum at Sunset* came from Zhang Ruoxu's poem *A Moon Evening by the Spring River*. The music of *Flute and Drum at Sunset* basically comes from the poem of *A Moon Evening by the Spring River*. *A Moon Evening by the Spring River* was a typical poem of the transition from the early Tang Dynasty to the prosperous Tang Dynasty, which had both the temperament of the early Tang and the atmosphere of the prosperous Tang. Broadness, enterprise, tolerance, and aestheticism, became a kind of "temperament" of Tang Dynasty. There was only one song of *A Moon Evening by the Spring River* and only one such poet in Tang Dynasty. The sound of the Pipa in *Flute and Drum at Sunset* is heard in bursts, the picturesque and poetic scenes are vividly described in *A Moon Evening by the Spring River*, making people feel like dreaming back to Tang Dynasty, and then infinitely feel the prosperous and diversified world of the flourishing Tang Dynasty.

7.《渔樵问答》——古今多少事，都付笑谈中

Questions and Answers between Fisherman and Woodcutter：Many things in the past and present are just put in a joke.

《三国演义》开篇词中的几句"白发渔樵江渚上，惯看秋月春风。一壶浊酒喜相逢。古今多少事，都付笑谈中。"可做古曲《渔樵问答》的妙解。《渔樵问答》是一首古琴曲。中国自古以来有渔樵耕读的说法，民间的屏风上就常画有渔、樵、耕、读四幅图。渔图和樵图画的分别是严子陵和朱买臣的故事，耕图和读图画的分别是舜教民众耕种的场景和战国时苏秦埋头苦读的情景。渔樵耕读是农耕社会的四业，代表了民间的基本生活方式。这四业一定程度上反映了古代不同价值取向，其中渔为首，樵次之。如果说耕读面对的是现实，蕴涵入世向俗的道理。那么渔樵的深层意象是出世问玄，充满了超脱的意味。

A few lines in the opening of *The Romance of the Three Kingdoms* are "White-haired fisherman and woodcutter are on the river, used to watching the autumn moon and spring wind; over the wine they are happy to meet, many things in the past and present, which in a joke they just put." Those can be considered the wonderful interpretation of *Questions and Answers between Fisherman and Woodcutter*, the ancient Chinese lyre music. There has been a saying of fishing, woodcutting, farming and reading in China since ancient times. The four pictures of fishing, woodcutting, farming and reading are always spotted on folk screens. The pictures of fishing and woodcutting respectively are the stories of Yan Ziling, a hermit, and Zhu Maichen, a woodcutter at first, later a senior official. The pictures of farming and reading are about the scenes of King Shun teaching people to farm, Su Qin in the Warring States period immersed in studying. Fishing, woodcutting, farming and reading were four walks of life in the farming society and represented the basic lifestyle of the folks. To a certain extent, these four walks reflected different values in ancient times. Among them, fishing was the first, followed by woodcutting. If farming and reading is to face reality, implying the secular truth of joining the world, fishing and woodcutting is deep images of out of the world, full of detached meanings.

《渔樵问答》一曲是几千年文化的沉淀。"青山依旧在，几度夕阳红"，尘世间万般滞重，在《渔樵问答》飘逸潇洒的旋律中烟消云散。这种境界令人叹服，然古往今来几人能够做到？虽向往之，实不能也。

The music *Questions and Answers between Fisherman and Woodcutter* is the accumulation of thousands of years of culture. "Still there are the green hills, the sunset time and again gilds", the dull stagnancy of the world disappears in the natural and elegant melody of *Questions and Answers between Fisherman and Woodcutter*. This kind of realm is impressive, but how many people have been able to achieve that? Although longing for it, it is impossible.

8. 《胡笳十八拍》——胡笳本自出胡中，响有余兮思无穷

Eighteen Songs of a Nomad Flute：Hujia was born in Huns, and much more in minds.

以文采武功来看，曹操应该是历史上最杰出的人物之一。一个连魏武都欣赏倍至的人物，虽是女流，理应属绝顶人物。此人就是蔡琰（文姬）。蔡琰

在匈奴生活了十二年，因而她通晓汉、胡音乐。据传《胡笳十八拍》是蔡文姬根据匈奴乐器胡笳的特点而创作的乐曲。她在该曲中将汉、胡音乐完美地融合在一起，从而使《胡笳十八拍》成为古代少有的中外结合的结晶。《胡笳十八拍》只是一首琴曲，虽表达的是悲怨之情，但也是"浩然之怨"。宋亡后，也许正是有这类流传广泛的"不胜悲"、充满"浩然之怨"的曲子，才有了"心如石铁"的坚持到底，从而使种族和文化的血脉不绝于缕，不断延续下去。

In terms of literary and martial arts, Cao Cao should be one of the most outstanding heroes in history. A figure whom even King Cao Cao admired very much, although she was a female, should be a super character. This person was Cai Yan (Cai Wenji). Cai Yan lived in Huns, an ancient nationality in China for twelve years, so she was familiar with Han and Hu (northern minority in China) music. According to legend, *Eighteen Songs of a Nomad Flute* was a piece of music composed by Cai Wenji based on the characteristics of Hujia, a Huns instrument. In this music, she perfectly blended the music of Han and Hu, so that *Eighteen Songs of a Nomad Flute* became a rare combination of Chinese and foreign music in ancient times. *Eighteen Songs of a Nomad Flute* is just a piece of lyre music, although it expresses sadness and resentment, it is also "awesome resentment". After death of the Song Dynasty, perhaps it was precisely this kind of "unconquerable sadness" and "awe-inspiring resentment" tunes widely circulated in society brought about the "iron-hearted" persistence, thus making the blood of race and culture continue endless.

9. 《汉宫秋月》——故国三千里，深宫二十年

Autumn Moon In the Han Palace：3000 miles from the homeland, 20 years in the deep palace.

《汉宫秋月》本是一首琵琶曲，后改编为二胡曲。有的认为此曲旨在表现古代受压迫宫女幽怨悲愁的情绪。有的则以为此曲细致地刻画了宫女面对秋夜明月，内心无限惆怅，流露出对爱情的强烈渴望。

Autumn Moon in the Han Palace was originally Pipa (the Chinese lute) music, which was later adapted into Erhu (another traditional Chinese instrument) music. It's believed that this music aims to express the sad and sorrowful emotions of the oppressed court ladies in ancient times. Some think that this music meticulously portrays the palace lady facing the autumn night and the moon, with infinite melancholy, showing a strong desire for love.

10. 《阳春白雪》——其曲弥高，其和弥寡

White Snow on a Warm Spring Day：The more elegant the music is, the less resonance it receives.

相传这是春秋时期晋国的乐师师旷或齐国的刘涓子所作。"阳春"取万物知春，和风淡荡之意；"白雪"取凛然清洁，雪竹琳琅之音。《阳春白雪》这个典故说明了不同的欣赏者之间审美情趣和审美能力存在着的巨大差异。乐曲的艺术性越高，能欣赏的人就越少。不得不承认，这种差异又和欣赏者的主观趣味有很大关系，有时很难得到一个客观公允的评价。对于听惯桑间濮上之曲、下里巴人之声的人，当然无法理解阳春白雪的高贵雅致。

According to legend, this was done by the musician Shi Kuang of Jin State or Liu Juanzi of Qi State in the Spring and Autumn Period. "A Warm Spring Day" means all things knowing the spring coming and gentle wind breezing; "White Snow" refers to awe-inspiring cleanness of snow bamboo. The allusion of Sunny Spring and White Snow illustrates the huge difference in aesthetic taste and aesthetic ability between different people. The more artistic the music, the fewer people can appreciate it. It's true that this difference has a lot to do with the subjective taste of the listener, and sometimes it is difficult to get an objective and fair evaluation. For those who are used to listening to popular music and songs, they cannot understand the sublimity, nobility and elegance of Yang Chun Baixue.

四、中华古代音乐名家 Famous Traditional Chinese Musicians

1. 伯牙 Boya

先秦琴师。《吕氏春秋》记载了伯牙鼓琴志在高山、流水，而能为钟子期领悟的故事。《琴操》记载伯牙学琴三年不成，老师成连带他到东海蓬莱山去实地领略"移情"的功夫，于是创作出《水仙操》。现存琴曲《高山流水》（已分为《高山》《流水》二曲）、《水仙操》都是源于这些传说的作品。

The Lyre master in pre-Qin Dynasty. *Mister Lv's Spring and Autumn Annals* recorded the story of Boya's aspirations for high mountain and flowing water while playing lyre, which could be understood by Zhong Ziqi. *Qin Cao* (*Lyre Music*) recorded that Boya failed to learn the lyre for three years. His teacher Cheng Lian took him to Penglai Mountain in East China Sea to experience the "empathy" skills on the spot, so he created *Water Fairy Music*. The existing lyre music *High Mountain and Flowing Water* (divided into *High Mountain* and *Flowing Water*) and *Water Fairy Music* are all works derived from these legends.

2. 冷谦 Leng Qian

冷谦精音律，善鼓琴。其琴风飘飘然有尘外之趣。明太祖置太常司，任冷谦为太常协律郎。他的名著《琴声十六法》，至今流传于世，是重要琴著。

Leng Qian had a good knowledge of music, and was an expert at playing lyre. His lyre style had the taste beyond human world. Emperor Ming Taizu set up Imperial Department of Music Affairs, and appointed Leng Qian as the minister in charge of it. His masterpiece *Sixteen Methods of the Lyre*, which has been passed down to the present, is an important lyre work.

3. 刘伯温 Liu Bowen

刘伯温善于琴，曾作琴曲《客窗夜话》。此曲是刘基功成身退，于篷窗之下，怀今忆古的写照。另外，古琴形制中的"蕉叶式"，亦称为"刘伯温式"。

Liu Bowen was good at playing lyre, and once composed the music *Night Talk on the Journey*. This music was a portrayal of his reminiscing about the past and pondering on the present by the window when he retired as a master counsellor. In addition, the "banana leaf style" in the Chinese lyre is also called "Liu Bowen style".

4. 孔子 Confucius

春秋时著名的教育家、音乐家。他作琴曲《陬操》，以伤悼被赵简子杀害的两位贤大夫。现存琴曲《龟山操》《获麟操》《猗兰操》相传都是孔子的作品。

The Famous educator and musician in the Spring and Autumn Period. He composed the lyre music *Zou Music* to mourn the two wise senior officials who were killed by Minister Zhao Jianzi. The existing lyre music *Guishan Music*, *Huolin Music* and *Yilan Music* are said to be the works by Confucius.

5. 师旷 Shi Kuang

春秋后期晋国著名宫廷乐师。目盲，精于审音调律，对于音感极为敏感。

明、清琴谱中说《阳春白雪》等琴曲是他所作。

He lived in the late Spring and Autumn Period, the famous court musician of Jin State, blind, good at tuning and sound distinguishing, extremely sensitive to tone. In the Ming and Qing dynasties, it was said that the music *White Snow on A Warm Spring Day* was composed by him.

五、中国传统音乐文化的主要特点 The Main Characteristics of Traditional Chinese Music Culture

中国传统音乐在长期的历史发展过程中，形成了自己的文化特点。概括说来，有如下三点：

Traditional Chinese music has formed its own cultural characteristics in the long historical development. Generally speaking, there are three points as follows:

（1）传统音乐的构成以五声调式为基础。所谓五声调式，是指由宫、商、角、徵、羽这五个音组成的调式，类似于简谱中的1、2、3、5、6。中国传统音乐一般都是由五声音阶写成的，如民歌《茉莉花》《小河淌水》，器乐曲《梅花三弄》。过去经常有人把唱歌不准的人称为"五音不全"，这里说的"五音"就是指五声调式中的这五个音。

The composition of traditional Chinese music is based on the pentatonic scale. The so-called pentatonce scale is a scale composed of the five tones of Gong, Shang, Jue, Zhi, and Yu, which are similar to 1, 2, 3, 5, and 6 in the numbered musical notation. Traditional Chinese music is generally written in pentatonic scales, such as folk songs *Jasmine*, *Little River Flowing*, instrumental music *Three Variations of the Plum Blossoms*. In the past, people often referred to those who were inaccurate in singing as "five notes incomplete". The "five notes" are the five notes mentioned in the pentatonic scale.

（2）传统音乐的表现注重音乐横向进行。所谓音乐的横向进行，即旋律的表现性。与中国的书法、绘画等艺术一样，在艺术风格上，中国传统音乐讲究旋律的韵味处理，强调形散神不散。传统的中国音乐作品在旋律进行上常常以单旋律的方式进行，对和声的运用较少。如人们熟悉的中国传统的十大名曲，基本上都是某一种乐器的独奏曲目。合奏音乐一般用在宫廷典礼、宗教仪式、迎神赛会等大型场合，这与讲求和声效果的西方音乐是有较大区别的。

The performance of traditional Chinese music focuses on the horizontal progress of music. The so-called horizontal progress of music is the expressiveness of the melody. Like other traditional Chinese arts such as calligraphy and painting, in terms of artistic style, traditional Chinese music pays attention to the charm of melody, emphasizing that the form is scattered but the spirit is condensed. Traditional Chinese music works are often performed in a single-melody way in stead of harmony. For example, the ten famous pieces of traditional Chinese music that people are familiar with are basically solo repertoires of a certain kind of instrument. Ensemble music is generally used on large-scale occasions such as palace ceremonies, religious ceremonies, and welcoming god processions, which is quite different from Western music that emphasizes harmony effects.

（3）传统音乐与舞蹈诗歌关系密切。在古代，音乐一般都离不开舞蹈，唐朝的歌舞大曲以及唐宋以后兴起的戏曲音乐都体现了音乐与舞蹈结合。即使中国传统音乐发展到现在，它与舞蹈、歌唱的关系仍然密切，常常同台演出，相映生辉。

Traditional Chinese music is closely related to dance and poetry. In ancient times, music was generally inseparable from dance. Songs and dances in Tang Dynasty and opera music that emerged after the Tang and Song Dynasties reflected the combination of music and dance. Even when traditional Chinese music has developed to the present, it is still closely related to dancing and singing, and they are often performed together on the stage, shining each other brightly.

中国传统文学的文化精神

一、中国的传统文学概况 Overview of Traditional Chinese Literature

中国传统文学广义指自先秦至清代末年的中国文学，包括作家、作品、文学事件，文体起源与发展历程，文学运动、流派，文学理论，作家作品的考据、研究，等等。类似中国古代文学史。狭义的指中国古典文学作品。按文学史的习惯，可以划分为先秦文学、秦汉文学、魏晋南北朝文学、隋唐五代文学、宋元文学、明清文学。代表性的文学作品形式有诗、词、曲、赋、散文、小说等。中国古典文学是中华民族最宝贵的文化遗产之一。

Traditional Chinese literature broadly refers to Chinese literature from the pre-Qin to the end of Qing Dynasty, including writers, works, literary events, the origin and development of styles, literary movements, genres, literary theories, textual research and research on writers' works, etc. similar to the history of ancient Chinese literature. Narrowly it refers to Chinese classical literature. According to the habits of literary history, it can be divided into pre-Qin literature; the literature in Qin and Han Dynasties; the literature in Wei, Jin, Southern and Northern Dynasties; the literature in Sui, Tang and Five Dynasties; the literature in Song and Yuan Dynasties, the literature in Ming and Qing Dynasties. Representative forms of literary works include poem, ci, opera, ode, prose, and novel. Chinese classical literature is one of the most precious cultural heritages of the Chinese nation.

（一）先秦两汉文学的代表作品 The representative works of pre-Qin and Han literature

1.《诗经》。中国第一部诗歌总集。编成于春秋时期，大抵收录西周初年至春秋中叶 500 年间的作品，共 311 篇（其中 6 篇只有标题），代表了 2500 多年以前诗歌创作的最高成就。《诗经》里的作品都是合乐的唱词，分属于"风""雅""颂"三大部分。风是乐调，国风就是各国土乐的意思，共 160 篇。雅本是乐曲名，分"大雅"和"小雅"，是周王朝直接统治地区的音乐，共 105 篇。《颂》是赞美诗，是祭祀时的乐曲，共 40 篇。《诗经》内容非常丰富，分别从不同角度反映了当时 500 多年间的社会生活。《诗经》在艺术创作上很有特色。其一，《诗经》里的作品多方面描写了现实生活，表现了不同阶层人民在现实生活中的各种感受，真实地反映了现实生活。其二，《诗经》大量运用了比、兴手法，取得了显著的艺术效果。其三，《诗经》在结构形式上也很有特色，最突出的是重章叠句。重章有时表示事物进展的程度和顺序。重章叠句更增强了诗歌的音乐性和节奏感，也更好地表达了诗人的感情，使人读之余味无穷。其四，《诗经》在体裁上也颇具特色。《诗经》多是四言一句，隔句用韵，但并不拘泥，且富于变化。

The Book of Songs. It is the first collection of poems in China. Compiled in the Spring and Autumn Period, it covered probably the 500 years from the beginning of the Western Zhou Dynasty to the middle of the Spring and Autumn Period. There were 311 poems in total with 6 only with titles, representing the highest achievement of poetry creation more than 2,500 years ago. The works in *The Book of Songs* are the words of chorus, which are divided into three parts: "wind", "elegance" and "hymns". The wind is the music tune, and the national wind means the local music of various states. There are 160 winds in total. Ya was originally the name of the music, divided into "Daya" (Great Elegance) and "Xiaoya" (Lesser Elegance). It was the music of the regions directly ruled by Zhou Dynasty. There are 105 pieces in total. Hymns, the music for sacrificial rituals, with a total of 40 pieces. *The Book of Songs* is very rich in content, reflecting the social life of more than 500 years at that time from different angles. *The Book of Songs* is very distinctive in artistic creation. First of all, the works in *The Book of Songs* describe the real life in many ways,

show the various feelings of people of different classes in real life, and truly reflect real life. Secondly, *The Book of Songs* makes extensive use of analogy, and Xing (top-
ic association) techniques and has achieved remarkable artistic effects. Third, the
Book of Songs is also very distinctive in terms of structure and form, the most prominent being repetition and refrain. Repetition and refrain can sometimes indicate the
degree and order of the development, but more enhance the musicality and rhythm of
the poems, and better express the poet's feelings, making people have a strong feeling of aftertaste. Fourth, *The Book of Songs* is also quite distinctive in genre. Most
sentences in *The Book of Songs* are four-character, with rhymes every other line,
but they are not rigid and full of changes.

2. 先秦散文。主要可分为历史散文和诸子散文。就大体情况而言，历史
散文主要是叙事的，诸子散文主要是说理的。历史散文有《春秋》《左传》
《战国策》《国语》等。《春秋》是孔子编订的一部编年史。《左传》仿照其体
例，详细记叙了春秋时代各国的政治、外交、社会事件以及某些代表人物的
活动。诸子散文可分为三个时期：一期是春秋末年和战国初年，主要作品中，
《论语》是语录体，《老子》多用韵，它们都辞约义丰，《墨子》开始向组织
结构严密的论说文形式发展。二期是战国中叶，主要作品有《孟子》《庄
子》，它们的文辞比前一个时期繁富，说理也畅达。三期是战国末期，主要作
品有《荀子》《韩非子》等。诸子散文中有代表性的文章均逻辑谨严、分析
深入、文辞绚丽，达到了很高成就。

Pre-Qin proses. They can be divided into historical proses and the proses by the
philosophers. Generally speaking, historical proses were mainly narrative, while the
proses by the masters were mainly persuasive. Historical proses included *Spring and
Autumn*, *Zuo Zhuan*, *Warring States Policy*, and *Guoyu*. *Spring and Autumn* was a
chronicle compiled by Confucius. Following its style, *Zuo Zhuan* described in detail
the political, diplomatic, and social events of various countries in the Spring and Autumn Period and the activities of certain representatives. The philosophers' proses
could be divided into three periods: the first period was the late Spring and Autumn
Period and the early Warring States Period. Among the main works, *The Analects of
Confucius*was a quotation style, and *Lao Tzu*was concise and informative, using
rhymes. *Mozi* began the development of a well-organized argumentative prose. The

second period was the middle period of the Warring States Period. The main works were *Mencius* and *Zhuangzi*. Their writings were more prosperous than the previous period, and their reasoning was smoother. The third period was the end of the Warring States Period. The main works included *Xunzi* and *Han Feizi*. The representative essays in the philosophers' proses were all rigorous in logical reasoning, with in-depth analysis and brilliant rhetoric, and they made very high achievements.

3. 辞。因产生于战国楚地而称楚辞；赋即铺陈之意，以"铺采摛文""直书其事"为特点。两者都兼有韵文和散文的性质，是一种半诗半文的独特文体。结构宏大，辞藻华丽，讲究文采、韵律，常用夸张、铺陈的手法。《楚辞》是战国时代以屈原为代表的楚国人创作的文学作品。屈原的《离骚》是楚辞的代表作，后人故又称楚辞这种文体为"骚体"。

Ci. Ci is called Chu Ci because it originated in the state Chu of the Warring States Period; Fu (rhapsody) means to narrate, and it is characterized by "narrating" and "telling the matter directly". Both Ci and Fu have the properties of verse and prose, and are a unique style of half poetry and half prose. The structure is magnificent, the rhetoric is gorgeous, and it pays attention to literary grace and rhythm. It often uses exaggeration and presentation. "*Chu Ci*" was a literary work created by Chu people represented by Qu Yuan in the Warring States Period. Qu Yuan's "Li Sao" (or *The Lament*) was the representative work of Chu Ci, and later generations also called the style of Chu Ci "Sao Style".

《离骚》是屈原（约公元前 340 年~公元前 278 年）的代表作，是中国古代最长的一首抒情诗，共 373 句，2490 字。这是一部浪漫主义杰作，在这首诗中，诗人以崇高的理想和炽热的感情，迸发出了异常灿烂的光彩。

Li Sao is a representative work by Qu Yuan (about 340 BC to 278 BC), and was the longest lyric poem in ancient China, with 373 sentences and 2,490 characters. This is a masterpiece of romanticism. In this poem, the poet demonstrated an unusual brilliance with lofty ideal and passionate feelings.

4. 汉赋。主要特点是铺陈写物，不歌而诵，是中国古代特有的一种文学体裁。汉赋代表作家在汉初主要有贾谊和枚乘。贾谊继承了屈原的骚体风格，他的《吊屈原赋》即拿屈原的遭遇来比自己。《七发》是枚乘的代表作，《七发》标志着汉赋的正式形成。汉武帝和汉成帝时代，是汉赋的全盛时期，代表作家有司马相如、扬雄等。

Han Fu (Odes in Han Dynasty). The main feature of Fu in Han Dynasty was to narrate in detail which was a literary genre unique to ancient China. The representative writers of Fu in Han Dynasty in the early Han Dynasty mainly were Jia Yi and Mei Cheng. Jia Yi inherited the style of Qu Yuan's *Li Sao*, and his *The Fu to Condole with Qu Yuan* compared Qu Yuan's experience to himself. *Qi Fa* (*Seven Wonder Drugs*) was a masterpiece of Mei Cheng, and *Qi Fa* marked the official formation of Fu in Han Dynasty. The era of Emperor Wu and Emperor Cheng in Han Dynasty was the heyday of Fu in Han Dynasty. The representative writers included Sima Xiangru and Yang Xiong.

（二）魏晋南北朝文学 Literature of Wei, Jin, Southern and Northern Dynasties

这一时期的代表为建安文学。东汉末年的黄巾起义重创了东汉王朝，代表中小地主利益的曹操、刘备、孙权三分天下。曹操力量最强，在文学方面成就也最大。以"三曹"和"建安七子"为代表的"建安文学"在古代文学史上占有重要的一席之地。所谓"三曹"即指曹操与其子曹丕、曹植；"七子"即指汉末作家孔融、陈琳、王粲、徐干、阮瑀、应场、刘桢。他们均能文善诗，且与曹氏父子关系密切。建安时期，是中国文学史上一个"俊才云蒸"的时代，大量作家和作品涌现出来，使各种文体都得到了发展，尤其是诗歌方面打破了汉代四百年沉寂的局面。五言诗从这时开始兴盛，七言诗也在这时奠定了基础。历代文学评论家都把建安时期看作文学的黄金时代。

Jian'an Literature is the representative school in this period. The Yellow Turban Uprising in the late Eastern Han Dynasty dealt a heavy blow to the Eastern Han dynasty Cao Cao, Liu Bei, and Sun Quan, representing the interests of small and medium landlords, divided the country into three kingdoms. Cao Cao had the strongest strength and the greatest achievement in literature. "Jian'an Literature", represented by "Three Caos" and "Jian'an Seven Masters", occupied an important place in the history of ancient literature. The so-called "three Caos" refer to Cao Cao and his sons Cao Pi and Cao Zhi; "Seven Masters" refer to the writers of the late Han Dynasty, Kong Rong, Chen Lin, Wang Can, Xu Gan, Ruan Yu, Ying Yang, and Liu Zhen.

They could all write good poems and were closely related to the Cao family. The Jian'an period was an era in the history of Chinese literature, when a large number of writers and works emerged, leading to the development of various styles, especially poetry, which broke the 400-year silence of Han Dynasty. The Five-Character Poems began to flourish at this time, and the foundation was also laid for Seven-Character Poens at this time. Literary critics of the dynasties regarded the Jian'an period as the golden age of literature.

建安七子中，以王粲的文学成就最高。王粲（公元 177 年~公元 217 年），字仲宣。代表作有《七哀诗》《从军诗》，除了诗以外，王粲还善于作赋，代表作有《登楼赋》等。从西晋建立到东晋灭亡的一百多年间，产生了左思、刘琨、郭璞、陶渊明等一批杰出的诗人，其中以陶渊明成就最高。

Among the seven masters of Jian'an, Wang Can's literary achievement was the highest. Wang Can (177~217 AD), by names Zhongxuan, has a number of representative works included *Seven Sorrowful Poems* and *Joining the Army Poems*. In addition to poems, Wang Can was also good at composing Fu, and his representative works included *Rhapsody on Ascending the Tower*. During the more than one hundred years from the establishment of the Western Jin Dynasty to the end of the Eastern Jin Dynasty, a group of outstanding poets such as Zuo Si, Liu Kun, Guo Pu, Tao Yuanming came into being known. Among them, Tao Yuanming had the highest achievement.

（三）唐宋文学 Literature in Tang and Song Dynasties

1. 初唐诗歌。初唐是唐诗繁荣的准备时期，重要诗人有被称为"初唐四杰"的王勃、杨炯、卢照邻、骆宾王，此外还有陈子昂、沈佺期、宋之问等。"四杰"通过自己的诗作抒发愤激不平之情和壮烈的抱负，拓宽了诗歌题材。继"四杰"而起的是陈子昂，他从理论上对南朝以来衰弱的诗风提出批评，认为这类诗专门玩弄华丽的辞藻，内容空虚，抛弃了《诗经》重视思想性的传统。对此他耿耿于心，提倡学习"汉魏风骨"，主张恢复建安时代的诗风。

The poems in the early Tang dynasty. The early Tang Dynasty was a period of preparation for the prosperity of Tang poetry. Important poets included Wang Bo, Yang Jiong, Lu Zhaolin, and Luo Binwang, who were known as the "four masters of the early Tang Dynasty", as well as Chen Zi'ang, Shen Quanqi, and Song Zhiwen. The "four masters" expressed their indignation and heroic embrace through their poems, and broadened the subject matters of their poems. Following the "Four Masters" was Chen Zi'ang, who theoretically criticized the weak poetic style since the Southern Dynasties. He believed that this type of poems were exclusively playing with gorgeous rhetoric and the content was empty, and abandoned the tradition of emphasizing ideology in *The Book of Songs*. Regarding this, he advocated learning the "Han and Wei style and spirit" to restore the poetic style of the Jian'an era.

2. 盛唐诗歌。唐代（公元 618 年~公元 907 年）是中国古典诗歌发展的全盛时期。唐代的诗人特别多。李白、杜甫、白居易就是世界闻名的伟大诗人。保存在《全唐诗》中的有四万八千九百多首。唐诗的题材非常广泛。在创作方法上，既有现实主义的流派，也有浪漫主义的流派，而许多伟大的作品，则又是这两种创作方法相结合的典范，形成了中国古典诗歌的优秀传统。

The poems in the Prime period of Tang Dynasty. Tang Dynasty (618~907 AD) was the heyday of the development of Chinese classical poetry. There were particularly many poets in Tang Dynasty. Li Bai, Du Fu, and Bai Juyi were world-renowned great poets. There are more than 48,900 poems preserved in the *Complete Tang Poems*. The subject matters of Tang poetry were very wide. In terms of creative methods, there were both realistic and romantic schools, and many great works were examples of the combination of these two creative methods, forming an excellent tradition of Chinese classical poetry.

唐诗的形式是多种多样的。唐代的古体诗，基本上有五言和七言两种。近体诗也有两种，一种叫做绝句，一种叫做律诗。绝句和律诗又各有五言和七言之不同。所以唐诗的基本形式基本上有这样六种：五言古体诗，七言古体诗，五言绝句，七言绝句，五言律诗，七言律诗。

The forms of Tang poetry were diverse. For Ancient Style Poetry in the Tang Dynasty, there were basically five-character and seven-character poems. There were also two types of Modern Style Poetry (or Regulated Verse), one was called quatrains and the other was called rhymed poems. Quatrains and rhymed poems can also adopt five-character or seven-character format. Therefore, there were basically six basic forms of Tang poetry: five-character archaic poems, seven-character archaic poems, five-character quatrains, seven-character quatrains, five-character rhymed poems, and seven-character rhymed poems.

　　唐诗的形式和风格丰富多彩、推陈出新。它不仅继承了汉魏民歌、乐府的传统，并且大大发展了歌行体的样式；不仅继承了前代的五言、七言古诗，并且发展为叙事言情的鸿篇巨制；不仅扩展了五言、七言形式的运用，还创造了风格特别优美整齐的近体诗。近体诗是当时的新体诗，它的创造和成熟，是唐代诗歌发展史上的一件大事。它把中国古曲诗歌的音节和谐、文字精练的艺术特色，推到前所未有的高度，为古代抒情诗找到一个最典型的形式，至今还特别为人民所喜闻乐见。

The forms and styles of Tang poetry were rich and colorful, and brought forth the new. It not only inherited the traditions of Han and Wei folk songs and Yuefu, but also greatly developed the style of song; not only inherited the five-character and seven-character ancient poems of the previous generation, but also developed into a long narrative and romantic poem; Tang poetry created modern style poems with a particularly beautiful and neat style by extending five-character and seven-character poems. Modern Style Poetry was new in style at that time. Its creation and maturity were a major event in the history of poetry development in the Tang Dynasty. It pushed the syllable harmony and refined artistic characteristics of Chinese ancient poetry to an unprecedented height, and found the most typical form of ancient lyric poetry, which is still especially popular among the people.

　　3. 宋词，是中国古代诗歌的一种。它始于梁代，形成于唐代而极盛于宋代。据《旧唐书》上记载："自开元（唐玄宗年号）以来，歌者杂用胡夷里巷之曲。"由于音乐的广泛流传，当时的都市里有很多以演唱为生的优伶乐师，根据唱词和音乐节拍配合的需要，创作或改编出一些长短句参差的曲词，这便是最早的词。

Song Ci. It is a type of ancient Chinese poetry. It began in Liang Dynasty, formed in Tang Dynasty and flourished in Song Dynasty. According to the *Old Tang Book*, "Since Kaiyuan (the reign of Emperor Xuanzong of Tang Dynasty), singers had mixed the folk songs." Due to the widespread distribution of music, there were many musicians who lived by singing in the city at that time. According to the needs of the lyrics and the musical rhythm, some songs with long and short sentences were created or adapted. This was the earliest Ci.

到了宋代，通过柳永和苏轼在创作上的重大突破，词在形式上和内容上得到了巨大的发展。宋词，大体上可分类为婉约派和豪放派。婉约派的词，其风格是典雅涪婉、曲尽情态；豪放词作是从苏轼开始的，是一种独立的抒情艺术。词大致可分小令（58 字以内）、中调（59 至 90 字）和长调（91 字以上，最长的词达 240 字）。一首词，有的只有一段，称单调；有的分两段，称双调；有的分三段或四段，称三叠或四叠。

In Song Dynasty, through Liu Yong and Su Shi's major breakthroughs in creation, Ci developed tremendously in form and content. Song Ci could be roughly classified into graceful and unrestrained schools. The style of the Ci of the graceful school was elegant, graceful, and expressive; the bold and unrestrained school started from Su Shi, which was an independent lyrical art. Ci can be roughly divided into Small Tune (within 58 characters), Middle Tune (59 ~ 90 characters) and Long Tune (more than 91 characters, the longest Ci is 240 characters). A Ci, some only has one paragraph, is called single tune; some is divided into two paragraphs, called double tune; some is divided into three or four paragraphs, called triple or quadruple tunes.

词有词牌。词牌的产生大体有以下几种情况：沿用古代乐府诗题或乐曲名称，如《六州歌头》；取名人诗词句中几个字，如《西江月》；据某一历史人物或典故，如《念奴娇》；还有名家自制的词牌。词发展到后来逐渐和音乐分离，成为一种独立的文体。

Ci has Ci titles. The generation of Ci titles generally had the following situations: the ancient Yuefu poem title or the name of the music was used; such as *Liuzhou Getou*; a few words in the poems of celebrities, such as *Xijiang Yue*; according to a historical figure or allusion, Such as *Niannujiao*; there were also Ci titles made by famous poets. Ci gradually separated from music and became an independent style.

4. 唐宋八大家。又称唐宋古文八大家，是中国唐代韩愈、柳宗元和宋代苏轼、苏洵、苏辙、欧阳修、王安石、曾巩八位散文家的合称。其中韩愈、柳宗元是唐代古文运动的领袖；欧阳修、三苏四人是宋代古文运动的核心人物；王安石、曾巩是临川文学的代表人物。他们先后掀起的古文革新浪潮，使诗文发展的陈旧面貌焕然一新。

The Eight Great Masters of Tang and Song Dynasties. They are also known as the Eight Great Masters of Ancient Literature in Tang and Song Dynasties, which is the collective name of the eight essayists including Han Yu, Liu Zongyuan in Tang Dynasty and Su Shi, Su Xun, Su Zhe, Ouyang Xiu, Wang Anshi, and Zeng Gong in Song Dynasty. Among them, Han Yu and Liu Zongyuan were the leaders of the ancient literature movement in Tang Dynasty, Ouyang Xiu and three Su's were the core figures of the ancient literature movement in Song Dynasty, and Wang Anshi and Zeng Gong were representatives of Linchuan literature. They successively set off a wave of ancient Chinese literature innovation, which gave the poetry development a new look.

（四）元明清文学 Literature in Yuan, Ming and Qing Dynasties

1. 元曲。盛行于元代的一种文艺形式，包括杂剧和散曲，有时专指杂剧。元代的戏剧活动，实际上形成两个戏剧圈。

The Yuan Opera. The Yuan Opera was an art form that prevailed in Yuan Dynasty, including Zaju (Miscellaneous operas) and Sanqu (detached songs), sometimes the term Yuan Opera is also used to specifically refer to Zaju. The opera activities in Yuan Dynasty actually formed two opera circles.

北方戏剧圈以大都（即今天的北京）为中心，包括长江以北的大部分地区，流行杂剧，涌现了大批杂剧艺人。南方戏剧圈以杭州为中心，包括温州、扬州、建康、平江、松江乃至江西、福建等东南地区。和北方情况不同，这里的城乡舞台，既流行南戏，也演出北方传来的杂剧，呈现出两个剧种相互辉映的局面。南戏产生于浙江永嘉（温州）一带，所以又被称为"永嘉杂剧"。它形成于南宋初年，在东南地区广泛流传，并渐渐进入杭州。许多艺人在这里创作、演出、出版南戏，使这座繁华的城市成了南戏的中心。

The northern opera circle was centered on the Yuan Dynasty Capital (that is, today's Beijing), including most of the area on the north of the Yangtze River, where Zaju was popular, and a large number of Zaju artists emerged. The southern opera circle was centered on Hangzhou, including Wenzhou, Yangzhou, Jiankang (now Nanjing), Pingjiang, Songjiang and even other southeast regions such as Jiangxi and Fujian. Unlike in the north, on the city and rural stages both southern operas and Zaju from the north were popular, presenting a situation where the two types of operas paralleled. Southern opera was produced in the area of Yongjia (Wenzhou), Zhejiang Province, so it was also called "Yongjia Zaju". It was formed in the early years of the Southern Song Dynasty, spread widely in the southeast, and gradually entered Hangzhou. Many artists created, performed and published Southern Operas here, making this bustling city the center of Southern Operas.

2. 明清小说。明清是中国小说史上的繁荣时期。这个时代的小说从思想内涵和题材表现上来说，最大限度地包容了传统文化的精华，而且经过世俗化的图解后，传统文化以可感的形象和动人的故事走进了千家万户。

Ming and Qing Novels. Ming and Qing Dynasties were a prosperous period in the history of Chinese novels. In terms of ideological connotation and subject perform-ance, the novels of this era contained the essence of traditional culture to the greatest extent. After secularized illustrations, traditional culture entered thousands of house-holds with sensible images and moving stories.

明代文人创作的小说主要有白话短篇小说和长篇小说两大类。明代的长篇小说按题材和思想内容，又可概分为五类，即讲史小说、神魔小说、世情小说、英雄传奇小说和公案小说。明代的短篇小说主要是白话短篇小说，白话短篇小说取得了辉煌的成就，明人创作的白话短篇小说是模拟学习宋元话本的产物，故被称为"拟话本"。收集白话短篇作品较多而且对后世影响较大的是明末天启年间冯梦龙编辑的"三言"（《喻世明言》、《警世通言》和《醒世恒言》）。其后，凌濛初模仿"三言"创作了《初刻拍案惊奇》和《二刻拍案惊奇》，合称"二拍"，均为拟话本。"三言""二拍"是明代白话短篇小说的代表作品。

The novels written by literati in Ming Dynasty mainly included vernacular short stories and novels. Ming Dynasty novels could be divided into five categories accord-ing to their themes and ideological content, namely, historical novels, novels of gods and demons, novels of society, heroic legends, and crime-case fictions. The short stories in Ming Dynasty were mainly vernacular short stories, and the vernacular short stories made brilliant achievements. The vernacular short stories created by Ming people were the product of imitating the Song and Yuan story-telling scripts, so they were called "simulation scripts". The collection of more short stories in the vernacular with greater influence on later generations was the Three Words edited by

Feng Menglong during the Tianqi period at the end of Ming Dynasty (*Wise Words to Enlighten People*, *Common Words to Warn People* and *Eternal Words to Awaken People*). Later, Ling Mengchu imitated Three Words and created *The First Engraved Surprise Stories to Make One Slap on the Desk* and *The Second Engraved Surprise Stories to Make One Slap on the Desk*, collectively known as Two Slaps. All were imitative scripts. Three Words and Two Slaps were representative works of vernacular short stories in Ming Dynasty.

清代的阶级矛盾、民族矛盾和思想文化领域里的斗争，给小说创作以深刻影响。清初至乾隆时期是清小说发展的全盛时期，数量和质量、内容和形式、风格和流派与前代相比都有较大发展。清代小说基本是文人的创作，虽有历史、传说等素材的借鉴，但作品多取材于现实生活，较充分地体现了作者个人的意愿，在结构、叙述和描写人物各方面也多臻于成熟的境界。康乾年间产生的《聊斋志异》和《红楼梦》，分别把文言小说和白话小说的创作推向顶峰。

The class contradictions, national contradictions, and struggles in the ideological and cultural fields in Qing Dynasty had a profound impact on novel creation. The period from the early Qing Dynasty to the Qianlong period was the prime time of the development of Qing novels. Compared with the previous generations, the quantity and quality, content and form, style and genre all developed greatly. Qing Dynasty novels were basically the creations of literati. Although they were borrowed from materials such as history and legends, their works were mostly based on real life and fully reflected the authors' personal wishes. They were also more advanced and more mature in terms of structure, narration and description of characters. The *Strange Stories from a Chinese Studio* and *Dream of the Red Chamber* produced during the Kangxi and Qianlong period respectively pushed the creation of novels in classical Chinese and in vernacular Chinese to the top.

二、中国传统文学之最 The Superlatives in Traditional Chinese Literature

1. 《诗经》是中国最早的一部诗歌总集，相传是孔子所删、汉代毛亨、毛苌所传。

2.《山海经》是中国最早的富有神话传说的一部地理志，作者无法考究。

3.《穆天子传》是中国最早的一部历史小说，作者无法考究。

4.《吕氏春秋》是中国哲理散文最早的总集，是秦国宰相吕不韦及其门客所著。

5.《新书》是中国最早的一部政论文总集，作者是西汉杰出的思想家、文学家、政治家贾谊。

6.《世说新语》是中国最早的笔记体小说集，作者是南北朝宋的著名文学家刘义庆。

7.《搜神记》是中国最早的一部志怪小说，作者是东晋文学家、史学家干宝。

8.《国语》是中国第一部国别体史书，作者据《史记》记载是左丘明，据考证是后人伪托。

9.《史记》是中国第一部纪传体通史，作者是西汉著名史学家、文学家、思想家司马迁。

10.《资治通鉴》是中国第一部编年体通史，作者是北宋史学家司马光。

1. *The Book of Songs* is the earliest collection of poems in China. According to legend, it was edited by Confucius and passed on by Mao Heng in Han Dynasty.

2. *The Book of Mountains and Seas* is the earliest geographical book rich in myths and legends in China, and the author is unknown.

3. *The Biography of Emperor Mu* is the earliest historical novel in China, and the author is unknown.

4. *Mister Lü's Spring and Autumn* is the earliest collection of Chinese philosophical essays, written by Lü Buwei, the prime minister of State Qin and his followers.

5. *New Book* is the earliest collection of political essays in China. The author is Jia Yi, an outstanding thinker, writer and statesman of the Western Han Dynasty.

6. *A New Account of the Tales of the World* is the earliest collection of notebook novels in China. The author is Liu Yiqing, a famous writer from the State Song in Southern and Northern Dynasties.

7. *Stories of Immortals* is China's first earliest mystery novel. The author is Gan Bao, a writer and historian of the Eastern Jin Dynasty.

8. *Conversation from the States* is China's first national history book. The author

is Zuo Qiuming according to the "*Historical Records*", who is believed to be a false trust of later generations.

9. *Historical Records* is China's first biographical general history. The author is Sima Qian, a famous historian, writer, and thinker in the Western Han Dynasty.

10. *History as a Mirror* is China's first chronicle general history, the author is the historian Sima Guang in the Northern Song Dynasty.

11.《燕歌行》是第一首完整的七言诗，作者是三国著名的诗人魏文帝曹丕。

12.《孔雀东南飞》是中国第一首优秀的长篇叙事诗，作者无法考究。

13.《离骚》是中国第一首优秀的长篇抒情诗，作者是战国时楚国的伟大诗人屈原。

14.《论语》是中国第一部语录体散文，作者是孔丘的弟子及再传弟子。

15.《春秋》是中国第一部私人编撰的史书，作者是春秋时代著名的思想家、教育家孔丘。

16.《汉书》是中国第一部纪传体断代史，作者是东汉文学家、史学家班固。

17.《文心雕龙》是中国最早的一部文学批评专著，作者是南北朝梁代文学理论批评家刘勰。

18.《诗品》是中国最早的一部品评诗歌的专著，作者是南北朝梁代文学理论批评家钟嵘。

19.《文选》（《昭明文选》）是中国现存最早的一部文章总集，作者是南北朝梁代的萧统。

20.《老子》（《大乘起信论》）是中国最早的典籍外文译本，译者是唐代僧人、佛教学家、翻译家、旅行家玄奘（法号），原名陈袆。

11. *A Song of the Yan Country* is the first complete seven-character poem written by the famous poet King Cao Pi of the Three Kingdoms.

12. *Peacocks Fly Southeastward* is China's first outstanding long narrative poem, and the author is unknown.

13. *The Lament* is China's first outstanding long lyric poem. The author is the great poet Qu Yuan of the State Chu during the Warring States Period.

14. *The Analects of Confucius* is China's first quotation style prose, the author is

the Confucius's disciples and their disciples.

15. *Spring and Autumn* is China's first privately compiled history book. The author is the famous thinker and educator Confucius in the Spring and Autumn Period.

16. *The History of Han Dynasty* is China's first biographical dynastic history, written by Ban Gu, a writer and historian of the Eastern Han Dynasty.

17. *Carving a Dragon at the Core of Literature* is China's earliest monograph on literary criticism, and the author is Liu Xie, a literary critic of Liang Dynasty in the Southern and Northern Dynasties.

18. *Critique of Poetry* is the earliest monograph on poetry in China. The author is Zhong Rong, a literary theory critic of Liang Dynasty in the Southern and Northern Dynasties.

19. *Selected Works* (or *Selected Works of Zhaoming*) is the earliest surviving collection of articles in China. The author is Xiao Tong in Liang Dynasty of the Southern and Northern Dynasties.

20. *Lao Tzu* (*Mahayana Uprising of Faith*) is the earliest foreign translation of Chinese classics. The translator was a monk, Buddhist scholar, translator, and traveler Xuanzang in Tang Dynasty. His original name was Chen Yi.

21.《徐霞客游记》是中国一部价值最高的游记体地理学著作，作者是明代杰出的旅行家、地理学家、散文家徐霞客。

22.《西厢记》是中国艺术成就最高的杂剧，号称"天下夺魁"，作者是元代著名戏剧家王实甫。

23.《原君》是中国最早的一篇具有民主思想的政论文，作者是明末清初杰出的思想家、文学家黄宗羲。

24.《三国演义》是中国第一部优秀的长篇历史小说，作者是明代著名的通俗小说家罗贯中。

25.《水浒传》是中国第一部优秀的描写农民革命斗争的小说，作者是明代著名的小说家施耐庵。

26.《西游记》是中国第一部长篇神话小说，作者是明代小说家吴承恩。

27.《金瓶梅》是中国第一部以家庭为写作题材的小说，作者是明代小说家兰陵笑笑生（笔名）。

28.《梦溪笔谈》是中国第一部用笔记文体写成的综合性学术专著，作者是北宋科学家、政治家沈括。

29.《聊斋志异》是中国第一部优秀的文言短篇小说集，作者是清代著名小说家蒲松龄。

30.《儒林外史》是中国第一部优秀的长篇讽刺小说，作者是清代伟大的小说家吴敬梓。

21. *Xu Xiake's Travel Notes* is one of the most valuable geographies in China. The author is Xu Xiake, an outstanding traveler, geographer and essayist in Ming Dynasty.

22. *The West Chamber* is the most accomplished drama in China. It is valued as "No. 1 in The World". The author is the famous dramatist Wang Shifu in Yuan Dynasty.

23. *Of the Emperor* is the earliest political essay with democratic thought in China. The author is Huang Zongxi, an outstanding thinker and writer in the late Ming and early Qing Dynasties.

24. *The Romance of the Three Kingdoms* is China's first outstanding long historical novel, written by Luo Guanzhong, a famous popular novelist in Ming Dynasty.

25. *The Water Margin* is China's first excellent novel describing the revolutionary struggle of the peasants. The author is the famous novelist Shi Naian in Ming Dynasty.

26. *A Pilgrimage to the West* is China's first full-length mythical novel, written by Wu Chengen, a novelist in Ming Dynasty.

27. *The Plum in the Golden Vase* is China's first novel with family as its theme. The author is Ming Dynasty novelist Lanling Xiao Xiaosheng (pen name).

28. *Written Notes at the Mengxi Garden* is China's first comprehensive academic monograph written in note-based style. The author is Shen Kuo, a scientist and politician in the Northern Song Dynasty.

29. *Strange Stories from a Chinese Studio* is China's first excellent collection of short stories in classical Chinese. The author is the famous Qing Dynasty novelist Pu Songling.

30. *The Scholars* is the first outstanding satirical novel in China. The author is Wu Jingzi, a great novelist in Qing Dynasty.

31. 《红楼梦》是中国艺术成就最高的早期白话小说，作者是清代伟大的小说家曹雪芹。

32. 《官场现形记》是中国第一部谴责小说，作者是清代的谴责小说家李宝嘉。

33. 屈原是中国第一个伟大的爱国诗人，作品收在《楚辞》里。

34. 许穆夫人是中国第一个女诗人，作品有《载驰》、《泉水》、《竹竿》。

35. 班昭是中国第一个女史学家，将其兄班固的《汉书》续成。

36. 李清照是中国第一个女词人，作品收在《李清照集》里。

37. 李白是盛唐时期最伟大的浪漫主义诗人，作品收在《李太白全集》里。

38. 杜甫是盛唐时期最伟大的现实主义诗人，作品收在《杜工部集》里。

39. 白居易是中唐时期最伟大的现实主义诗人，作品收在《白氏长庆集》里。

40. 杨万里是中国历史上写诗最多的诗人，一生写诗两万多首，作品收在《诚斋集》里。

41. 关汉卿是中国最伟大的戏剧家，代表作是杂剧《窦娥冤》。

31. *Dream of the Red Chamber* is an early vernacular novel with the highest artistic achievement in China. The author is the great novelist Cao Xueqin in Qing Dynasty.

32. *The Records of Officialdom Exposure* is the first condemnation novel in China. The author is Li Baojia, a condemnation novelist in Qing Dynasty.

33. Qu Yuan was the first great poet in China, and his works are included in *The Songs of Chu*.

34. Mrs. Xu Mu is the first female poet in China, and her works include *Zai Chi*, *Spring Water* and *Bamboo Pole*.

35. Ban Zhao is the first female historian in China, who continued to finish her brother Ban Gu's *The History of Han Dynasty*.

36. Li Qingzhao is the first female Ci poet in China, and her works are included in *The Collection of Li Qingzhao*.

37. Li Bai was the greatest romantic poet in the heyday of Tang Dynasty, and his works are included in *The Complete Works of Li Taibai*.

38. Du Fu was the greatest realist poet in the heyday of Tang Dynasty, and his works are included in *The Collection of Du Gongbu.*

39. Bai Juyi was the greatest realist poet in the Mid-Tang Dynasty, and his works are included in the *Mr. Bai's Everlasting Collection.*

40. Yang Wanli is the poet who wrote the most poems in Chinese history. He wrote more than 20, 000 poems in his lifetime, and his works are included in *Cheng Zhai Collection.*

41. Guan Hanqing is China's greatest dramatist, and his masterpiece is *Snow in Midsummer.*

三、中国传统文学的主要特点 Major Characteristics of Traditional Chinese Literature

（一）独特文字表达形式 Unique expression of Chinese characters

（1）容易引起具体意象。（2）汉字一般为单文独义、一字一音，这就使中国诗歌的音节变化有了一整套独特的谨严的格律，并且在外观上构成整齐对称的形式美。（3）汉语有四声，诗人们利用汉语言的这种特性，写诗时注意字声安排，于是近体诗（五言律诗、绝句，七言律诗、绝句）、词、散曲等诗歌体应运而生。（4）文言文作为特殊的书面语言，可与日常用语长期分离而保持官方语言的地位，这就发生了文学在文言和白话两个不同的轨道上运行、内容与形式皆有巨大的差异的现象。

（1）Chinese characters easily create specific images. （2）A Chinese character generally has a single meaning and one sound. This makes the syllable changes of Chinese poetry have a unique set of rigorous rhythms, and in appearance constitutes a neat and symmetrical form of beauty. （3）There are four tones in Chinese. Poets take advantage of this characteristic of the Chinese language and pay attention to the arrangement of words and sounds when writing poems. So the poems (five-character rhymed poems, five-character quatrains; seven-character rhymed poems, seven-character quatrains), Ci, and Sanqu came into being. （4）Classical Chinese, as a special written language, could be separated from everyday language for a long time and maintain its status as an official language. This has led to the phenomenon that literature runs on two different tracks, classical Chinese and vernacular, with huge differences in content and form.

（二）独特文学观念体系 Unique literary ideological system

这种观念体系受中国传统的思想体系所支配，其思想渊源在于孔子创立的儒家学派。

其一，"修身、齐家、治国、平天下"（《礼记·大学》）为核心的入世思想；

其二，"仁、义、礼、智、信"为标准的道德观念；

其三，"天、地、君、亲、师"为次序的伦理观念；

其四，"允执其中"（《论语》）为规范的中庸哲学。

This conceptual system is dominated by traditional Chinese ideological systems, and its ideological origin lies in the Confucian school founded by Confucius.

First is the thought of entering into the world with "cultivating oneself, managing the family, governing the country, and paeifying the world" (*Book of Rites · The Great Learning*) as the core;

Second, "benevolence, righteousness, manners, wisdom, and credit" are the standard moral concepts;

Third, the ethical concept of "heaven, earth, monarch, ancestors, teachers" as the order;

Fourth, "sincerely adhering to the golden mean" (*The Analects of Confucius*) is the normative philosophy of the mean.

（三）独特宗教特点表现 Unique religious characteristics

在中国思想史上，儒、道两家的思想体系是互为补充的，儒、道、释三家也常常合流。儒家、道家、佛教思想分别给予中国文学以不同侧面的影响。在中国文人身上，积极入世和消极避世思想往往交织在一起，彼此消长。在文学作品中，这种现象有着鲜明的表现。佛教鄙视现实、尊重自然、保持自然本性的思想，道教鄙视权贵、愤世嫉俗的思想都对作家起过作用，由李白、杜甫、王维、李商隐、柳宗元、韩愈、白居易、苏东坡这类大家及其作品就足以证明。

In the history of Chinese thought, the ideological systems of Confucianism and

Taoism are complementary to each other, and the three schools of Confucianism, Taoism and Buddhism often merge. Confucianism, Taoism, and Buddhism have different influences on Chinese literature. Among the Chinese literati, actively entering into the world and passively escaping from the world are often intertwined in ebb and flow. In literary works, this phenomenon has a clear manifestation. Buddhism despises reality, respects nature, and maintains the innate nature; Taoism despises the power cynically; both have worked on writers. Li Bai, Du Fu, Wang Wei, Li Shangyin, Liu Zongyuan, Han Yu, Bai Juyi, Su Dongpo and their works offer us the evidence.

（四）特别注重情感表达 Special attention to emotional expression

中国传统文学具有强烈的情感特征。对于诗文的评价，文人也总喜欢首先从"性情"或"性灵"来着眼，把有无强烈的抒情的感动，提高为衡量文学的价值、区别文学与非文学的首要标识。

Traditional Chinese literature has strong emotional characteristics. For the evaluation of poetry, literati like to look at "disposition" or "spirituality" first, and raise the presence or absence of strong lyrical touch as the primary indicator for evaluating the value of a literary work and distinguishing between literature and non-literature.

（五）特别注重伦理道德 Special attention to ethics and morality

中国传统文学通常具有强烈的道德感。中国文化是一种富有人文精神的文化，尤为注重人文领域内的问题，伦理道德与现实政治成为中国文化关注的两大核心，从而使中国文化呈现出道德型文化与政治型文化的特征。

Traditional Chinese literature usually has a strong sense of morality. Chinese culture is a culture full of humanistic spirit. It pays particular attention to issues in the humanistic field. Ethics and real politics have become the two core concerns of Chinese culture, thus making Chinese culture present the characteristics of moral culture and political culture.

四、中国传统文学的文化精神 The Cultural Spirit of Traditional Chinese Literature

中国文学的产生和发展有其广阔的文化背景，中国文化的基本特征普遍而深刻地渗透在文学作品中。文化塑造作家，作家创作文学，文学自然地承载了中国文化的一些精神特质，二者相生相存。

The emergence and development of Chinese literature have its broad cultural background, and the basic characteristics of Chinese culture permeate literary works universally and deeply. Culture shapes writers, writers create literature, and literature naturally carries some spiritual characteristics of Chinese culture, and the two coexist.

（一）忧患意识 Sense of worry and hardships

一部中国传统文学史，以《诗经》《楚辞》为发端，直至古典文学终结，忧患的情绪贯穿始终。可以这样说，《离骚》为屈原之哭泣，《庄子》为庄子之哭泣，《史记》为司马迁之哭泣，《草堂诗集》为杜甫之哭泣。李后主以词哭，八大山人以画哭，王实甫以《西厢记》哭，曹雪芹以《红楼梦》哭。这些经典的中国古代文学作品，充满了忧患情绪。忧患表现为对现实、对人生的关切。

For the history of traditional Chinese literature, starting with *The Book of Songs* and *Chu Ci* until the end of classical literature, the sense of worry and hardships runs through. It can be said that *Li Sao* is the cry of Qu Yuan, *Zhuangzi* is the cry of Zhuangzi, *Historical Records* is the cry of Sima Qian, and *The Caotang Poetry Collection* is the cry of Du Fu. Later King Li cried with poetry, Bada Shanren cried with paintings, Wang Shifu cried with *The Story of the West Chamber*, and Cao Xueqin cried with *Dream of the Red Chamber*. These classic Chinese ancient literary works are full of worry and hardships. The sense of worry and hardships is manifested as a concern for reality and life.

中国传统文学中的忧患意识可以归纳为三种类型：第一，对国家前途和民族命运的忧患；第二，对民生多艰的忧患；第三，对人生的忧患。上述忧患意识以文学为表现形式，昭示了中国传统文化是一种非宗教的、世俗的文化，具有鲜明的人文精神。传统作家大都把儒家的诗教奉为信条，以国家社稷为重，以民生疾苦为怀，直面社会与人生。

The sense of worry and hardships in traditional Chinese literature can be summarized into three types: first, the worry about the future of the country and the destiny of the nation; second, the worry about the hardships of the people's livelihood; and third, the worry about life. The above-mentioned sense of worry is expressed in literature, which shows that traditional Chinese culture is a non-religious and secular culture with a distinct humanistic spirit. Most traditional writers regarded Confucian poetry as a creed, focused on the country and the people's livelihood, and faced society and life directly.

（二）超脱意识 Consciousness of detachment

在封建中国，正直的文人士大夫常常以超脱来对付严峻现实，并借此保持高洁的节操和审美创造的自由精神。士大夫文人超脱意识的产生，以古代社会的集权制度和农耕生活的社会形态为背景，以儒道佛三者的互补融汇为思想和哲学基础，以"士志于道"的群体心理为内在动因。其旨在超越的价值取向，使中国传统文学呈现如下重要特征：注重表现人品的高洁淡泊，游心自然、乐至畅神的美学趣味，静观默察、心随物化的审美态度，以及缘此而旷达、闲适、宁静致远的艺术境界。

In feudal China, honest literati and officialdom often used detachment to deal with the harsh reality, and in this way maintained the noble morals and the free spirit of aesthetic creation. The emergence of the consciousness of detachment of the literati and scholars was based on the centralized system of ancient society and the social form of farming life, and on the ideological and philosophical basis of the complementation and fusion of Confucianism, Taoism and Buddhism, and the internal group psychology of "the scholars are committed to the Way" as the motivation. Its value orientation aiming at transcendence made Chinese classical literature present the following important characteristics: focusing on the expression of one's nobility and indifference, of the aesthetic taste of appreciating the nature and enjoying oneself, of the aesthetic attitude of quiet observation and mind materialization, and of the artistic realm of broad-mindedness, leisure and tranquility.

第一，中国传统文学注重对自我人品的表现，并且认为这种表现应该排斥矫饰，无须关注取悦他人，从其内外表里相统一的风仪和心境出发，随心所致，遣性抒怀，使其人品跃然纸上。第二，中国文人旨在超越尘俗的文化心理，使他们自觉地把山水自然视为自己的精神乐园，并力图创造同生命与造化同体的艺术境界，这是中国山水文学发达的原因之一。第三，超脱意识作用于审美活动和文学创作，便形成素朴人性与客体本性在静默观察中的自然契合，从而把握和反映事物的特点。第四，超越尘俗和个人忧患，使作者在外在行为上表现为洒脱不羁，逍遥自在，在精神上则耿介绝俗，卓然自立。其表现于文学，便使作品充溢着旷达的精神。

First of all, traditional Chinese literature pays attention to the expression of self-character, and believes that this kind of expression should reject pretentiousness, and doesn't need to pay attention to pleasing others. Starting from their internal and external appearance and mood, writers express their feelings in literary works at will, making their character lively and lyrically on paper. Secondly, Chinese literati's cultural psychology of transcending the mundane makes them consciously regard beautiful mountains and rivers as their spiritual paradise, and strive to create an artistic realm of integrating life and nature. This is one of the reasons for the prosperity of Chinese landscape literature. Thirdly, the consciousness of detachment acts on aesthetic activities and literary creation, and it forms a natural affinity between simple human nature and objective nature in silent observation, thereby grasping and reflecting the characteristics of things. Fourthly, to transcend mundane and personal worry and anxiety, the author appears to be free and unrestrained in external behavior, while in spirit, he is upright, self-reliant and far from vulgar. The performance in literature makes the works full of broad-minded spirit.

（三）家国情怀 Love for one's home and country

家国情怀集中表现为对乡土、对国家执着的热爱。中国传统文学中有难以计数的作品表现了对于乡土的眷恋，对于国家的深情。传统诗文中，对于故乡家园的执着思念是一个永恒的主题，它发端于先秦，绵延不绝于中国文学发展的长河中。与乡情紧密关联的是对国家的爱恋。尤其是在家国存亡之际，对家国的挚爱深情表现得更为集中和充分。

The love for one's home and country is concentratedly expressed as a persistent love for the native land and the country. There were countless works in traditional Chinese literature that showed nostalgia for the countryside and deep affection for the country. In traditional poetry, the persistent yearning for the homeland was an eternal theme. It originated in the pre-Qin Dynasty and continued in the long river of Chinese literature development. Closely related to nostalgia is the love for the country. Especially when the country is at the critical time of life and death, the affection for the country is expressed more fully and intensively.

家国情怀作为中国文学的一种文化精神，其思想文化的来源之一是大一统思想。大一统思想形成于春秋末年，在多民族国家形成、巩固和发展的历史进程中，这一思想不断充实和深化。尽管中国历史上治乱更迭，然而在分裂的时代，企盼统一是人心所向。其思想来源之二是宗法制度与宗法精神。血缘、地缘观念一直是古代中国人根深蒂固的观念。诸如"父母在，不远游""叶落归根"等都是由此派生的社会心理。因此，家国情怀的思想与尽孝尽人伦之间有着内在的联系，思乡恋土实为道德人伦的一种特殊表现。宗法精神与古代农业型自然经济结合，造就了人们安土重迁的恋乡情结，这都给中国文学刻下了深刻的文化烙印。

As a kind of cultural spirit of Chinese literature, the idea of great unification is one of the ideological culture sources for the love for home and country. The idea of great unification was formed at the end of the Spring and Autumn Period. In the historical process of the formation, consolidation and development of multi-ethnic countries, this idea has been continuously enriched and deepened. In spite of the changes in China's history of order and chaos, especially in the era of division, the desire for reunification is what people most want. The second source for the love of home and country is the patriarchal system and the patriarchal spirit. The concepts of blood relationship and geographical relationship were deeply ingrained in ancient Chinese. Such as "Now that parents are alive, the children do not travel afar" and "Falling leaves return to their roots" are social psychology derived from the love of home and country. Therefore, there is an inherent connection between thinking and fulfilling filial piety. Homesickness and love for the motherland are a special manifestation of morality. The combination of the patriarchal spirit and the ancient agriculturally natural economy created a complex for people to be attached to the land and reluctant to move elsewhere, which has carved a deep cultural imprint on Chinese literature.

（四）亲情情结 Affection complex

表达爱情和友情，是中国传统文学又一个永恒的主题。从民间文学到文人之作，表现男女相悦的作品不仅数量众多，而且较充分地展示了人性的特点。在民间，从《诗经》"国风"到两汉乐府民歌，对爱情的表白以大胆热烈为显著特点，很少受到礼的束缚。

Expressing love and friendship was traditional eternal theme in traditional Chinese literature. From folk literature to literati's works, there were not only a large number of works that expressed the love between men and women, but also fully demonstrated the characteristics of human nature. Among the folks, from the "Guo Feng" of *The Book of Songs* to the folk songs of the Han Dynasties, the confession of love is characterized by boldness and enthusiasm, and is rarely restrained by rite.

较之于民歌的直白与本真，文人对爱情的描写则体现出多样化的特点。首先是含蓄深婉；其次，文人在歌咏人间深挚纯真的爱情时，往往加入富有浪漫诗意的情节和理想的信念，以此表达对人性自由的追求与渴望。除讴歌爱情外，讴歌友情是文学中人伦情结的又一大系。在大量的行旅怀思、酬答赠别之作中，对友情的忠贞，对朋友的诚信与关爱，汇集成极富人伦意味的情感洪流。传统文人在其求学、游历和仕宦生涯中，多好结交朋友，文学史上留下无数患难见真情、视友情如生命的佳话。

Compared with the straightforwardness and authenticity of folk songs, the description of love by literati reflects diverse characteristics. On the one hand it is implicit and euphemistic; On the other hand, when literati sing the deep and pure love in the world, they often add romantic and poetic plots and ideal beliefs to express their pursuit and desire for human freedom. In addition to sing love, to praise friendship is another major line of affection complex in literature. In a large number of travel thoughts, rewards and farewell works, the loyalty to friendship, the honesty to and care of friends, converge into a torrent of emotions that is very humane. Traditional literati were so good at making friends during their studies, travels, and official careers. In the history of literature, there are numberless stories about friendship in need and seeing friendship as life.

亲情情结赋予中国传统文学以浓厚的人文情味，它植根于伦理型文化深厚的土壤中。儒家文化把人伦关系归结为君臣、父子、兄弟、夫妇、朋友"五伦"，一方面强调等级和威严，一方面又主张合乎人情，顺乎人情，强调"爱人"。对于交友，中国传统文化历来主张以诚待友，君子之交应该淡于利而重乎义，道相同则视朋友如兄弟。赞美纯真爱情和友情的作品，在中国传统文学的发展史中始终占据着重要地位，代表着文学发展的方向。

Affection complex gives traditional Chinese literature a strong humanistic flavor, which is rooted in the deep soil of ethical culture. Confucian culture attributed human relations to the "five constant values" of monarchs and subjects, fathers and sons, brothers, couples, and friends. On the one hand, it emphasizes rank and majesty; and on the other hand, it advocates being human, conforming to human feelings, and emphasizing love. With regard to making friends, traditional Chinese culture advocates treating friends with sincerity. Gentlemen's friendship should be less profitable but more righteous, and friends should be regarded as brothers if their Way is the same. Works that praise pure love and friendship have ever occupied an important position in the history of traditional Chinese literature and represent the direction of literature development.

五、中国传统艺术的美学追求 The Aesthetic Pursuit of Traditional Chinese Arts

（一）道——中国传统艺术的精神性 Tao: the spirituality of traditional Chinese Arts

"天人合一"决定了中国古代哲学的基本精神是追求人与人、人与自然的和谐统一。"天人合一"是中国传统文化的核心范畴，它不仅是一种人与自然关系的学说，而且也是一种关于人生理想、人生价值的学说。"天人合一"强调人性即天道，道德原则和自然规律是一致的，人生的最高理想应当是天人协调，包括人与万物的一体性，还包括人与人的一体性。中国传统文化与西方文化最根本的区别之一，就在于前者强调"天人合一"，后者强调"主客分立"。"道"体现了天、人的统一，也就是"天人合一"。老子认为，天地万物都是由"道"产生的，"道"是有与无的统一体，是宇宙天地万事万物存在的根据和本原。

"The unity of nature and man" determines that the basic spirit of traditional Chinese philosophy is the pursuit of harmony between man and man, and man and nature. "Harmony between man and nature" is the core of traditional Chinese culture. It is not only a doctrine of the relationship between nature and man, but also a doctrine of ideals and values of life. "The unity of nature and man" emphasizes that human nature is the way of nature, and the moral principles are consistent with the laws of nature. The highest ideal of life should be the harmony between man and nature, including the unity of man and all things, as well as the unity of man and man. One of the most fundamental differences between traditional Chinese culture and Western culture is that the former emphasizes "the unity of nature and man", while the latter emphasizes "the separated establishment of subject and object." "Tao" embodies the unity of nature and man, that is, "the unity of man and nature". Lao Tzu believed that all things in the universe are produced by "Tao", which is the unity of being and non-being, and is the basis and origin of the existence of all things in the universe.

（二）气——中国传统艺术的生命性 Qi: the vitality of traditional Chinese arts

物质的气被精神化、生命化，这可以说是中国"气论"的本质特征。"气"在中国传统文化中占有十分重要的地位，不但中医讲"气"，气功讲"气"，戏曲表演讲"气"，绘画书法也要首先运"气"。中国传统美学用"气"来说明美的本原，提倡艺术描写和表现宇宙天地万事万物生生不息、元气流动的韵律与和谐。中国美学十分重视养气，主张艺术家要不断提高自己的道德修养与学识水平，"气"是对艺术家生理心理因素与创造能力的总概括；又要求将艺术家主观之"气"与客观宇宙之"气"结合起来，使得"气"成为艺术作品内在精神与艺术生命的标志。"气韵生动"成为中国画创作的总原则，深刻地反映了中国传统美学的基本特色。

Material Qi (Air) is spiritualized and vitalized, which can be said to be the essential feature of Chinese "Qi theory". "Qi" occupies a very important position in traditional Chinese culture. Not only "Qi" is taught in Chinese medicine, "Qi" is taught in Qigong, and "Qi" is expressed in operas. Painting and calligraphy must also first to use Qi. Traditional Chinese aesthetics uses "Qi" to explain the origin of beauty, and advocates artistic description and expression of the endless rhythm and harmony of vitality and vivacity in the universe. Chinese aesthetics attaches great importance to the cultivation of Qi, and advocates that artists should continuously improve their moral and academic level. "Qi" is a general summary of an artist's physiological and psychological factors and creative ability; it also requires that the artist's subjective "Qi" (Inner Vital Force) and the objective universe's "Qi" (Outer Vital Force) be combined, "Qi" has become a symbol of the inner spirit and artistic life of art works. "lively and vivid inner Qi" has become the general principle of Chinese painting creation, which deeply reflects the basic characteristics of Chinese classical aesthetics.

（三） 心——中国传统艺术的审美性

Heart: the aesthetics of traditional Chinese arts

中国传统美学和中国传统艺术，一开始就十分重视人的主体性，认为艺为心之表、心为物之君，主张心乐一元、心物一元。因此，中国传统美学和中国传统艺术，一贯强调审美主客体的相融合一，认为文学艺术之美在于情与景的交融合一、心与物的交融合一、人与自然的交融合一。

Traditional Chinese aesthetics and traditional Chinese arts have attached great importance to human subjectivity from the very beginning, holding that art is the expression of the heart and heart is the king of things, and advocates the unity of heart and happiness, and the unity of mind and matter. Therefore, traditional Chinese aesthetics and traditional Chinese arts have often emphasized the integration of aesthetic subject and object. They believe that the beauty of literature and art lies in the integration of emotion and scenery, the integration of heart and object, and the integration of man and nature.

（四） 舞——中国传统艺术的音乐智慧

Dance: the musical wisdom of traditional Chinese arts

远古的中华大地上，原始的图腾歌舞与狂热的巫术仪式曾经形成过龙飞凤舞的壮观场面。在中国古代艺术中，诗、乐、舞最初是三位一体的，只是到后来才逐渐发生了分化，形成了各具特色的艺术门类。具有强烈生命力的"乐舞"精神，并没有消失，后来逐渐渗透与融会到中国各个艺术门类中，体现出飞舞生动的形态和风貌。

On the ancient land of China, primitive totem singing and dancing and fanatical witchcraft rituals once formed spectacular scenes of dragons and phoenixes. In ancient Chinese art, poetry, music, and dance were originally a trinity, but only later did they gradually differentiate, forming different arts with their own characteristics. However, the spirit of "musical dance" with strong vitality did not disappear at all. Later, it gradually penetrated and merged into various art categories in China, reflecting the vivid forms and styles.

（五）悟——中国传统艺术的直觉思维

Epiphany: the intuitive thinking of traditional Chinese arts

重直觉是中国传统思维方式的重要特点之一。而这种传统思维方式，对中国的传统艺术思维和审美思维也产生了巨大的影响，尤其是形成了以"悟"为核心的感性直觉的审美思维方式。"悟"，作为中国美学与艺术学的重要范畴之一，在中国传统艺术创造与艺术鉴赏中，都具有十分重要的作用，并且衍生出"顿悟""妙悟"等一系列相关范畴。真正的艺术家必须具有"悟性"。艺术家与艺术匠人最大的区别就在于：前者是以道驭技，而后者是有技无道。

Emphasis on intuition is one of the important characteristics of traditional Chinese thinking. This traditional way of thinking has had a huge impact on Chinese traditional artistic thinking and aesthetic thinking, especially the formation of a perceptual and intuitive aesthetic thinking with "epiphany" as the core. "Epiphany", as one of the important categories of Chinese aesthetics and art, plays a very important role in traditional Chinese artistic creation and art appreciation, and it derives a series of related categories such as "epiphany" and "insight". A true artist must have "insightful and epiphanic understanding". The biggest difference between an artist and an art craftsman is that the former uses Tao to control skills, while the latter has skills without Tao.

（六）和——中国传统艺术的辩证思维

Harmony: the dialectical thinking of traditional Chinese arts

"和"指事物的多样统一或对立统一，是矛盾各方统一的实现。对立统一思想成为具有中国传统哲学特色的朴素辩证思维观，并对中国传统美学和艺术学产生了极大的影响。中国传统美学与艺术学的许多经典语汇都是以对立统一的形式出现，如"刚柔""虚实""动静""形神""文质""情理""情景""意象""意境"等。其中，偏于精神性的一面，更多地在矛盾统一中处于主导地位，如"形神"中的"神"，"情景"中的"情"，"意象"中的"意"等。正是这种闪烁着中华民族理性智慧光芒的辩证思维，对中国传统艺术和美学思想产生了巨大的影响，并且形成了中国传统艺术和美学思想中极富民族特色的辩证和谐观——"和"。

"Harmony" refers to the unity of diversified things or the unity of opposites, and is the realization of the unity of the contradictory parties. The idea of unity of opposites has become a distinctive and simple dialectical thinking of traditional Chinese philosophy, and has had a great impact on Chinese traditional aesthetics and arts. Many classic vocabularies of traditional Chinese aesthetics and arts appear in the form of unity of opposites, such as "rigid and soft", "virtual and real", "dynamics and statics", "form and spirit", "text and quality", "sense and sensibility" and "emotion and scene", "implication and image" and "conception and context", among them, the spiritual side is more dominant in the unity of contradictions, such as the "spirit" in "form and spirit" and the "emotion" in "emotion and scene", "implication" in "implication and image". It is this dialectical thinking shining with the light of the rational wisdom of the Chinese nation that has had a huge influence on Chinese traditional arts and aesthetics, and has formed a dialectical and harmonious view of traditional Chinese arts and aesthetics that is rich in national characteristics-"harmony".

中国的传统武术文化

一、中国传统武术的起源 The Origin of Traditional Chinese Martial Arts

（一）武术的原始起源 The origin of martial arts

武术是中华民族在长期的历史演进过程中不断创造、逐渐形成的一个体育项目。在原始社会，兽多人少，自然环境十分恶劣，在"物竞天择，适者生存"的严酷斗争中，人们自然产生了拳打脚踢、指抓掌击、跳跃翻滚一类的初级攻防手段。后来又逐渐学会了制造和使用石制或木制的工具作为武器，并且产生了一些徒手和使用器械的搏斗捕杀技能，这便是武术的萌芽。

Martial arts is a sport created and gradually formed by the Chinese nation in the course of long-term historical evolution. In primitive society, there were many beasts and few people, and the natural environment was very harsh for them. In the harsh struggle of "natural selection and survival of the fittest", people naturally produced elementary offenses and defenses such as punching and kicking, finger-grabbing, jumping and rolling means. Later, people gradually learned to make and use stone or wooden tools as weapons, and developed some unarmed and weapon fighting and killing skills. These were the germination of martial arts.

原始社会末期，部落战争的频繁发生，进一步促进了武术的发展。在部落战争中，远则使用弓箭、投掷器，近则使用棍棒、刀斧、长矛，凡是能用于捕斗搏击的任何生产工具都成为战斗的武器。古代的"武舞"与中国传统武术具有紧密的联系。

At the end of primitive society, the frequent occurrence of tribal wars further promoted the development of martial arts. In tribal wars, bows, arrows and throwers were used at a distance, and sticks, axes, and spears were used if at a nearer distance. Any production tool that could be used for hunting and fighting became a combat weapon. The ancient "armed dance" laid the foundation for the later formation of martial arts routines.

（二）武术的概念 Concept of martial arts

武术概念，是人们认识、研究武术的基本依据。在漫长的历史进程中，不同的时期对武术概念的表达不尽相同，它的内涵和外延是随着社会历史的发展和武术本身的发展而发展、变化的。

The concept of martial arts is the basic foundation for people to understand and study martial arts. In the long historical process, expressions of the concept of martial arts have not been the same, its connotation and extension developed and changed along the development of social history and the development of martial arts itself.

从历史上看，有不少归属武术类的名称，春秋战国时称"技击"；汉代出现了"武艺"一词，并沿用至明末；清初又借用南朝《文选》中"偃闭武术"（当时泛指军事）的"武术"一词；民国时称"国术"；新中国成立后仍沿用"武术"一词。

Historically, there are many names that belong to the Martial Arts. It was called "combat techniques" in the Spring and Autumn and Warring States period; the term "Wuyi" appeared in Han Dynasty and was extended to the end of Ming Dynasty; in the early Qing Dynasty, it borrowed the term "Wushu" from "a closed Wushu" of the *Selected Works* edited in the Southern Dynasty, referring to military at that time; Later it was called "national martial arts"; the term "Wushu" (martial arts) was still used after the founding of PRC.

武术属于中国传统的技击术。它是以踢、打、摔、拿、击、刺等技击动作为主要内容，通过徒手或借助于器械的身体运动表现攻防格斗的能力。无论是对抗性的搏斗运动，还是势势相承的套路运动，都是以中国传统的技击方法为核心。中国武术在技击方法上更为丰富，在运动形式上，既有套路的，也有散手的，既是结合的，又是分离的，这种发展模式，也迥然有别于世界上其他技击术。在演练方法上注重内外兼修，演练风格上要求神形兼备。这些都是中国传统武术的运动特点。

"Wushu" (Kung Fu) belong to traditional Chinese martial arts. It is based on kicking, beating, throwing, taking, striking and stabbing. The main content is the attacking and stabbing action, and the offensive and defensive ability is demonstrated through unarmed or physical movement with the aid of equipment. Whether it is a confrontational fighting or a routine movement, it is based on traditional Chinese combat methods. Chinese martial arts are richer in attacking methods. In terms of sports forms, there are both routines/sets and Sanshou (free combat) techniques; they can be combined and separated. This development model is also very different from other martial arts in the world. Pay attention to both internal and external training in the drill method, and the drill style requires unity of both spirit and form. These are the sports characteristics of traditional Chinese martial arts.

随着历史的变迁，冷兵器的逐步消亡，专用武术器械的生产及拳械套路的大量出现，对抗性项目、武术竞赛规则的制定，武术已演化成为体育运动项目之一。武术的体育化使其内容、形式及训练手段等都发生了很大变化，反映事物本质属性的概念也在不断变化。发展到今天，武术的基本定义可概括为：武术是以技击为主要内容，以套路和搏斗为运动形式，注重内外兼修的中国传统体育项目。

With the changes in history, the gradual disappearance of cold weapons, the production of special martial arts equipment and the emergence of a large number of boxing and weapon routines, the formulation of confrontational events and martial arts competition rules, Wushu has evolved into one of the sports events. The physicalization of martial arts has caused great changes in its content, form, and training methods. The concepts that reflect the essential attributes of things are also constantly changing. To this day, the basic definition of martial arts can be summarized as: martial arts is a traditional Chinese sport that takes the art of attack and defence as the main content, routines and fighting as sports forms, and focuses on both internal and external training.

二、中国传统武术的哲学基础 The Philosophical Foundation of Traditional Chinese Martial Arts（Wushu）

中国武术，作为民族传统体育项目之一，是以中国传统文化为理论基础，伴随着人类社会的历史进程产生和发展起来的，并以内外兼修、术道并重为鲜明特点的运动。它根植于中国传统文化之沃土，与传统文化有着深厚的血缘和形神相依的联系，蕴含着中国传统哲理之奥妙，形成了内涵广泛、层次纷杂的庞大理论体系。

Chinese martial arts, as one of the national traditional sports, is based on traditional Chinese culture and has developed along with the historical process of human society. It is a sport with distinct characteristics of both internal and external training and equal emphasis on martial arts and self-cultivation. It is deeply rooted in the fertile soil of traditional Chinese culture, has a deep blood relationship and a close relationship with traditional culture, contains the mystery of traditional Chinese philosophy, and has formed a huge theoretical system with a wide range of connotations and multiple levels.

中国传统哲学、伦理、中医理论和古典兵法思想等都是武术的理论基础。中国哲学与武术关系最为密切的是《易经》以及后来发挥《易经》思想的《易传》。阴阳五行、八卦生化的哲学观念，被作为拳理的哲理依据，运用在拳技理论中。"天人合一"观对武术文化影响至深，各种象形取意的拳种和拳式，都是在这一哲学观念指导下发展起来的。"知行合一"的哲学观念，也成为其理论指导原则。武术要求"动静相生""刚柔互补""快慢相间""后发先至"等，这都是以阴阳辩证观念为指导的。

Traditional Chinese philosophy, ethics, traditional Chinese medicine theory and classical art of war are the theoretical basis of traditional Chinese martial arts. The closest relationship between Chinese philosophy and martial arts is the *Book of Changes* and later the *Essays on Book of Changes*, which interprets the ideas of the *Book of Changes*. The philosophical concepts of yin and yang, five elements, the generation and change of eight trigrams are used as the philosophical bases of boxing theory. The concept of "Heaven and Man as One" (Unity of Nature and Man) has a profound impact on martial arts culture. Various types of animal-like boxing forms and ideas have been developed under the guidance of this philosophy. The philosophical concept of "Unity of knowledge and action" has also become its theoretical guiding principle. Martial arts requires "dynamics and statics in mutual generation", "hardness and softness in mutual complementation", "speediness and slowness in alternation", and "starting late but arriving first". These are all guided by the dialectical concept of yin and yang.

中国传统武术追求内在自我修养、整体和谐与抽象的武德武道，还蕴含着丰富的民族传统伦理，处处表现着仁义之国、礼仪之邦的民族特征，形成了重传统、重经验、尊师爱徒的人伦观念，在儒家仁义精神的基础上，融汇了禅宗佛学的"持戒""化解"的慈悲胸怀，又以道家的"不争""虚静"修身养性来调处，深刻地反映了中华民族善良、诚信、热爱和平的美德。

Traditional Chinese martial arts pursues inner self-cultivation, overall harmony and abstract martial morality. It also contains a wealth of traditional national ethics, in which the national characteristics of benevolence, righteousness and etiquette of China are demonstrated. The ethic philosophy that emphasizes tradition and experience, respecting the teacher and loving the apprentice has been formed. Traditional Chiness Martial Arts is based on the spirit of Confucian benevolence, incorporating the compassionate minds of "observing the precepts" and "dissolving" of Zen Buddhism, and at the same time the Taoist "non-contention", "void and peau" of Taoism. It profoundly reflects the Chinese nation's virtues of kindness, integrity, and love of peace.

三、中国传统武术的特点 Characteristics of Traditional Chinese Martial Arts

（一）技击与实用基本一致 Skills and practicality are basically the same

武术最初作为军事训练手段，与古代军事斗争紧密相连，其技击的特性显而易见。在实用中，其目的在于杀伤、限制对方，它常常以最有效的技击方法，迫使对方失去反抗能力。武术攻防格斗的特点，在技术上与实用技击基本上是一致的，可以说武术的搏斗运动具有很强的攻防技击性，但又与实用技击有所区别。

Martial arts was originally used as a means of military training and was closely connected with ancient military struggles. Its fighting characteristics are obvious. In practice, its purpose is to kill and limit the opponent, and it often uses the most effective combat methods to force the opponent to lose the ability to resist. The characteristics of offense and defense in martial arts are generally the same both technically and practically. It can be said that martial arts sports have strong offensive and defensive methods, but they are different from practical martial arts.

（二）内外合一形神兼备 Combination of the internal and the external with both form and spirit

中国传统武术既讲究形体规范，又要求精神传意。内外合一的整体观，是中国武术的一大特色。所谓内，指心、神、意等心志活动和气的运行；所谓外，即手、眼、身、步等形体活动。内与外、形与神是相互联系统一的整体。

Traditional Chinese Martial Arts not only pays attention to the physical norms, but also requires spiritual communication. The holistic view of the unity of inside and outside is a major feature of Chinese Martial Arts. The so-called inner means the activities of heart, spirit and mind, and the movement of breath; the so-called external, that is, physical activities such as hands, eyes, body and steps. Inside and outside, form and spirit are a united whole closely related with one another.

（三）适应性广泛 Broad adaptability

武术的练习形式丰富多样，有竞技对抗性的散手、推手，有适合演练的各种拳术、器械和对练，还有与其相适应的各种练功方法。不同的拳种和器械有不同的动作结构、技术要求、运动风格和运动量，分别适应人们不同年龄、性别、体质的需求。人们可以根据自己的条件和兴趣爱好选择练习，同时它对场地、器材的要求较低，俗称"拳打卧牛之地"，练习者可以根据场地的大小变化练习内容和方式，即使一时没有器械也可以徒手练功。一般来说，受时间、季节限制也很小。

The forms of martial arts exercises are rich and varied, including competitive free combat and Pushing Hands, various martial arts, equipment and pair exercises suitable for training, as well as various exercise methods suitable for them. Different

types of boxing and equipment have different movement structures, technical requirements, exercise styles and exercise volumes, which are adapted to the needs of people of different ages, sexes, and physiques. People can choose to practice according
to their own conditions and hobbies, and at the same time, it has lower requirements
for venues and equipment, commonly known as "One can practice Shaolin fist within
a place of a crouching cow size", practitioners can change the content and methods
of practice according to the size of the field, even if there is no equipment for a
while, they can practice with bare hands. Generally speaking, it is not limited by
time or season.

四、武术内容与分类 Wushu content and classification

（一）对练 Pair training

对练是两人或两人以上，按照预定的程序进行的攻防格斗套路。其中包
括徒手对练、器械对练、徒手与器械对练等几种练法。

It is an offensive and defensive fighting routine of two or more people in accordance with a predetermined procedure. It includes several training methods: bare-handed training, equipment-based training, and bare-handed and equipment training.

1. 徒手对练。其是运用踢、打、摔、拿等方法，按照进攻、防守、还击的
运动规律编成的拳术对练套路，有打拳、擒拿对练、南拳对练、形意拳对练等。

Bare-handed pair training. It is a martial arts pair training routine compiled according to the law of offense, defense, and counter-attacking using methods such as
kicking, hitting, throwing, and holding. Sometimes boxing, pair catching and grap-
ping, pair Nanquan (Southern Boxing), and pair Xingyiquan (Boxing of Form and
Mind).

2. 器械对练。其是以器械的劈、砍、击、刺等技击方法组成的对练套路，
主要有长器械对练、短器械对练、长与短对练、单与双对练等多种形式，常
见的有单刀进枪、三节棍进棍、双匕首进枪、对刺剑等。

Weapon pair training. It is a pair routine training composed of weapon chopping,
slashing, hitting, and stabbing. It mainly includes long weapon pair training, short
weapon pair training, long and short pair training, single and double pair train-

ing. The common forms include single knife against spear, three-section sticks against stick, double daggers against spear, swords confrontation.

3. 徒手与器械对练。其是一方空手、另一方持器械进行的攻防对练套路,如空手夺刀、空手夺棍、空手进双枪等。

Bare-handed and weapon pair training. It is an offensive and defensive pairing exercise performed by one side with empty hands and the other with equipment, such as grabbing a knife bare-handedly, grabbing a club bare-handedly, and entering double spears bare-handedly.

4. 集体演练。其是集体进行的徒手、器械或徒手与器械的演练。在竞赛中通常要求六人以上,可变换队形、图案,也可用音乐伴奏,要求队形整齐、动作协调一致。

Group exercises. It refers to exercises conducted collectively with bare hands, equipment, or bare hands versus equipment. In the competition, more than six people are usually required. The formation and pattern can be changed, and music accompaniment can also be used. The formation is required to be neat and coordinated.

（二）搏斗运动 Combating sports

搏斗运动是两人在一定条件下,按照一定的规则进行斗智较力的对抗练习形式。目前武术竞赛中正在逐步开展的有散手、推手、短兵三项。

It is a form of antagonistic exercise in which two people under certain conditions, according to certain rules, compete in wit and in strength. At present, there are three events in the martial arts competition, namely Sanshou, Pushing Hands and Short Weapons.

1. 散手。是两人按照一定的规则使用踢、打、摔、拿等方法制胜对方的竞技项目。

2. 推手。是两人遵照一定的规则,使用棚、扳、挤、按、采、肘、靠等手法,双方粘连粘随,通过肌肉的感觉来判断对方的用劲,然后借劲发力将对方推出,以此决定胜负的竞技项目。

3. 短兵。是两人手持一种用藤、皮、棉制作的短棒似的器械,在 8 米直径的圆形场地内,按照一定的规则使用劈、砍、刺、崩、点、斩等方法进行决胜负的竞技项目。

1. Sanshou（Free combat）. It is the competition in which two people use kicking, beating, throwing, taking according to certain rules to win the opponent.

2. Pushing Hands. It is the competition in which two people follow certain rules and use shed, pull, squeeze, press, pick, elbow, and lean. The two sides lean against each other, judge the other's strength with the muscle, and then use the other's strength to put the other aside to determine the outcome of the competition.

3. Short Weapons. Two people holding a short rod–like device made of rattan, leather, and cotton, in a circular field with a diameter of 8 meters, in accordance with certain rules, use methods such as slashing, hacking, stabbing, pointing, smashing, and chopping to win over the opponent.

五、中国传统武术的流派 Schools of Traditional Chinese Martial Arts

中国武术如同浩瀚大海，深不可测，门派拳种，枝繁叶茂，穷毕生精力能得其皮毛，已属不易。主要流派如下：

Chinese Martial Arts are like the vast ocean that is unfathomable, the schools of which are like luxuriant branches and it is not easy for one to get a basic sense of each. The main genres are as follows：

（一）少林派 Shaolin School

少林派是武术中一个约定俗成的技术流派。因以少林寺所传习拳械为基础形式，曾一度被民间誉为武林的"泰山北斗"，又称少林拳、少林武功等。少林武术的形成，大都来自民间和军旅武术。少林僧人中，有的不容于世，遁入空门，削发为僧，以致把武术带进寺院，也有武林名家将自己的艺业传于少林，这些武技传入少林寺后，形成了少林派的基本部分。在流传过程中，由于社会需要的制约和禅宗文化的影响，逐步演进成相对稳定的少林拳派。少林寺武术推崇达摩老祖，只不过借助达摩在佛教中崇高的地位罢了。发展到近现代，少林拳派的运动特点表现为拳禅一体，神形一片，硬打快攻，齐进齐退。

Shaolin School is a conventional technique school in martial arts. It was once known as the "Mount Tai and North Star" (the most respectable) of martial arts by the folks because of its basic form of boxing and weapons taught by Shaolin Temple, also known as Shaolin Boxing or Shaolin Martial arts. Most parts of the Shaolin martial arts originated from folk and military martial arts. Among the Shaolin monks, some of them were not allowed to live in society. They escaped into the empty door (the temple world) and cut their hair to become monks. As a result, they brought the martial arts into the temple. There were also famous martial arts masters who passed on their art to Shaolin. After the martial arts were introduced to Shaolin Temple, they formed a basic part of Shaolin School. In the process of spreading, due to the constraints of social needs and the influence of Zen culture, Shaolin Boxing School gradually evolved and became relatively stable during Ming and Qing Dynasties. The martial arts of Shaolin Temple respected Bodhidharma, but with the help of Bodhidharma's lofty position in Buddhism. Developed in modern times, the characteristics of Shaolin Boxing School are manifested as a combination of boxing and Zen, a unity of form and spirit, fighting hard and fast, advancing and retreating together.

（二）武当派 Wudang School

内家拳俗称武当派，源于湖北武当山。近代有人将太极拳、八卦拳、形意拳合并为"内家拳"，称为"武当派"。武当拳具有代表性的拳术还有"九宫神行拳""九宫十八腿""太乙五行擒扑"等，更以武当剑法为最。

Commonly Neijiaquan (Inner Boxing) is known as Wudang School, it originated from Wudang Mountain in Hubei province. In modern times, some people merged Taiji Boxing, Eight Trigram Boxing and Form and Spirit Boxing into "Inner Boxing" and called "Wudang School". The representative martial arts of Wudang Boxing include "Nine-grid Speedy Boxing", "Nine-grid Eighteen Legs", and "Taiyi Five-element Boxing", and Wudang swordsmanship is the most amazing.

（三）峨眉派 Emei School

峨眉派是中国武术的著名门派之一。该系武技崇奉四川峨眉山为发祥地。清初湛然法师在《峨眉拳谱》中写道："一树开五花，五花八叶扶；皎皎峨眉月，光辉满江湖。""峨眉月"即指峨眉派武术。有人将近代四川流传的僧、岳、杜、赵、洪、化、字、会等八门，黄林、点易、铁佛、青城、青牛等五派，统归为峨眉派，即《峨眉拳谱》所谓"五花八叶扶"。其中，僧、岳、杜、赵称四大家，洪、化、字、会称四小家。

Emei School is one of the famous schools of Chinese martial arts. This system of martial arts considers Mount Emei in Sichuan as its birthplace. In the early Qing Dynasty, Master Zhan Ran wrote in the *Emei Boxing Book*："A tree blooms with five flowers, five flowers with eight leaves support；Hence Emei moon full bright，the glory shines the sky.""Emei moon" refers to the martial arts of Emei school. The eight doors of Seng，Yue，Du，Zhao，Hong，Hua，Zi，and Hui；the five branch-schools of Huanglin，Dianyi，Tiefo，Qingcheng，and Qingniu，all these are collectively classified as Emei School，which refers to the so-called "five flowers with eight leaves support" in the *Emei Boxing Book*. There are also Yumenquan and Baimeiquan（White-brow Boxing）. And Hong，Hua，Zi，and Hui are called the four small families.

（四）内家拳 Inner Boxing School

内家拳是一种"主于御敌"的拳种。所谓内家是相对于主于搏人的外家拳技而言。内家拳又被统称为武当派。传习者说此拳传自宋代武当山道士张三丰。清末年初，有将太极拳、八卦拳、形意拳等概括为内家拳的说法，这种说法在民间一直沿用着。太极拳是武术拳种之一。清初始见传于河南温县陈家沟。

Neijiaquan is a type of boxing that "defends against the enemy". The so-called inner boxing is relative to the outer boxing skills，which mainly focus on fighting people. Neijiaquan is collectively referred to as Wudang School. The practitioners said that this boxing was passed on from Zhang Sanfeng, a Taoist priest in Wudang Mountain in Song Dynasty. At the end of Qing Dynasty, Taijiquan（Tai Chi），Baguaquan（Eight Trigram Boxing），and Xingyiquan were summarized as Neijiaquan，which has been used in the folk. Tai Chi（Taiji）is one of the martial arts types. In early Qing Dynasty, it was spread in Chenjiagou，Wen County，Henan province.

关于太极拳的起源，有几种不同说法。一说传自唐朝许宣平或李道子；一说传自宋代张三丰；一说传自陈家沟陈氏始祖陈卜。太极拳分为：陈式太极拳，创始人陈王庭；杨式太极拳，创始人杨露禅；武式太极拳，创始人武禹襄；孙式太极拳，创始人孙禄堂；吴式太极拳，创始人吴鉴泉；赵堡太极拳，因在赵堡镇流传，故名。

There are several different stories about the origin of Taijiquan, one is from Xu Xuanping or Li Daozi of Tang Dynasty; one is from Zhang Sanfeng in Song Dynasty, and another is from Chen Bu, the ancestor of the Chen family in Chenjiagou. Taiji is divided into: Chen style Taiji, founder Chen Wangting; Yang style Taiji, founder Yang Luchan; Wu style Taiji, founder Wu Yuxiang; Sun style Taiji, founder Sun Lutang; Wu style Taiji, founder Wu Jianquan; Zhaobao Taiji is called because it is spread in Zhaobao town.

（五） 自然门 Natural School

自然门为武术的一种，湖南慈利县人杜心五（公元 1869 年～公元 1953 年）所传。杜自称此术得自四川武师徐矮师。近代由万籁声广为传播。自然门无固定拳套，不讲招，不讲相，以气为归，以不失自然为本旨；所谓：动静无始，变化无端，虚虚实实，自然而然。

Natural School is a kind of martial arts, passed on by Du Xinwu (1869–1953 AD) from Cili County, Hunan Province. Du claimed to have obtained this technique from Sichuan martial master Xu Aishi. It was widely spread by Wan Laisheng in modern times. The natural school has no fixed routines, no fixed routines, no forms, relies on Qi as the goal, and does not lose nature; it says: dynamic and static movement has no beginning, change has no reason, virtuality and reality go on naturally.

（六） 南少林派 South Shaolin School

南少林派是武术流派之一。此派传习者崇嵩山少林寺为祖庭，以福建少林寺为发祥地。为与嵩山少林寺相别，该寺称"南少林寺"，所传拳技称"南少林拳"。

South Shaolin School is one of the martial arts schools. The inheritors of this school takes Shaolin Temple as the ancestral place, and Fujian Shaolin Temple is the birthplace. In order to distinguish it from Songshan Shaolin Temple, the temple is called "South Shaolin Temple", and its boxing skills are called "South Shaolin Boxing".

（七）龙行派 Longxing School（The Dragon Walk School）

龙行派起源于山西五台山铁林寺，有人称其为五台派。龙行派最初仅有三掌，其三掌要诀是"熟能生巧、巧能生精、精神融汇，变化无穷。"要求动则暴发寸劲，发即排山倒海。另外五台地区还流传着五郎棍、鞭杆等，也都可列为五台派之内。

The Longxing School originated from Tielin Temple in Wutai Mountain, Shanxi province, and some people call it Wutai School. The Dragon Walk School had only three palms at first, and the key to the three palms was "Familiarity makes skill, skill makes essence, essence and spirit integrate; infinite changes come on." Movement requires powerful and explosive strength in a very short distance and time. In Wutai area, there are also Wulang sticks and whip sticks, which can also be classified as Wutai School.

（八）昆仑派 Kunlun School

据传昆仑派源于昆仑山地区，后来随移民传至河南一带，至今已有二百余年历史。昆仑派独树一帜，技法奇特，内容丰富，既有技击护身之功，又有健身益年之术。其中昆仑拳是其代表之一。昆仑拳矫健有力，动作迅速快猛。讲究：刁滑、凶猛、吞吐、浮沉八法。手型多变，攻防结合，手脚并用，步法灵活、扎实。昆仑派长期秘传之气功——大雁功，则是模仿大雁的形态，结合气功导引法编成的一套高级功法，其功效为舒筋活血，防治疾病，保健强身。

According to legend, Kunlun School originated in Kunlun Mountains, and later spread to Henan province with immigrants. It has a history of more than 200 years. Kunlun School is unique, with peculiar techniques and rich content. It not only has the skill of martial arts protection, but also has the skill of fitness and longevity. Among them, Kunlun Boxing is one of its representatives. Kunlun boxing is strong and vigorous, and its movements are fast and fierce. Pay attention to the eight methods of slyness and slipperiness, fierceness and violence, swallow and spit, ups and downs. Changeable hand shapes, combination of offense and defense, combined use of hands and feet, flexible and solid footwork. The Kunlun School's long-term secret Qigong——Big Goose, is a set of advanced exercises that imitates the form of a wild goose, combined with the Qigong Guiding Method. It can relax muscles and blood, prevent diseases, and strengthen the body.

武林中还有天山派、崆峒派等说法，由于未见其传人或流传不广，其内容不详。还有很多著名拳种。曾有人将少林、武当、峨眉、昆仑、华山（华拳）、青城、五台（龙行）、崆峒列为中国武术的八大门派。

There are also Tianshan (Tianshan Mountain) School and Kongtong School in the boxing, and their contents are not known because of no descendants or not widespread. There are many famous boxing types. Shaolin, Wudang, Emei, Kunlun, Huashan (Huaquan), Qingcheng, Wutai (Longxing), and Kongtong are listed as the eight martial arts schools in China.

六、中国传统武术的拳派 Famous Boxing Schools of Traditional Chinese Martial Arts

几千年来，中华武术，博大精深，门派众多，历史上产生无数英雄豪杰。

For thousands of years, Chinese martial arts have been broad and profound, with many schools, and numerous heroes have appeared in history.

（一）少林拳 Shaolin Boxing

少林武术创始人相传为达摩祖师。自古以来，有"天下功夫出少林"之说，就是说，天下各大门派武术多数是从少林寺传出。但后代武林史学家经研究后认为，"天下武功汇少林"之说，更为妥当。因为少林寺汇集了全国各地僧众，还有些武林人士为了躲避仇家或者犯了命案，逃到少林寺剃发为僧，躲避官府追查，然后将一身武功传给僧众。所以，少林寺内武术种类繁杂，罗汉拳、龙拳、蛇拳、心意把，等等，应有尽有。少林拳主要特点为硬打快攻、刚劲威猛。

The founder of Shaolin Wushu is said to be Bodhidharma. Since ancient times, there has been a saying that "Kung Fu in the world comes from Shaolin", that is to say, most martial arts came from Shaolin Temple. However, after research, later generations of martial arts historians believe that "the world's martial arts are absorbed and integrated in Shaolin" is more appropriate. Because Shaolin Temple gathered monks from all over the country, some martial arts people fled to Shaolin Temple to shave their hair and became monks in order to avoid enemies, or avoiding investigation by the government after having commited murders, and then passed on martial arts to the monks. Therefore, there are many types of martial arts in Shaolin Temple, including Arhat Boxing, Dragon Boxing, Snake Boxing, Mind Boxing and so on. The main characteristics of Shaolin Boxing are hard, fast and mighty.

（二）心意拳 Xinyiquan （Mind Boxing）

心意拳祖师相传为岳飞，但后人经考证，多数认可祖师为明末姬龙峰。心意拳有三大主要流派。一是以马学礼为代表的河南心意拳，二是山西祁县的戴氏心意拳，以金道人为代表的重庆金家功夫。心意拳特点为模仿十种动物搏斗方法，俗称"十大形"，讲究拳功一体，身形高低起伏，以打击人体要害为目标。少林拳的镇山拳法心意把，就来源于心意拳。

According to legend, the ancestor of Xinyiquan （Mind Boxing）was Yue Fei, but after research, the ancestor as Ji Longfeng in the late Ming Dynasty is recognized. There are three main schools of Xinyi quan. One is Henan Xinyiquan represented by Ma Xueli, another is Daishi Xinyiquan in Qixian County of Shanxi province, another is Jin family's Kungfu in Chongqing city represented by Taoist Jin. Xinyiquan is characterized by imitating ten kinds of animal fighting methods, commonly known as the "ten forms". The most treasurable Mind Boxing of Shaolin Boxing is derived from Xinyiquan.

（三）形意拳 Xingyiquan （Form and Mind Boxing）

形意拳祖师为李洛能。其是在戴氏心意拳基础上创立的一种实战拳法。形意拳拔高身形，更接近于现代搏击站姿，启动更快。形意五行拳与现代拳击动作神似，可谓是中国版拳击。形意拳讲究"硬打硬进无遮拦"，拳势勇猛，动作如电闪雷鸣。"太极十年不出门，形意拳一年打死人！"形意拳的高效实用实战能力，可见一斑！

The ancestor of Xingyiquan was Li Luoneng, which is a boxing method designed for actual combat based on the Dai family's Xinyiquan. Xingyiquan takes a taller position, closer to the modern fighting stance, and starts faster. Xingyi Wuxing Boxing is similar to modern boxing, and it can be described as a Chinese version of boxing. Xingyiquan pays attention to "fighting hard and entering without blocking". The boxing is brave and moves like lightning and thunder. "Taiji will not go out for ten years, while Xingyiquan can kill people with one year's practice!" Xingyiquan's effective and practical combat ability is evident!

（四）八卦掌 Bagua Palm （Eight Diagrams Palm）

八卦掌祖师为董海川。八卦掌自董海川在清朝同治年间在北京首创始传。八卦掌以掌法多变、步法灵活、身法灵动为特色。出手成招，刚柔相济，踢打摔拿融为一体；拧裹钻翻，避正打斜，围圆打点，循循相生无有穷尽。

The ancestor of Bagua Palm was Dong Haichuan. Bagua Palm was first spread in Beijing by Dong Haichuan in the Tongzhi period of Qing Dynasty. Bagua Palm is characterized by variable palms, flexible steps, and agile body skills. Strikes into action, combining strength and softness, kicks, beats and throws into an integration. Twisting, drilling and turning, avoiding straight and fighting slanting, making rounds and pointing, with numerous changes.

（五）太极 Taiji Boxing

太极祖师相传为张三丰。太极拳含蓄内敛、连绵不断、急缓相间、行云流水，讲究借力打力、以柔克刚。现代，太极拳发展为世界最著名的养生拳。

The forefather of Taiji is said to be Zhang Sanfeng. Taijiquan is implicit and restrained, continuous, rapid and alternate, like clouds and flowing water, and emphasizes leveraging strength and with softness to overcome rigidity. In modern times, Taiji Boxing has developed into the most famous health-preserving boxing in the world.

（六）通臂拳 Tongbi Boxing

通臂拳祖师是清末浙江人祁信。通臂拳特点为以柔为主，刚柔相济，以背力为法，放长击远先发制人。

The ancestor of Tongbi Boxing was Qi Xin from Zhejiang province in the late Qing Dynasty. Tongbi Boxing is characterized mainly by softness, with alternate hardness and softness, using back force as the method, with long-term strikes and preemptive strikes.

（七）八极拳 Bajiquan （Eight-extremities Boxing）

相传为明末一外号"癞"的云游高人所创，后传吴钟。八极拳是非常讲求实战、打练结合的拳种之一。猛起硬落、硬开对方之门，连连进发是八极拳技击中的最大特色。

A legend has it that it was created by a nicknamed person "Lai" (meaning scab-headed) in the late Ming Dynasty, who later taught Wu Zhong. Bajiquan is one of the boxing types that emphasizes practical combat and combination of fighting and practice. Fighting forcefully and violently to open the opponent's door, and attacking again and again are the major features of Bajiquan.

（八）意拳 Yiquan（Mind Boxing）

意拳是在形意拳、心意拳、鹤拳、少林拳基础上创立的一种实战拳法。意拳抛弃传统招法训练，以"站桩、试力、走步、试声、发力、推手、实作"七妙法门为训练方法，以培养人体搏斗本能为目标。

Mind Boxing was a practical boxing based on Xingyiquan（Form and Mind boxing）, Xinyiquan（Heart and Mind boxing）, Hequan（Crane boxing）and Shaolin boxing. Mind Boxing abandons the traditional technique training, uses the seven methods of "stand, try strength, walk, test sound, exert force, push hands, and practice" as the seven training methods, aiming at cultivating the human body's combating instinct.

（九）咏春拳 Wing Chun

咏春拳相传为清朝女子严咏春所创。咏春拳长于近身搏击，拳速快、防守紧密，马步灵活和上落快，攻守兼备、刚柔并济。近代咏春拳师叶问赴香港传拳，其徒弟众多。晚年叶问收了一位徒弟，名唤李小龙，后来成为功夫巨星和截拳道创始人。咏春拳因李小龙而风靡世界。

According to legend, Wing Chun was created by Yan Wing Chun, a woman in Qing Dynasty. Wing Chun was good at close combat, with fast fists, tight defense, flexible stance and fast ups and downs, both offensive and defensive, both rigid and flexible. Modern Wing Chun boxer Ip Man went to Hong Kong to teach the boxing, and his apprentices were numerous. In his later years, Ye Wen accepted an apprentice named Bruce Lee, who later became a Kung Fu star and founder of Jeet Kune Do. Wing Chun has become popular all over the world because of Bruce Lee.

（十）长拳 Changquan School（Long-distance Boxing School）

长拳泛指遐举遥击、进退疾速的徒手攻防技术和运动形式，所谓长是相对短而言。长拳是相对短打而言。现代长拳拳术架式舒展、工整，动作灵活、敏捷，腿法和鼠跳动作较多。

Changquan（Long-distance Boxing）generally refers to unarmed offensive and defensive techniques and forms of movement that use remote strikes and rapid advance and retreat. Long-distance Boxing is relatively said in contrast with short-distance boxing. Modern Changquan boxing is stretched, neat, flexible and agile, with more legwork and rat jumping.

（十一）象形拳 Imitative Boxing School

象形拳是武术中的一类，泛指模仿某一动物的技能、特长和形态，或模仿某种特定人物的动作形态，结合攻防技法而编的拳术。

Imitative boxing is a type of martial arts. It generally refers to a boxing technique that imitates the skills, specialties and forms of a certain animal, or imitates the action of a certain person, combined with offensive and defensive techniques.

中国的传统姓名文化

一、中国人姓氏的产生与发展 The Appearance and Development of Chinese Surnames

姓的起源可以追溯到人类原始社会的母系氏族制时期。姓是作为区分氏族的特定标志符号。中国的许多古代姓氏都是女字旁，这说明祖先曾经经历过母系氏族社会。各姓氏互相通婚，同姓氏族内禁婚，子女归母亲一方，以母亲为姓。姓的出现是原始人类逐步摆脱蒙昧状态的一个标志。

The origin of the surname can be traced back to the matrilineal clan period of human primitive society. The surname was used as a specific symbol to distinguish clans. Many ancient Chinese surnames were related to female radicals, which showed that the ancestors experienced matrilineal clan society. The different surnamed people intermarried each other, and marriages within the same surname clan were forbidden. The children belonged to the mother and were surnamed after the mother. The appearance of the surname was a sign that primitive humans gradually got rid of ignorance.

"氏"的产生要比"姓"晚一些，这是因为同一母系血统的氏族子孙繁衍，人口增加，同一母族分为若干支族迁往不同的地方生活和居住，每个支族都要有一个区别于其他支族的称号，这就是"氏"。因此可以说，姓代表母系血统，氏代表氏族分支；姓是不变的，氏是可变的；姓区别血统，氏区别子孙。这是姓与氏在最初的区别。

"Shi" came into being later than "Xing". This was because the descendants of the same matrilineal lineage multiplied and the population increased. The same mother clan was divided into several tribes and moved to different places to live, and each tribe must have its own name to differentiate their tribe from other tribes, this was the "Shi", meaning sub-surname. Therefore, it can be said that the surname represented the matrilineal lineage, the sub-surname represented the clan branch; the surname was unchanged, the sub-surname was variable; the surname distinguished the lineage, and the sub-surname distinguished the descendants. This was the initial difference between surname and sub-surname.

随着社会生产力的发展，母系氏族制度过渡到父系氏族制度，姓改为从父，氏反为女子家族之用。后来，氏族制度逐渐被阶级社会制度所替代，赐土以命氏的治理国家的方法、手段便产生了。在阶级社会，男子有氏，女子无氏。男子称氏以别贵贱，女子称姓以别婚姻。姓和氏，是人类进步的两个阶段，是文明的产物。后来，在春秋战国时期，姓与氏合一，不再区分，即姓与氏都是姓，表明个人及其家族的符号。这就是我们今天理解的姓氏含义。

With the development of social productive forces, the matrilineal clan system transitioned to the patrilineal clan system, and the surname was named from after mother to after father. Later, the clan system was gradually replaced by the class social system, and naming a person after the land came into being as a means to govern a country. In a class society, men had sub-surnames but women had no sub-surnames. Men were called with their sub-surnames to differentiate their positions; women were called with their surnames to show to what family they were married. Surnames and Sub-surnames were the two phases of human progress and both the product of civilization. Later, in the Spring and Autumn Period and the Warring States Period, the surname and the sub-surname were unified and no longer distinguished, thus the surname and the sub-surname were both surnames, indicating the symbols of individuals and their families. This is the meaning of surnames as we understand today.

二、姓氏的影响 The Influences of the Surnames

在中国的封建社会，姓氏是一个非常重要的问题。它不但标志着一个人的血统，还标志着一个人的门第和地位。汉魏以来，盛行门阀制度，姓氏有了高低贵贱之分。帝王、功臣、贵戚之姓拥有尊贵地位，享有社会的某些特权，可以左右当时的政治局面，逐渐形成了一些豪门大族。隋唐时代，科举盛行，寒门庶族大量进入统治阶层，但门第观念依然盛行。由于推崇高门大户，便产生了所谓的"郡望意识"。"郡望"是指某一姓氏世居某郡而为人们所仰望之意，实际指某一姓氏在当时的社会影响很大。中国文化中在婚姻方面有句名言，那就是"门当户对"，也就是指结婚的两家要门第相当，地位相当，财富相当。

In the feudal society of China, surname was a very important issue. It not only marked a person's blood, but also marked a person's family and status. Since the Han and Wei Dynasties, the system of dominant family prevailed, and surnames were distinguished between high and low. The surnames of emperors, heroes, and nobles had noble status and enjoyed certain social privileges, which could influence the political situation at that time, and gradually formed some noble families. During Sui and Tang Dynasties, imperial examinations prevailed, and a large number of common people entered the ruling class, but the concept of family status still prevailed. The so-called "consciousness of Junwang", which means consciousness of prestige at a "Junwang" (certain area) came into being due to the admiration of noble families. "Junwang" referred to a certain surname living in a certain county and being looked up to by the local people. It actually meant that a certain surname had a great social influence at that time. There is a well-known saying in Chinese culture in terms of marriage, that is, "properly matched marriage", which means that the two families who get married should have the same rank, status and wealth.

三、家谱 Genealogy

姓氏的产生和变化是社会发展的结果，姓氏的混杂则是社会变动的反映。由于宗法制的统治和影响，一姓一族常用家谱或宗谱记载他们的变迁始末及家族承袭关系。家族变动的原因主要有四点：(1) 帝王分封子弟功臣；(2) 战乱；(3) 官宦；(4) 移民。姓氏和家庭的变迁，往往记录在家谱里。

The generation and changes of surnames are the result of social development, and the mixing of surnames is a reflection of social changes. Due to the rule and influence of the patriarchal system, a surname and a clan often used family genealogy or clan genealogy to record their changes and family inheritance relationships. There were four main reasons for the changes of a family: (1) the enfeoffment to the sons and nephews and rewards to the meritorious statesmen and heroes by the kings or emperors; (2) wars; (3) holding official positions; (4) immigration. Changes in surnames and families were often recorded in the genealogy.

四、中国人的名字 Chinese Names

中国人注重姓氏，以姓氏为自己的根基和归属；中国人也注重名字，因为名字才是自我的存在。我们现在所说的名字，其实只是古代的"名"。自古以来，中国人很讲究命名，而命名的出发点与那个时代的社会生活密切相关。周朝建立，礼制规范对如何命名有许多规定："名有五：有信、有义、有象、有假、有类。"即以出生时的情况命名为"信"，以道德品行命名为"义"，以某一物的形象命名为"象"，借用某一物体的名称为"假"，取婴儿与其父相同之处命名为"类"。此外还规定不以国名、官名、山川、隐疾、牲畜、器帛等六种事物命名。

Chinese people value surnames and take surnames as their root and belonging; Chinese people also pay attention to given names, because given names are the existence of one's self. The names we are talking about now are actually just ancient "given names". Since ancient times, Chinese people have been very particular about naming, and the starting point of naming is closely related to the social life of that era. Since Zhou Dynasty was established, there had been many rules on how to name people: "There are five namings: faith, righteousness, image, borrowing, and kind." That is, it is "faith" if named according to the birth situation; it is righteousness if named based on moral character; it is image if named after the image of a certain object; it is borrowing if named borrowing the name of a certain object, and it is kind if named after the father for they share some quality. In addition, it is stipulated not to name a person after the six things, including country names, official titles, mountains and rivers, hidden diseases, livestock, and utensils.

古代的中国人不但有名，而且有字。字由名演化而来，所以统称为"名字"。由于古人注重礼仪，因此称名称字大有讲究。在人际交往中，名一般用于谦称、卑称，或上对下、长对少；而字用于下对上、少对长或对他人尊称。在多数情况下，直呼其名是很不礼貌的。从历代的取字情况看，名与字有密切关系，可以说是"因名取字"。古人说"名之与字，义相比附"。名与字大致有五种关系：（1）名与字意义相同；（2）名与字意义相关；（3）名与字意义相反；（4）名与字的意义取自五行相生相克；（5）按伯、仲、叔、季的排行。

The ancient Chinese had not only names, but also had bynames, which evolved from names, so they were generally called "names". Because the ancients paid attention to rite, they were very particular about using names or bynames. In interpersonal communication, the name was generally used for modest, humble, or senior-to-junior, elder-to-younger; while bynames were used for junior-to-senior, younger-to-elder, or to address others respectfully. In most cases, it is impolite to call a person directly by his given name. From the perspective of byname selection in the past dynasties, names were closely related to bynames, and it could be said that "bynames are taken from names". The ancients said that "names and bynames are attached in meanings". There are roughly five relationships between names and bynames: (1) Names and bynames have the same meaning; (2) Names and bynames are related in meaning; (3) Names and bynames are opposite in meaning; (4) The names and bynames are derived in meaning from mutual promotion or mutual restraint between the five elements (metal, wood, water, fire, earth). (5) According to the ranking of brothers as Bo (the eldest), Zhong (the second eldest), Shu (the third eldest), Ji (the youngest).

古人在名字之外还有"号"，这也是中国文化的一个独特现象。号的起源虽然很早，但其流行是在唐宋以后，明清时为盛。一方面，是社会对文人学士的一种推崇和敬佩心理；另一方面，是骚人墨客企图用一种委婉曲折的方式表达自己超然物外的理想与情趣。取号皆由文人士大夫的性情、爱好及其所处环境而定。

The ancients had "Hao" (referring to nicknames) besides their names and bynames, which is also a unique phenomenon in Chinese culture. Although the origin of the nickname was very early in history, its popularity was since Tang and Song Dynasties, and it was flourishing in Ming and Qing Dynasties. On the one hand, it was the society's esteem and admiration for scholars and officials; on the other hand, it was the writers and poets who attempted to express their transcendental ideals and interests in an euphemistic and circumlocutory way. The nickname was determined by the temperament, hobbies of the literati and the environment they lived in.

五、中国传统姓名文化的特点 Characteristics of Traditional Chinese Name Culture

（一）姓氏是重要标记 Surname is an important mark

中国人初次见面时总要问一声："您贵姓?""您怎么称呼?""怎么称呼您?"在表示自己敢作敢当、无所畏惧时，经常拍着胸脯说："男子汉大丈夫，行不更名，坐不改姓。"这就说明在人们的社会交际中，姓氏是一个人在社会上安身立命的重要标记。

When Chinese meet for the first time, they usually ask: "What's your name?" "How shall I call you?" "May I get your name?" When expressing their courage and fearlessness, they often pat their chests and say: "As a man, I don't change my name, let alone my surname." This shows that in people's social communication, the surname is an important mark for a person to settle down in society.

（二）姓氏来源多样 Surnames come from various sources

中国人的姓，大多是从几千年前代代相传下来的。有人统计，文献记载和现存的共有 5600 多个姓。其特点是：源远流长、内容丰富、出处具体。姓氏的形成各有不同的历史过程。同姓不一定是同源，如刘姓就有五处起源；异姓也可能是同出一宗，如古、吴两姓本是同源，都是古公的后裔。还有以名为氏，以国为氏，以邑为氏，以官职为氏，以职业为氏（如巫、卜、陶、匠）等；还有赐姓改姓等。

Most Chinese surnames were passed down from generation to generation thousands of years ago. According to statistics, there are more than 5,600 surnames recorded in the literature and in existence. Its characteristics are: a long history, rich content, and specific sources. The formation of surnames has different historical processes. The same surname is not necessarily of the same origin. For example, the

Liu surname has five origins. Different surnames may also originate from the same ancestry. For example, the two surnames of Gu and Wu are originally of the same origin, and both are descendants of Master Gu. There are also situations where people take name as surname, country as subsurname, town as subsurname, official position as subsurname, occupation as subsurname (such as witch, divination, pottery, craftsman); there are also some surnames honored or changed by kings or emperors.

每个姓氏的起源不同。比如"林"，林姓是一个有着悠久历史的姓氏，相传由商朝末年的名臣比干而来。比干原是商朝王室成员，在商纣王时担任少师之职，以忠正敢言闻名。纣王昏庸无道，他多次进言劝谏，后来因此获罪，被剖心而死。夫人陈氏为躲避官兵追杀，逃难于长林石室，生子名坚，因生于林被周武王赐以林为姓，史称林坚，被林姓人尊为受姓始祖。

The origin of each surname is different. For example, Lin (means forest), the surname Lin is a surname with a long history, according to legend, it was derived from Bi Gan, the famous minister Bi Gan in the last years of Shang Dynasty. Bi Gan was a member of the royal family in Shang Dynasty. He served as the teacher for the prince during the government of King Zhou, and he was known for his loyalty and boldness. King Zhou was fatuous and immoral; Bi Gan repeatedly offered the king advice and persuasion, but was later convicted and cut to death. His wife, Chen, fled to the stone cave of a forest in order to avoid the officers and soldiers. She gave birth to a son named Jian. Because he was born in Lin (the forest), he was given Lin as the surname by King Wu of Zhou Dynasty. He was named Lin Jian in history and was respected as the ancestor of the surname Lin.

（三）有单姓复姓之分 There are single and double surnames

单姓是只用一个字的姓，与复姓相对。复姓，指由两个及以上的汉字组成的姓氏。如：欧阳、司马、上官、西门。复姓的来源较多，如官名、封邑、职业等，有些则源于少数民族改姓。

Single surname is a one-character surname, as counterpart to double surname. Double surname refers to a surname composed of two or more Chinese characters. Such as: Ouyang, Sima, Shangguan, Ximen. There are many sources of double surnames, such as official names, fief, occupations and some are derived from minority surnames.

六、部分少数民族的姓氏习俗 Surname customs of some ethnic minorities

（一） 满族姓氏 Manchu Surnames

姓氏就是家族系统的称号。满族姓氏，也是构成满族民间氏族团体的称号。中国的满族人口中，历史上以女真族为主体，又加入了蒙古、索伦部、汉、朝鲜等，诸多民族经过多个世纪融合而成新的民族共同体"满洲族"，今天简称满族。满族八大姓有：佟佳氏、瓜尔佳氏、马佳氏、索绰罗氏、齐佳氏、富察氏、叶赫那拉氏、钮祜禄氏。冠以汉字姓为：佟、关、马、索、齐、富、那、郎。辽东地区是满族的发祥地，现今仍是满族人民集居的地方。

The surname is the title of the family system. The Manchu surname is also the title of the Manchu folk clan group. Among the Manchu population in China, in history, the Jurchen tribe was the main body, and Mongolia, Solun tribe, Han, and Korean, were added. Many ethnic groups have merged for more than eight centuries to form a new ethnic community "Manchu", today referred to as Manchu. The eight major surnames of Manchu are: Tong Jia, Guar Jia, Ma Jia, Suo Chuo Luo, Qi Jia, Fu Cha, Yehenala, Niu Hulu. Surnames with Chinese characters are: Tong, Guan, Ma, Suo, Qi, Fu, Na, Lang. The Liaodong region was the birthplace of the Manchu, and it is still the place where the Manchu people live.

（二） 蒙古族姓氏 Mongolian Surnames

20 世纪以来中国蒙古族逐渐取汉译姓氏。蒙古族的汉姓来源主要有四种：（1）以部落名称为姓；（2）以氏族名称为姓；（3）以祖先名字为姓；（4）直接取汉译姓氏为姓。

Since the 20th century, Mongolians in China have gradually adopted Han-translated surnames. There are four main sources of Han surnames of Mongolian people: (1) Take tribal name as surname; (2) Take clan name as surname; (3) Take ancestor's name as surname; (4) Take the Han surname directly as the surname.

（三）回族姓氏 Hui Surnames

回族有多少姓氏，至今未有准确的答案，估计有 500 个左右。从这些姓氏资料中发现，回族人口虽然少，但姓氏数量较为可观。通常的汉姓，回族有；古老的汉姓，回族也有；而一些传统的回族姓氏，汉族很少甚至没有，使回族姓氏仍保持本民族的特点。西北地区是中国回族人口最集中的地区，作为中国回族第一大姓——马姓，在这里表现得尤为突出。西北除了较多的马姓外，还保留了许多回族的传统姓氏和稀僻姓氏。

There is no accurate answer as to how many surnames the Hui people have, and there are estimated to be about 500. From these surname data, it is found that although the Hui nationality has not so many people, the number of surnames is relatively large. The usual Han surnames are available for the Hui nationality, the ancient Han surnames can be found in the Hui nationality; and some traditional Hui surnames, the Han nationality has few or no such surnames. Those surnames still retain the characteristics of the nation. The northwestern region is the region with the most concentrated Hui population in China. As the largest Hui surname in China, Ma (meaning horse) is particularly prominent here. In addition to it in the northwest, many traditional Hui surnames and rare surnames have been retained.

世界上许多古文化早已连同创造它们的种族一起销声匿迹了，而中国姓氏文化则历经了四五千年始终延续和发展着。姓氏一直是代表中国传统的宗族观念主要的外在表现形式，以一种血缘文化的特殊形式记录了中华民族的形成，在中华民族的文化同化和国家统一上曾起过独特的民族凝聚力的作用。

Many ancient cultures in the world have already disappeared along with the races that created them, while the culture of Chinese surnames has continued and developed for four to five thousand years. Surnames have been the main external manifestation of traditional Chinese family concepts. They record the formation of the Chinese nation in a special form of blood relationship culture, and have played a unique role of the national cohesion in the cultural assimilation of the Chinese nation and in the national unity.

中国的传统节日文化

一、中国传统节日的产生 The Birth of Traditional Chinese Festivals

中国传统节日，形式多样、内容丰富，是中华民族悠久历史文化的重要组成部分。传统节日的形成，是一个民族或国家的历史文化长期积淀凝聚的过程。中华民族的古老传统节日，其形成与原始信仰、祭祀文化以及天象、历法等人文与自然文化内容有关，涵盖了哲学、人文、历史、天文等方面的内容，蕴含着深邃丰厚的文化内涵。从远古先民时期发展而来的中华传统节日，清晰地记录着中华民族丰富而多彩的社会生活文化内容，也积淀着博大精深的历史文化内涵。

Traditional Chinese festivals are diverse in form and rich in content. They are an important part of the long history and culture of the Chinese nation. The formation of traditional festivals is a process of long-term accumulation and cohesion of the history and culture of a nation or country. The formation of the ancient traditional festivals of the Chinese nation is related to primitive beliefs, sacrificial culture, astronomical phenomena, calendars and other human and natural cultural content, covering philosophy, humanities, history, and astronomy, and contains profound cultural connotations. The traditional Chinese festivals which developed from the time of the ancient ancestors clearly record the rich and colorful social life and cultural content of the Chinese nation, and also accumulate extensive and profound historical and cultural connotations.

传统节日的起源和传承发展，是人类社会逐渐形成，逐渐完善的文化过程，是人类文明进化发展的产物。据现代人类学、考古学的研究成果表明，人类最原始的两种信仰：一是天地信仰，二是祖先信仰，均产生于人类初期对自然界以及祖先的崇拜，由此产生了各种崇拜祭祀活动。古老传统节日的形成与上古原始信仰、祭祀文化以及天象、历法等人文与自然文化内容有关。古老传统节日多数形成于古人择吉日祭祀，以谢天地神灵、祖先恩德的活动。祭祀，是一种信仰活动，源于天地和谐共生的信仰理念。心怀敬畏，方行之高远。上古历法为节日的产生提供了前提条件，原始信仰与祭祀文化是多数传统节日形成的重要因素。传统节日文化反映了源远流长、博大精深的中华文化内涵。

The origin, inheritance and development of traditional festivals are the gradual formation and gradual improvement of the cultural process of human society, and the product of the evolution and development of human civilization. According to the research of modern anthropology and archaeology, there are two most primitive beliefs of mankind: one is belief in heaven and earth, and the other is belief in ancestors. They originated from the worship of nature and ancestors in the early stage of mankind, which resulted in various worship and sacrifice activities. The formation of traditional festivals is related to ancient primitive beliefs, sacrificial culture, astronomical phenomena, calendars and other human and natural cultural contents. Most of the traditional festivals were formed when the ancients chose auspicious days to make sacrifices to thank the gods and ancestors. Sacrifice is a kind of religious activity, derived from the belief concept of harmony between heaven and earth. With awe, people can walk far and wide. The ancient calendar provided prerequisites for the creation of festivals. Primitive beliefs and sacrificial culture were important factors in the formation of most traditional festivals. The traditional festival culture reflects the long-standing and profound Chinese cultural connotation.

二、中国的传统节日 Traditional Chinese Festivals

中国的传统节日主要有春节（正月初一）、元宵节（正月十五）、龙抬头（农历二月二）、上巳节（农历三月初三）、清明节（阳历 4 月 5 日前后）、端午节（农历五月初五）、七夕节（农历七月初七）、七月半（农历七月十四/十五）、中秋节（农历八月十五）、重阳节（农历九月九）、冬至节（阳历 12

月 21~23 日）、除夕（年尾最后一天）等。

Traditional Chinese festivals mainly include Spring Festival (first day of the first lunar month), Lantern Festival (fifteenth day of the first lunar month), Longtai tou Fesrival (Festival of the Dragon Rising its Head, the second day of the second lunar month), Shangsi Festival (third day of the third lunar month), Qingming Festival (around April 5th in the solar calendar), Dragon Boat Festival (the fifth day of the fifth lunar month), the Qixi Festival (the seventh day of the seventh lunar month), Ghosts' Festival (the fourteenth or fifteenth day of the seventh lunar month), the Mid-Autumn Festival (the fifteenth day of the eighth lunar month), the Double Ninth Festival (the ninth day of the ninth lunar month), Winter Solstice Festival (December 21st~23rd in the solar calendar), and New Year's Eve (the last day of the lunar year).

中华民族的传统节日，承载着原始信仰、祭祀文化、天文、术数、历法等人文与自然文化内容。早期的节日文化，反映的是上古社会古人自然崇拜、天人合一的人文精神；一系列的祭祀活动，蕴含着礼乐文明的深邃文化内涵。每个中华传统节日都有自己的来源之处与形成的必要条件。由于上古文献缺失，现存下来的文献对传统节日的记录最早只见于《夏小正》。在历史演变中，由于朝代更迭、历法变动，有些节日在日期上有所改动。古时代一些流传至今的节俗活动，清晰地记录着古人丰富多彩的社会生活内容。

The traditional festivals of the Chinese nation carry human and natural cultural contents such as primitive beliefs, sacrificial culture, astronomy, number, and calendar. The early festival culture reflected the humanistic spirit of ancient people's natural worship and harmony between man and nature; a series of sacrificial activities contained profound cultural connotations of ritual and music civilization. Each Chinese traditional festival has its own source and necessary conditions for formation. Due to the lack of ancient documents, the earliest records of traditional festivals in existing documents can only be found in the works of *Xia Dynasty's Almanac*. In the course of historical evolution, due to dynasties and calendar changes, some festivals have changed dates. Some festivals and customs that have been passed down from ancient times clearly record the rich and colorful social life content of the ancients.

三、二十四节气 Twenty four Solar Terms

二十四节气

春	立春 The Beginning of Spring 02 月 03 ~ 05 日	雨水 Rain Water 02 月 18 ~ 20 日	惊蛰 Awakening of Insects 03 月 05 ~ 07 日
	春分 Spring Equinox 03 月 20 ~ 22 日	清明 Pure Brightness 04 月 04 ~ 06 日	谷雨 Grain Rain 04 月 19 ~ 21 日
夏	立夏 The Beginning of Summer 05 月 05 ~ 07 日	小满 Grain Buds 05 月 20 ~ 22 日	芒种 Grain in Ear 06 月 05 ~ 07 日
	夏至 Summer Solstice 06 月 21 ~ 22 日	小暑 Minor Heat 07 月 06 ~ 08 日	大暑 Major Heat 07 月 22 ~ 24 日
秋	立秋 The Beginning of Autumn 08 月 07 ~ 09 日	处暑 The End of Heat 08 月 22 ~ 24 日	白露 White Dew 09 月 07 ~ 09 日
	秋分 Autumnal Equinox 09 月 22 ~ 24 日	寒露 Cold Dew 10 月 08 ~ 09 日	霜降 Frost's Descent 10 月 23 ~ 24 日
冬	立冬 The Beginning of Winter 11 月 07 ~ 08 日	小雪 Minor Snow 11 月 22 ~ 23 日	大雪 Major Snow 12 月 06 ~ 08 日
	冬至 Winter solstice 12 月 21 ~ 23 日	小寒 Minor Cold 01 月 05 ~ 07 日	大寒 Major Cold 01 月 20 ~ 21 日

二十四节气是中国人通过观察太阳周年运动，认知一年中时令、气候、物候等方面变化规律形成的知识体系和社会实践。由于历史上中国的主要政治、经济、文化、农业活动中心多集中在黄河流域、中原地区，二十四节气是以这一带为依据建立起来的。远在春秋时期，中国古代先贤就定出仲春、仲夏、仲秋和仲冬等四个节气，以后不断地改进和完善。到秦汉年间，二十

四节气已完全确立，成为中国古代一种用来指导农事的补充历法。二十四节气指导着传统农业生产和日常生活，被誉为"中国的第五大发明"。

The Twenty-Four Solar Terms is a knowledge system and social practice formed by the Chinese people through observing the annual movement of the sun and cognizing the changing laws of the season, climate, and phenology of the year. As China's main political, economic, cultural, and agricultural centers were mostly concentrated in the Central Plains of the Yellow River Basin in history, the twenty-four solar terms were established based on this area. As far back as the Spring and Autumn Period, ancient Chinese sages set out the four solar terms: Mid-Spring, Mid-Summer, Mid-Autumn and Mid-Winter, which were continuously improved and perfected. By Qin and Han Dynasties, the twenty-four solar terms were fully established and became a kind of guidance in ancient China as a supplementary calendar for farming. The twenty-four solar terms guided traditional agricultural production and daily life, and are hailed as "China's fifth greatest invention."

2006 年 5 月 20 日，"二十四节气"作为民俗项目经中国国务院批准列入第一批国家级非物质文化遗产名录。2016 年 11 月 30 日，联合国教科文组织正式通过决议，将中国申报的"二十四节气——中国人通过观察太阳周年运动而形成的时间知识体系及其实践"列入联合国教科文组织人类非物质文化遗产代表作名录。二十四节气这一非物质文化遗产十分丰富，其中既包括相关的谚语、歌谣、传说等，又有传统生产工具、生活器具、工艺品、书画等艺术作品，还包括与节令关系密切的节日文化、生产仪式和民间风俗。

On May 20, 2006, the "Twenty-Four Solar Terms" as a folk custom project was approved by the State Council to be included in the first batch of national intangible cultural heritage lists. On November 30, 2016, UNESCO formally passed a resolution to include the "Twenty-Four Solar Terms—The Time Knowledge System and Practices Formed by the Chinese through Observing the Movement of the Sun's Anniversary" declared by China as a UNESCO Human Representative list of intangible cultural heritage. The intangible cultural heritage of the twenty-four solar terms is very rich. It includes not only related proverbs, ballads, legends, but also traditional production tools, living utensils, handicrafts, calligraphy and other artistic works, and also covers festival culture that is closely related to the festival, production ceremonies and folk customs.

《二十四节气歌》全文是：

春雨惊春清谷天，夏满芒夏暑相连。

秋处露秋寒霜降，冬雪雪冬小大寒。

每月两节不变更，最多相差一两天。

上半年来六廿一，下半年是八廿三。

Song of "Twenty-four Solar Terms"：

Beginning of Spring, Rain Water, Awakening of Insects, and Spring Equinox,

Pure Brightness, Grain Rain, Beginning of Summer, Grain Full, and Grain in Ear,

Summer Solstice, Minor Heat, Major Heat, Beginning of Autumn appear,

End of Heat, White Dew, follow the Autumnal equinox.

Cold Dew, Frost's Descent, Beginning of Winter,

Minor Snow, Major Snow, Winter solstice, Minor Cold, Major Cold over.

Every month two terms solar,

one or two days different at most；

On the sixth and twenty first day in the first half year,

On the eighth and twenty third day in the second half year.

四、月份、季令、节令之别称 Alternative Mames for Months, Seasons and Festivals

另：二十四节气当中，也有个别既是节气也是节日。如：清明、冬至等，这些节日兼具自然与人文两大内涵，既是自然节气也是传统节日。此外，中国各少数民族也都保留着自己的传统节日，诸如傣族的泼水节、蒙古族的那达慕大会、彝族的火把节、瑶族的达努节、白族的三月街、壮族的歌圩、藏族的藏历年和望果节、苗族的跳花节等。

What's more, among the twenty-four solar terms, there are a few that are both solar terms and festivals. Such as：Pure Brightness Festival (Qingming Festival), Winter Solstice. These festivals have both natural and humanistic connotations. They are both natural solar terms and traditional festivals. In addition, all ethnic minorities in China also retain their own traditional festivals, such as Dai's Water Splashing Festival, Mongolian Naadam Conference, Yi's Torch Festival, Yao's Danu Festival, Bai's March Market Festival, Zhuang's Song Fair, and Tibetan Calendar New Year and Ongkor Festival (to move round the fields), and Miao's Treading on Flower Festival.

五、七大传统节日 Seven Important Traditional Festivals

(一) 春节 Chinese New Year/ Spring Festival

春节，是农历正月初一，又叫阴历年，俗称"过年"。这是中国民间最隆重、最热闹的一个传统节日。春节的历史很悠久，它起源于殷商时期年头岁尾的祭神祭祖活动。按照中国农历，正月初一古称元日、元旦等，俗称年初一。后来改用公历，公历的一月一日称为元旦，把农历的一月一日叫春节。

The Spring Festival is the first day of the first month of the lunar calendar, also known as the lunar year, commonly known as the "New Year". This is the most solemn and lively traditional festival in China. The Spring Festival has a long history. It originated from the worship of gods and ancestors at the turning time of two years in Shang Dynasty. According to the Chinese lunar calendar, the first day of the first lunar month was called Yuanri, New Year's Day, commonly known as the first day of a new year. Later, the first day of the first solar month is called Yuandan, and the first day of the lunar year is called the Spring Festival.

春节到了，意味着春天将要来临，万象复苏、草木更新，新一轮播种和收获季节将要开始。人们刚刚度过冰天雪地、草木凋零的漫漫寒冬，早就盼望着春暖花开的日子。当新春到来之际，自然要充满喜悦、载歌载舞地迎接这个节日。千百年来，人们使年俗庆祝活动变得异常丰富多彩，每年从农历腊月二十三日起到年三十，民间把这段时间叫做"迎春日"，也叫"扫尘日"，在春节前扫尘搞卫生，是中国人民素有的传统习惯。

The Spring Festival has arrived, which means that spring is coming, everything is reviving, the vegetation is renewing, and a new round of planting and harvesting season will begin. People have just passed the long and cold winter with icy and snowy vegetation, and have long been looking forward to the warmth of Spring. When the new year comes, they will naturally greet this festival with joy, singing and dancing. For thousands of years, people have made New Year celebrations extremely colorful. Every year, from the 23rd day to the 30th day of the twelfth lunar month, folks call this time "Welcoming Spring Days" or "Dust Sweeping Days". It is a traditional custom for the Chinese people to clean up the dust before the Spring Festival.

　　在节前要在住宅的大门上粘贴红纸黄字的新年寄语，也就是用红纸写成的春联。屋里张贴色彩鲜艳、寓意吉祥的年画，心灵手巧的姑娘们剪出美丽的窗花贴在窗户上，门前挂大红灯笼，贴福字及财神、门神像等，福字还可以倒贴，路人一念福倒了，也就是福气到了。所有这些活动都是要为节日增添足够的喜庆气氛。

　　Before the festival, the New Year's message written in red paper and yellow characters should be pasted on the door of the residence, which is called the Spring Festival couplets. Brightly colored New Year pictures with auspicious meanings are posted in the hall. The ingenious girls cut out beautiful window grilles and paste them on the windows. In front of the door hang red lanterns, paste characters meaning good fortune or good luck, and the god of wealth and door gods. The character Fu (means good luck) for blessing can also be pasted upside down, that is, the blessing has come, all these activities are to add enough festive atmosphere to the festival.

　　春节的另一名称叫过年。在过去的传说中，"年"是一种为人们带来坏运气的想象中的动物。"年"一来，树木凋敝，百草不生；"年"一过，万物生长，鲜花遍地。"年"如何才能过去呢？需用鞭炮轰。于是有了燃鞭炮的习俗，这其实也是烘托热闹场面的又一种方式。

　　Another name for the Spring Festival is Guo Nian. In the past legends, Nian is an imaginary animal that brings bad luck to people. When Nian comes, the trees are withered, and the grass does not grow; when Nian leaves, everything grows and flowers are everywhere. How can Nian pass? Firecrackers are needed, so there is a custom of burning firecrackers, which is actually another way to highlight the lively scene.

　　春节是个欢乐祥和的节日，也是亲人团聚的日子，离家在外的孩子在过春节时都要回家欢聚。过年的前一夜，就是旧年的腊月三十夜，也叫除夕，又叫团圆夜。在这新旧交替的时候，守岁是最重要的年俗活动之一。除夕晚上，全家老小都一起熬年守岁，欢聚酣饮，共享天伦之乐。北方地区在除夕有吃饺子的习俗。饺子的做法是先和面，"和"字就是合；饺子的"饺"和交谐音，合和交有相聚之意。在南方有过年吃年糕的习惯，甜甜的、黏黏的年糕，象征新一年生活甜蜜蜜，步步高。

The Spring Festival is a joyous and peaceful festival, and it is also a day for family reunion. Children away from home must go home to get together during the Spring Festival. The night before the New Year is the 30th Eve of the Twelfth Lunar Month, known as New Year's Eve, also known as Reunion Night. At this time of the transition between the old and the new year, people stay up late and wait for the first dawn of the bright new year which is called "Shousui", is one of the most important annual activities. On New Year's Eve, the whole family will stay together, sharing the joy. There is a custom of eating dumplings on New Year's Eve in the north. The practice of eating dumplings (Jiaozi) is to mix flour first that means harmony; Jiao and meeting are homophonic in Chinese, referring that harmony and peace gather together. In the south, there is a custom of eating rice cakes during the New Year. The sweet and sticky rice cakes symbolize the sweetness of life and that people progress step by step in the new year.

（二）元宵节 Lantern Festival

元宵节，是中国的传统节日之一，时间为每年农历正月十五。正月是农历的元月，古人称"夜"为"宵"，正月十五是一年中第一个月圆之夜，所以称正月十五为"元宵节"。根据道教"三元"的说法，正月十五又称为"上元节"。元宵节习俗自古以来就以热烈喜庆的观灯习俗为主。

The Lantern Festival is one of the traditional Chinese festivals. The first lunar month is the first month of the lunar calendar. The ancients called "night" as "xiao". The fifteenth night of the first lunar month is the first full moon night of the year, so the fifteenth night of the first lunar month is called the "Lantern Festival" (moonlight/lantern light). According to the Taoist idea of "Three Yuan's", the 15th night of the first lunar month is also called "Shangyuan Festival" (upper night). The Lantern Festival custom has been dominated by warm and festive lantern viewing since ancient times.

元宵节习俗的形成有一个较长的过程，据一般的资料与民俗传说，正月十五在西汉已经受到重视，皇帝要在宫中祭祀，被后人视作正月十五祭祀天神的先声。不过，正月十五元宵节真正成为民俗节日是在汉魏之后。正月十五燃灯的习俗与佛教东传有关。唐朝时，佛教大兴，仕官百姓普遍在正月十五这一天"燃灯供佛"，佛家灯火于是遍布民间。从唐代起，元宵张灯即成为法定之事，并逐渐成为民间习俗。

The formation of the Lantern Festival custom took a long time. According to general information and folklore, the fifteenth night of the first lunar month was valued in the Western Han Dynasty. The emperor needed to sacrifice in the palace, which was regarded as the forerunner of sacrificing the gods on the fifteenth night of the first month. However, the Lantern Festival on the 15th night of the first lunar month was really treated as a folk festival after Han and Wei Dynasties. The custom of burning lanterns on the fifteenth night of the first lunar month is also said relating to the east spread of Buddhism. During Tang Dynasty, Buddhism flourished, officials and people generally "lightened lamps for Buddha" on the fifteenth day of the first lunar month, and Buddhist lamps spread throughout the people. Since Tang Dynasty, decorating with lanterns on the fifteenth night of the first lunar month has become a legal affair and gradually a folk custom.

元宵节主要有赏花灯、吃汤圆、猜灯谜、放烟花等一系列传统民俗活动。此外，不少地方元宵节还增加了耍龙灯、耍狮子、踩高跷、划旱船、扭秧歌、打太平鼓等传统民俗表演。2008 年 6 月，元宵节入选第二批国家级非物质文化遗产。

Lantern Festival mainly includes a series of traditional folk activities such as viewing lanterns, eating sweet dumplings, guessing lantern riddles, and setting off fireworks. In addition, many local Lantern Festivals have also added traditional folk performances such as dragon lantern playing, lion playing, walking on stilts, land boat dancing, twisting Yangge (a popular rural folk dance), and beating drums while dancing. In June 2008, the Lantern Festival was selected as the second batch of National Intangible Cultural Heritage.

（三）清明节 Qingming Festival

清明节是农历二十四节气之一，在仲春与暮春之交，也就是冬至后的 108

天。中国汉族传统的清明节大约始于周代，距今已有二千五百多年的历史。《历书》："春分后十五日，斗指丁，为清明，时万物皆洁齐而清明，盖时当气清景明，万物皆显，因此得名。"清明一到，气温升高，正是春耕春种的大好时节，故有"清明前后，种瓜点豆"之说。清明节是一个祭祀祖先的节日，传统活动为扫墓和踏青。2006 年 5 月 20 日，该民俗节日经国务院批准列入第一批国家级非物质文化遗产名录。

Qingming Festival is one of the twenty-four solar terms in the lunar calendar. It is at the turn of mid spring and late spring, that is, 108 days after the winter solstice. The traditional Qingming Festival of the Han people in China began approximately in Zhou Dynasty and has a history of more than 2, 500 years. *Almanac* says: "On the fifteenth day after the spring equinox, the dipper directs to the Ding, which is Qingming (Pure Brightness), when everything is clean and clear, and when the weather is clear and the scenery is clear, everything is visible, so it is named." It is a good time for plowing and planting, so there is a saying of "around Qingming, plant melons and cast beans". Qingming Festival is a festival to worship ancestors. The traditional activity is tomb sweeping and taking the green stroll. On May 20, 2006, the folk festival was approved by the State Council to be included in the first batch of national intangible cultural heritage lists.

清明节的习俗是丰富有趣的，除了讲究禁火、扫墓，还有踏青、荡秋千、蹴鞠、打马球、插柳等一系列风俗体育活动。相传这是因为清明节要寒食禁火，为了防止寒食冷餐伤身，所以大家来参加一些体育活动，以锻炼身体。因此，这个节日中既有祭扫祖宗生别死离的悲酸泪，又有踏青游玩的欢笑声，是一个富有特色的节日。

The customs of Qingming Festival are rich and interesting in activities. In addition to paying attention to fire bans and tomb sweeping, there are also a series of custom sports activities such as taking the green stroll, swinging, Cuju (playing Chinese football), playing polo, and planting willow branches. According to legend, this was because cold food and fire were prohibited during Qingming Festival. In order to prevent cold food from hurting the body, everyone came to participate in some sports activities to exercise. Therefore, this festival has both the sad tears of sacrificing the ancestors, and the laughter of green outings. It is a unique festival.

（四）端午节 The Dragon Boat Festival

端午节，为每年农历五月初五，又称端阳节、午日节、五月节、龙舟节、浴兰节等。是流行于中国以及汉字文化圈诸国的传统文化节日。

The Dragon Boat Festival is the fifth day of the fifth month of the lunar calendar year. It is also known as the Duanyang Festival, the Wuri Festival, the May Festival, the Dragon Boat Festival, and the Bath Orchid Festival. It is a traditional cultural festival popular in China and other countries in the Chinese character culture circle.

端午节起源于中国，最初为祛病防疫的节日。春秋之前，在吴越之地有在农历五月初五以龙舟竞渡形式举行部落图腾祭祀的习俗；后因诗人屈原抱石自投汨罗江身死，又成为华人纪念屈原的传统节日；部分地区也有纪念伍子胥、曹娥等说法。端午节自古便有食粽、饮雄黄酒的习俗。受中华文化的影响，中秋节也是汉字文化圈国家以及世界各地华人华侨的传统节日。

The Dragon Boat Festival originated in China. It was originally a festival for curing diseases and preventing epidemics. Before the Spring and Autumn Period, there was a custom of holding tribal totem sacrifices in the area of State Wu and State Yue in the form of dragon boat races on the fifth day of the fifth month of the lunar calendar. Later, because the patriotic poet Qu Yuan killed himself in Miluo River with a boulder bound on him, that day became the traditional Chinese festival to commemorate Qu Yuan; in some areas there were also sayings to commemorate Wu Zixu and Cao E. The Dragon Boat Festival has had the custom of eating rice dumplings (Zongzi) and drinking realgar wine since ancient times. Affected by Chinese culture, the Dragon Boat Festival is also a traditional festival for Chinese character culture circles and overseas Chinese around the world.

自 2008 年起端午节被列为国家法定节假日。2006 年 5 月，国务院将其列入首批国家级非物质文化遗产名录。2009 年 9 月，联合国教科文组织正式审议并批准中国端午节列入世界非物质文化遗产，成为中国首个入选世界非遗的节日。

The Dragon Boat Festival has been listed as a national legal holiday since 2008. In May 2006, the State Council included it in the first batch of national intangible cultural heritage lists. In September 2009, UNESCO formally reviewed and approved the Chinese Dragon Boat Festival to be included in the world's intangible cultural heritage, becoming China's first festival to be selected as a world intangible cultural heritage.

（五）七夕节 Chinese Valentine's Day

在中国，农历七月初七的夜晚，天气温暖，草木飘香，这就是人们俗称的七夕节，也有人称之为"乞巧节"或"女儿节"。这是中国传统节日中最具浪漫色彩的一个节日，也是过去姑娘们最为重视的日子。

In China, on the night of the seventh day of the seventh lunar month (Double Seven), the weather is warm and the vegetation is fragrant. This is commonly known as the Qixi Festival (the Seventh Night), and it is also called the "Qiqiao Festival" (Begging for Skills) or "Girls' Day". This is the most romantic traditional Chinese festival. The festival was also a day that girls valued most in the past.

在晴朗的夏秋之夜，天上繁星闪耀，一道白茫茫的银河横贯南北。在河的东西两岸，各有一颗闪亮的星星，隔河相望，遥遥相对，那就是牵牛星和织女星。

On a clear night between summer and autumn, the sky is shining with stars, and a white Milky Way traverses north and south. On the east and west side of the Way, there is a shining star respectively, looking at each other feelingly but remotely, they are Altair and Vega.

七夕坐看牵牛织女星，是民间的习俗。相传，在每年的这个夜晚，是天上织女与牛郎在鹊桥相会之时。织女是一个美丽聪明、心灵手巧的仙女，凡间的妇女便在这一天晚上向她乞求智慧和巧艺，也少不了向她求赐美满姻缘，所以七月初七也被称为乞巧节。

It is a folk custom to sit and watch Altair and Vega on Chinese Valentine's Day. According to legend, this evening of every year is the time when the Heavenly Weaver and Cowherd meet at Magpie Bridge. The Weaver Girl is a beautiful, clever, and ingenious fairy. On this evening, mortal women beg her for wisdom and skill, and indispensable to ask her for a happy marriage, so the seventh day of July is also called the Qiqiao Festival.

人们传说在七夕的夜晚，抬头可以看到牛郎织女的银河相会，或在瓜果架下可偷听到两人在天上相会时的脉脉情话。女孩们在这个充满浪漫气息的晚上，对着天空的朗朗明月，摆上时令瓜果，朝天祭拜，乞求天上的女神能赋予她们聪慧的心灵和灵巧的双手，让自己的针织女红技法娴熟，更乞求爱情婚姻的姻缘巧配。过去婚姻对于女性来说是决定一生幸福与否的终身大事，所以，世间无数的有情男女都会在这个晚上，夜深人静时刻，对着星空祈祷自己的姻缘美满。

It is said that on the night of Qixi Festival, we can see the Milky Way meeting of the Cowherd and the Weaver Girl when we look up, or we can overhear the honeyed words of the two people meeting in the sky under the melon and fruit stand. On this romantic evening, facing the bright moon in the sky, the girls place seasonal melons and fruits, praying to the sky, begging the goddess in the sky to give them clever minds and dexterous hands, so that their female knitting skills are adept. What's more, begging for a good marriage in full love. In the past, marriage was a lifelong event for women to determine the happiness of their lives. Therefore, countless loving men and women in the world would pray to the starry sky for their happy marriage on this night, in the quiet of the night.

（六）中秋节 The Mid-Autumn Festival

中秋节是上古天象崇拜——敬月习俗的遗痕。二十四节气的"秋分"时节，是古老的"祭月节"，中秋节则是由传统的"祭月节"而来。在传统文化中，月亮和太阳一样，这两个交替出现的天体成了先民崇拜的对象。中秋节庆源自古人对月亮的祭祀，是中华民族祭月习俗的遗存和衍生。祭月，在中国是一种十分古老的习俗，实际上是古时中国一些地方的古人对"月神"的一种崇拜活动。据考证，最初"祭月节"是定在干支历二十四节气"秋分"这天，不过由于后来历法变动使用阴历（夏历），"秋分"这天在夏历八月里的日子每年不同，不一定都有圆月，后来就将"祭月节"由干支历二十四节气的"秋分"调至夏历（农历）八月十五日。中秋节是秋季时令习俗的综合，其所包含的节俗因素，大都有着古老的渊源。

The Mid-Autumn Festival is a trace of the ancient celestial phenomenon worship: the custom of respecting the moon. In the "autumn equinox" season of the twenty-four solar terms, it was the ancient "Moon-worship Festival", and the Mid-

Autumn Festival is derived from the traditional "Moon-worshiping Festival". In traditional culture, the moon was the same as the sun, and these two alternating celestial bodies became objects of worship by the ancestors. The Mid-Autumn Festival was derived from the ancient people's sacrifice to the moon, and it was the legacy and derivation of the custom of the Chinese nation to worship the moon. Sacrificing the moon was a very ancient custom in China. It was actually a worship activity for the "moon goddess" by ancient people in some places in China in ancient times. According to some research, the original "Jiyue Festival" was set on the 24th solar term "autumn equinox" in the Ganzhi (Stem and branch) calendar. However, due to the later calendar changes, the lunar calendar was used. The day of the "autumn equinox" in the eighth month of the lunar calendar was different every year. There may not always be a full moon. Later, the "Jiyue Festival" was adjusted from the 24th solar term "autumn equinox" in the Ganzhi calendar to August 15th in the Xia calendar (lunar calendar). The Mid-Autumn Festival is a synthesis of autumn seasonal customs, and most of the festival factors it contains have ancient origins.

中秋节成为官方认定的全国性节日，大约是在唐代。《唐书·太宗记》记载有"八月十五中秋节"。中秋赏月的风俗在唐代极盛，许多诗人的名篇中都有咏月的诗句。并将中秋与嫦娥奔月、吴刚伐桂、玉兔捣药、杨贵妃变月神、唐明皇游月宫等神话故事结合起来，使之充满浪漫色彩。唐代是传统节日习俗糅合定型的重要时期，其主体部分传承至今。

The Mid-Autumn Festival became an officially recognized national holiday, probably in Tang Dynasty. "*Book of Tang: Record of Emperor Taizong*" recorded "August 15 Mid-Autumn Festival". The custom of admiring the moon during the Mid-Autumn Festival was very popular in Tang Dynasty, and many poets wrote verses about the moon. The Mid-Autumn Festival is combined with myths and stories such as Chang'e Flying to the Moon, Wu Gang's Cutting the Osmanthus, Jade Rabbit Making Medicine, Imperial Noble Concubine Yang's Turning into Moon Goddess, and her lover the Emperor's Visiting the Moon Palace, which made it full of romance. Tang Dynasty was an important period when traditional festivals and customs were combined and finalized, and the main part has been passed down to the present.

中秋节自古就有祭月、赏月、吃月饼、玩花灯、赏桂花、饮桂花酒等习俗，流传至今，经久不息。中秋节时，云稀雾少，月光皎洁明亮，民间除了要举行赏月、祭月、吃月饼祝福团圆等一系列活动，有些地方还有舞草龙、砌宝塔等活动。发展至今，吃月饼已经是中国南北各地过中秋节的必备习俗。除月饼外，各种时令鲜果干果也是中秋夜的美食。

Since ancient times, the Mid-Autumn Festival has the custom of worshipping the moon, enjoying the moon, eating moon cakes, playing with lanterns, appreciating osmanthus, and drinking osmanthus wine, which have been passed down for a long time. During the Mid-Autumn Festival, there are few clouds and little fog, and the moon is clear and bright. In addition to these activities, some places also have activities such as grass dragon dance and pagoda building. Since its development, eating moon cakes has become a must for the Mid-Autumn Festival in all parts of China. In addition to moon cakes, various seasonal fresh and dried fruits are also delicacies for the Mid-Autumn Festival.

（七）重阳节 Chongyang Festival/ Double Ninth Festival

农历九月九日，为传统的重阳节。因为古老的《易经》中把"六"定为阴数，把"九"定为阳数，九月九日，日月并阳，两九相重，故而叫重阳，也叫重九，古人认为这是个值得庆贺的吉利日子，并且从很早就开始过此节日。

The 9th day of the 9th lunar month is the traditional Double Ninth Festival. Because the ancient *Book of Changes* set "six" as the yin (moon) number and "nine" as the yang (sun) number. On September 9th, the numbers of the month and day are both yang, and the two nines become a double, so it is called Double yang and Double Ninth. The ancients thought it was an auspicious day worth celebrating, and they celebrated this festival very early.

秋季也是一年收获的黄金季节，重阳佳节，寓意深远，人们对此节历来有着特殊的感情。唐诗宋词中有不少贺重阳、咏菊花的诗词佳作。另外，在中国人的传统观念中，九九重阳，因为与"久久"同音，九在数字中又是最大数，有长久长寿的含意，因此双九还有生命长久、健康长寿的意思，所以后来重阳节被立为老人节。

Autumn is also the golden season of harvest of the year. The Double Ninth Festival has far-reaching implications. People have had special feelings for this festival. There are many poems about Celebrating Double Ninth and chanting chrysanthemums in Tang and Song poetry. In addition, in the Chinese traditional concept, the double nine, because it is the same as "jiujiu" (meaning forever), nine is the largest in the number, so double nine also means health and longevity. That's why later the Double Ninth Festival was established as Elders' Day.

在古代，民间有在重阳登高的风俗，人们把重阳节登高看作是免灾避祸的活动，故重阳节又叫"登高节"。相传此风俗始于东汉。唐代文人所写的登高诗很多，大多是写重阳节的习俗；杜甫的七律《登高》，就是写重阳登高的名篇。登高所到之处，没有划一的规定，一般是登高山、登高塔。还有吃"重阳糕"的习俗。

In ancient times, the folks had the custom of climbing on Double Ninth Festival. People regarded climbing on the Double Ninth Festival as an activity to avoid disasters, so the Double Ninth Festival is also called "Climbing Festival". According to legend, this custom began in the Eastern Han Dynasty. There were many poems of mountain-climbing written by literati in Tang Dynasty, most of which were the custom of writing about the Double Ninth Festival; Du Fu's seven-character poem *Deng Gao* (*Climbing up*) is a famous piece about Double Ninth ascending. There is no uniform rule wherever you go ascending, usually climbing up mountains and towers. There is also the custom of eating "Chongyang Cake".

中国的传统中医文化

一、中国中医的起源和发展 The Origin and Development of Traditional Chinese Medicine（TCM）

（一）中医的发展历程 The development history of Traditional Chinese Medicine

中医发源于中国黄河流域。中医在漫长的发展过程中，历代都有不同的创造，涌现了许多名医，出现了许多重要学派和名著。中医产生于原始社会，春秋战国时期中医理论已经基本形成，出现了解剖和医学分科，已经采用"四诊"，治疗法有砭石、针刺、汤药、艾灸、导引、布气、祝由等。而且自古以来就有"医道相通"的说法。

Traditional Chinese medicine originated in the Yellow River basin in China. In the long development process, there had been different creations in the past dynasties. Many famous doctors emerged, and many important schools and masterpieces appeared. Traditional Chinese medicine was born in primitive society. The theory of Chinese medicine in the Spring and Autumn Period and the Warring States Period was basically formed. Anatomy and medical divisions appeared. The "four methods of diagnosis" were adopted. The treatment methods included stone acupuncture needle, acupuncture, decoction, moxibustion, breathing exercise, spread of harmonious breath, and Zhu You, Since ancient times, there has been a saying that "medicine and Tao are interlinked".

"中医"二字最早见于《汉书·艺文志》，"有病不治，常得中医"。在这里"中"字念去声，中（zhòng）。两千多年前，《汉书》里的那个中医概念，倒是体现了中国医学中的一个最高境界。

The word "Chinese medicine" was first seen in the *Hanshu · Yiwenzhi* (*History of Han Dynasty · Records of Arts and Literature*), "If you have a disease but don't cure it, you will always get/Zhong (zhòng) medicine." Here, the Chinese character is pronounced in falling tune (zhòng). More than two thousand years ago, the concept of Chinese medicine in "Han Shu" (*History of Han Dynasty*) embodied the highest level of Chinese medicine.

中国历史上有"神农尝百草……一日而遇七十毒"的传说，反映了古代劳动人民在与自然和疾病作斗争的过程中发现药物、积累经验的艰苦过程，也是中药起源于生产劳动的真实写照。

There was a legend in Chinese history that "Shennong (God of Agriculture) tasted a hundred herbs... met seventy poisons in a day", reflecting the painstaking process of discovering medicine and accumulating experience by the working people in the struggle against tough nature and disease. It is also a true portrayal of traditional Chinese medicine coming from productive labor.

早在夏商周时期（约公元前 22 世纪末~公元前 256 年），中国就已出现药酒及汤液。西周（约公元前 11 世纪~公元前 771 年）的《诗经》是中国现存文献中最早记载有药物的书籍。现存最早的中医理论典籍《内经》提出了"寒者热之，热者寒之""五味所入""五脏苦欲补泻"等学说，为中药基本理论奠定了基础。

As early as Xia, Shang and Zhou Dynasties (approximately the end of the 22nd century BC~256 BC), medicated wines and soups appeared in China. *The Book of Songs* in the Western Zhou Dynasty (approximately 11th century BC~771 BC) is the earliest book containing medicines in existing Chinese documents. The earliest existing TCM theoretical classics *Neijing* (*The Inner Canon of Huangdi*) puts forward the theories of "the cold is cured by hot, the hot by cold", "the five flavors enter", and "if the five internal organs are bitter, cured by reinforcing or reducing", which laid the foundation for the basic theory of traditional Chinese medicine.

现存最早的药学专著《神农本草经》是秦汉时期（公元前 221 年~公元 220 年）众多医学家搜集、总结了先秦以来丰富药学资料而成书的。本书载药 365 种，至今尚为临床所习用。它的问世，标志着中药学的初步确立。

The earliest existing pharmacy monograph Shennong Bencaojing (*Shennong's*

Herbal Classics）was a book compiled by many medical scientists in Qin and Han Dynasties（221 BC~220 AD）, summarizing the rich pharmacy materials since the pre-Qin period. This book contains 365 kinds of medicines, which are still used in clinical practice. Its advent marked the initial establishment of traditional Chinese medicine.

周代已经使用望、闻、问、切等诊病方法和药物、针灸、手术等治疗方法。秦汉时期，形成了《黄帝内经》这样具有系统理论的著作。此书是现存最早的一部中医理论性经典著作。张仲景所著的《伤寒杂病论》，专门论述了多种杂病的辨证诊断、治疗原则，为后世的临床医学奠定了发展的基础。汉代外科学已具有较高水平。据《三国志》记载，名医华佗已开始使用全身麻醉剂"麻沸散"进行各种外科手术。

In Zhou Dynasty, the four methods of diagnosis such as observation, auscultation and smell, inquiry, pulse feeling and palpation were used as well as treatment methods such as medicine, acupuncture, and surgery. During Qin and Han Dynasties, a book with systematic theory such as *Huangdi Neijing*（*The Inner Classic of the Yellow King*）was formed. This book is the earliest extant theoretical classic of Chinese medicine. *Treatise on Febrile and Miscellaneous Diseases* by Zhang Zhongjing specifically discussed the principles of diagnosis and treatment of various miscellaneous diseases, laying the foundation for the development of clinical medicine in later generations. Surgery in Han Dynasty reached a relatively high level. According to *The History of the Three Kingdoms*, the famous doctor Hua Tuo started to use the general anesthetic "Ma Fei San"（anesthesia powder）for various surgical operations.

从魏晋南北朝（公元220年~公元589年）到隋唐五代（公元581年~公元960年），脉诊取得了突出的成就。晋代名医王叔和所著的《脉经》归纳了24种脉象。该书不仅对中国医学有很大影响，而且还传到了国外。这一时期医学各科的专科化已趋成熟。针灸专著有《针灸甲乙经》；《抱朴子》和《肘后方》是炼丹的代表著作；制药方面有《雷公炮炙论》；外科有《刘涓子鬼遗方》；《诸病源候论》是病因专著，《颅囟经》是儿科专著；《新修本草》是世界上第一部药典；眼科专著有《银海精微》等。另外，唐代还有孙思邈的《千金要方》和王焘的《外台秘要》等大型方书。

From Wei, Jin, Southern and Northern Dynasties（220~589 AD）to the Sui,

Tang and Five Dynasties (581 ~ 960 AD), pulse diagnosis made outstanding a-chievements. The *Pulse Classic* by Wang Shuhe, a famous doctor in Jin Dynasty, summarized 24 kinds of pulse conditions. The book not only had a great influence on Chinese medicine, but also spread abroad. During this period, the specialization of various medical disciplines matured. Monographs on acupuncture and moxibustion in-cluded *A−B Classic of Acupuncture and Moxibustion*; *Baopuzi* and *Back Elbow Pre-scriptions* were representative works of alchemy; *Master Lei on Drug Preparation and Processing* in pharmaceuticals; *Ghostly Prescriptions by Liu Juanzi* in Surgery; *Gener-al Treatise on the Cause and Symptoms of Diseases* was a monograph on etiology, *A Baby's Skull Classic* was a pediatric monograph; *Newly−Edited Materia Medica* is the world's first pharmacopoeia; ophthalmology monographs included *Yinhai Jingwei* (*Incisive Exposition on Eye Diseases*). In addition, in Tang Dynasty, there were also large−scale prescriptions such as Sun Simiao's Qianjin Yaofang (*Essential Recipes for Emergent Use Worth A Thousand Gold*) and Wang Tao's *Waitai Secret and Important Prescriptions*. (Waitai, an official title)

唐代（公元 618 年 ~ 公元 907 年）经济繁荣，促进了中药学的发展。唐政府率先完成了世界第一部药典性著作——《唐本草》的编修工作。全书载药 850 种，还增加了药物图谱，进一步完善了中药学的规模格局。

The economic prosperity of Tang Dynasty (618 ~ 907 AD) promoted the devel-opment of traditional Chinese medicine. The Tang government took the lead in com-pleting the compilation of the world's first pharmacopoeial book——*Tang Materia Medica*. The book contained 850 kinds of medicines, and a drug map was added to further improve the scale and pattern of Chinese medicine.

在宋代（公元 960 年 ~ 公元 1279 年）医学教育中，针灸教学有了重大改革。王惟一著有《铜人腧穴针灸图经》。后来，他又设计制造等身大针灸铜人两具，教学时供学生实习操作。这一创举，对后世针灸的发展影响很大。明代（公元 1368 年 ~ 公元 1644 年）时，有一批医学家提出把伤寒、温病和瘟疫等病区分开。到了清代，温病学说达到成熟阶段，出现了《温热论》等专著。

For the medical education in Song Dynasty (960 ~ 1279 AD), acupuncture teaching had a major reform. Wang Weiyi was the author of *Acupuncture and Moxi-bustion Diagrams for Bronze Figures*. Later, he designed and manufactured two large acuncture and moxibustion bronze figures for students to practice in teaching. This pioneering work had a great influence on the development of acupuncture and moxibustion in later generations. In Ming Dynasty (1368~1644 AD), a group of medical scientists proposed to distinguish typhoid fever, febrile disease and epidemic disease. In Qing Dynasty, the theory of febrile disease reached its maturity stage, and monographs such as *On Febrile Diseases* appeared.

到了明代 (公元 1368 年~公元 1644 年), 医药学家李时珍历时 27 年, 完成了中药学巨著《本草纲目》, 全书载药 1892 种, 成为中国本草史上最伟大的集成之作。《中庸》一书中至关重要的哲学命题是 "致中和" 这一思想。中和是世界万物存在的理想状态, 通过各种方法达到这一理想状态就是致中和。中医学所阐明的 "阴阳和合""阴平阳秘" 生理机制正是儒家致中和思想的最佳体现。在这个终极目标下, 中医是用精气学说、阴阳学说和五行学说这三大学说来具体解释生命的秘密。

In Ming Dynasty (1368~1644 AD), the medical scientist Li Shizhen took 27 years to complete the masterpiece *Compendium of Materia Medica* in Chinese pharmacy. The book contained 1892 kinds of medicines and became the greatest integrated work in the history of Chinese Materia Medica. The most important philosophical proposition in the book *The Doctrine of the Mean* is the idea of "achieving the golden mean and harmony". The golden mean and harmony is an ideal state, to achieve such an ideal state through various ways is to achieve the state of the golden mean and harmony. The physiological mechanism of "Harmony between Yin and Yang" and "Dynamic Balance between Yin and Yang" explained in Chinese medicine is the best embodiment of the Confucian thought of "achieving the golden mean and harmony". Under this ultimate goal, Chinese medicine uses the three theories of essence and qi, yin and yang, and five elements to explain the secrets of life.

(二) 中医的代称 The Nicknames of Chinese Medicine

第一个代称是岐黄。这个名字来源于《黄帝内经》。因其是黄帝与岐伯讨论医学的专著, 便称《黄帝内经》为岐黄之术。自然, 岐黄也就成了中医的别名。

The first nickname was Qihuang. The name came from the *Huangdi Neijing*, which was a monograph of the Yellow King discussing medicine with Qi Bo, therefore the *Huangdi Neijing* was called the art of Qihuang. Naturally, Qihuang became the nickname for Chinese medicine.

第二个代称叫青囊。它的来源与三国时期的名医华佗有关。据说，华佗被杀前，为报一狱吏酒肉侍奉之恩，曾将所用医书装满一青囊送与他。华佗死后，狱吏亦行医，使华佗的部分医术流传下来。据此，后人称中医为青囊。

The second nickname was called Qing Nang (Black Bag) . Its origin was related to the famous doctor Hua Tuo in the Three Kingdoms period. It was said that before Hua Tuo was killed, in order to repay a jailer for serving him alcohol and meat, he sent him a bag full of medical books he used. After Hua Tuo's death, the jailer also practiced medicine, so that part of Hua Tuo's medical skills were passed down. According to this, later generations referred to Chinese medicine as Qing Nang (Black Bag).

第三个代称唤杏林。这个名字的起始，也与三国有关。有资料介绍，三国时吴国有位名医叫董奉，他一度在江西庐山隐居。附近百姓闻名求医，但董奉从不收取钱财，只求轻症被治愈者种一棵杏树，大病重病被治愈者种五棵杏树。数年后，董奉门前杏树成林，一望无际。从此，人们便唤中医为杏林。

The third nickname was called Xinglin (Apricot Forest). The beginning of this name was also related to the Three Kingdoms. According to information, during the Three Kingdoms period, State Wu had a famous doctor named Dong Feng. He once lived in seclusion in Lushan Mountain, Jiangxi province. The nearby people learned about his medical talent and came for his medical treatment, but Dong Feng never collected money. He only asked those who were cured of mild illness to plant an apricot tree, and those who were cured of serious illness to plant five apricot trees. A few years later, the apricot trees in front of Dong Feng's door became a forest, endless. Since then, people have called Chinese medicine Xinglin.

第四个代称是悬壶。传说河南汝南的费长房在街上看到一卖药老者的竿杆上挂一葫芦，奇怪的是，天黑散街后，老者就跳入那葫芦中。为弄清底细，费长房以酒款待。老者后来约他同入葫芦中，只见玉堂俨丽，甘肴旨酒。费长房即拜老者为师，学修仙之道。数载后，他术精业成，辞师出山，又得壶翁传赠的治病鞭鬼之竹杖，从此悬壶行医。从那时起，医生腰间挂的和诊所前悬的葫芦，便成了中医的标志。

The fourth nickname was called Xuanhu (Hanging Gourd). A legend has it that Fei Changfang in Runan, Henan Province, saw a gourd hanging on the pole of an old man selling medicine on the street. Strangely, the old man jumped into the gourd after it was dark and the fair was over. In order to make it clear, Fei Changfang treated him with wine. The old man later asked him to join him into the gourd, only to see a splendid house and delicious food. Fei Changfang took the old as his teacher and learned the way of immortality. A few years later, he succeeded in his skills, resigned from his teacher and went out of the mountain, and obtained the bamboo stick for treating diseases and whipped ghosts given by the old man of gourd, and from then on hanging the gourd to practice medicine. Since then, the gourd hung on the waist of the doctor and the gourd hung in front of the clinic has become a symbol of Chinese medicine.

二、中医的特点 Characteristics of Traditional Chinese Medicine

中医的主要特点有三点：

There are three main characteristics of TCM：

（一）整体观念 The concept of the whole

整体观念在于"天人合一""天人相应"的观念，指人体的统一性和完整性。

1. 中医认为人体是一个有机整体，是由若干脏器和组织、器官所组成的。各个组织、器官都有着各自不同的功能，决定了机体的整体统一性。

2. 人与自然是统一的，自然界存在着人类赖以生存的必要条件。自然界的变化可直接或间接地影响人体，而机体则相应地产生反应。在功能上相互协调、相互为用，在病理上相互影响。

The concept of the whole lies in the concept of "Nature and Man are one" (Unity of Man and Nature) and "Nature and Man correspond" (Correspondence between Man and Nature), which refers to the unity and integrity of the human body.

1. Chinese medicine believes that the human body is an organic whole, composed

of tissues and organs. Various tissues and organs have their own different functions, which determine the overall unity of the body.

2. Man and nature are unified, and there are necessary conditions for human survival in nature. Changes in nature can directly or indirectly affect the human body, and the body responds accordingly. They coordinate with each other in function, serve each other, and influence each other in pathology.

（二）辨证论治 Determination of the treatment based on the differentiation of symptoms and signs

所谓"证"是机体在疾病发展过程中某一阶段的病理概括。包括病变的部位、原因、性质以及邪正关系，能够反映出疾病发展过程中，某一阶段的病理变化的本质，因而它比症状能更全面、更深刻、更准确地揭示出疾病的发展过程和本质。所谓"辨证"，就是将四诊（望、闻、问、切）所收集的资料，症状和体征分析综合，辨清疾病的原因、性质、部位以及邪正之间的关系，从而概括、判断为某种性质证候的过程。所谓"论治"又叫施治，则是根据辨证分析的结果来确定相应的治疗原则和治疗方法。辨证是决定治疗的前提和依据，论治则是治疗疾病的手段和方法，所以辨证论治的过程，实质上是中医学认识疾病和治疗疾病的过程。

The so-called "symptom" is the pathological summary of the body at a certain stage in the development of the disease. Including the location, cause, nature, and the relationship between negative and positive factors, it can reflect the nature of pathological changes at a certain stage in the development of the disease, so it can reveal the development process and nature of the disease more comprehensively, more in depth and more accurately than symptoms. The so-called "differentiation" is the process of summarizing and judging the syndroms of a certain nature by analyzing and comprehending the information, symptoms and signs collected by the four diagnosis methods and identifying the cause, nature, location of the disease and the relationship between negative and positive factors. The so-called "treatment" is to determine the corresponding treatment principles and treatment methods based on the results of dialectical analysis. Syndrome differentiation is the prerequisite and basis for deciding treatment. Discussion and treatment are the means and methods of treating diseases. Therefore, the determination of treatment based on the differentiation of symptoms and signs is essentially the process of understanding and treating diseases in traditional Chinese medicine.

疾病是具有特定的症状和体征的，而证则是疾病过程中典型的反应状态。中医临床认识和治疗疾病是既辨病又辨证，并通过辨证而进一步认识疾病。

A disease has specific symptoms and signs, while a symptom is a typical response state in the course of the disease. The clinical understanding and treatment of diseases in traditional Chinese medicine is both to distinguish the disease, the symptom and sign, and to further understand the disease through the differentiation of the symptom.

（三）相似观念 The concept of similarity

相似观念在中国几千年前就有，如著名的阴阳、五行就是最古老的分形观，即通过类比、象征方式把握对象世界联系的思维方法，运用带有感性、形象、直观的概念、符号表达对象世界的抽象意义。

The concept of similarity existed in China thousands of years ago, such as the famous yin and yang, Five Elements, they were the oldest fractal view, that is, the way of thinking that grasps the connection between objects through analogy and symbolism, and expresses the abstract meaning of the objects with perceptual, visual, and intuitive concepts and signs. .

三、中医的治疗手段 The Treatment Methods of Traditional Chinese Medicine

（一）中药 Chinese herbs

中药即中医用药，为中国传统中医特有药物。中药按加工工艺分为中成药、中药材。

Chinese herbs are medicine specially used by traditional Chinese doctors. Chinese herbs are classified into Chinese patent medicines and Chinese medicinal materials according to their processing technology.

Observation is to observe the patient's body, complexion, tongue, and tongue coating, and determine the location and disease nature according to the changes in shape and color.

2. 闻诊 Auscultation and smelling

闻诊包括听声音和嗅气味两方面，从病人发生的各种声音，从其高低、缓急、强弱、清浊测知病性的方法；嗅气味可分为病人身体的气味和病室内的气味。

Auscultation and smelling include two aspects: listening to the sound and smelling the smell. Listening is to detect the disease from the height, emergency, strength, and turbidity of the various sounds of the patient; smelling can be divided into the smell of the patient's body and the smell of the patient's room.

3. 问诊 Inquiry

问诊是询问病人及其家属，了解现有证象及其病史，为辨证提供依据的一种方法。

Inquiry is a method of asking patients and their families to understand the existing symptoms and medical history, and to provide a basis for the differentiation of symptoms and signs.

4. 切诊 Pulse feeling and palpation

切诊是指用手触按病人身体，借此了解病情的一种方法。

Pulse feeling and palpation is a method of touching the patient's body with the hands to understand the condition of the patient.

（五）医科分类 Medical classification

中医主要可以分成六类：

Traditional Chinese Medicine can be divided into six categories:

1. 内科 Internal Medicine

中医内科主要治疗外感病和内伤病两大类。外感病是由外感风、寒、暑、湿、燥、火六淫及疫疠之气所致疾病。内伤病主要指脏腑经络病、气血津液病等杂病。

The Department of Internal Medicine of Traditional Chinese Medicine mainly treats two types of externally-infected diseases and internal injuries. Exogenous diseases are diseases caused by exogenous wind, cold, heat, dampness, dryness, fire, and epidemic qi (air). Internal injuries and diseases mainly refer to miscellaneous diseases such as viscera and meridian diseases, qi, blood and body fluid diseases.

2. 外科 Surgical Department

中医外科主要治疗包括疮疡、瘰、瘤、岩、肛肠疾病、男性前阴病、皮肤病及性传播疾病、外伤性疾病与周围血管病等。

The main treatments of TCM surgery include sores and ulcer, goitres, tumours, carbuncles, anorectal diseases, male genital diseases, skin diseases and sexually transmitted diseases, traumatic injuries and peripheral vascular diseases.

3. 儿科 Pediatric Department

中医儿科主要治疗小儿疾病。由于小儿的生理特点和病理特点与成人不同，因而治疗的方法和用药也与成人不同。

The Department of Pediatrics of TCM mainly treats pediatric diseases. Because the physiological and pathological characteristics of children are different from those of adults, the treatment methods and medications are also different from those of a-dults.

4. 妇科 Gynecology Department

中医妇科主要治疗妇女月经病、带下病、妊娠病、产后病、乳房疾病、前阴疾病和妇科杂病。

The Department of Gynecology in Traditional Chinese Medicine mainly treats women's menstrual disorders, leukorrheal diseases, pregnancy-related conditions, postpartum diseases, breast diseases, genital diseases and other gynecological disea-ses.

5. 针灸科 Acupuncture Department

中医针灸是针刺法和灸法的合称。针法是把毫针按一定穴位刺入患者体内，用捻、提等手法，通过对经络腧穴的刺激来治疗疾病。灸法是把燃烧着的艾绒按一定穴位熏灼体表的经络腧穴，利用热的刺激来治疗疾病。针灸疗法适用于各科疾病，包括许多功能性疾病和传染病，以及部分器质性疾病。

Acupuncture in traditional Chinese medicine is the collective name of acupuncture and moxibustion. The acupuncture method is to pierce the filiform needle into the patient's body at a certain point, and use twisting, and lifting to treat the disease by stimulating the meridian acupoints. The moxibustion method is to press the burning moxa to burn the meridians and collaterals on the body surface at a certain point, and use the heat to treat the disease. Acupuncture therapy is suitable for various diseases, including many functional diseases and infectious diseases, as well as some organic diseases.

6. 五官科 Ophthalmology and otorhinolaryngology

主要治疗耳、鼻、咽喉、口腔疾病、眼睛疾病。

Mainly treat ear, nose, throat, oral cavity and eye diseases.

7. 骨伤科 Orthopedics department

中医骨伤科学是一门防治骨关节及其周围筋肉损伤与疾病的学科。古属"疡医"范畴，又称"接骨""正体""正骨""伤科"等。

Orthopedics and Traumatology of Traditional Chinese Medicine is a discipline that prevents and treats injuries and diseases of bones, joints and surrounding muscles. In ancient times, it belonged to the category of "ulcer medicine", also known as "bone fixation", "rectification", "bone setting", and "traumatology".

四、中医理论 Theories of Traditional Chinese Medicine

中医理论来源于对医疗经验的总结及中国古代的阴阳五行思想。战国至西汉初期，中医专著《黄帝内经》问世，奠定了中医学的基础。时至今日，中国传统医学相关的理论、诊断法、治疗方法等，均可在此书中找到根源。中医理论主要包括下面几种学说：

The theories of Chinese medicine come from the summary of medical experience and the ancient Chinese thought of Yin and Yang and the Five Elements. During the Warring States period through the early Western Han Dynasty, the TCM monograph *Huangdi Neijing* came out, laying the foundation of TCM. Today, the theories, diagnostic methods, and treatment methods related to traditional Chinese medicine can all find their roots in this book. TCM theories mainly include the following theories:

1. 运气学说 The theory of destinies and weathers

运气学说又称五运六气，是有关自然界天文、气象、气候变化对人体健康和疾病的影响的学说。五运包括木运、火运、土运、金运和水运，指自然界一年中春、夏、长夏、秋、冬的季候循环。六气则是一年四季中风、寒、暑、湿、燥、火六种气候因子。运气学说是根据天文历法参数来推算、预测来年的天象、气候、疾病发生流行的规律，并提供预防、养生的方法。

The theory of destinies and weathers, also known as the five destinies and six weathers, focuses on studying how astronomical pattevns, meteorological changes, and climatic cycles in nature influences human health and disease. The Five Destinies include wood destiny, fire destiny, earth destiny, metal destiny, and water destiny. It refers to the seasonal cycle of spring, summer, long summer (the sixth month of the Lunar calendar), autumn and winter in the natural world. The Six Weathers refer to the six climatic factors of wind, cold, heat, dampness, dryness and fire throughout the year. The theory of destinies and weathers is based on the astronomical calendar parameters to calculate and predict the astronomical phenomena, climate, and the laws of disease occurrence and prevalence in the coming year, and to provide methods for prevention and health preservation.

2. 精气学说 The theory of essence and Qi

气是构成天地万物的原始物质。气的运动称为"气机"，有"升降出入"四种形式。由运动而产生的各种变化，称为"气化"。

Qi (the Air) is the primitive substance that constitutes everything in the world. The movement of qi is called "qi mechanism", and there are four forms of "lifting, falling, coming in and going out". The various changes caused by movement are called "Change of Air of Yin and Yang".

3. 阴阳学说 The theory of yin and yang

阴阳是宇宙中相互关联的事物或现象对立双方属性的概括。最初是指日光的向背，向日光为阳，背日光为阴。阴阳的交互作用包括：阴阳交感、对立制约、互根互用、消长平衡、相互转化。

Yin and Yang are the generalization of the attributes of the opposite sides of the interconnected things or phenomena in the universe. They originally referred to the directions of the sun's back and forth, with the side to the sun is yang, and the side back to the sun is yin. The interaction of yin and yang includes: mutual induction and intermingling, oppositional restriction, mutual root and interaction, balance of growth and decline, and mutual transformation.

阴阳学说认为世界是物质的，物质由阴阳二部分组成。凡是剧烈运动的、外向的、上升的、温热的、明亮的都属于阳。相对静止的、内守的、下降的、寒冷的、晦暗的都属阴。中医运用阴阳对立统一的观念来阐述人体上下、内外各部分之间，以及人体生命同自然、社会这些外界环节之间的复杂联系。阴阳对立统一的相对平衡，是维持和保证人体正常活动的基础；阴阳对立统一关系的失调和破坏，则会导致人体疾病的发生，影响生命的正常活动。

The theory of yin and yang believes that the world is material, and matter is composed of yin and yang. Anything that is vigorously moving, outgoing, rising, warm, and bright belongs to yang. The relatively static, inwardly guarded, descending, cold, and gloomy are all Yin. Traditional Chinese medicine uses the concept of the unity of opposites between yin and yang to explain the complex connection between the upper and lower parts of the human body, between the internal and external parts, and between the human life and the external links of nature and society. The relative balance of the unity of yin and yang is the basis for maintaining and guaranteeing the normal activities of the human body; the imbalance and destruction of the unity of yin and yang will lead to the occurrence of human diseases and affect the normal activities of life.

4. 五行学说 Five Elements Theory

五行学说是中国传统哲学的重要成就。五行学说即是用木、火、土、金、水五个哲学范畴来概括客观世界中的不同事物属性，并用五行相生相克的动态模式来说明事物间的相互联系和转化规律。五行学说以五脏配五行：肝与木、心与火、脾与土、肺与金、肾与水。五行于中医则体现了具备这五种属性的人体五大系统的相互关系。

The Five Elements Theory is an important achievement of traditional Chinese philosophy. The Five Elements Theory uses the five philosophical categories of wood, fire, earth, metal, and water to summarize the attributes of different things in the objective world, and uses the dynamic model of the five elements to grow and restrain each other to illustrate the interaction laws of connection and transformation between things. In the theory of the five elements, the five internal organs are matched with the five elements: liver and wood, heart and fire, spleen and earth, lung and metal, kidney and water. The Five Elements Theory in Chinese Medicine embodies the interrelationship of the five major systems of the human body with these five attributes.

5. 气血津液 Qi, blood and body fluid

气血津液是构成人体的基本物质，是腑脏、经络等组织器官进行生理活动的物质基础。

气是构成人体和维护人体生命活动的最基本物质，在生理上具有推动、温煦、防御、固摄、气化等功能。血也是构成人体和维持人体生命活动的基本物质，具有很高的营养和滋润作用。津液是指各腑脏组织器官的内在体液及正常分泌物，是机体一切正常水液的总称。津是指性质较清稀，流动性较大，分布于体表皮肤肌肉，并能渗注于血脉，起着滋润的作用；液是指性质较稠厚，流动性较小，流注于骨节、腑脏、脑髓等组织，起着濡养作用。

Qi, blood and body fluid are the basic substances that constitute the human body, and the material basis for the physiological activities of organs, meridians and other tissues.

Qi is the most basic substance that constitutes the human body and maintains the life activities of the human body. It has physiological functions such as promotion, warmth, defense, solidification, and change of breath. Blood is also the basic substance that constitutes the human body and maintains the life activities of the human body, and has a high nutritional and moisturizing effect. Body fluid (Jin and Ye) refers to the internal body fluids and normal secretions of various organs, and is the general term for all normal water fluids in the body. Jin refers to the nature of relatively clear and thin fluid, distributed in the skin and muscles of the body surface, and can infiltrate into the blood vessels, playing a moisturizing effect; Ye refers to the thicker, less moving fluid, flowing into the joints, organs, and brain marrow to play a nourishing role.

气血津液都是机体腑脏、经络等组织器官进行生理活动所需要的能量，而气血津液又依赖于腑脏、经络等组织器官正常的生理活动。如果气血津液代谢不正常或腑脏、经络等组织器官不能进行正常的生理活动，就会引起疾病的发生。

Qi, blood and body fluid are all the energy required for the body's organs, and meridians to perform physiological activities, and qi, blood and body fluid depend on the normal physiological activities of organs, such as viscera, and meridians If the metabolism of qi, blood and body fluid is not normal or the organs, meridians cannot carry out normal physiological activities, it will cause the occurrence of diseases.

6. 脏腑学说 The viscera theory

脏腑学说主要是研究五脏（心、肝、脾、肺、肾）、六腑（胆、胃、小肠、大肠、膀胱、三焦）和奇恒之腑（脑、髓、骨、脉、胆、女子胞）的生理功能和病理变化。"脏腑"是包括解剖、生理、病理在内的综合概念。

The viscera theory mainly studies the physiological functions and pathological changes of the five internal organs（heart, liver, spleen, lung and kidney）, the six hollow organs（gall bladder, stomach, small intestine, large intestine, urinary bladder, and San Jiao）and Unusual viscera（brain, marrow, bone, pulse, gall, and womb）. "Viscera" is a comprehensive concept including anatomy, physiology, and pathology.

7. 经络学说 The theory of channels and collaterals

经络是人体运行气血、联络脏腑形体官窍、沟通上下内外的通道。经络学说是研究人体经络的生理功能、病理变化与脏腑相互关系的学说。在病理情况下，经络系统功能发生变化，会呈现相应的症状和体征。通过这些表现，可以诊断体内脏腑疾病。

Meridians are the channels through which the human body runs qi and blood, connects the organs, the upper and lower internal and external bodies. The theory of channels and collaterals is a theory that studies the relationship between the physiological functions, pathological changes and viscera of the human body's meridians. Under pathological conditions, the function of the meridian system changes, and corresponding symptoms and signs will appear. Through these manifestations, the internal organs diseases can be diagnosed.

8. 病因学说 The etiology theory

病因学说将病因分为外感性致病因素、内伤性致病因素和其他致病因素三大类。

The etiology theory divides the disease causes into three categories: exogenous pathogenic factors, internal traumatic pathogenic factors and other pathogenic factors.

9. 元气学说 The vitality theory

中医认为，元气为先天之精所化生，是人体最基本最重要的气，由先天之肾所藏，后天脾胃来濡养，借三焦和经络流行分布并弥散全身。

Traditional Chinese medicine believes that vitality is transformed by the innate essence and is the most basic and most important qi in the human body. It is stored by the innate kidneys and nourished by the spleen and stomach. It is distributed and diffused throughout the body through the use of Sanjiao and meridians.

五、中医名家 Great Masters of Traditional Chinese Medicine

1. 黄帝——针灸之祖。黄帝是传说中中原各族的共同领袖。现存《黄帝内经》即系托名黄帝与岐伯、雷公等讨论医学的著作。此书治疗方法多用针刺，故对针刺的记载和论述特别详细。

The Yellow King, the ancestor of acupuncture. The Yellow King was the common leader of the various ethnic groups in the Central Plains in the legend. The existing *Huangdi Neijing* is a work on medicine under the name Huang Di, Qi Bo and Lei Gong. Acupuncture is mostly used in the treatment of this book, so the record and discussion of acupuncture are also particularly detailed.

2. 扁鹊——脉学介导者，姓秦，名越人，战国渤海郡郑（今河北任丘）人。《史记·战国策》载有他的传记病案，并推崇他为脉学的倡导者。

Bian Que, the introducer of pulse studies, whose surname was Qin, named Yueren, from Bohai County (now Renqiu, Hebei province) of the Warring States Period. *The Historical Records · Intrigues of the Warring States* contains his biographical medical records and is highly regarded as an advocate of pulse studies.

3. 华佗（约公元 145 年~公元 208 年）——外科之祖，又名敷，字元化，后汉末沛国（今安徽亳州）人。精内、外、妇、儿、针灸各科，对外科尤为擅长。

Hua Tuo (about 145~208 AD), the ancestor of surgery, also known as Fu, by names Yuanhua, was born in Peiguo (now Bozhou, Anhui province) at the end of Han Dynasty. He was particularly good at surgery in various departments of internal medicine, external medicine, gynecology, pediatrics, acupuncture and moxibustion.

4. 张仲景——医圣，名机，汉末向阳郡（今河南南阳）人，他的著作《伤寒杂病论》总结了汉代 300 多年的临床实践经验，对中国医学的发展有重大贡献。

Zhang Zhongjing, the medicine sage, named Ji, was born in Xiangyang County（now Nanyang, Henan province）at the end of Han Dynasty. His book *Treatise on Febrile Diseases and Miscellaneous Diseases* summarized more than 300 years of clinical practice experience in Han Dynasty and made a significant contribution to the development of Chinese medicine.

5. 葛洪——预防医学的介导者，字稚川，自号抱朴子，晋朝丹阳句容（今属江苏）人，著有《肘后备急用方》。书中最早记载一些传染病如天花、恙虫病症候及诊治。"天行发斑疮"是全世界最早有关天花的记载。

Ge Hong, the introducer of preventive medicine, whose name was Zhichuan, self-named Baopuzi, a native of Danyang Jurong（now Jiangsu province）in Jin Dynasty, authored *Handbook of Prescriptions for Emergency*, which first recorded the diagnosis and treatment of the symptoms of some infectious diseases such as smallpox and tsutsugamushi disease. "Smallpox Variola" was the earliest record of smallpox in the world.

6. 孙思邈（公元 581 年～公元 682 年）——药王，唐朝京兆华原（今陕西铜川耀州区）人，医德高尚，医术精湛。因治愈唐太宗唐太后头痛病，太宗封孙思邈为药王。

Sun Simiao（581~682 AD）, Medicine King, a native of Huayuan, Capital of Tang Dynasty（present-day Yaozhou District, Tongchuan, Shaanxi province）, with noble medical ethics and superb medical skills. Emperor Taizong entitled Sun Simiao the king of medicine for curing the emperor and empress's headache.

7. 钱乙——儿科之祖，字仲阳，北宋郓州（今山东东平）人。著有《小儿药证直诀》三卷。以脏腑病理学说立论，根据其虚实寒热而立法处方，比较系统地作出了辨证诊治的范例。

Qian Yi, the ancestor of pediatrics, whose name was Zhongyang, was born in Yunzhou（now Dongping, Shandong province）in the Northern Song Dynasty. He was the author of "The Direct Formula of Children's Medicine Symptoms"（3 volumes）. Based on the theory of viscera pathology, formulating prescriptions according to its deficiency, actuality, cold and heat, and systematically made an example of determination of treatment accordingly.

8. 宋慈——法医之祖，宋朝福建人。1247 年宋慈总结宋代前法医方面的经验及他本人四任法官的心得，写成《洗冤集录》，是世界上最早的法医文著。

Song Ci, the ancestor of forensic medicine, was a native of Fujian province in Song Dynasty. In 1247, he summarized the experience of forensic medicine before Song Dynasty and the experience of himself as four judges, and wrote *The Records of Redressing Injustices*, which is the earliest forensic writing in the world.

9. 李时珍——药圣，字东壁，号频湖山人，明朝蕲州（今湖北蕲春）人。他参考历代医书 800 余种，经 27 年的艰苦，著成《本草纲目》，所载药物共 1892 种，被译为日、法、德、俄等国文字。

Li Shizhen, the Pharmacy sage, named Dongbi, nicknamed Pinhu Shanren, was born in Qizhou (now Qichun, Hubei province) of Ming Dynasty. With reference to more than 800 medical books of the past dynasties, he wrote *Compendium of Materia Medica* after 27 years of hard work, in which there are 1, 892 kinds of medicine. The book has been translated into Japanese, French, German, and Russian.

10. 吴谦——《医宗金鉴》总修官，字文吉，清朝安徽歙县人，乾隆时为太医院院判。《医宗金鉴》是清代御制钦定的一部综合性医书，全书 90 卷，它是中国综合性中医医书最完善又最简要的一种。

Wu Qian, the chief editor of Yi Zong Jin Jian (*The Golden Mirror of Medicine*), named Wen Ji, was born in Shexian County, Anhui Province during Qing Dynasty. He was a judge of the Imperial Hospital in Emperor Qianlong. Yi Zong Jin Jian was a comprehensive medical book imperially edited in Qing Dynasty. It has 90 volumes. It is the most complete and concise type of comprehensive Chinese medical books in China.

六、四大中医经典 Four Classics of Traditional Chinese Medicine

1. 《黄帝内经》 *The Inner Classic of the Yellow King*
简称《内经》，原书 18 卷。其中 9 卷名《素问》；另外 9 卷无书名，汉晋

时被称为《九卷》或《针经》，唐以后被称为《灵枢》，非一人一时之作，主
要部分形成于战国至东汉时期。每部分各为 81 篇，共 162 篇。《素问》主要
论述了自然界变化的规律、人与自然的关系等。《灵枢》的核心内容为脏腑经
络学说。它是中国现存最早的研究人的生理学、病理学、诊断学、治疗原则
和药物学的传统医学巨著。它总结了春秋至战国时期的医疗经验和学术理论，
并吸收了秦汉以前有关天文学、历算学、生物学、地理学、人类学、心理学
等学科，运用阴阳、五行、天人合一的理论，对人体的解剖、生理、病理以
及疾病的诊断、治疗与预防做了比较全面的阐述。在理论上建立了中医学上
的 "阴阳五行学说" "脉象学说" "藏象学说" "经络学说" "病因学说" "病
机学说" "病症" "诊法" "论治" "养生学" "运气学" 等学说，反映了中国
古代天人合一的思想，确立了中医学独特的理论体系，成为中国医药学发展
的理论基础和源泉。

　　Shortly referred to as "*Nei Jing*", the original book had 18 volumes. Among
them, 9 volumes were entitled "*Su Wen*"; the other 9 volumes had no titles, later
called "*Nine Volumes*" or "*Needle Classic*" in Han and Jin Dynasties. They were
called "*Lingshu*" after Tang Dynasty. They were not written by one person at a
time. The main part formed from the Warring States Period to the Eastern Han Dynasty. There are 81 articles in each part, 162 articles in total. "*Su Wen*" mainly dis-
cusses the laws of nature change, and the relationship between man and nature. The
core content of "*Lingshu*" is the theory of viscera and meridians. It is the earliest
surviving traditional medical masterpiece in China that studies human physiology,
pathology, diagnostics, therapeutic principles and pharmacology. It summarized the
medical experience and academic theories from the Spring and Autumn Period to the
Warring States Period, and absorbed related subjects such as astronomy, calendar
math, biology, geography, anthropology, and psychology before Qin and Han Dynasties, and used the theories of Yin and Yang, the Five Elements, and the unity of
nature and man to give a more comprehensive explanation of the anatomy, physiology, pathology of the human body, as well as the diagnosis, treatment and prevention
of diseases. The theories of "Yin and Yang and Five Elements", "Pulse Theory",
"Store Theory", "Theory of Channels and Collaterals", "Etiology Theory", "Path-
ogenesis Theory", "Symptoms", "Diagnosis Methods", "Treatment Theory"

"Health Preservation Theory" and "Theory of Destinies and Weathers" have been established theoretically in traditional Chinese medicine. These theories reflect the traditional Chinese idea of harmony between man and nature, establish a unique theoretical system of traditional Chinese medicine, and become the theoretical foundation and source of the development of traditional Chinese medicine.

2. 《难经》 Nanjing (The Yellow King's Canon of Eighty-One Difficult Issues)

中医理论著作。原名《黄帝八十一难经》，共三卷。原题秦越人撰。"难"是"问难"之义，或作"疑难"解。"经"乃指《内经》，即问难《内经》。作者把自己认为的难点和疑点提出，然后逐一解释阐发，部分问题做出了发挥性阐释。该书以问难的形式，亦即假设问答、解释疑难的体例予以编纂。全书共分八十一难，对人体脏腑功能形态、诊法脉象、经脉针法等诸多问题逐一论述。但据考证，该书是一部托名之作，约成书于东汉以前（一说在秦汉之际）。该书还明确提出（"伤寒有五"）包括中风、伤寒、湿温、热病、温病，并对五脏之积、泻痢等病多有阐发，为后世医家所重视。全书内容简扼，辨析精微，在中医学典籍中常与《内经》并提，被认为是最重要的古典医籍之一。

TCM theoretical work. Formerly known as The Yellow King's Canon of Eighty-One Difficult Issues (3 volumes), originally by Qin Yueren. "Issues" means "answering the problems" or "difficult problems". "Canon" refers to "The Yellow King's Inner Classic", that is, "Inner Classic". The author put forward the difficult problems and doubts he thought, and then explained and elaborated one by one, and made an initiative explanation of some problems. The book was compiled in the form of questions, that was, hypothetical questions and answers, and explanations of difficult problems. The book is divided into eighty-one difficult problems, discussing many problems one by one, such as the functional morphology of the human body's internal organs, diagnosis and pulse conditions, and meridian acupuncture. But according to research, the book was just a work under the name. The book was finished about before the Eastern Han Dynasty (or it was in Qin and Han Dynasties). The book also clearly stated ("typhoid fever has five") including stroke, typhoid fever, damp fever, fever, and febrile disease, and explained the long standing diseases of the five internal organs, and diarrhea, which were valued by later generations of doctors. The content of the book is concise, and the analysis is subtle. It is often mentioned together with *The Inner Canon of Huangdi* in the classics of traditional Chinese medicine. It is regarded as one of the most important classical medical books.

3. 《伤寒杂病论》*Treatise on Febrile and Miscellaneous Diseases*

东汉张仲景所著。张仲景（公元 150 年～公元 219 年）名机，字仲景，南阳人。《伤寒杂病论》是中国传统医学著作之一，是一部论述外感病与内科杂病为主要内容的医学典籍。《伤寒杂病论》系统地分析了伤寒的原因、症状、发展阶段和处理方法，创造性地确立了对伤寒病的"六经分类"的辨证施治原则，奠定了理、法、方、药的理论基础。该书成书约在公元 200 年～210 年左右。原书失散后，经王叔和等人收集整理校勘，分编为《伤寒论》和《金匮要略》两部。《伤寒论》共十卷，专门论述伤寒类急性传染病。《金匮要略》又称《金匮要略方论》，为原《伤寒杂病论》中的杂病部分，共三卷。

Written by Zhang Zhongjing in the Eastern Han Dynasty. Zhang Zhongjing（150～219 AD）was named Ji, by names Zhongjing, from Nanyang, Henan Province. *Treatise on Febrile and Miscellaneous Diseases* is one of the traditional Chinese medical works, systematically analyzed the causes, symptoms, development stages and treatment methods of typhoid fever, creatively established the principles of differentiation and treatment of "Six meridians classification" of typhoid fever, and laid the theoretial foundation of theory, methods, prescriptions, and medicines. The book was written about 200～210 AD. After the original book was lost, it was collected and collated by Wang Shuhe and others, and divided into two parts: *Treatise on Febrile Diseases* and *Synopsis of the Golden Chamber*. *Treatise on Febrile Diseases* consists of 10 volumes, specifically discussing acute infectious diseases such as typhoid fever. *Synopsis of the Golden Chamber*, also known as *On the Prescriptions of Synopsis of the Golden Chamber*, is the miscellaneous part of the original *Treatise on Febrile and Miscellaneous Diseases* （3 volumes）.

4. 《神农本草经》*Shen Nong's Materia Medica*

《神农本草经》又称《本草经》或《本经》，托名"神农"所作，实成书于汉代，成书非一时，作者亦非一人，是对中国中医药的第一次系统总结，是中医四大经典著作之一，是已知最早的中药学著作。《神农本草经》全书分三卷，以三品分类法，分上、中、下三品，文字简练古朴，成为中药理论精髓。《神农本草经》记载了365种药物的疗效，多数真实可靠，至今仍是临床常用药；它提出了辨证用药的思想，所论药物适应病症能达170多种，对用药剂量、时间等都有具体规定，这也对中药学起到了奠基作用。其中规定的大部分中药学理论和配伍规则以及提出的"七情和合"原则在几千年的用药实践中发挥了巨大作用，是中医药药物学理论发展的源头。

Shen Nong's Materia Medica, also known as Materia Medica or Ben Jing, was written under the name "Shen nong". It was actually written in Han Dynasty. The book was not written at a time and the author was not alone. It was the first systematic summary of traditional Chinese medicine. It is one of the four classic works of traditional Chinese medicine and the earliest known works of traditional Chinese medicine. The book Shennong's Materia Medica is divided into three volumes. It is classified into upper, middle and lower grades according to the classification of three grades. The text is concise and simple, which has become the essence of traditional Chinese medicine theory. Shennong's Materia Medica records the curative effect of 365 kinds of drugs, most of which are true and reliable, and are still commonly used in clinical medicine. In the book there are specific regulations for the doses and time, which also laid the foundation for traditional Chinese medicine. Most of the traditional Chinese medicine theories and compatibility rules as well as the principle of "Seven Emotions Harmony" have played a significant role in the medication practice for thousands of years, and are the source of the development of traditional Chinese medicine pharmacology.

中国文化类词汇中英对照表

Aa	
阿尔金山	Alkin Mountain
阿尔泰山	Altai Mountain
艾灸	Moxibustion（Aijiu）
安史之乱	An Shi Rebellion
安土重迁	Be happy to stay where they are and reluctant to move their home/Affachment to One's Homeland
Bb	
八大菜系：鲁、川、粤、淮扬、湘、闽、徽、浙	Eight Major Cuisines：Shandong, Sichuan, Guangdong, Huaiyang, Hunan, Fujian, Huizhou, Zhejiang
八卦拳	Bagua Quan（Eight Trigram Boxing）
八极拳	Baji Boxing（Eight-extremities Boxing）
巴蜀地区	Bashu Region
巴蜀文化	Bashu Culture
拔火罐	Cupping Therapy
霸王鞭	King Whip
白茶	White Tea
白话小说	Novels in Vernacular Chinese（vernacular novel）
白酒	Chinese White Liquor（Baijiu）
白鹿洞书院	Bailu Cave Academy（Bailudong Academy）
白露	White Dew

白云观	Baiyun Temple
《百家姓》	*The Hundred Family Surnames*
《百骏图》	*Hundred Horses Painting*
百日酒	100-day Celebration Drink
百戏	Baixi (Variety Show), a comprehensive form of performances that included various folk skills such as music, dance, acrobatics, martial arts, and burlesque
拜师酒	Apprenticeship Initiation Drink
包子	Steamed Stuffed Bun (Baozi)
杯酒释兵权	To Relinquish Military Power Over a Drink
北京猿人	Peking Man
《本草纲目》	*Compendium of Materia Medica*
《本草经集注》	*Materia Medica Scripture Collected Notes*
比	Analogy
闭关锁国政策	The Closed-door Policy
碧螺春茶	(Jiangsu) Biluochun tea
兵部	Ministry of Military
伯、仲、叔、季	Bo (the eldest), Zhong (the second eldest), Shu (the third eldest), Ji (the youngest)
《伯远帖》	*Boyuan Copybook* (Boyuantie)
不朽	immortal
不争	indisputableness
《步辇图》	*Emperor Taizong Receiving the Tibetan Envoy*
Cc	
采茶戏	the tea picking opera
彩陶文化	Painted Pottery Culture
菜	the general term for vegetables and edible wild vegetables
参军	Canjun, act as an officer
参军戏	Canjun opera, a kind of farce
参知政事	Administrator
苍鹘	Canghu, act as a clown
草书	cursive script
《草书诗帖》	*Cursive Copybook of Poems*

插柳	plant willow branches
茶道	tea ceremony
茶道引导	tea ceremony guidance
茶德	tea ethics
《茶经》	*The Tea Classic*
茶礼	tea etiquette
茶理	tea theory
茶情	tea love
茶圣：陆羽	Tea Sage：Lu Yu
茶学说	tea philosophy
茶艺	tea art
长调	Long Tune（more than 91 characters, the longest Ci is 240 characters）
长江	Yangtze River
长江流域	Yangtze River Basin
长拳	Changquan（Long-distance Boxing）
长阳人	Changyang people
禅让制	the Abdication System
唱、念、做、打	sing, recite, act, and fight
巢居	nest
潮商	Chaozhou merchants
承宣布政使司	Department of Proclamation
持戒	observe the precepts
出妇	women out of the family
出师酒	graduation drinking
除夕（年尾最后一天）	New Year's Eve（the last day of the lunar year）
楚辞	Chu Ci
楚文化	Chu culture
处暑	the End of Heat
传道、授业、解惑	preach, teach, solve puzzles

传奇	legends
春分	the Spring Equinox
春节（正月初一）	Spring Festival（first day of the first lunar month）
《春秋》	The *Spring and Autumn Annals*
春秋战国	Spring and Autumn and Warring States
词	Ci, a kind of Chinese traditional poetry
祠庙	the temple
祠堂	ancestral hall
刺史	governor in the local
粗细	thickness and thinness
蹴鞠	Cuju（Chinese football）
皴、擦、点、染	dip, rub, dot, and dye
重阳节（登高节，农历九月九）	the Double Ninth Festival（Climbing Festival，the ninth day of the ninth lunar month）
Dd	
达努节	the Yao's Danu Festival
打马球	play polo
打油茶（吃豆茶）	Butter Tea（Eating Bean Tea）
《大藏经》	*Tripitaka*
大豆	soybeans
大寒	Major Cold
大荔人	Dali people
大麦	barley
大曲	Daqu（Big Music），a combination of music, dance, and poetry
大暑	Major Heat
大碗茶	Big Bowl Tea, named after serving tea in a large bowl
大汶口文化	Dawenkou Culture
大学	university

《大学》	*Great Learning*
大雪	Major Snow
大音希声	Da Yin Xi Sheng（the loudest and most beautiful music is no music at all）
大禹（夏后氏）	Yu the Great（Xiahoushi）
大篆	big seal script
大宗	major clan
旦	female characters in Peking Opera
淡墨	light ink
弹词	Tanci（Suzhou storytelling to the accompaniment of stringed instruments）
荡秋千	swing
道	Tao/Dao
《道藏》	*Tao Zang（Taoist Canon）*
道教	Taoism
道具舞	prop dance
道士	Taoist
稻	rice
德	morality
德治	rule of virtue
地藏菩萨	Ksitigarbha
地主	landlord
嫡长子继承制	the inheritance system by the eldest son of the lineage
帝喾（高辛氏）	King Ku（Gaoxin）
滇红茶	black tea in Yunnan province
颠张醉素	Lunatic Zhang and Drunk Su
殿试	court examination
丁村人	Dingcun people
东厂	Dongchang（East Arresting Agency）
东林书院	Donglin Academy
冬至	the Winter Solstice

冬至节（阳历12月21～23日）	Winter Solstice Festival (December 21–23 in the solar calendar)
动静相生	dynamics and statics in mutual generation
都指挥使司	Department of Commanding Envoys
斗拱	bracket
端午节（龙舟节、五月节，农历五月初五）	Dragon Boat Festival (the May Festival, the fifth day of the fifth lunar month)
短兵	Short weapons
队舞	team dance
敦煌石窟	Dunhuang Caves in Dunhuang, Gansu province
顿挫	pause
顿悟	epiphany
多元通和	pluralistic harmony
Ee	
峨眉派	Emei School in boxing
峨眉山	Mount Emei in Emeishan City, Sichuan province
二胡	erhu, a traditional Chinese instrument
二里头文化	Erlitou Culture
二十四节气	Twenty-Four Solar Terms
Ff	
发面饼	leavened pancake
法门寺	Famen Temple in Fufeng County, Shaanxi province
方圆	squareness and roundness
分封制	the enfeoffment system
汾酒	Fenjiu, from Xinghua Village in Shanxi
风、雅、颂	wind, elegance, hymns
风、寒、暑、湿、燥、火	wind, cold, heat, dampness, dryness and fire
封禅	Feng Shan, a large-scale ceremony in which the emperor came to worship heaven and earth

封建土地所有制	the feudal land ownership system
《封神演义》	*Fengshen Yanyi*（*The Romance of the Investiture of the Gods*）
夫为妻纲	husband as wife's master
伏羲（羲皇）	Fuxi（King Xi）：Fishing and Hunting Man
佛诞节（盂兰盆会）	the Buddha's Birthday Festival（the Bon Fair）
复姓	double surname
赋	Fu（rhapsody）
《富春山居图》	*Dwelling in the Fuchun Mountains*
Gg	
干、湿、浓、淡	dryness, wetness, thickness and lightness
干栏式建筑	stilt-style building
刚柔互补	hardness and softness in mutual complementation
高跷	stilts
《高山流水》	*High Mountain and Flowing Water*
歌圩	the Zhuang's Song Fair
歌舞戏	musical dance drama
歌仔戏	Taiwanese opera
耕读传家	farm and study from generation to generation
更戍法	Army Rotating
工笔画	elaborate-style painting
工部	Ministry of Engineering
公案小说	crime-case story
功夫茶	Kung Fu Tea
勾栏	Goulan（Circular Rail for play）
古琴	Chinese zither
谷	grain, the general term for gramineous crops
谷雨	Grain Rain
骨法（骨力）	Bone Technique（Bone Strength）
鼓词	drumming

关公	Guan Gong, the Greatest Master of Martial Arts
观音菩萨	Avalokitesvara
官腔	official tune
官营手工业	official handicraft industry
《广陵散》	*Guanglingsan Music*
《归风送远之曲》	*The Song of Gone with the Wind*
贵州茅台酒	Kweichow Moutai
国清寺	Guoqing Temple in Tiantai County, Zhejiang province
国学	national school/Studies of Chinese culture
国子学	Guozixue（National School）
	Hh
海禁政策	the maritime prohibition policy
《韩熙载夜宴图》	*Han Xizai's Night Banquet*
寒露	Cold Dew
寒门庶族	common people
《汉宫春晓图》	*Han Palace Spring Morning*
《汉宫秋月》	*Han Palace Autumn Moon*
汉魏风骨	Han and Wei style
豪放派	unrestrained school in Ci
号	Hao, nickname
和	Harmony
和而不同	harmony in differences
和为贵	harmony is precious
河姆渡文化	Hemudu Culture
河套人	Hetao people
黑茶	Dark tea
黑陶文化	Black Pottery Culture
横断山	Hengduan Mountain
红茶（乌茶）	Black tea
《红楼梦》	*Dream of Red Mansions/Dream of the Red Chamber*

红山文化	Hongshan Culture
鸿鹄之志	great ambition
后发先至	starting late but arriving first
后土	Thick Earth, the god of earth
厚德载物	to hold the world with virtue/the man of great virtue takes great responsibility
《胡笳十八拍》	*Eighteen Lectures of Hujia*
户部	Ministry of Households
户籍制度	the household registration system
花部	huabu (Flower part, that means not elegant at all)
花茶	Scented tea
花灯戏	the flower lantern show
花鼓戏	the flower drum opera
花鸟画	flower and bird painting
华山	Huashan Mountain in Huayin County, Shaanxi
化成天下	transform people into the world
化解	resolving
画圣：吴道子	Painting Sage：Wu Daozi
皇帝	Emperor
皇天上帝	God of Grand Heaven, the god of heaven
黄白术	Huangbaishu, refining and production of golden elixir and immortal medicine
黄茶	Yellow tea
黄帝（有熊氏）	Yellow King (Youxiong)
《黄帝内经》	*The Yellow King's Inner Classic*
黄河	Yellow River
黄河流域	Yellow River Basin
黄酒	yellow rice wine
黄梅戏	Huangmei Opera
徽商	Huizhou merchants
徽州民居	Huizhou folk house
会试	national examination
馄饨	wonton

火把节	the Yi's Torch Festival
Jj	
疾徐	rapidity
几分耕耘，几分收获	some hard work, some harvest/no pains, no gains
计白当黑	reckon blank as inked
技击	strike
祭坛	the altar
《祭侄文稿》	*Draft of a Reguiem to My Nephew*
稷	millet
家国同构	the same structure of family and country
家谱	genealogy
家天下	Family Country
家庭手工业	cottage handicraft industry
甲骨文	oracle-bone inscription
饯别酒	farewell drinking
建安文学	Jian'an Literature
健舞	Jian Wu, referring to those dance moving with vigorous and bold style
江汉流域	the Jianghan River Basin
江南水乡民居	houses in Jiangnan Water Town
《江山万里图》	*The Vast Motherland*
"讲会"制度	the "lecture" system
讲史小说	historical novel
焦墨	burnt ink
饺子	dumpling（Jiaozi）
教坊	Jiaofang, imperial music office
教学相长	teaching is learning
教子义方	teach children righteously
金骏眉	Jin Junmei tea from Wuyi Mountain
金沙江	Jinsha River
金文	bronze inscription

锦衣卫	Secret Service Guard
晋商	Shanxi merchant
京剧	Peking Opera
经世致用	practical management for practical use
荆楚文化	Jingchu culture
惊蛰	the Awakening of Insects
精耕细作	farm intensively
井底之蛙	frog at the bottom of the well
井田制	the "nine squares" system（well-like system）
敬茶	offer tea
静观	contemplation
九华山	Mount Jiuhua in Qingyang County, Anhui province
酒令	drinking game
绝句	quatrain
军机处	Department of Military and State Affairs
均田制	the land equalization system
君	kings and emperors
君、臣、父、子	emperors, subjects, fathers, and sons
君权神授	sovereign power is granted by God
君师崇拜	worship of emperors and teachers
君子	gentleman
郡望	Junwang, referring to a certain surname living in a certain county and being looked up to by the local people
郡县制	the county system
Kk	
开门七件事：柴、米、油、盐、酱、醋、茶	the seven things for Chinese people in daily life：firewood, rice, oil, salt, sauce, vinegar and tea
科举制	the imperial examination system
客家土楼	Hakka Tulou, earth building
崆峒派	Kongtong School in boxing

孔子	Confucius
《苦瓜和尚画语录》	*Bitter Gourd Monk Painting Quotations*
《苦笋帖》	*Bitter Bamboo Shoots Copybook*
《快雪时晴帖》	*When the Sun Shines after the Heavy Snow/Timely clearing After Snowfall*
狂草	crazy cursive
傀儡戏	puppet shows
昆仑派	Kunlun School in boxing
昆仑山	Karakoram Mountain
昆曲	Kun Tune
Ll	
腊八节（过小年）	the Laba Festival（the Lesser New Year）
《兰亭集序》	*The preface to Lanting Pavilion Collection/the preface of the Orchid Pavilion*
蓝田猿人	Lantian Ape Man
澜沧江	Lancang River
崂山	Mount Lao in Qingdao, Shandong province
《老子》	*Lao Tzu*
乐府	Yuefu, the Music Bureau
乐府诗	Yuefu poems
《离骚》	*Li Sao*（*The Lament*）
梨园	Pear Garden, the operatic circle
梨园子弟	Liyuan children, opera actors
《礼》	The*Book of Rites*
礼崩乐坏	disintegration of rite and music
礼部	Ministry of Rite
礼乐之邦	the country of rite and music
礼乐制	the rite music system
礼有五论，莫重于祭	there are five theories about rite, and nothing is more important than sacrifice

礼治	rule of rite
历史散文	historical proses
立春	the Beginning of Spring
立德、立功、立言	make a moral person, make achievements, make publication
立嫡以长不以贤	to establish a son as the head for he is the eldest but not for he is the virtuous
立冬	the Beginning of Winter
立秋	the Beginning of Autumn
立夏	the Beginning of Summer
立子以贵不以长	to establish the son for he is the noblest, but not for he is the eldest
吏部	Ministry of Officials
隶书	official script/clerical script
良渚文化	Liangzhu Culture
粱	fine millet
量资循序	step-by-step measures
灵岩寺	Lingyan Temple in Jinan, Shandong province
岭南文化	Lingnan culture
柳江人	Liujiang people
六安瓜片茶	Lu'an Guapian tea from Lu'an, Anhui province
六畜	six livestock such as horses, cattle, sheep, chickens, dogs, and pigs
六腑：小肠、大肠、胃、膀胱、胆、三焦	the six hollow organs: small intestine, large intestine, stomach, bladder, gallbladder, and San Jiao
六艺：礼、乐、射、御、书、数	six arts: rite, music, shooting, driving, calligraphy, and mathematics
龙井茶	Hangzhou West Lake Longjing tea
龙门石窟	Longmen Caves in Luoyang, Henan province
龙山文化	Longshan Culture

龙抬头（农历二月二）	Longtaitou Festival (Festival of the Dragon Rising its head, the second day of the second lunar month)
龙舞	dragon dance
龙行派	Longxing School (The Dragon Walk School) in boxing
楼观台	Louguantai in Zhouzhi County, Shaanxi province
泸州老窖特曲	Luzhou Laojiao Special Yeast Liquor, from Sichuan province
《论语》	*The Analects of Confucius*
罗浮山	Luofu Mountain in Boluo County, Guangdong province
《洛神赋图》	*Nymph of the Luo River*
律诗	rhymed poem
绿宝石茶	Guizhou green gem tea
绿茶	Green tea
Mm	
麻	sesame
麻沸散	Ma Fei San, anesthesia powder
马坝人	Maba people
马家浜文化	Majiabang Culture
马家窑文化	Majiayao Culture
脉象	pulse conditions
馒头	steamed bun (Mantou)
满汉全席	the Manchuria and Han Feast
满月酒	full-moon celebration drinking
满族	Manchus
芒种	Grain in Ear
毛峰茶	Maofeng tea from Huangshan Mountains, Anhui province
茅山	Maoshan in Jurong City, Jiangsu province
《梅花三弄》	*Three Times on Plum Blossoms*
门当户对	the two families of marriage should match each other/well-matched marriage
门阀制度	the System of Dominant Family
门下省	Province of Assessment
孟子	Mencius

《孟子》	*The Book of Mencius*
庙会	temple fairs
民营手工业	private handicraft industry
闽商	Fujian merchants
明经修行	understanding the Classics and cultivating oneself
墨分五色	ink is divided into five colors
墨子	Mozi
《墨子》	*Mozi*
木骨泥墙	wood bone and mud wall
Nn	
那达慕大会	the Mongolian Nadam Fair
男耕女织	male farming and female weaving
男尊女卑	male superior, female inferior
南少林派	South Shaolin School in boxing
南戏	South China folk Operas
《难经》	*Classic on 81 Medical Issues*
内阁大学士	Grand Secretary
内家拳	Neijiaquan (Inner Boxing)
内圣	inner sage
内外兼修，形神兼备	combination of internal and external cultivation in form and spirit
《霓裳羽衣舞》	*Rainbow Skirt and Feather Garment Dance*
农本商末	farming is fundamental and business is trivial
农恒为农	farmers being farmers generation after generation
浓墨	thick ink
女乐舞蹈	female musical dance
女娲	Nvwa
Oo	
欧体	Ouyang Xun's style
Pp	
俳优	Paiyou, comedian

跑旱船	dry boat running
跑竹马	bamboo horse running
裴李岗文化	Peiligang Culture
皮影	shadow puppets
琵琶	Pipa, a traditional Chinese instrument
品茶	taste tea
《平沙落雁》	*On the Sandbank Falls a Wild Goose/Wild Geese on the Sandbank*
评剧	Ping Opera
泼水节	the Dai's Water Splashing Festival
鄱阳湖	Poyang Lake
普洱茶	Pu'er tea
普陀山	Putuo Mountain in Zhejiang Province
普贤菩萨	Samantabhadra
Qq	
七夕节（乞巧节、女儿节，农历七月初七）	the Qixi Festival (Qiqiao Festival, Girls' Day, the seventh day of the seventh lunar month)
沏茶	make tea
栖霞寺	Qixia Temple in Nanjing, Jiangsu province
齐家文化	Qijia Culture
齐鲁文化	Qilu culture
祁红茶	Qi black tea in Anhui province
祁连山	Qilian Mountain
岐黄	Qihuang, the nicknames of Chinese medicine
气	Qi (Air)
《千金要方》	*A Thousand Gold Prescriptions/Essential Recipes for Emergent Use Worth a Thousand gold*
《千里江山图》	*A Thousand Miles of Rivers and Mountains*
《千字文》	*One Thousand Character Primer*
《前后赤壁赋》	*Fomer and Latter Ode to the Red Cliff*
潜移默化	imperceptible influence
羌族碉楼	Qiang Diaolou, blockhouse-like building

切诊	pulse feeling and palpation
亲贤远佞	close to the virtuous and far away from the vicious
秦腔	Qin Opera
青藏高原	Qinghai-Tibet Plateau
青茶（乌龙茶）	Oolong tea
青城山	Qingcheng Mountain in Dujiangyan City, Sichuan
青海湖	Qinghai Lake
青囊	Qing Nang（Black Bag），the nicknames of Chinese medicine
卿大夫	master
清、敬、怡、真	quietness, respect, joy and truth
清净无为	purity and inaction
清明	Pure Brightness
清明节（阳历4月5日前后）	Qingming Festival（around April 5th in the solar calendar）
清明前后，种瓜点豆	before and after Qingming, plant melons and cast beans
《清明上河图》	*Sightseeing along the River on Qingming Festival*
清墨	clear ink
清商乐	Qingshang music
清商署	Qingshang Office
情景合一	the unity of sense and scene
庆功酒	celebration drinking
秋分	the Autumnal equinox
曲	opera
屈家岭文化	Qujialing Culture
拳打卧牛之地	one can play boxing at a place where an ox can lie down
Rr	
人法地，地法天，天法道，道法自然	people follow the earth, the earth follows the sky, the sky follows the Way（Tao），and the Way follows the nature

人文	humanity
人物画	figure painting
仁、义、礼、智、信	benevolence, righteousness, propriety, wisdom, and credit
仁政	benevolent governance
儒释道	Confucianism, Buddhism and Taoism
入世	entry into the world
Ss	
萨彦岭	Sayan Mountain
三纲五常	Three Guidlines and Five Constant Values
三公九卿制度	the system of three prime ministers and nine ministers
三皇五帝	Three Sovereigns and Five Kings
三亩地一头牛，老婆孩子热炕头	one cow and 3 mu of land; the wife, children, and the warm bed
三秦文化	Three Qin culture
三省六部制度	system of three provinces and six ministries
三司使	Envoy
三月街	the Bai's March Fair
《三字经》	*San Zi Jing* (*Three Character Primer*)
散曲	Sanqu, detached songs
散手	Sanshou
散文	prose
丧酒	funeral drinking
骚体	Sao Style
扫墓	tomb sweeping
色、受、想、行、识	form, feeling, meditation, behavior, and consciousness
色、香、味	color, arome and taste
山顶洞人	the Upper Cave Man
山高皇帝远，村落犹一国	the mountain is high and the emperor is far away, so a village is like a country

山水画	landscape painting
《伤寒杂病论》	*Treatise on Febrile and Miscellaneous Diseases*
上清宫	Shangqing Palace in Guixi County, Jiangxi province
上巳节（农历三月初三）	Shangsi Festival（third day of the third lunar month）
上下相维	the upper and lower are mutually dependent
尚书省	Province of Shangshu（Imperial Enforcing Secretary）
少林派	Shaolin School in boxing
少林拳	Shaolin Boxing
社火	Shehuo（Community Fire）
神魔小说	novel of gods and demons
神农	Shennong：God of Agriculture
《神农本草经》	*Shen Nong's Materia Medica*（*The Herbal Canon of Shen Nong*）
生	male characters in Peking Opera
师	those saints who can serve as teachers for all generations
诗	poem
《诗》	The *Book of Songs*
诗佛：王维	Poetry Buddha：Wang Wei
诗礼之教	teaching of poetry and rite
诗情画意	poetic and picturesque
诗圣：杜甫	Poem Sage：Du Fu
狮子舞	lion dance
十二平均律	the twelve equal temperament
十里不同天，百里不同日	different skies for ten miles and different days for hundreds of miles
《十面埋伏》	*Ambush on All Sides*
石鼓书院	Shigu Academy
石峡遗址	Shixia Site
《食鱼帖》	*Eating Fish Copybook*
士	official
氏族公社	clan communes

世不徙业	not change their walks of life for generations
世情小说	novel of worldly love
世袭制	the hereditary system
《尚书》	*The Book of Documents*
书画同源	calligraphy and painting have the same origin
书圣：王羲之	Calligraphy Sage：Wang Xizhi
书院	academy
枢密使	Privy envoy
枢密院	Privy Council
秫	glutinous rice
黍	yellow rice
《蜀素帖》	*Shu Silk Copybook*
术道并重	equal emphasis on skill and self-cultivation
霜降	Frost's Descent
《水浒传》	*Water Margin*
舜（有虞氏）	King Shun（Youyushi）
说书	storytelling
司隶校尉	comptroller in the center
丝绸之路	Silk Road
四川盆地	the Sichuan Basin
四合院	Siheyuan（Quadrangle Courtyard）
四书五经	the Four Books and Five Classics
四诊	four methods of diagnosis
俗令	popular game
粟	millet
燧人（燧皇）	Suiren（King Sui）：Flinting man
Tt	
踏青	a green outing
台湾岛	Taiwan Island
太常寺	Taichangsi（Department of Music Affairs）
太湖流域	the Taihu Lake Basin

太极拳	Taiji Boxing
太清宫	Taiqing Palace of Heaven in Luyi County, Henan province
太上老君	Taishang Laojun, the very high lord
太学	Taixue（Large School）
泰山	Mount Tai in Tai'an, Shandong province
泰山北斗	Mount Tai and North Star, the most respectable
《唐宫仕女图》	*Ladies in the Tang Palace*
踢、打、摔、拿、击、刺	kick, beat, throw, take, strike and stabbing
提味	to enhance flavor
提刑按察使司	Department of Prosecutors
天、地、君、亲、师	heaven, earth, monarch, parents, teachers
天、地、人	heaven, earth, and human beings
天地山川崇拜	worship of heaven, earth, mountains and rivers
天府之国	Land of Paradise/Land of Plenty
天人感应	interaction between nature and man
天人合一	the unity of nature and man
天山	Tianshan Mountain
天山派	Tianshan（Tianshan Mountain）School in boxing
天下武功汇少林	the world's martial arts gather in Shaolin Temple
天下之人，唯利是求	people in the world only pursue profits
天圆地方	Round Sky and Square Earth
天子	the Son of Heaven
跳花节	the Miao's Flower Jumping Festival
铁犁牛耕	iron plow and cattle farming technology
通臂拳	Tongbi Boxing
吐鲁番盆地	the Turpan Basin
团圆酒	reunion drinking

推恩令	the Grace Order
推手	pushing hands
屯田制	the station farm system
Ww	
瓦舍	Washe, tile market, tile-roofed houses
外王	outer king
外兴安岭	Outer Khingan Range
婉约派	graceful schools in Ci
万事不求人	asking no help for everything
王道	kingly way
王民相依	the king and the people depend on each other
望果节	the Tibetan Ongkor Festival
望诊	observation
为仁由己	be benevolent on one's own
文人墨客	Literati
文殊菩萨	Manjushri
文舞	literary dance
文言小说	novels in classical Chinese
闻诊	auscultation and smelling
问诊	inquiry
乌江	Wujiang River
巫舞	witch dance
吴越文化	Wuyue culture
五谷杂粮	various grains
《五牛图》（《唐韩滉五牛图》）	*Five Bulls*
五台山	Mount Wutai in Wutai County, Shanxi province
五味：酸、甜、苦、辣、咸	Five-Flavor: sour, sweet, bitterness, spiciness and saltiness
五味调和	Five-Flavor Harmony

五行：木、金、火、水、土	five elements：wood, gold, fire, water, and earth
五音戏	the five-tone drama
五蕴	five aggregates
五脏：心、肝、脾、肺、肾	the five internal organs：heart, liver, spleen, lung and kidney
武当派	Wudang School in boxing
武当山	Wudang Mountain in Danjiangkou City, Hubei province
武术	martial arts/Kung Fu
武舞	martial dance
武艺	Wuyi
舞剑	sword dance
舞象	weapon dance
舞旋	dance spin
Xx	
《夕阳箫鼓》	*Flute and Drum at Sunset*
西厂	Xichang（West Arresting Agency）
《西游记》	*A Pilgrimage to the West*
戏曲舞蹈	opera dance
夏至	the Summer Solstice
先贤	sages，those outstanding figures who have made sacrifices and contributions to the historical development of the Chinese nation
献茶	offer tea
乡试	provincial examination
乡学	countryside school
相和歌	mutual response songs
《响屐舞》	*Sound Clogs Dance*
象形拳	Animal-like Boxing/Imitative Boxing
小豆	Adzuki beans
小寒	Minor Cold

小令	Small Tune（within 58 characters）
小麦	wheat
小满	Grain Full
小农经济	the small farm economy
小暑	Minor Heat
小说	novel
小学	elementary school
小雪	Minor Snow
小篆	small seal script
小宗	minor clan
协和万邦	concord among all nations/harmony between nations
写意	freehand
写意画	freehand brushwork
谢师酒	drinking to thank the teachers
心意拳	Xinyiquan（Mind Boxing）
信而勿诳	be faithful and don't lie
信阳毛尖	Xinyang Maojian Tea from Xinyang, Henan province
刑部	Ministry of Justice
行书	Xing Shu（semi-cursive scripts）
行中书省（行省）	Province of Secretary（the Province）
形神兼备	have both form and spirit
形意拳	Xingyiquan（Form and mind Boxing）
兴	Xing, topic association
兴于诗，立于礼，成于乐	beginning in *Book of Songs*, establishing in rite, and completing in music
杏林	Xinglin（Apricot Forest）, the nickname of Chinese medicine
修身、齐家、治国、平天下	cultivate oneself, manage the family, govern the country, and pacify the world
馐	delicious food

虚静	emptiness and quietness
虚心	humility
宣政院	Promoting Administration
玄览	esotericism
玄学	metaphysics
悬壶	Xuanhu (Hanging Gourd), the nickname of Chinese medicine
穴居	cave dwell
学官	academic official
荀子	Xunzi
《荀子》	*Xunzi*
Yy	
雅部	Yabu, elegant part
雅乐	Yayue, elegant music
雅令（文字令）	elegant game, a character game
雅舞	elegant dance
言谏制度	the remonstrance system
颜筋柳骨	Yan Tendon Liu Bone
颜柳	Yan Zhenqing and Liu Zongyuan
《颜氏家训》	*Home Instructions of Yan Family*
颜体	Yan Zhenqing's style
宴会舞蹈	Yanyue, banquet dance
燕赵文化	Yanzhao culture
秧歌	Yangko
《阳春白雪》	*The Spring Snow*
仰韶文化	Yangshao Culture
尧（陶唐氏）	King Yao (Taotangshi)
肴	meat dishes
窑洞	cave dwelling
徭役制度	the corvee system
药酒	medicinal wine

药圣：李时珍	Pharmacy sage：Li Shizhen
药王：孙思邈	Medicine King：Sun Simiao
叶落归根	Falling leaves return to their roots
一分耕耘一分收获	one effort, one gain/no pain, no gain
医圣：张仲景	medicine sage：Zhang Zhongjing
以德治国	rule the country by virtue
以文教化	educate people with culture
以形写神	convey spirit through form
弋腔	Yi Opera
《易》	*The Book of Changes*
逸品	graceful works
逸士	hermit
意拳	Yiquan（mind boxing）
因材施教	to teach students in accordance with their aptitude
阴阳	Yin and Yang
阴阳和合	Harmony between Yin and Yang
应天府书院	Yingtianfu Academy
英雄传奇小说	legends
迎宾酒	welcome drinking
迎春日（扫尘日）	Welcoming Spring Days (Dust Sweeping Days, from the 23rd day to the 30th day of the twelfth lunar month)
《营造法式》	*Building Methods*
永乐宫	Yongle Palace in Ruicheng, Shanxi province
咏春拳	Wing Chun Boxing
有容乃大	One will be greater with tolerance
《幼学琼林》	*For the Children to Learn By*
鬼节（农历七月十四或十五）	Ghosts' Festival (the fourteenth or fifteenth day of the seventh lunar month)
渔樵耕读	fishing, woodcutting, farming, and studying

《渔樵问答》	*Questions and Answers between Fisherman and Woodcutter*
雨水	Rain Water
玉泉寺	Yuquan Temple in Dangyang, Hubei province
浴佛节（傣族泼水节）	the Desire Buddha Festival (the Splashing Water Festival of the Dai people)
豫剧	Yu Opera
元谋猿人	Yuanmou Ape Man
元宵节（上元节，正月十五）	Lantern Festival (Shangyuan Festival, fifteenth day of the first lunar month)
元杂剧	Zaju Operas
岳鹿书院	Yuelu Academy
越剧	Yue Opera
粤剧	Cantonese opera
云冈石窟	Yungang Caves in Datong, Shanxi
Zz	
藏历年	the Tibetan Calendar NewYear
藏族碉房	Tibetan blockhouse
张颠素狂	Zhang Lunatic and Su Crazy
赵体	Zhao Mengfu's style
针灸	acupuncture and moxibustion
正山小种	Lapsang Souchong, a tea
知行合一	the unity of knowledge and action
至善	the best/supreme good
志怪小说	mystery novel
《治家格言》	*Guidelines for Family Management*
中调	Middle Tune (59-90 characters)
中国书法	Chinese calligraphy
中秋节（农历八月十五）	the Mid-Autumn Festival (the fifteenth day of the eighth lunar month)
《中秋帖》	*Mid-Autumn Copybook*

中书省	Province of Imperial Secretary
中央集权制度（封建君主专制）	centralized system（feudal monarchy）
中药	Chinese herbs
中医	Traditional Chinese medicine（TCM）
《中庸》	*The Doctrine of the Mean*
中原地区	the Central Plains region
忠、孝、节、义	loyalty, filial piety, integrity and righteousness
种瓜得瓜，种豆得豆	plant melons to get melons, sow beans to get beans
《仲尼梦奠帖》	*Dream of Confucius at the Alta*
重民轻神	value the people and despise the gods
重墨	heavy ink
"重农抑商"政策	the policy of "emphasizing agriculture and restraining commerce"
重实际而黜玄想	emphasize reality and abandon fantasy
重土安迁	preferring staying at home to moving elsewhere
《肘后备急方》	*Elbow Reserve Emergency Recipe/Recipes for Emergent Use*
珠江流域	the Pearl River Basin
诸宫调	Miscellaneous Modes of Music
诸侯	vassal（lords）
诸子散文	the proses by the masters
祝寿酒	birthday celebration drinking
颛顼（高阳氏）	King Zhuanxu（Gaoyangshi）
转折	turning
《庄子》	*Zhuang Zi*
资阳人	Ziyang people
自己食自己	support oneself
自然门	Natural School in boxing

《自叙帖》	*Autobiography Copybook*
字	byname
宗法制（奴隶制宗法贵族君主制）	the patriarchal system（slavery patriarchal aristocratic monarchy）
走会	Zouhui（walking meeting）
祖先崇拜	worship of ancestors
坐忘	forgetfulness

参考文献

1. 白钢：《中国基层治理的变革》，载《民主与科学》2003 年第 6 期。

2. 常修泽：《中国经济发展模式的特点和内在支撑》，载《前线》2008 年第 7 期。

3. 陈蓉、颜鹏飞：《近代中国保险业百余年历史特征的考察》，载《财经问题研究》2022 年第 12 期。

4. 陈晓：《江山之助：地理环境对艺术的影响研究》，西南大学 2009 年硕士学位论文。

5. 陈颖等：《追溯中国农耕文化的渊源与发展——以贵州贵定县多元文化发展为例》，载《贵州大学学报（自然版）》2015 年第 1 期。

6. 程爱民主编：《中国概况》，上海外语教育出版社 2018 年版。

7. 程家福等：《新中国来华研究生教育历史研究》，载《学位与研究生教育》2012 年第 10 期。

8. 程家福、黄美旭：《略论来华留学生教育历史分期问题》，载《中国高教研究》2008 年第 12 期。

9. 崔乐泉：《中国近代体育史话》，中华书局出版社 1998 年版。

10. 崔友平：《中国经济体制改革：历程、特点及全面深化——纪念改革开放 40 周年》，载《经济与管理评论》2018 年第 6 期。

11. 邓洪波、宗尧：《明代书院教育及其对现代大学的启示》，载《大学教育科学》2018 年第 5 期。

12. 《邓小平文选》（第 3 卷），人民出版社 1993 版。

13. 樊志刚：《改革开放 40 年中国银行业的发展》，载《前线》2019 年第 1 期。

14. 方龄萱：《试论中国古代学校教育及其教学思想》，载《兰州工业学院学报》2016 年第 6 期。

15. 费孝通：《中国文化的重建》，华东师范大学出版社 2014 年版。

16. 冯泉清：《从〈中国文化通论〉导论部分的翻译浅谈中国文化汉译英的策略与技巧》，复旦大学 2013 年硕士学位论文。

17. 高飞：《改革开放 40 年中国外交的历程与启示》，载《当代世界》2018 年第 5 期。

18. 公丕祥：《新中国 70 年社会主义法治建设的成就与经验》，载 http://theory. people. com. cn/n1/2019/0823/c40531-31312237. html。

19. 公丕祥：《法治现代化的中国方案》，载《江苏社会科学》2020 年第 4 期。

20. 顾伟列：《中国文化通论》，华东师范大学出版社 2005 年版。

21. 顾长声：《传教士与近代中国》，上海人民出版社 2013 年版。

22. 郭秀晶、王霁霞：《来华留学高等教育的政策分析与制度变迁》，载《北京科技大学学报（社会科学版）》2008 年第 4 期。

23. 郭燕来、程竹汝：《论中国当代政治发展的特色》，载《长白学刊》2011 年第 4 期。

24. 国家体委体育文史工作委员会、中国体育史学会编：《中国近代体育史》，北京体育学院出版社 1989 年版。

25. 韩鉴堂编著：《汉字文化》，北京语言大学出版社 2010 年版。

26. 郝先中：《近代中国西医本土化与职业化研究》，人民出版社 2019 年版。

27. 胡适：《中国文化的反省》，华东师范大学出版社 2013 年版。

28. 湖南中医学院编：《中国医学发展简史》，湖南科学技术出版社 1979 年版。

29. 黄其洪、郑人杰：《中国当代政治模式的独特性及比较优势》，载《中共山西省委党校学报》2015 年第 6 期。

30. 黄伟宏、温红祥：《试谈武术中的"击"与"艺"》，载《宜春学院学报》2008 年第 S1 期。

31. 黄夏玉：《论宗法制对中国历史的影响》，载《广播电视大学学报（哲学社会科学版）》2003 年第 4 期。

32. 黄新华：《变革社会中的基层治理现代化：思考与建议》，载《国家治理》2020 年第 2 期。

33. 黄元丰、王红光：《人民幸福：当代中国社会发展的价值旨归》，载《广东石油化工学院学报》2015 年第 2 期。

34. 季敦山：《武德：武术文化发展的重中之重》，载《搏击·武术科学》2009 年第 1 期。

35. 贾兆义、魏礼庆：《来华留学教育事业回顾与思考》，载《国际教育交流》2019 年第 7 期。

36. 江必新、戢太雷：《中国共产党百年法制建设历程回顾》，载《中南大学学报（社会科学版）》2021 年第 4 期。

37. 江飞涛：《中国工业发展政策的演进和启示》，载《产业经济评论》2022 年第 2 期。

38. 江生忠：《中国保险业发展成果的经验与问题的反思》，载《保险研究》2018 年第 12 期。

39. 金灿荣、刘冰若：《中国外交的特点和趋势》，载《前线》2020 年第 1 期。

40. 金干：《西方医学教育的传入发展及历史经验（上）》，载《中国高等医学教育》1992年第6期。

41. 金鹏、王海军：《在中华优秀传统文化教育中培育社会主义核心价值观》，载《辽宁教育行政学院学报》2017年第4期。

42. 孔宪丽、梁宇云：《2017年中国工业景气运行态势及特点分析》，载《科技促进发展》2017年第11期。

43. 李国豪等主编：《中国科技史探索：国际版》，上海古籍出版社1982年版。

44. 李宏斌、钟瑞添：《当代中国社会转型的内容、特点及应然趋向》，载《科学社会主义》2013年第4期。

45. 李璐：《浅析汉代乐舞和魏晋南北朝乐舞发展特点及异同》，载《大江周刊：论坛》2009年第9期。

46. 李鹏、唐静：《新中国开启留学教育的历史考察》，载《当代中国史研究》2015年第4期。

47. 李涛：《中国医学发展史大纲》，载《中医杂志》1954年第5期。

48. 李涛：《中国医学发展史》，载《中级医刊》1954年第10期。

49. 李滔：《中华留学教育史录：1949年以后》，高等教育出版社2000年版。

50. 梁勇、邓显洁：《基于社会学视域的中西方饮酒礼仪的比较研究》，载《酿酒科技》2014年第8期。

51. 林崇德主编：《中国少年儿童百科全书（科学·技术）》，浙江教育出版社1991年版。

52. 刘利民：《多措并举提升来华留学质量》，载 http://www.jyb.cn/rmtzgjyb/201907/t20190726_250414.html。

53. 刘宓庆：《文化翻译论纲》，中译出版社2019年版。

54. 刘其芸：《黄自元书法研究》，湖南师范大学2019年硕士学位论文。

55. 刘升平：《论新中国法律的发展及其历史经验——为庆祝建国35周年而作》，载《中国法学》1984年第3期。

56. 路遥：《简论中国近代外交的转型》，外交学院2010年硕士学位论文。

57. 栾凤池：《实施四大发展战略提升来华留学生教育水平》，载《中国高等教育》2013年第1期。

58. 吕建中：《中国古代书院制度述略》，载《青海民族大学学报（社会科学版）》2004年第3期。

59. 马伯英：《中医科学性的内涵兼论科学、非科学和伪科学》，载《科学文化评论》2007年第2期。

60. 马德浩：《新中国成立以来我国竞技体育发展方式演进历程与展望》，载《中国体育科技》2021年第1期。

61. 马德浩：《新发展理念视域下的中国体育发展方式转变》，载《上海体育学院学报》2019 第 6 期。

62. 马庆钰：《中国政治文化论纲》，载《理论导刊》2002 年第 6 期。

63. 彭国强、舒盛芳：《中国体育发展走向的研究》，载《体育学刊》2016 年第 2 期。

64. 皮德宁：《中国古代书院与欧洲中世纪大学的比较研究》，载《南昌教育学院学报》2004 年第 4 期。

65. 钱穆：《中国文化史导论》，商务印书馆 1994 年版。

66. 秦爽：《与君共醉——浅析酒的文化》，载《新疆广播电视大学学报》2013 年第 1 期。

67. 任应秋：《通俗中国医学史话》，重庆人民出版社 1957 年版。

68. 申万里：《元代官学的教与学》，载《首都师范大学学报（社会科学版）》2019 第 6 期。

69. 沈春敏、李书源：《近代科技在中国的引进与传播》，载《社会科学战线》2000 年第 6 期。

70. 沈国明：《中国法治建设的经验与进路——在新的历史方位上的思考》，载《地方立法研究》2020 年第 3 期。

71. 孙广丰：《我国大众体育发展历程的特征和未来发展趋势》，载《通化师范学院学报》2008 年第 8 期。

72. 孙祁祥、范娟娟：《新中国保险业发展的经验》，载《中国金融》2019 年第 19 期。

73. 孙振民：《中国传统教育文化的体认特征及其价值意义》，载《理论导刊》2007 年第 4 期。

74. 唐珂：《关于农业与文化的关系》，载《古今农业》2011 年第 1 期。

75. 田玲等：《建国 60 年我国医学教育发展回顾与思考》，载《医学研究杂志》2009 年第 11 期。

76. 汪力平、冷树青：《当代中国社会风气的守与变》，载《中国人民大学学报》2019 年第 5 期。

77. 王春艳等：《综述我国食品安全标准体系建设现状》，载《中国食品学报》2021 年第 10 期。

78. 王国刚：《中国银行业 70 年：简要历程、主要特点和历史经验》，载《管理世界》2019 年第 7 期。

79. 王开玺：《中国近代的外交与外交礼仪》，载《史学月刊》2001 年第 2 期。

80. 王磊：《孟子义利思想辨析》，载《齐鲁学刊》2005 年第 5 期。

81. 王利伟：《中国古典文学的思想政治教育功能研究》，西安科技大学 2012 年硕士学位论文。

82. 王刘玉、高军：《当代中国社会阶层分化现状及其走势》，载《学术交流》2009 年第 6 期。

83. 王顺洪编著：《中国概况》，北京大学出版社 2015 年版。

84. 王伟、王声跃：《论中国传统文化与地理环境的关系》，载《玉溪师范学院学报》2003 年第 11 期。

85. 王晓：《表现中国传统美学精神的现代建筑意研究》，武汉理工大学 2008 年硕士学位论文。

86. 王毅：《以习近平新时代中国特色社会主义思想引领中国外交开辟新境界》，载 http://www.qstheory.cn/dukan/qs/2017-12/31/c_1122175289.htm，最后访问日期：2017 年 12 月 19 日。

87. 王运涛：《儒学人文精神在经典文学中的传承及其当代意义》，载《辽宁教育行政学院学报》2006 年第 5 期。

88. 文雯等：《"一带一路"倡议与来华留学教育》，载杨东平主编：《中国教育发展报告》，社会科学文献出版社 2018 年版。

89. 吴素雄等：《医疗卫生服务体系整合的过程、结构与治理边界：中国实践》，载《浙江学刊》2022 年第 3 期。

90. 吴天智：《中国传统文化视域中的和谐观念及其当代转换》，南开大学 2009 年博士学位论文。

91. 吴文忠：《中国体育发展史》，三明书局出版社 1981 年版。

92. 习近平：《在庆祝改革开放 40 周年大会上的讲话》，载 http://www.xinhuanet.com/politics/leaders/2018-12/18/c_1123872025.html，最后访问日期：2022 年 1 月 25 日。

93. 习近平：《习近平谈治国理政》，外文出版社 2014 年版。

94. 习近平：《习近平谈治国理政》（第四卷），外文出版社 2022 年版。

95. 习近平：《习近平谈治国理政》（第三卷），外文出版社 2020 年版。

96. 习近平：《习近平谈治国理政》（第二卷），外文出版社 2017 年版。

97. 习近平：《决胜全面建成小康社会，夺取新时代中国特色社会主义伟大胜利——在中国共产党第十九次全国代表大会上的报告》，人民出版社 2017 年版。

98. 肖川：《论当代教育思想的基本特征》，载《全球教育展望》2006 年第 8 期。

99. 谢立奎：《中国医学发展史纵向观》，载《湖南中医杂志》1986 年第 2 期。

100. 曾雄生等：《中国科技史》，文津出版社 1998 年版。

101. 徐冠华：《当代科技发展六大趋势》，载《文汇报》2002 年 05 月 27 日，第 11 版。

102. 徐汉明：《"习近平公共卫生与健康治理理论"的核心要义及时代价值》，载《法学》2020 年第 9 期。

103. 徐小跃：《论中国古代宗教的特点》，载《江苏行政学院学报》2012 年第 4 期。

104. 阎国华：《"当代科技发展的特征、趋势与建设世界科技强国"教学设计》，载《马克思主义理论学科研究》2020 年第 6 期。

105. 燕国材：《论中国当代教育发展的轨迹》，载《云梦学刊》1996 年第 3 期。

106. 杨芳：《中国历代教育制度与教育思想的发展历程》，北京工业大学出版社 2019 年版。

107. 杨国勇：《元代教育的几个特点》，载《山西大学学报（哲学社会科学版）》1985 年第 1 期。

108. 杨洁篪：《改革开放以来的中国外交》，载 http://www.fmprc.gov.cn/chn/gxh/wzb/zxxx/t512782.htm。

109. 杨月梅等：《近二十年中国工业结构发展特点分析——基于资源 环境 经济综合因素的视角》，载《能源与节能》2017 年第 12 期。

110. 叶自成：《中国崛起——华夏体系 500 年的大历史》，人民出版社 2013 年版。

111. 叶自成：《春秋战国时期的中国外交思想》，香港社会科学出版社有限公司 2003 年版。

112. 殷奎英：《清代教育制度的变化》，载《菏泽学院学报》2008 年第 1 期。

113. 于富增：《改革开放 30 年的来华留学生教育：1978-2008》，北京语言大学出版社 2009 年版。

114. 于玲玲：《民国时期公民教育思想的若干特点——基于对教育人士的考察》，载《教育探索》2016 年第 4 期。

115. 袁铮一：《70 年来中国外交思想核心论点的演进解析》，载《中共济南市委党校学报》2019 年第 6 期。

116. 张福国：《论古代语文的德性教化》，湖南师范大学 2006 年硕士学位论文。

117. 张建仁：《试论明代教育管理的特点》，载《华东师范大学学报（教育科学版）》1992 年第 1 期。

118. 张文显：《中国法治 40 年：历程、轨迹和经验》，载《社会科学文摘》2018 年第 11 期。

119. 赵佳楹：《中国近代外交史》，世界知识出版社 2008 年版。

120. 周彭等：《佛医思想对中医哲学思想体系构建的研究与探索》，载《整理，传承，发展——中医医史文献研究的新思路——中华中医药学会第十五次中医医史文献学术年会论文集》，中华中医药学会医史文献分会、山东中医药大学中医文献研究所 2013 年版。

121. 周世举：《当代科技发展新趋势及其影响》，载《发展研究》2003 年第 5 期。

122. 周祖成、万方亮：《党的政策与国家法律 70 年关系的发展历程》，载《现代法学》2019 年第 6 期。

123. 朱小略：《龙与奇美拉——中国外交的起源兼论春秋时期诸侯国行为性质》，载《儒学评论》第 14 辑。

124. 朱永新、马国川：《中国当代教育改革历程评述》，载《阴山学刊》2015 年第 4 期。

125. 邹相：《中医文化，国之瑰宝》，载《第十二届全国中医药文化学术研讨会论文集》，中华中医学会中医药文化分会、福建中医学院 2009 年版。